The Transnational Beat Generation

THE TRANSNATIONAL BEAT GENERATION

EDITED BY

NANCY M. GRACE AND JENNIE SKERL

First published in 2012 by
PALGRAVE MACMILLAN®
in the United States—a division of St. Martin's Press LLC,
175 Fifth Avenue, New York, NY 10010.

Where this book is distributed in the UK, Europe and the rest of the world,
this is by Palgrave Macmillan, a division of Macmillan Publishers Limited,
registered in England, company number 785998, of Houndmills,
Basingstoke, Hampshire RG21 6XS.

Palgrave Macmillan is the global academic imprint of the above companies
and has companies and representatives throughout the world.

Palgrave® and Macmillan® are registered trademarks in the United States,
the United Kingdom, Europe and other countries.

ISBN: 978–0–230–10840–0 (hardback)
ISBN: 978–0–230–10841–7 (paperback)

Library of Congress Cataloging-in-Publication Data

The transnational beat generation / edited by Nancy M. Grace,
Jennie Skerl.
      p. cm.
Includes bibliographical references and index.
ISBN 978–0–230–10840–0 (hardback)—
ISBN 978–0–230–10841–7 (paperback)
    1. Beat generation—Influence. 2. American literature—20th century—
History and criticism. I. Grace, Nancy McCampbell. II. Skerl, Jennie. III. Title.

PS228.B6T73 2012
810.9′0054—dc23   2011029790

A catalogue record of the book is available from the British Library.

Design by Newgen Imaging Systems (P) Ltd., Chennai, India.

First edition: January 2012

10 9 8 7 6 5 4 3 2 1

Printed in the United States of America.

For Tom L. Milligan
For John L. Hynes

Contents

Part 3   Global Circulation

Acknowledgments

We both thank participants in the October 2008 Beat Generation Symposium held at Columbia College Chicago and co-sponsored by the Beat Studies Association. At the conclusion of this conference, an exciting conversation took place about "global Beats," which provided the impetus for this project. We thank our contributors for their hard work in creating insightful essays, and for their patience and good humor during the editorial process. Peter Hale, with the Allen Ginsberg Project, deserves a heartfelt thanks for assisting us to secure a beautiful cover image. We thank Brigitte Shull, our editor at Palgrave-Macmillan, for her faith in this project, and her editorial assistant, Joanna Roberts, for her expertise and patience as she guided us through the publication process. Thank you as well to The College of Wooster for providing funding for the indexing of this volume.

Jennie Skerl wishes to thank colleagues at West Chester University and in the Beat Studies Association, especially the board members, for encouragement and support throughout this project.

Nancy Grace also thanks the Beat Studies Association board members for encouragement and support throughout this project. Thanks to Ronna C. Johnson for a long-standing and inspirational professional collaboration and friendship. A special thank you to DeeDee Milligan, Marianne Bowden, and Marcia Holbrook for providing moral support.

And, as always, thank you Tom and John for always being there and believing in the value of our dedication to Beat studies.

Permissions

Introduction to Transnational Beat: Global Poetics in a Postmodern World

Nancy M. Grace and Jennie Skerl

Beat Generation writers and artists are most often unequivocally identified as American, and there exists a strong body of Beat scholarship delineating the literary and political traditions within American cultural history that engendered the many manifestations of Beat writing. However, that same scholarship foregrounds distinct threads that speak to Beat borrowings and blendings of various traditions from other Western and non-Western cultures. Some of these easily come to mind when Beat is mentioned, such as Buddhism, pan-cultural hallucinogenic practices, and European surrealism and romanticism. These borrowings and blendings, accomplished through traditional reading practices, reflect extensive migratory or travel experiences. In fact, travel both within and outside the United States for many Beat writers—including Jack Kerouac, Allen Ginsberg, William S. Burroughs, Lawrence Ferlinghetti, Gary Snyder, Joanne Kyger, Philip Whalen, Janine Pommy Vega, and Anne Waldman—characterized a method for fusing life as art and vice versa. However, the migratory character of the Beat movement is much more than the fact that a number of Beat writers traveled extensively outside the United States. Granted, their interactions sometimes fit compatibly with a common understanding of tourism. But some, most notably Burroughs and Ted Joans, lived abroad for extended periods of time, interacting with writers and artists outside the United States and often making concerted efforts to live as members of the local community. Equally important is the fact that many American Beat writers saw themselves as part of the twentieth-century international avant-garde—here, Ginsberg, Waldman, and Ferlinghetti are representative—and were received as such outside the United States. In turn, writers and literary movements beyond U.S. borders were affiliated with or influenced by the Beats in the 1950s and 1960s and beyond. Most significantly, Beat writing became a model of resistance or dissidence within Cold War cultures and is now seen as initiating a critique of hegemony.

In light of these realities, Beat immersion in cultures as varied as North African, Meso-American, Japanese, South Asian, East European, Central American, and South American—in addition to multiple racial/ethic cultures within the United States—must be synthesized with earlier understandings of how the Beat movement fashioned personal and artistic identities as specifically American and as "Other."

While the Beat literary project, the "New Vision" that Jack Kerouac, Allen Ginsberg, and William S. Burroughs imagined as a new literary nationalism or national literature, remains the core of Beat literature and its subsequent political and social incarnations, contemporary theories of globilization and transnationalism can elucidate constituent elements of that core, providing a more nuanced understanding of both Beat and the United States.

Anyone who accepts the challenges of this project learns quickly that the terms globalism and transnationalism border on the vexed. Anthropology, sociology, political science, cultural area studies, and economics have all offered perspectives on these concepts. *Transnationalism*, especially, a term coined early in the twentieth century by Randolph Bourne to describe a new way of thinking about relationships between cultures, has been defined in various divergent and convergent forms. Some of the most salient include involving or operating in several nations or nationalities; extending beyond national boundaries; referring to human migration as well as the flow of ideas, money, and credit; a social movement grown out of heightened interconnectivity; an economic process involving the global reorganization of the production process, in which various stages of the production of any product can occur in various countries with the aim of reducing costs; the loosening of cultural boundaries; identities that defy the nation-state; identities tied to multiple nation-states; the prelude to a nationless, global-wide state; and an ongoing movement between two or more social spaces. It is sometimes used synonymously with internationalism and cosmopolitanism, as well as migratory and diasporic processes. With respect to the latter two, the conflation of terms has emerged as the social sciences have recognized both migration and diaspora as not only forced movement of peoples but also voluntary movements for a multitude of purposes and sometimes within existing state boundaries. The expansion of the definition has subsumed expatriate movements such as those of American and British modernists and arcs back to claim the earliest of human movements out of Africa and around the globe.

Economic transnationalism is another term for globalization, which many social scientists agree has accelerated in the latter half of the twentieth century, characterized by the development of the Internet and wireless communication, as well as the development of more efficient forms of global transportation. Globilization is also defined as the intensifying global reach of capitalism and the market; the Americanization of the world through economic strategies and the dominance of the English language; the widening chasm between a developed northern hemisphere and a considerably less developed southern hemisphere; the homogenization (i.e., Westernization) of world cultures, especially at the level of popular culture; and the reality of global power shifting from nation-states to multinational corporations and other nongovernmental enterprises. Both transnationalism and globalization in their broadest definitions can be analyzed from economic, power/political, communication, linguistic, and technology perspectives. And no matter which perspective one chooses, it fast becomes clear that neither transnationalism nor nationalism are inherently emancipatory or reactionary (Ramazani 48).

In the literary context, Mao and Walkowitz explain this "transnational turn" as embracing three approaches: alternate traditions, centrality of transnational circulation and translation, and responses to imperialism. These analyses have begun with methods and perspectives including Marxism, feminisms, hermeneutics, post-colonial studies, African American and Africanist studies, and deconstructivism. Certainly innovators such as Michel Foucault, Franz Fanon, Henry Louis Gates, Barbara Christian, Gilles Deleuze and Felix Guattari, Homi Bhabha, Michael Hardt and Antonio Negri, Donna Haraway, George Landow, and others have transformed the spatial and imaginary landscapes within and by which we identify self and other, the nation and the world. However, as Linda Basch et al. point out, "individuals, communities, or states rarely identify themselves as transnational [or global]" (8). They argue that most transmigrants do not have a transnational form of identity since identity discourse remains grounded in "loyalty to a nation and nation-states." Consequently, they maintain, "*it is only in contemporary fiction . . . that this state of 'in-betweenness' has been fully voiced*" (8, emphasis ours).

Basch et al. rightly cite writers Gloria Anzaldua and Salmon Rushdie as authors who have more fully articulated the reality of living in a transnational and global-ized environment. Others, including Haruki Murakami and Michael Ondaatje, can be easily added to this list of artists who have produced narratives that in essence situate transnational and global literature as a genre that "operates outside the national canon, addresses issues facing deterritorialized cultures, and speaks for those in . . . 'paranational' communities and alliances" (Seyhan 7). As Azade Seyhan explains, "[t]hese are communities that exist within national borders or alongside the citizens of the host country but remain culturally or linguistically distanced from them and, in some instances, are estranged from both the home and the host culture" (7). No argument can be convincingly made that any American Beat writer fits this definition with the smoothness of an Anzaldua, Murakami, or Rushdie. But many, including Kerouac, Ginsberg, Burroughs, Snyder, Kyger, Amiri Baraka, Waldman, and others, fashioned for themselves or found themselves in physical zones cultur-ally or linguistically separate from the perceived boundaries of the states in which they lived. Others, such as ruth weiss and Alexander Trocchi, were born in countries other than the United States, but became part of the American Beat movement: in that space, they carried with them—ruth weiss especially, who was born in Berlin in 1928 and escaped with her Jewish family to the United States in 1939—an identity that bridged both nation-of-birth and adopted country. Still others, perhaps best exemplified by the young people in Prague who elected Ginsberg King of May, forged a paranational identity of liberation and resistance through the fusion of an American Beat hero (Ginsberg) with a local anti-Soviet agenda.

What links them all is the world into which they were born—"the American Century." Marked by industrialization, military dominance, and consumerism, the United States in the twentieth-century produced a culture awash in the convergence of advertising, public relations, and media culture. The latter was engineered to a great extent during World War I by Edward Bernays, a nephew of Sigmund Freud and known as "the Father of public relations/spin." Covertly linking advertising and news reportage, Bernays's propagandistic techniques were staggeringly success-ful from his clients' perspectives: they convinced many Americans that President Woodrow Wilson's decision to enter the war was democratically necessary, that women in the late 1920s should buy and smoke The American Tobacco Company's "Lucky Strikes," and that the United Fruit Company truly did have a right to the economic and political largess of Guatemala in the 1950s (See Tye). The rise of this conflation of economically based tools, used by those in government as well as industry, produced what Edward Said describes as the "unprecedented growth in the apparatus for the diffusion and control of information" (*Culture* 291) underpinning American empire and hegemony in the capitalist world. Following World War II, asserting hegemony abroad was paralleled by "the containment culture" at home in the United States, which saw the rise of the conflation of nationalism and religion as well as the repression of women and the government-sponsored oppression of so-called sexual and political deviants. The Soviet/communist/socialist world was not untouched by these impulses as it attempted to assert a counter global hegemony through military supremacy and space technology. Global, transnational flows intensified as transportation and communication networks reduced distance and time lags. These flows, a concept associated with Arjun Appanduri's seminal work, were not all one way, since cultural, economic, and diasporic transmissions move from periphery to margins to center, as well as from the center. In the process, "world cities," of which New York City is one, emerged as loci of transnational flows, connecting with each other as well as with more peripheral/national/regional locations. The Beats responded to this globalization and American hegemony, particularly by reacting against political/social conformity, class/ethnic barriers, sexual mores, consumerism, and media dominance. At the same time, they responded creatively to the cultural diversity of transnational encounters and the nodes of resistance found in popular culture, ethnic/racial minorities, dissident writers, and artists/the avant-garde. The art and social dissent of the 1940s, 1950s, and early 1960s of the Beat Generation and parallel groups in other countries fed into the broader and more politicized counterculture of the 1960s and early 1970s, which is when, for the most part, Beat writers become known outside the United States. Thus, Beat Generation writers provided a critique and a counter-culture within the United States, while participating in a transnational critique. By so doing, they embody the transnational role of the intellectual, appropriately defined by Said as one whose role is "to challenge and defeat both imposed silence and the normalized quiet of unseen power" (*Humanism* 135). In fact, Czech President and poet Václav Havel, in his preface to the collected interviews of Ginsberg (2001), reiterates this definition, declaring Beat literature "a potential instrument for resistance to the totalitarian system that had been imposed on our existence" (ix).

The state of this project varies, of course, from writer to writer, but the result is a vast body of literature that, while inherently contradictory and in some cases representing less criticality than others, in unison responds to the post–World War II reconfiguring of geographic, political, and economic maps. Within these spheres, the writers negotiated identities, by no means static within the lifetime of the writers or uniform across Beat perspectives, that embrace transnationalism and globalism as complex processes, while simultaneously distrusting these processes as injurious to selfhood, liberation, and literary production. In the latter guise, they act to resist capitalistic and other broad-sweeping cultural forces. Both guises (and their many variations within Beat discourse) imagine America as physical space/s and as a device for connectivity: imaginary landscapes with which the artist/citizen dismisses, or at least questions, myths of nationalism, but refuses to relinquish his or her right to re-dream the culture(s) that nurtured them. Both guises emerge from a 300-year-old national (U.S.) history of creating literature from multiple languages and thus promoting a global character while resisting that character through the dominance of the English language. Working within these histories, Beat writers crafted literature that has modeled a range of responses to post–World War II political and economic regimes—many of which have continued to resonate for post–World War II generations around the world.

Beat literature from a transnational/global perspective began to receive scholarly attention in the 1990s and has grown since 2000. Perhaps most comprehensively, A. Robert Lee has fashioned a broad scholarship on the Beats, arguing over time for an expanded multicultural and international Beat canon. He has articulated transnational currents in his essays on African American Beat writers Ted Joans, Amiri Baraka, and Bob Kaufman (1996, 2004); Chicano writer Oscar Zeta Acosta (2000); and examples of what he calls "Beat International," such as Michael Horovitz, Andrei Vosnesensky, and Kazuko Shiraishi (2010). He has also traced the geography of Beat both inside and outside the United States and has explored the complex affiliations of Beat-inflected writing around the globe—most comprehensively in his book *Modern American Counter Writing* (2010).

In his essay in *Beat Culture* (1999), Jaap van der Bent surveyed the interaction of Beat and Western European writers in France, England, Germany, and the Netherlands, with attention to literary exchange and collaboration through magazines such as *Merlin* (France), *Fragmente* (Germany), and *Litterair Paspoort* (Netherlands). His essay on the Dutch poet Simon Vinkenoog (2000) not only discusses the Vinkenoog/Ginsberg connection but also the broader American/Dutch Beat scene in Amsterdam—with its publications, readings, jazz, cafes, and clubs—and the Amsterdam poetry festivals (1978–1985), which brought together Beat-related poets from many countries.

Jennie Skerl, as the editor of two collections, a special issue of *College Literature* in 2000 and *Reconstructing the Beats* in 2004, has addressed the international scope of Beat as part of a reconceptualization of the Beat Generation as a movement. These collections feature essays by Lee and van der Bent, as well as a frequently cited essay by Daniel Belgrad, "The Transnational Counterculture: Beat-Mexican Intersections," which argues that the American Beats and Mexican Magical Realists were part of a counter-culture organized against the emerging corporate capitalist postwar order. The *College Literature* issue also included Robert Kern's essay on the East/West hybridity of Snyder's *Mountains and Rivers Without End* and Anthony Waine and Jonathan Woolley's essay on the Beat-influenced German poets of the postwar generation born after 1940. In *Reconstructing the Beats*, Deshae Lott and Tony Trigilio discuss the hybrid Western Buddhist philosophies and literary forms of Kerouac and Ginsberg, respectively.

Literary historians have also noted Beat affiliations with the transatlantic, Franco-American avant-garde. Christopher Sawyer-Lauçanno's chronicle of American expatriate writers in Paris after World War II (1992) includes chapters on Ferlinghetti, several Beat writers residing at what became known as the Beat Hotel, and Alexander Trocchi's involvement with *Merlin*. Barry Miles devoted an entire book to a narrative history of the Beat Hotel from 1958 to 1965 (2000), noting that the international aspect of the Beat Generation had been underappreciated, thus excluding writers such as Brion Gysin from the Beat canon. Timothy S. Murphy (2004) and Andrew Hussey (2009) have recently discussed the relationship between Burroughs's cut-up productions and the Situationists, an important Parisian avant-garde movement during the time that Burroughs was living in Paris, one with many parallels to Burroughs's theories of word and image. Hussey also makes an argument for a postcolonial political perspective on Burroughs's work in the context of France's war with Algeria. Kathryne V. Lindberg, in a special issue of *Discourse* (1998), examines Ted Joans's tri-continental internationalist and anticolonial aesthetic, which began with the Beats and French surrealists in New York and Paris as well as Joans's subsequent travels to Africa.

Because of his long-term expatriation and his prescient critique of the post–World War II consumer capitalism, Burroughs, more than any other Beat writer, has recently been the subject of criticism that analyzes his response to globalization, neo-imperialism, and transnational phenomena. Greg Mullins, in *Colonial Affairs: Bowles, Burroughs, and Chester Write Tangier* (2002), situates Burroughs's critique of language and subjectivity within the sexual politics of colonialism and American hegemony. Davis Schneiderman and Philip Walsh's *Retaking the Universe: William S. Burroughs in the Age of Globalization* (2004) collects sixteen essays devoted to reading Burroughs in the context of theories about globalization and resistance. International conferences have also recently taken place in Mexico (2006), Tangier (2008), and Paris (2009), bringing together Burroughs critics from many countries and cross-cultural approaches to his work.

In his conclusion to *The Beat Generation: A Beginner's Guide* (2008), Christopher Gair points out the global dimensions of the Beat Generation, commenting on the American writers' incorporation of other literatures and communities, the Beat-inflected writers in both Western and Eastern Europe in the 1960s and 1970s, and the continuing global circulation of Beat ideals of freedom up to the present. He identifies Beat-inspired movements in the United Kingdom and the former Czechoslovakia, as well as the Beat influence on the post-Soviet Czech Republic and Havel. While the Americanization of cultures poses serious threats to local autonomies, Gair recognizes the paradox that ideals of Beat freedom continue to reify America as the very opposition to the globalization of Americanness.

Testimony to Beat global circulation in specific locations can be found in Philip Mead's essay, "American Model II" (2003), Deborah Baker's *A Blue Hand: The Beats in India* (2008), and Todd F. Tietchen's *Cubalogues: Beat Writers in Revolutionary Havana* (2010). Mead describes the impact of Donald Allen's *The New American Poetry* in Australia in the 1960s, which led to an engagement with American culture (as opposed to English) and its contradictory "emancipatory and imperialist meanings"(180). He particularly notes that Beat narratives of freedom and resistance to authority catalyzed the Australian "Generation of '68." Baker's book is a biographical narrative of the travels of several Beat writers and bohemians with the main focus on Ginsberg and Hope Savage in India, but it also includes the perspectives of their Indian interlocutors, especially the Bengali poets known as the Hungry Generation. As Keith Abbott wrote in a review of the book, "Through the ethnic and artistic values of these exchanges, Baker shows a wider panorama for the influence of India on the American pilgrims"

(Abbott). Tietchen's *Cubalogues* analyzes male Beat writers' travel to and writing about Cuba after the revolution, illuminating the significant roles of Baraka, Ferlinghetti, Harold Cruse, Ginsberg, and journalist Marc Schleifer in the prefiguring of the New Left. He argues that, for these writers, the Cuban Revolution functioned as a transnational and collaborative catalyst for experimenting with new concepts of inter-American politics.

Finally, two scholars in fields other than literature have made important contributions to analysis of Beat transnationalism. Religious studies scholar Stephen Prothero explicates the Beats' religious eclecticism and radical ecumenism, based on their own varied ethnic/cultural backgrounds, interaction with racially marginal and low status social groups, non-Western cultures, and nonorthodox Western spiritual philosophies, revealing multicultural and transnational cross-currents of spiritual resistance to mainstream religion in the post-war period (1991). He later provided the introduction to Tonkinson's *Big Sky Mind* (1995), an anthology of Beat Buddhist writing, which documents the key role that the Beats played in the transmission of Buddhism to America. Anthropologist Howard Campbell, in "Beat Mexico," examines the writing of Beats based on their experiences in Mexico as valid and valuable examples of postmodern ethnography and engagement with non-Western Others who are not members of the cultural elite or the tourist industry (2003).

The essays in this volume touch on many of the themes expressed in the published literature on the transnational dimensions of Beat literature, while opening for critical discussion new areas of the field. Certainly, the essays extend existing discussions, such as the impact of Burroughs's writing in and on transnational zones, Ginsberg's trans-global political experiences, the complexity of U.S./British Beat connections, and the Beat presence in Japan. Further questions are raised about the differences between tourism and cosmopolitanism, exile, textual hybridity, the legacy of colonialism, and the shared values of freedom and democracy. However, the volume also introduces gender, race, and class into these discussions, as well as feminist studies, genre studies, the importance of little magazines, environmental activism through poetics, strengths and weakness of nationalism, technology and cyberspace, the role of translation as both art and political action, and the impact of Beat literature on cultures in Greece, Vienna, Prague, Nicaragua, and Quebec, Canada. As we hope to illustrate in the tripartite construction of this volume, Beat aesthetics and politics create(d) a dialectical movement of ideas across time and space, perpetuating beliefs in the fundamental democratic rights of free speech and liberty for all, while attempting to awaken readers transnationally to the pressing problems facing us as a post–World War II global community.

Part one collects essays on American Beat writers that examine the transnational currents in their writing and their responses to globalizing forces, colonialism, U.S. neo-imperialism, and postwar conformist repression. A number of the essays foreground the politics of Beat aesthetics and the protest in experimental literary styles. Allen Hibbard points out in "William S. Burroughs and U.S. Empire" that Burroughs's life coincided with the expansion of U.S. imperial power, especially after World War II with the spread of American global capitalism, decolonization by European powers, and wars on the periphery. Burroughs's writing both participates in and critiques American imperialist impulses. In this comprehensive essay, Hibbard traces the evolution of Burroughs's political analysis over time—from ironic ambivalence to a more critical response, concluding with Burroughs's prescient fictions of the end of empire and the nation-state in his later works.

The exploration of the transnational heterogeneity of U.S. cultures in Kerouac's fiction is the subject of Hassan Melehy's "Jack Kerouac and the Nomadic Cartographies of Exile." Melehy analyzes the "poetics of exile" derived from Kerouac's experience of French-Canadian ethnicity, the Québécois diaspora, and the anti-assimilationist ideology of *survivance*. Through close readings of *On the Road* and other Kerouac texts, Melehy argues that Kerouac's sense of a loss of origins leads to a nomadism of geographical and linguistic exile, specifically within a series of culturally heterogeneous zones that occur around borders and American identities that resist strict national and territorial fixity, thus challenging stereotypes.

Brenda Frazer has stated that her fictional memoir *Troia* was composed in the style of Kerouac's "spontaneous prose," but her story of Beat travel to Mexico and the transnational hipster culture found there, including her experiences as a mother and prostitute, exposes the gendered constructions that Kerouac's work elides. Ronna C. Johnson's "Beat Transnationalism under Gender: Brenda Frazer's *Troia*" reveals that Beat freedom through travel is limited by the dynamics of the female body as well as gender, race, and class. Frazer's border-crossing—in the company of her husband, Ray Bremser, and their baby daughter, Rachel— triggers policing, vulnerability, and marginality for a woman subjected to patriarchal Madonna-whore roles in two cultures and who experiences the liminality of the border as abjection. Johnson's essay, which critiques the generic Beat road tale and the transnational road tale, challenges scholars of transnationalism and global studies to take seriously gender and feminist perspectives.

As Frazer's memoir attests, Beat writers were often travelers, and Beat travel raises questions about tourism, exploitation, expatriation, Orientalism, exile, and cosmopolitanism—all subject to redefinition in the context of contemporary globalization theory. Jane Falk's essay, "Two Takes on Japan: Joanne Kyger's *The Japan and India Journals* and Philip Whalen's *Scenes of Life at the Capital*," describes Japan as a site of resistance and contested identity as the poets oscillate among the roles of foreign tourist, Zen student, urban flaneur, dissenting expatriate, and cosmopolitan. Both produced generic hybridity in their poems as they adapted Japanese literary forms and images from traditional culture into their American open forms. Gender also marks their experience: Kyger's journal shows how both Japanese and Western patriarchy constrained her, while Whalen could more easily take on the role of the flaneur and social critic.

In examining Beat writers' relationship to Nicaraguan poetry and politics in her essay "'If the Writers of the World Get Together': Allen Ginsberg, Lawrence Ferlinghetti, and Literary Solidarity in Sandinista Nicaragua," Michele Hardesty analyzes the history of this current of Beat transnational poetics through anthologies and journals in the 1960s, the proclaimed solidarity of poets in the "Declaration of Three" in the 1980s, and the post-revolutionary political differences of Nicaraguan poets in power and American outsider poets. Her essay explores claims for a transcendent humanist transnational community of poets as a counter-power to the state, and the responsibilities of the writer to self and nation. As she argues, Ferlinghetti and Ginsberg, in their poetic responses to their travel to post-revolutionary Nicaragua, elucidate the particularities of place, time, and politics that problematize universalist notions of a transnational poetic community.

The internationalism of Beat writing, particularly its relationship to the European avant-garde—especially surrealism—is approached by Jimmy Fazzino through the work of African American Beat writers in "The Beat Manifesto: Avant-Garde Poetics and the Worlded Circuits of African American Beat Surrealism." In his discussion of the manifesto or "manifesto function" in the works of Baraka, Ted Joans, and Bob Kaufman, Fazzino theorizes the transnational, mixed genre of the avant-garde manifesto, which simultaneously serves both artistic and political purposes. He defines African American Beat surrealism as a transatlantic and tri-continental poetics that is anti-imperialist, anticolonialist, and community building. Fazzino also employs the "worlded" concept to position these authors' works in opposition to global hegemony.

Nancy M. Grace's "The Beat Fairy Tale and Transnational Spectacle Culture: Diane di Prima and William S. Burroughs" addresses the theme of textual hybridity and border-crossing in popular culture. She notes that the fairy tale itself is a complex hybrid with polygenetic roots whose iterations in the modern era have often been tied to political or economic goals, a claim exemplified by the globalized commodification of Disney productions. Employing Guy Debord's Situationist theory of spectacle culture, Grace analyzes di Prima's use of the fairy tale in *Dinner and Nightmares* as a bohemian, feminist critique of Cold War culture. Grace's discussion of *The Black Rider*, a theatrical collaboration by Burroughs, Tom Waits, and Robert Wilson, in terms of Situationist *detournement* is the first extended critical analysis of this recent work. Both writers, she argues, paradoxically critique and perpetuate transnational spectacle.

Part Two is devoted solely to an interview with poet Anne Waldman on the transnational dimensions of the Beat literary movement. Waldman is one of the most well-traveled of all the Beat-associated writers, a lived experience reflected in much of her artistic production. In the interview, she defines transnationalism and globalization, reflects on the importance of core American values disseminated globally by the Beats, and discusses the global features of her own poetry; additionally, she addresses the state of publishing in the age of cyberspace, the place of literature as a vehicle for transnational social protest, the critical reception of Beat writers by artists outside the United States, and the ways in which literature is transmitted and translated across state boundaries. Her remarks convincingly demonstrate that art endeavors to persevere no matter what the global or local conditions may be—and in the process serves a vital human function.

Part Three explores Beat-influenced communities and artists outside the United States. The section opens with R. J. Ellis's essay "'They . . . took their time over the coming': The Postwar British/Beat 1957–1965," which maps the scene of British/Beat poetry as an index of postwar British culture. Most British poets, as Ellis reveals through extensive interviews, do not identify as Beat; hence the hyphenated term British/Beat. But Ellis argues that nonetheless the Beats served as significant catalysts for the development of British poetry. The Beat influence began in the

1960s after late 1950s Beat publications reached the United Kingdom; it was both a literary and a cultural phenomenon that redefined poetry, art, and culture, contributing to the rising counter-culture. As Ellis reveals, British/Beat poetry is a matter of complex hybrid cultural transnationalisms with multiple Atlantic crossings involved as well as strong regional and class elements.

The reality of shared cultural visions, as noted in Ellis's essay, is highlighted in Jaap van der Bent's exploration of the Weiner Gruppe (Vienna Group). "Beating Them to It? The Vienna Group and the Beat Generation" argues that in both the United States and Austria small groups of artists rebelled against postwar conformity and conservatism—but as a matter of synchronicity, *not* mutual influence. The Vienna Group's social criticism and artistic forms were similar to those of the Beats, both being concerned with liberation of language and self. Artists such as Conrad Bayer and Oswald Wiener experimented with multimedia collages and were influenced by Dada/surrealism and language philosophy, sharing affinities with Burroughs especially. Café, cabaret, jazz, and performance were also fundamental parts of the scene. Van der Bent concludes with the claim that it was after American Beat literature reached Austria in the 1960s that the Beat influence on Austrian writers really seemed to expand, and to exemplify this point he discusses the work of Walter Buchebner and the development of the Schule für Dichtung/School for Poetry, established in 1991 by the Austrian poet Ide Hintze.

One of the most well-known cross-national Beat events is Ginsberg's 1965 trip to Prague, where he was elected King of May. In "Prague Connection," Josef Rauvolf concentrates on the political dynamics of then-Czechoslavakia, including a discussion of the Midnight group, a parallel, synchronic movement that published samizdat from 1949 to 1953. He then surveys the reception and influence of the Beats, especially Ginsberg, on Czech literature after the Beats became known there from the late 1950s on. The essay details the problems of censorship and political repression that made the Beats highly attractive as models of dissidence, freedom, and outsiderdom. It also presents a nuanced account of Ginsberg's travails in Prague and the ways in which the Czech government used Beat artists and values to reprimand Czech artists and intellectuals who were engaged in dissent.

Similarly, Christopher Gair and Konstantina Georganta, in "Greece and the Beat Generation: the Case of Lefteris Poulios," explore the ways in which Greek artists, especially in the 1970s, drew from Greek tradition as well as American dissident and popular cultures to address regional issues of urban alienation, consumerism, and censorship. Using as a case study the Greek poet Poulios, who acknowledged Beat influence on his work, they analyze the period of the junta in Greece as a time during which Beat writers, who served as quintessentially American and counter-hegemonic in the United States, represented American freedom abroad, particularly in Greece. The essay features an extended discussion of Poulios's poem "An American Bar in Athens," written in 1973, which reflects in theme and form Ginsberg's "A Supermarket in California," and thus illustrates Poulios's role as a poet seeking to shock society in the name of political reform.

The section also includes two essays that examine specific non-U.S. poets who were associated with the American Beat coterie. Fiona Paton, in "*Cain's Book* and the Mark of Exile: Alexander Trocchi as Transnational Beat," positions Trocchi as moving between and within American Beat, Scottish Renaissance, and French Situationist cultures, his insider/outsider status fraught with ambiguity and ambivalence. While Trocchi is probably (and unfortunately) best known as a sexual libertine and voracious drug taker, Paton's analysis reveals the limitations of opposing American and European traditions on a Beat-influenced author such as Trocchi rather than synthesizing them. Her focus on his major work, *Cain's Book*, which fuses neo-Jamesian complexity with the Kerouacian overtones and the forceful pungency of street-slang, argues that the text must be recognized as an essential component of emerging postmodernism.

In "Japan Beat: Nanao Sakaki," A. Robert Lee takes on the complex, comedic poetry of Sakaki, an environmental activist and global traveler/pilgrim/itinerant who had longstanding relationships with Snyder, Ginsberg, Waldman, Kyger, and Ferlinghetti. He was also a founder of The Tribe, Banyan Ashram, with which Snyder was associated, and he was a frequent visitor to Naropa's poetry school. Lee's meticulous reading of a rich collection of Sakaki poems testifies to the fusion of Japanese, Western, and Beat literature in his poetry, as well as his interest in multiple cultures, geographies, and identities. Unlike Trocchi, Sakaki emerges as a cosmopolitan, one who was at home everywhere.

The essays in this volume expand and complicate our understanding of the Beat writers, who participate in a global circulation of a poetics that is also a form of dissent, beginning in the immediate post–World War II period both inside and outside the United States. When viewed through the lens of transnationalism, with its many complicated and contradictory definitions and interpretations, the Beat Generation emerges as a global configuration of artists whose work in total resists the simplistic binaries of square versus hip 1950s culture and the equally simplistic binary of bad nationalism versus good transnationalism. Exploring transnational and trans-generational dimensions of Beat literature also illuminates the biases and blind spots in the transnational studies/Beat studies "interzone," exposing as lacunae, for instance, treatments of genres, gender/sexualities, translation, dissent, and cyberspace. Of course, this volume, built upon an already stimulating collection of foundation texts, is only the next step in the development of what we consider a fertile turn for Beat studies.

Part 1

Transnational Flows

Chapter 1

William S. Burroughs and U.S. Empire

Allen Hibbard

"[Allen] Ginsberg felt strongly that the Beat Generation was an international phenomenon," Barry Miles writes in his introduction to *The Beat Hotel*. "[I]t embodied an approach to life, a set of beliefs that transcended national barriers, and in virtually every country he was able to find a local 'Beat' scene" (6). In addition to the transnational, global reach of Beat influence, there is the transnational, global dimension of various Beat writers' lives, travels, and literary production. Among the borders Beat writers crossed—seeking to extend the realm of experience and escape from prevailing domestic norms—were the actual boundaries between nation-states. Movement and pursuit of freedom, central to the Beat experience, are inextricably linked conceptually, often in an antithetical relationship to stasis, boredom, oppression, and authoritarianism. The same kind of dynamism and freewheeling drama celebrated in Jack Kerouac's *On the Road* is extended from a domestic space into an extra-national space, as our travelers cross the border into Mexico. That quest—that audacity, if you will—is entangled with the operating conditions of empire, as both an enabling condition for travel and the potential for radical critique of the construction and effects of American Empire.

William S. Burroughs is a key figure in this context. Of all those associated with the Beats, it is probably safe to say that Burroughs spent the most time abroad.[1] For about a quarter of a century, from the late 1940s to mid-1970s, Burroughs was somewhat nomadic, responding to various impulses and desires, moving beyond the borders of the United States, and returning from time to time for one reason or another. "Have no base but not much of a voyager," Burroughs stated in a somewhat fictionalized interview conducted by Ann Morrisett in 1963 (Hibbard, "Conversations" 7). His residence in Mexico City and 1953 South American journeys (chronicled in *The Yage Letters* and *Everything Lost*), his sojourn in Tangier at the time Morocco gained its independence, the time he spent in Paris, then London, and his return to the United States in the mid-1970s are all important elements in the story of Burroughs becoming Burroughs—of Burroughs becoming writer.

Burroughs's life coincided with the expansion of U.S. imperial power, particularly after World War II, seen in the growth of global capitalist enterprise as well as attendant wars on the periphery of empire. Michael Hardt and Antonio Negri, in their astute, magisterial study *Empire*, trace the development of American Empire, noting various phases and means by which hegemony is established and maintained.[2] "During the cold war," they write, "this imperialist temptation—or really the ambiguity between protector and dominator—became most intense and more extensive. In other words, protecting countries across the entire world from communism (or, more accurately, Soviet imperialism) became indistinguishable from dominating and exploiting them with imperialist techniques" (178). They see the Vietnam War as "the pinnacle of this tendency." The consolidation of U.S. global power during this period was aided by a number of historical developments, including the waning of European colonial power. The United States moved in to fill a vacuum, propelled by a rhetoric championing its constitution, proclaiming the spread and protection of democracy and liberty. Following the end of the Cold War, the United States entered a new phase of empire, "a global project of network power" marked by a new "open space of imperial sovereignty" (179–180; 182). These power relations are characterized and shaped by patterns of flows described by Arjun Appadurai— flows of media, money, people, ideas, military operations, and so on. Burroughs's Latin American travels in the 1950s coincided with the Cold War, the containment policies of George Kennan, McCarthyism at home, and the Korean War abroad, involving tens of thousands of American soldiers. A decade later, Burroughs viewed the 1960s largely from abroad. In the late 1970s, he returned to the United States in time to live most of the last phase of his life in the Reagan-Bush era.

What I propose to do in this essay is consider Burroughs's story—his personal narrative—alongside this unfolding of the national narrative. Key questions will be: To what extent does Burroughs participate in dominant American imperialist impulses and dynamics? To what extent does he offer a critique of those forces? And how do his attitudes evolve (if indeed they do) in response to his encounters with the world beyond the borders of the United States? Burroughs's direct acquaintance with places beyond the borders of the United States (but sometimes still within the sphere of U.S. influence), I suggest, made him more aware of the forces and dynamics of the so-called third world, authoritarianism, independence movements, and the postcolonial scene, resulting in a perspective that extended beyond Cold War, parochial, containment views of the United States and the world. His thinking and presentation of notions of empire, control, and power respond to the circumstances he observed in his own journeys through liminal spaces on the fringes of empires as well as time he spent in old imperial capitals. He was an astute witness to the process and arc of U.S. imperial expansion and (over time) its subsequent decline. While his stance is often ambivalent or ironic—particularly during his early ventures beyond national borders—increasingly he registers stronger critical positions vis-à-vis the operation of the U.S. Empire.[3] Certainly Burroughs would not have become the writer he became and written what he wrote if he had not taken these journeys outside the borders of the United States, as they afforded him a chance to gain a broader understanding of empire, an understanding that is frequently registered in his work. The evolution of that understanding, I argue, is displayed in his work and is integrally connected to an awareness obtained from his movements abroad during a critical phase of U.S. history.

Take One: South of the Border

Burroughs's first major ventures outside the United States, beginning in 1949, were south of the border to Mexico.[4] We might recall lines near the opening of *Naked Lunch* that describe a sense of relief associated with crossing the border:

> Something falls off you when you cross the border into Mexico, and suddenly the landscape hits you straight with nothing between you and it, desert and mountains and vultures; little wheeling specks and others so close you can hear their wings cut the air (a dry husking sound), and when they spot something they pour out of the blue sky, that shattering bloody blue sky of Mexico, down in a black funnel. (14)

Of course, one of the reasons for this easing of pressure, as he crossed the border, was the fact that he, an outlaw running away from a court appearance to face drug charges in New Orleans, was out of reach of the American legal system. Issues of freedom and control become important; somewhat ironically, Burroughs leaves the United States in order to escape systems of control and preserve personal liberty. During these first journeys, Burroughs often displays a rather naïve or ironic attitude toward this position of privilege as an American traveler. Yet, at the same time, we see signs of a developing consciousness of both his position and global historical forces. These ambivalent postures resemble those of the Western travelers Ali Behdad discusses in his study *Belated Travelers: Orientalism in the Age of Colonial Dissolution*. In his analysis of works by writers such as Gerard de Nerval, Gustave Flaubert, Rudyard Kipling, Lady Anne Blunt, Isabel Eberhardt, and others, Behdad describes what he terms "split discursive practice": sympathy with the colonial subject and, at the same time, a residual alliance with the power structures of societies from which they traveled—a foot in both camps, if you will.

The time Burroughs spent in Mexico and his trips into regions farther south, into South America, were critical for his development as a writer. In Mexico, he found the space, time, psychic conditions, and material needed to write. *Junky, Queer,* and *The Yage Letters*—his first trio of works that must be thought of as interrelated texts—all owe their existence to Burroughs's extended sojourn south of the border.[5] It was also in Mexico City, on September 6, 1951, in his apartment at 210 Calle Orizaba, that one of the most notorious events in Burroughs's life took place: the famous enactment of his William Tell routine that resulted in his deadly shooting of his wife, Joan Vollmer. The incident has become a defining component of the Burroughs legend. Lines from near the end of his introduction to *Queer*, written for the 1985 publication of the novel which he had penned while he was in Mexico in the early 1950s, after Vollmer's death, are frequently cited to support the notion that this event is directly linked to his development as a writer: "I am forced to the appalling conclusion that I would never have become a writer but for Joan's death, and to a realization of the extent to which this event has motivated and formulated my writing" (134–135). He goes on to describe a kind of haunting, a fear of possession by the Ugly Spirit, either kept at bay or exorcized to some extent by the act of writing.

Despite the liberating sensation of being rid of "the U.S. drag" associated with crossing into Mexico as described in *Naked Lunch*, Burroughs nonetheless carried a lot of cultural baggage with him, even if unwittingly, simply because of his nationality, class, and race. While in Mexico, he could not help but become more aware of the dynamics between the United States and Mexico. One only has to read Cormac McCarthy's *Blood Meridian* to be reminded that U.S. incursions into Mexico have not been wholly benevolent and amicable. In the history of U.S. intervention in Latin American politics, and imperialist designs, one thinks of the Mexican-American War, the Spanish-American War, and, more recently, interventions in Cuba, Nicaragua, and Chile. It's been called the good neighbor policy, a phrase Burroughs alludes to satirically in *The Yage Letters*.

Queer owes itself to Burroughs's experience in Mexico and bears the traces of the place. In his introduction to the novel, Burroughs describes Mexico City— its poverty, corruption, deep association with Aztec culture, and air of immanent violence—as a kind of matrix for the novel's actions. And in his introduction to the twenty-fifth-anniversary edition of *Queer*, Oliver Harris cites and concurs with Jorge García Robles's claim that "if there exists a 'Mexican novel' in the Burroughs oeuvre, it is *Queer*" (xv). Harris examines a multitude of ways Mexico City (then later, of course, Ecuador) figures in the novel, starting with Amsterdam Avenue park in the opening scene of the book which "for many North American readers probably suggests the Upper West Side of Manhattan" (iv). The park Burroughs describes, however, is "the Parque México, around which runs the oval-shaped Calle Amsterdam" (xiv). Even the concrete bench "that was molded to resemble wood" has a real source in the park (2).

As a transnational novel of the 1950s in which American characters figure prominently, *Queer* also inscribes aspects of interactions between U.S. domestic politics and foreign policy during the Cold War period, where alleged communists and homosexuals, considered threats to the nation's ideology, were hounded out, prosecuted, suppressed, or banished. At work is containment policy writ large: threats to dominant American ideology can and should be kept outside national borders. The novel's central motivating force is the protagonist's, Lee's, preoccupation with and pursuit of the young American Allerton. Significantly, this drama is played out beyond the borders of the nation, rather as in James Baldwin's novel *Giovanni's Room*, set in France and published in 1956. Harris reminds us that *Queer* is produced at a time when we see "the demonization of homosexuality as an un-American, viral contagion and threat to the body politic" (xxv). And, at the same time, despite the personal, almost confessional, quality of the novel, it also invites consideration of an analogous relationship between the operation of an individual psyche (one that through its pursuit of an object of desire both attempts to establish control while almost inevitably losing control at the same time) and the operation of empire. Harris points to "the connection [the novel] repeatedly implies between the intimate world of individual desires and a global narrative of power." (xxvi).[6] At the same time that Lee "fantasizes a brutal imperialism," he "turns the argument inside out and seeks to reverse the demonized position of the queer in cold war America by fully identifying with American power at its most demoniacal" (xxvii).

Given this narrative stance, and the attendant anti-"fag," anti-Jew rhetoric, it is difficult to determine how straight to take things. (It is, after all, a novel called *Queer*.) The satirical, parodic potential of this early novel is not always entirely clear, perhaps reflecting the writer's own ambivalence and conflicting feelings at the time. The novel seems to display, recalling Hardt and Negri's characterization of U.S. Empire, "ambiguity between protection and domination," played out in Lee's obsession with Allerton. The analogous relationship between self and empire, thus, prompts consideration of the degree of Burroughs's complicity with those forces and ideology underpinning the creation and maintenance of empire. The issue is all at once specific to Burroughs and more generally philosophical. To what extent are we bound by our material conditions—culture, history, gender, and class? To what extent can we—through experience, thought, and reading— imaginatively transcend our own position, see it from the outside, and consider the place of the other? The move toward parody or irony can be seen as a step toward the recognition of one's place in the larger drama; writing *from*, or with a keen appreciation of, the other's point of view might be a further step. In his essay "With Imperious Eye," Manuel Martinez argues that American Beat writers acted within the framework of colonial privilege as they traveled and wrote about Mexico. Certainly evidence can be found to support that view. Daniel Belgrad counters that view, however, proposing that we see relations in terms of a "cross-cultural dialogue" that recognizes "the multiplicity of subject positions created by the power dynamics of imperialist hegemony" ("Transnational" 40). We should, Belgrad suggests, think of a dynamic relationship between Mexico and the United States, in which Beat writers' projects "intersected with the major currents of Mexican cultural and intellectual life" and Mexican writers such as Octavio Paz crossed into the United States (29).

Burroughs's ambivalent stance toward residual colonialism and its attendant privileges are acutely felt in *The Yage Letters*, a work that traces and inscribes Burroughs's travels beyond Mexico, into South America. One particular, perhaps iconic, moment memorialized in image and word, poignantly captures Burroughs's encounter with empire, and displays his ironic posture vis-à-vis the cultural forces surrounding him. I refer to the photograph of Burroughs in Mocoa, taken in March of 1953. The image easily takes hold in the mind and has become part of the Burroughs legend: the tall lanky American, wearing slacks (or perhaps jeans) and a white shirt with sleeves rolled up past his elbow, holds a pith helmet in one hand and an anyahuasca vine in the other; he is standing in profile, projecting his gaze upward, toward some distant El Dorado—the great white explorer in the jungles. We've seen the picture before in various forms. It could be Pizarro, or David Livingston, or Marlow in *Heart of Darkness*, or Bogart in *The African Queen*. It signifies the expansion of capitalism and empire into potentially resistant or hostile spaces, previously undisturbed by outside contact or force. Burroughs strikes the pose, and in so doing takes on a part, submits to a role, perhaps in a parodic mode, much as he does in his routines. It's a little act, a scene. We'll play along with it, see where it goes, and have some fun in the process. Still, the act of parody, by

mimicking the original pose, in some way perpetuates that order even as it admits
a critical perspective on it.

In a letter written to Ginsberg on April 15, 1953, from Hotel Nuevo Regis in Bogotá,
Burroughs reflects on his journey "through Cali, Popayan and Pasto to Mocoa":

> This trip I was treated like visiting royalty under the misapprehension I was a repre-
> sentative of the Texas Oil Company traveling incognito. (Free boat rides, free plane
> rides, free chow; eating in officers' mess, sleeping in the governor's house.)
>
> The Texas Oil company surveyed the area a few years ago, found no oil and pulled
> out. But everyone in the Putumayo believes the Texas Company will return. Like the
> second coming of Christ. (*Yage Redux* 24)

The only reason local residents, given previous experience, could think of that would
account for the presence of this white American man in the backwaters of Colombia—
looking like a businessman in the jungle—was that he was there to prospect, to find
something valuable to his home culture and find a means to extract and transport it
back to market, at minimal cost and maximum profit. Silver, rubber, oil. Little did
most know or suspect that his prospecting was for another kind of holy grail, that magical hallucinogenic substance, indigenous to the area—ya-heh, or yage. Perhaps more
important was the journey itself, the prospecting for raw material that he transformed
or processed in his writing. In his search for yage, Burroughs uncannily displays elements of a history of interactions between the United States and Latin America involving drugs, money, guns, and political struggles between right and left.

A noticeable degree of American exceptionalism can be detected in these portray-
als of Americans traveling through Latin America in the early 1950s, even though
the writer displays an ambivalent posture.[7] "Burroughs traveled through the region
always aware of the exile's ironic power to still exercise the master race's privileges—
his class identity projected here as the dark side of 'William Lee, the Ugly American,'"
as Harris puts it, in his introduction to *The Yage Letters Redux* (xxvi). Yet, as we have
seen, Burroughs's position was not so simple: "[He] played the Ugly American ambig-
uously, at times blind to its operation, at others holding the identity up for coruscat-
ing critique," Harris notes, pointing to signs of "the political education Burroughs
received in South America" (xxx). Evidence of this evolution in Burroughs's thought
is found toward the end of the series of letters when Burroughs concludes that "the
Colombian Civil War is basically about . . . the fundamental split between the South
American Potential and Repressive Spanish life-fearing character armadillos. I have
never felt myself so definitely on one side and unable to see any redeeming features in
the other" (38). It would have been far more unlikely, and more difficult, for him to
reach these conclusions had he remained within U.S. borders.

Take Two: Tangier/Interzone[8]

Burroughs left Latin America in August of 1953. By February of 1954 he had arrived
in Tangier. Once again—as always seems to be the case with Burroughs and certain
other Beats—we know the legend. Indeed, the legends often eclipse attempts to

find out what really happened—if in fact one ever can determine one true, reliable account of events. Tangier is where Burroughs took up with a Spanish-speaking young man named Kiki. It's where he was either feeding or trying to kick his drug habit. It's where—at the Villa Muneria—Ginsberg, Peter Orlovsky, Kerouac, and Alan Ansen came in 1957 to help assemble the manuscript that became *Naked Lunch*. Beyond this, however, Burroughs's experience in Tangier must be placed in relation to resistance to colonialism and the Moroccan independence movement. Despite some recent attention to these connections, the role his time in Morocco played in the development of his thinking has yet to be fully appreciated. If in Latin America Burroughs began to become aware of the fact of U.S. Empire and his implicit association with its machinery, in Morocco he found himself a witness to resistance to colonial rule, and the dismantling of that rule.

It is surprising, when we realize Tangier was where he did most of the work compiling the book, that the city doesn't figure more prominently than it does in *Naked Lunch*. Still, the city's presence is felt strongly throughout the novel. In my essay for the volume *NL@50*, I claim that "there would be no *Naked Lunch* at least not in the form we know it, without Burroughs's sojourn in Tangier from 1954–1958." I suggest that "the very nature of changing conditions in Tangier, as it moved from International Zone status toward integration within a newly independent Morocco, is registered in both the novel's making and its final form." Though Burroughs once characterized himself as "the most politically neutral man in Africa," ("Tangier" 118), there is plenty of evidence to suggest that he was aware of (and even interested in) the social and political transformations going on around him, as the colonial system crumbled and collapsed and was replaced by an independent Moroccan government, in the form of a monarchy, under the rule of Mohammed V.

Burroughs's ambivalent posture toward these events in Morocco is not unlike his responses to the scene he witnessed in Latin America. While he seemed to have little sympathy for the French colonial regime (one more system of domination and repression), neither did he openly embrace the nationalist movement, which itself (like any political party or movement) was prone to bend people to its agenda. (Burroughs was fairly consistently opposed to government interference in private personal liberties, whether in the form of Roosevelt New Dealism or McCarthyism in the United States, or nationalist/fundamentalist pressures elsewhere.) He did not succumb to the kind of "imperial nostalgia" that some of his more reactionary fellow expatriates felt and expressed.[9] "I have no nostalgia for the old days in Morocco, which I never saw," he wrote to Ginsberg on October 29, 1956. "Right now is for me" (*Letters* 337). And several months later (January 28, 1957), after the return of Mohammed V to the throne, he wrote again to Ginsberg: "ARABS ARE NOT VIOLENT . . . . Riots are the accumulated, just resentment of a people subjected to outrageous brutalities by the French cops" (*Letters* 349).

Naked Lunch contains a number of scenes and references to the contemporary political situation in Morocco. The section entitled "Ordinary Men and Women" opens with a scene depicting a "Luncheon of Nationalist Party on balcony overlooking the Market" (101). A character simply identified as "Party Leader" (supposedly associated with the nationalist movement and seeking support for the cause, and aka P.L.) surveys the market and remarks to his interlocutor, referred to simply as

Lieutenant, "*Ordinary* men and women going about their ordinary everyday tasks." The description of the Party Leader—who creates the impression of a "successful gangster in drag," dressed in a djellaba, hairy legs showing, wearing Western-style shoes, smoking a cigar and drinking whisky—is satirical. That the character is given no proper name suggests that he is simply playing a prescribed role, one that in fact becomes his identity. As the scene unfolds (characteristically without authorial comment) it seems as though the leader is more interested in gaining recruits from the nationalist cause (for the enhancement of his own position) than in the real needs of ordinary men and women.

Immediately after the scene is set, a boy from the street jumps the rail and approaches the two.

> *LIEUTENANT*: "No, we do not want to buy any used condoms! Cut!"
> *P.L.*: "Wait! . . . Come in, my boy. Sit down . . . Have a cigar. . . Have a drink."
> *He paces around the boy like an aroused tom cat.*
> *P.L.*: "What do you think about the French?"
> *"Huh?"*
> *P.L*: "The French. The Colonial bastard who is sucking your live corpuscles."
> *"Look mister. It cost two hundred francs to suck my corpuscule.. . .*
> *P.L.*: "Now look, kid, let's put it this way. The French have dispossessed you of your
>   birthright." (102)

The hustler is portrayed as being more concerned about his own business than about political issues, while the Party Leader is portrayed as being self-interested, hypocritical.

Later we return to the Nationalists. This time the Nationalists' encounter is with two capitalists, Clem and Jody, who show no interest in "ordinary men and women" beyond their interest in preying on them.

> A group of sour Nationalists sits in front of the Sargasso sneering at the queens and jabbering in Arabic. Clem and Jody sweep in dressed like the capitalist in a communist mural.
>
> *CLEM*: "We have come to feed on your backwardness."
> *JODY*: "In the words of the Immortal Bard, to batten on these Moors."
> *NATIONALIST*: "Swine! Filth! Sons of dogs! Don't you realize my people are
>   hungry?"
> *CLEM*: "That's the way I like to see them."
>
> The Nationalist drops dead, poisoned by hate. . . . Doctor Benway rushes up: "Stand back everybody, give me air." He takes a blood sample. "Well, that's all I can do. When you gotta go you gotta go." (119)

These references suggest that Burroughs was, on some level, to some extent, aware of the political turmoil around him in Morocco; they display an ambivalent if not critical attitude toward political actors and their motives, consistent with his

libertarian views and his distaste for bureaucracy and organized political movements.[10] Indeed, readers could easily take offense at depictions of Arabs in *Naked
Lunch*, particularly if the possibility of parody is not admitted. For instance, Kurt
Hemmer suggests that if the novel were published today "it would probably inspire a
mufti to declare a *fatwa* for Burroughs's immediate silencing" (65). He contends that
"while certain aspects of *Naked Lunch* bring into sharp focus the cruelty of imperialism in Tangier, other aspects appear to reify that oppression." While the disjunctive
narrative form itself signals a resistance to traditional representational schemes, the
content of the work at times is at odds with revolutionary impulses. Thus, Hemmer
proposes that the novel be seen as a text of "desistance" rather than "resistance" (66).
True, Burroughs did not openly embrace the cause of Moroccan independence. To
some extent, his views of liberty and freedom were not unlike those undergirding
the exceptionalist basis of the expansion of U.S. Empire and hegemony. The spread
of liberty and freedom have been (and still are) used as rhetorical justification for
American intervention and domination, yet the real motives often have more to do
with consolidating political and economic power. Burroughs was interested in the
spectacle of social disorder partly because it reflected a movement with potential
for disrupting if not overturning mechanisms of control and partly for aesthetic
reasons. In "Jihad Jitters," a routine contained in a letter to Ginsberg, he displays a
fascination with the 1955 riots. "Really, rioting must be the greatest, like snap, *wow*.
I mean I dug it watching them Arabs jumping around yelling and laughing, and
they laugh in serious riots" (*Letters* 341).

The extent to which Burroughs cared about or was affected by his sojourn in Tangier
remains a topic of debate. A consideration of Burroughs within the context of American
Empire, along with a reading of his letters and literary production from the period,
clearly shows the impact his experience in Tangier had on him. He benefited from
privileges associated with U.S. citizenship at a time when the country was emerging as
a power in the region, following its involvement in the North Africa campaign during
World War II, and during the subsequent collapse of the French colonial regime in
Morocco. Throughout the Cold War and since, Morocco has consistently tilted toward
Washington. Brian Edwards offers a clear and accurate summation of Burroughs's position in Morocco: Despite the writer's "Orientalist framework," he nonetheless "may
from this position imagine a contestatory position that undoes the more particular U.S.
political position in Tangier and within cold war domestic culture" (174).

Take Three: Paris

Burroughs moved from Tangier to Paris toward the end of the 1950s, at a critical
moment in his own career and in the cultural and political life of France. Once
again, we know the legend—Burroughs's residence, along with that of Ginsberg,
Gregory Corso, and Brion Gysin (at various times), at the Beat Hotel, 9 rue
Git-le-Coeur. To this day, Burroughs fans who find themselves in Paris make their
pilgrimages to the place, ready to worship at the shrine, only to discover a very

chi-chi hotel at the address. Beyond the legend, we might ask, what did Burroughs do in Paris, and what did Paris do to Burroughs? It was in Paris that he finished *Naked Lunch*, worked on a number of collaborative projects, and (under the influence of Gysin) developed the cut-up technique, producing *The Soft Machine* and part of *The Ticket that Exploded*. In other words, Burroughs's sojourn in Paris marks a key stylistic shift in his work. It might also mark a certain development of his thinking about the world around him. What we see in these novels is a supra-national world, rather like what we find in *Star Trek* or *Star Wars*, difficult if not impossible to locate in time or space, where the Nova Police battle the Nova Mob. Empire is extended into space. We might think of this time in Paris as a time during which Burroughs consolidated his understanding of experiences in Latin America and Morocco, in light of the visible, dramatic struggle France, as a colonial power, was engaged in with its colonies, particularly Algeria.

Miles's *The Beat Hotel*, published in 2000, several years after the deaths of Ginsberg and Burroughs, has a nostalgic tone. An era is over, we feel. The world has changed, and all we can do is look longingly back at a time when it was possible to live a carefree, bohemian life, unworried about where money would come from or what plans we should make for retirement. One gets the sense, also, in reading Miles, that the Beats did not venture far from the Beat Hotel, other than to go to museums, to bookstores, or in search of various (mainly forbidden) pleasures. "As non-French speakers," Miles writes, "they had no involvement with French culture and the issues of the day, nor were they restricted by rules with which the French lived, simply because they were ignorant of them." He goes on to quote Jean-Jacques Lebel: "They were on an island, isolated in this magic little paradise full of rats and bad smells" (19). Later Miles does acknowledge that the Beats, even though relatively isolated from French politics, could not help being aware of the war in Algeria and the heated debates surrounding the Algerian question.

The importance of Paris for Burroughs was much greater than often thought, as demonstrated in recent scholarship by Andrew Hussey and Timothy S. Murphy. In "'Paris is about the last place. . .': William Burroughs In and Out of Paris and Tangier, 1958–1960," first delivered in the form of a paper at a 2008 conference in Tangier, Hussey makes a strong case that in Paris the writer consolidated strands of thinking begun earlier. "Burroughs's itinerary between Paris and Tangier," Hussey proposes, should be seen as "tracing a growing political consciousness during this period" (74). The move from Tangier to Paris was from a postcolonial country to a center of colonial activity. The Paris Burroughs arrived in was in the throes of conflict over the Algeria question, with ferment among various avant-garde political organizations. Suggesting that we might think of *Naked Lunch* as a postcolonial novel, Hussey proposes a more nuanced "post-nationalist" relationship between Burroughs and Morocco, one not wholly colonialist or predatory. He shows how Burroughs would have been aware of (and perhaps influenced by) movements such as the Situationists (Guy Debord) and the Lettrists (Isidore Isou), groups with whom he would have found a good deal of affinity, both in terms of philosophy and method. Indeed, what Burroughs found in Paris "was a matrix of avant-garde movements, all of them deeply marked by the tensions of their age and with an absolute belief in revolution as real experience rather than metaphor or theory" (78–79).

Murphy also explores connections between Burroughs and Debord in his essay "Exposing the Reality Film: William S. Burroughs Among the Situationists." Both were keenly aware of the growing power of the image in the post–World War II period. And while both were acquainted with Alexander Trocchi, who may have served as a link between them, Murphy cautions that claims for direct influence remain speculative. Flows of communication would have gone from the Situationists to Burroughs. Murphy usefully draws comparisons between the key Situationist notion of spectacle and Burroughs's notion of the reality studio, citing Debord's description of the spectacle as "not a collection of images; rather, it is a social relationship between people that is mediated by images" (qtd. in Murphy 34). It is, furthermore "the self-portrait of power in the age of power's totalitarian rule over conditions of existence" (qtd. in Murphy 34). At once, then, we realize a shared concern for the operation of power, particularly through the careful construction and distribution of images, with corporate mass media playing a key, intermediary role in the process.

Burroughs and Debord, along with poststructuralist French theorists who were developing and refining their ideas at the same historical moment, began to articulate aspects of the global postmodern condition. Like thinkers such as Derrida and Althusser, Burroughs was interested in how dominant worldviews (ideologies) are constructed and maintained—by whom and to what purposes? And, like Michel Foucault and Gilles Deleuze and Félix Guattari, he thought about how dominant systems could be resisted. One tactic Burroughs proposed was to cut the tape and intersperse it with portions of other tapes. Take charge of your own narrative. Disrupt national narratives; "Storm the Reality Studio." Reshuffle material formed by traditional modes of production. Contemporary mythologies, worldviews produced electronically and disseminated widely, thus were formed and functioned much in the way Greek myths or tribal myths used to work in smaller societies. Both Burroughs's cut-up technique and the Situationist practice of *detournement* envisioned a transformation of everyday lived experience, springing from a consciousness of shaping forces and optimizing the capacity for individual self-determination.

Paris, a colonial center feeling the resistance of colonized subjects, thus was a critical place where Burroughs experimented with literary techniques and continued to develop his thinking about systems of control in a late-capitalist global scene. A revolutionary mood was in the air, with the spring of 1968 just around corner.

Take Four: London

Throughout the 1960s Burroughs frequently moved around, shuttling between Paris, London, Tangier, New York, Palm Beach, and other places. By the time he settled in London in 1966, he was fairly well acquainted with this colonial capital of empire that had been waning, through World War II and after. While London was his base, Burroughs published a string of works: *The Wild Boys, The Job, Port of Saints, The Last Words of Dutch Schultz,* and *Exterminator!* These works appeared in the context of the Vietnam War and growing insurgency and resistance movements, both on the periphery of empire (such as Che, Castro, the Vietcong) and within empire itself.

Burroughs had been living in England for several years when he went to cover the Democratic Convention in Chicago for *Esquire* in the summer of 1968. Jean Genet and Norman Mailer, both of whom he met at the time, were there to cover the convention, as well. The spectacle of violent clashes between young radicals and police forces fascinated Burroughs, just as riots in Morocco had fascinated him a decade earlier. At this point, Burroughs's stance was less ambivalent. His excitement and revolutionary sympathies are clearly felt in an interview conducted by Jeff Shero at the time of the convention and published in the radical rag *Rat*: "It seems to me to be the most antipolitical revolt that I've ever seen and perhaps that there's ever been in history," he said of the radical movements of the 1960s (Hibbard, *Conversations* 17).

He goes on to offer candid views on the obsolescence of the nation-state, the folly of the Vietnam War that extended American Empire in a way not unlike the French occupation of Algeria, the growing capacity of military technology to kill without direct contact with the enemy, and governments' forceful repression of dissidents in so-called democracies, as well as by authoritarian regimes. When asked about possibilities for revolution in Great Britain, Burroughs said, "It must happen after they get rid of the idea of this bloody Queen. . . . There's no hope for them until we have five thousand people out in Trafalgar Square screaming 'Bugger the Queen'" (Hibbard, *Conversations* 22, 23).

Some of these views can be felt strongly in fiction Burroughs wrote at the time, notably in *The Wild Boys* and *Port of Saints*, both of which respond to the revolutionary possibilities of this historical moment, presenting fictionalized possibilities of resistance. In *Wising Up the Marks*, Murphy underscores how "Burroughs's invention of a new set of fantasies [occurs] during the period of cultural unrest in the late sixties" (146). In *The Wild Boys*, for instance, young men from around the globe gather and form packs that stand in opposition to nation-states, families, and other established institutions of the status quo; they are bound together by mutually reinforcing, nonreproductive sexual energies. They cross national boundaries and resist the power of U.S. Empire:

> In Mexico, South and Central America guerrilla units are forming an army of liberation to free the United States. In North Africa from Tangier to Timbuctu corresponding units prepare to liberate Western Europe and the United Kingdom. Despite disparate aims and personnel of its constituent members the underground is agreed on basic objectives. We intend to march on the police machine everywhere. We intend to destroy the police machine and all its records. We intend to destroy all dogmatic verbal systems. (139–140)

The narrator of this section announces that he is on his way from London to Tangier and that while in North Africa he will "contact the wild-boy packs that range from the outskirts of Tangier to Timbuctu." He "will learn their specialized skills and transfer wild-boy units to the Western cities. We know that the West will invade Africa and South America in an all-out attempt to crush the guerrilla units" (140).

This world, as Murphy and other critics note, lies in the realm of fantasy, or (as the novel's subtitle indicates) the realm of the dead. The narrative voice in these works of the late 1960s registers sympathy for resistance to empire that is less ambiguous than earlier writing, from the 1950s, that we have examined. The writing from this period certainly draws from experiences of these other places and the revolutionary potential Burroughs witnessed there.

No Place Like Home

"In my beginning is my end," another St. Louis–born writer, T.S. Eliot, writes in *The Four Quartets* ("East Coker"). And: "Home is where one starts from." After a couple of decades of nomadic wandering abroad, Burroughs returned to the United States in February 1974 to live in New York. His final move, toward the end of 1981, was to Lawrence, Kansas, in the heartland of the country, the belly of empire, and akin to a return to his St. Louis childhood. Like Voltaire's Candide, after a life of picaresque wandering and adventure, during which he came to know parts of the world outside the boundaries of his native land, Burroughs chose to settle down, not to tend his garden but to commune with his cats and fire shotguns into paint canisters, producing new and unexpected designs.

It was in this last phase of his life, back in his homeland, that Burroughs wrote his final Western Lands trilogy, a crowning achievement to his already significant career as a writer. These works, that like *The Wild Boys* and *Port of Saints* at times occupy and depict a land of the dead, embark on a revisioning and rewriting of U.S. history, providing alternative scenarios that could perhaps have averted a course of empire predicated on the domination (or extermination) of others. I contend that these works could not have been written had it not been for Burroughs's time abroad, a time, as I have suggested, during which he came to know the extent and operation of U.S. Empire up close. The utopian social visions displayed in the Western Lands trilogy (notably in *Cities of the Red Night*) have their origins in the notion of the "composite city," which Burroughs wrote of as early as 1953, when he was in Latin America. Burroughs's writing from this period expresses his most mature and comprehensive narrative scope, geographically expansive and temporally unbound.

It is not possible to do justice to the trilogy in this essay.[11] A very brief glimpse of *Cities of the Red Night*, however, will at least point toward the relevance of these works within the context of U.S. global power. In the introductory chapter of the novel, we are given an overview of the premises underlying the following stories. Our attention is immediately drawn to "pirate communes" of the eighteenth century, in particular one established by a Captain Mission and based upon a set of Articles that included the prohibition of slavery, the abolition of the death penalty, citizen consent to public policies, and freedom of religious and sexual practice "without sanction or molestation" (xii). In other words, what is imaginatively created here in fictional form is a libertarian, Utopian space—outside traditional boundaries of time and nation-state—in which individual rights and freedoms (both those of the colonizers and colonized) are not violated. Such an alternative approach to the encounter with the other would has resulted in a vastly different present, one in which the United States was not in an antagonistic relationship with resistance and freedom fighters around the globe:

> At once we have allies in all those who are enslaved and oppressed through the world, from the cotton plantations of the American South to the sugar plantations of the West Indies, the whole Indian population of the American continent peonized and degraded by the Spanish into sub-human poverty and ignorance, exterminated by the Americans, infected with their vices and diseases, the natives of Africa and Asia—all these are potential allies. (xiii)

One of the subsequent narrative strands in the novel consists of the first person account of the travels of American gunsmith Noah Blake who signs up for service on what turns out to be a pirate ship, and whose travels around the globe resemble those of Captain Cooke and other explorers associated with colonial powers. The members of Blake's renegade group, however, develop new military technologies to use against colonial forces and distribute them to indigenous populations, thus altering the balance of power. These narratives stand in contrast to the historical account of colonization and expansion of empire.

Belief in the revolutionary potential of the youth movements of the 1960s had faded by the 1980s. Burroughs calls his vision a "retroactive Utopia," suggesting that the chance for such a revolutionary project had been missed.

> There is simply no room left for "freedom from the tyranny of government" since city dwellers depend on it for food, power, water, transportation, protection, and welfare. Your right to live where you want, with companions of your choosing, under laws to which you agree, died in the eighteen century with Captain Mission. Only a miracle or a disaster could restore it. (xv)

Coda: Empire's End?

In a scene toward the beginning of Book Three of *Cities of the Red Night*, Blake relates an account of traveling by train in twentieth-century United States. At the U.S.-French Canada border, the border control official takes his passport, along with those of fellow American travelers, and tosses them into a stove to burn. The documents are deemed forgeries, "lies": "Documents purportedly issued by a government which ceased to exist two hundred years ago" (253). Thus in one possible extension of an alternative history, Burroughs projects a point at which U.S. imperial power has dissolved. No longer does the U.S. passport assure the kind of privilege Burroughs enjoyed as a U.S. citizen during his travels. The scene also carries an implicit criticism of the way nation-states control human movement, calling to mind one of Captain Mission's articles: freedom of movement unrestricted by national boundaries.

Ginsberg recalls Burroughs talking to him and Kerouac about the "end of empire" as early as the 1940s. In the past decade, following Burroughs's death near the century's end, discussions of the end of American Empire have proliferated. Cullen Murphy, in *Are We Rome? The Fall of an Empire and the Fate of America*, compares our current situation to that of Rome during its period of decline. In *Colossus: The Rise and Fall of the American Empire*, Niall Ferguson notes an ambivalence toward the exercise of imperial power within the United States and argues the need for a confident, unapologetic use of U.S. power in the twenty-first century to spread social freedom, spur development, combat disease and tyranny, and support free market principles around the world. Johan Galtung, in *The Fall of U.S. Empire—and Then What?*, projects the end of U.S. Empire by 2020, accelerated five years by the actions of George W. Bush. Chalmers Johnson's fourth book on American imperialism, *Dismantling the Empire: America's Last Best Hope*, critically examines the vast and costly overextension of the U.S. military around the world and proposes a plan for divestiture. Once again, Burroughs was ahead of his time. He saw what was coming at us long before most observers.

Notes

This essay expands a talk I gave at the "Naked Lunch@50" celebrations in Paris in July 2009. I thank Oliver Harris for inviting me to participate and Andrew Hussey for hosting the event at the University of London in Paris. Thanks also go to my wife, Nora, and my friend and colleague Carl Ostrowski who read and commented on versions of this essay.

1. Paul Bowles would be the possible exception, should he be considered as part of the Beat movement, which I do not.
2. Over the past several decades, there has been a surge of interest in empire in U.S. literary studies responding to present historical conditions and views of the past afforded by the present moment, coinciding with Hardt and Negri's work. In 1993, a large volume of essays titled *Cultures of United States Imperialism*, edited by Amy Kaplan and Donald E. Pease, was published. Kaplan's own study, *The Anarchy of Empire in the Making of U.S. Culture*, was published nearly a decade later, in 2002. *Retaking the Universe: William S. Burroughs in the Age of Globalization*, edited by Davis Schneiderman and Philip Walsh, published in 2004, squarely focused critical attention on connections between Burroughs and globalization. This essay is situated within these discussions within American studies and Burroughs scholarship.
3. My position here parallels or complements Oliver Harris's view of Burroughs's paradoxical stance toward power, presented in *William Burroughs and the Secret of Fascination*: "His complicity in exercising power coincides absolutely with his writing, because it marks the material point of origin," Harris writes (31). Then, after citing Ann Douglas's reference to Burroughs as "revolutionary," Harris continues with a corollary: "that Burroughs, as the 'enemy within' the power structure, gains access to information about the structure of power only through the 'enemy within' *him*" (32).
4. Rob Johnson in *The Lost Years of Williams S. Burroughs: Beats in South Texas* convincingly argues that the trips Burroughs made across the border into Mexico from McAllen to Reynosa "undoubtedly served as a dress rehearsal for his later life in Mexico City since his behavior in Reynosa closely resembles his description of himself in *Queer*, written a few years later in Mexico City" (20).

5. In his splendid introductions to recent editions of these three books, Oliver Harris sorts out the intriguing and complicated textual history of these works in ways that make us radically and productively rethink them.

6. This argument calls to mind a similar case made almost four decades ago by Quentin Anderson in *The Imperial Self: An Essay in American Literary and Cultural History* (New York: Knopf, 1971). Anderson examines Emerson as a source of this quintessential American view of a boundless, ever-expanding notion of self.

7. For a thorough, thought-provoking discussion of the history of American Exceptionalism, see Donald E. Pease, "American Studies after American Exceptionalism? Toward a Comparative Analysis of Imperial State Exceptionalisms," in *Globalizing American Studies*, edited by Brian T. Edwards and Dilip Parameshwar Gaonkar, 47–83.

8. *Interzone* was a working title of *Naked Lunch*, and the volume so titled contains material that, in some form, ended up in the novel. As James Grauerholtz states in his introduction to *Interzone*, "The name of the piece refers . . . to the quadripartite administration of Tangier, divided between the U.S., French, Spanish and English sectors," before independence (xvii). The term "interzone," for Burroughs, refers as much to a surreal place of his imagination as it does to Tangier when it was an international zone.

9. The phrase is used by Renato Rosaldo in *Culture and Truth: The Remaking of Social Analysis* (Boston: Beacon, 1989).

10. Some of the previous material I have, in Burroughsian fashion, cannibalized from my introduction to *Bowles/Beats/Tangier*.

11. See the last chapters of Timothy S. Murphy's *Wising Up the Marks* for a smart discussion of the trilogy that appropriately draws on the theories of Deleuze and Guattari.

Chapter 2

Jack Kerouac and the Nomadic Cartographies of Exile

Hassan Melehy

With the 1950 publication of his first novel, *The Town and the City*, Jack Kerouac saw a measure of success. Although sales were disappointing, major outlets reviewed the book (Nicosia 300–310, 319), signaling the twenty-seven-year-old writer's obvious talent.[1] One milieu in which Kerouac's accomplishment was especially appreciated was the Franco-American or French-Canadian community of New England, in which he had grown up and to which he maintained close ties. Members of this population, who had left Quebec mainly between 1840 and 1930 under severe political, cultural, and economic pressures, were understandably pleased to see the mainstream prominence of "one of their own." This interest in traditional U.S.-American success was somewhat complicated by the Franco-American community's strong commitment to *survivance*, the set of practices designed to maintain cultural identity, especially with regard to the continued use of the French language. Certainly aware of the history and conditions of his home community, Kerouac was thrilled to read Yvonne Le Maître's review of *The Town and the City* in the French-language weekly *Le Travailleur*, published in Worcester, Massachusetts. His reaction to this review, a letter to its author, is a remarkable document for the way it reveals the major role of his relationship to his community in his approach to writing. This role is evident throughout his work—not just in his fictional depictions of French Canadians but also in his consistent fascination with the great variety of cultures in the United States and how they show signs of heterogeneous origins. As background for my assessment of this role, I will provide some brief observations on Franco-American life, especially those aspects of it that signal the massive cultural upheaval marking Kerouac's work.

Quebec in New England

Among the French Canadians of New England, *survivance* was a continuation of the disposition of the francophone population of Quebec: they responded to policies of the British Canadian government, which were heavily informed by cultural and linguistic disparagement of French Canadians and exerted pressure on them to assimilate (Dickinson and Young 158–168, 182–183). One of the effects of their marginalized position in Canada was the economic fact of restricted access to affordable credit; interest rates in the early 1860s went as high as 72 percent (Roby, *Franco-Americans* 12–14 and *Histoire* 19). Many peasant families knew overwhelming debt, which could best be alleviated by taking advantage of the growing industries south of the border (Roby, *Franco-Americans* 13). As many people and families fully intended to return, the importance of maintaining identity among the anglophone majority of New England remained strong: it entailed continuing fluency in French, consideration of Quebec as the homeland, avid devotion to French Catholicism, and a conception of cultural and "racial" kinship with France itself.[2] Survivance took place mainly through the churches, parochial schools, newspapers, and social clubs, against local pressures to assimilate.

By the turn of the twentieth century, Franco-Americans had firmly established their communities in New England; they numbered around 573,000, an astounding figure given that the French-Canadian population of Quebec at the time was just under 1,322,000. The total number of French Canadians in the United States and Canada at the time approached 2,413,000; so about 24 percent of the population lived in New England, in the range of half as many as in Quebec (Roby, *Histoire* 22–27). The French-speaking population of some New England cities exceeded 50 percent (Roby, *Histoire* 7). The region was literally understood on both sides of the border as an extension of Quebec, an idea captured in the term "le Québec d'en bas," "Quebec below" or "lower Quebec," that Pierre Anctil has signaled. At the same time, Franco-American community leaders were interested in establishing the population in the United States: education emphasized full bilingualism, and prominence in anglophone society could serve as a means of increasing awareness of the identity and culture of the Franco-Americans, hence paradoxically strengthening survivance against assimilationist forces. This part of Franco-American life was a resistance to U.S. melting pot ideology: it presented itself as a contribution to the broader culture by insisting on recognizing the latter as made up of multiple component cultures, each of which needed to look continually toward its ancestry.

Reviewing Survivance

Le Maître's review of *The Town and the City*, appearing in the March 23, 1950, issue of *Le Travailleur*, is a mostly laudatory assessment, no small feat on Kerouac's part. Besides her status as the most distinguished Franco-American journalist of the first half of the twentieth century, she was also very distinguished in anglophone circles.

From 1911, she covered the Paris literary scene for such magazines as *The New Yorker* and *The Smart Set*, of which H. L. Mencken was editor, counting among her close friends such authors as Colette (Dion-Lévesque, "Le Maître" 551). Le Maître calls the young John Kerouac (as the first edition of the book identifies him) "a first-class animator: he knows how to populate a location with a stirring, disturbing, frightening, and dense life. This is the strong point of a considerable talent, which already in this first attempt reaches a color and relief far beyond ordinary" (1, my translation). However, she is quick to point out her reservation: Kerouac "has succeeded in bringing to life in the American forest a vigorous tree that spreads an exuberant sap around itself, without once speaking to us of the old blood from which the tree has drawn life and vigor" (1). Missing, she finds, is the gaze and reverence toward the ancestors, which she holds to be the source of life and cultural identity. She signals this lack as a problem because she rightly sees in *The Town and the City* a novel that presents an acute challenge, as does all of Kerouac's work, to the U.S. ideology of assimilation, but that nonetheless avoids recourse to fully formed cultural identity. In much of Franco-American culture, such recourse was the vehicle of that challenge. In phrasing that uncannily prefigures Kerouac's later writing practices, Le Maître characterizes the tension in the novel:

> Spontaneous generation, then, this Lowell; a uniform mass from which none of the elements that have created this mass springs up with a face of its own. And nonetheless . . . nonetheless Lowell is everything except uniformity and fusion. Lowell—*Galloway* is the name of the city in the book—is the *melting pot* [in English in Le Maître's text, a signal that the very concept belongs to an anglicizing ideology] in which nothing is yet perfectly melted; Lowell is the French Canada of Quebec, the English Canada of the Maritime Provinces; Ireland, England, and Scotland; Portugal and the Azores; Italy, Sweden, Norway, Greece, Armenia, Syria, and Lebanon; Poland and Lithuania, Israel, and many more! I am but lightly touching the forty-seven varieties and their forty-seven *survivances*. (1)

It is interesting that Le Maître uses the very charged word survivance, which I leave in French because of its special sense, to describe the practices of all the immigrant groups in Lowell.

In connection with this novel, whose realist qualities are so powerful as to occasion an interrogation of the reality that it presents, Le Maître raises the following problem: in his Lowell/Galloway, Kerouac gives close attention to many of the signs of these survivances and almost none to the specificity of the surviving cultures, and hence makes a partial concession to the ideology of assimilation. She writes, "[T]he people of Lowell/Galloway know that the total eclipse of old times is not quite that, that the tenacious shadow of the buried ancestor still haunts the old houses. When John Kerouac himself calls the Holy Child 'the Little Jesus,' with English words he is still speaking French" (1). Le Maître is alluding to the fact that the French equivalent of the English expression "the baby Jesus" is "*le petit Jésus.*" She also states several times the author's first name, John, hence emphasizing the anglicization of his given name, Jean-Louis Lebris de Kérouac. Herself a long-time resident of Lowell (Dion-Lévesque, "Le Maître" 550–551), she knew the entire Kerouac family well. She characterizes them as "of purely French origin" and "pronounced *survivants*": their deep commitment to survivance shows in their excellent French, she writes, although "the young novelist himself speaks a chastened French [*un françaischâtié*]" (1). She excuses Kerouac somewhat for departing from family and community linguistic traditions, explaining that his education took place only partly in the parochial schools and mostly at Lowell High School and Columbia University. But this qualification of his French would seem to be her chastening of him for this departure and for translating it into his novel.

Nonetheless, the rest of her review is maximally positive. She praises Kerouac for the intensity of his realism and the quality of his prose, defending him from the charge, which some reviewers made, of overwriting: "The beautiful style here simply seeks to express in beauty what is felt as such" (1–2). Indeed, her assessment of Kerouac is remarkably perceptive, as she hones in on aspects of his writing in *The Town and the City* that become more important and distinct in his later work. Among these is his lyrical realism—his interest in describing the gritty details of hidden, sometimes frightening parts of social reality in a poetic language that seems to emanate directly from that reality, and his close attention to the passions that accompany it. In citing his practice of using English words in what amount to French expressions, she notes a distinct mark of his style, which he would subsequently cultivate. But more importantly, she delineates quite precisely his effort to capture a social whole that is America, as well as the innumerable component cultural currents that make it up, which render it close to indefinable. Later, Kerouac announces this effort in such phrases as the dedication of *Visions of Cody*: "Dedicated to America, whatever that is" (dedication page). Even in a largely glowing review, Le Maître chastens Kerouac for hiding his origins; in effect, she speaks in the voice of the Franco-American community to call the young author back to the ancestral traditions from which he has wandered away.

What she does not quite see, though, is that, for Kerouac, the deracination of the many different cultures that make up the United States, and more broadly America (which for Kerouac includes parts of Canada and Mexico), is precisely their opportunity to wander and come together in the heterogeneous festival that he seeks and finds in his writing. Le Maître passes over the funeral of the novel's father, George Martin, in part of one sentence, although it is a stunningly lyrical section of the book that closes the plot of this panorama of life in the United States (480–498). She presents it as the occasion for the errant, scattered Martin family to reunite on ancestral territory in New Hampshire, only to reaffirm their deracination. She omits consideration of the final chapter, in which Peter Martin goes on the road, beginning the vagabondage that already in 1950 is integral to the next phase of Kerouac's literary career. In her effort to bring the nomad cultures of Kerouac's America back to the survival of the identity of the fathers, she overlooks the fact that the father's death directly precedes a new affirmation of life in the joy of travel. Of course, hindsight makes it easy to identify these oversights as such. Her review is sharply insightful and indeed comes very close to discerning two poles that continue to operate throughout Kerouac's work: the mournful knowledge of the loss of origins and the ecstasy of wandering that this loss precipitates.

On the Franco-American Road

Kerouac's passionate concern with his origins in the Franco-American community of New England, as well as his distance from it in the time that the project of survivance was losing force, is patent in his response to Le Maître. In September 1950, he wrote to her expressing his great joy at being honored among the people to whom he felt a familial connection: "What amazed me most about your review—which I read and reread in Mexico City all summer—is the beautiful and elegant French tone that made it seem as though a very *aunt* of mine had reviewed the book" (*Selected Letters* 228). He signals that it is not simply in the community but in the French language that he feels at home, a sense he took with him in the form of her review to the expatriate community in Mexico City in which he was a frequent guest. Curiously, though, his feeling of being at home amounts to an awareness that there is no home. He continues, "Because I cannot write my native language and have no native home any more, and am amazed by that horrible homelessness all French Canadians abroad in America have—well, well, I was moved" (228). In affirming his connection between his stay in Mexico City and his awareness of the exile of the Québécois[3] community—his own wandering south of the border that mirrors his community's having come south of another border—he makes explicit the relationship between his fascination with the road and the geographic displacement of his people. Also notable is the close connection he draws between geographic exile and linguistic exile—along with the suggestion that, although he is distant from the French language in his avowed inability to write it, it is nonetheless in that language that one might find a reprieve from the pain of exile. The language is mobile, part of the displacement, but it also becomes the mobile home, so to speak, of the person and the community in exile, a vehicle of American nomadism.

Kerouac informs the *grande dame* of Franco-American journalism that, as a writer, he wishes to contribute to the community and its linguistic identity, hence to overcome his avowed inability to write in French: "Someday, *Madame*, I shall write a French Canadian novel, with the setting in New England, in *French*" (228, author's emphasis). With that statement, Kerouac points to a literary homecoming to both his native New England and his native French—the word *someday* places it in an indeterminate future, which would presumably come after further wandering. That is, his own engagement in survivance through writing incorporates the very displacement that it purports to address. It is evident that the various homes at issue involve a multiple exile: that of the French Canadians from France, in the mid-twentieth century, still cited as an ethnic and linguistic homeland; that of the Franco-American population in "le Québec d'en bas"; and that of the French language itself in predominantly anglophone New England, an extension and furtherance of its exile in British Canada. Mainly at issue is Kerouac's own exile from his native French—in the English he tells Le Maître he learned only at the age of six or seven (228)—in which most of his education took place, and in which he is on his way to becoming an established author. Kerouac continues the letter with a bold claim about his identity: "All my knowledge rests in my 'French-Canadianness' and nowhere else" (228). One should not overlook the complications of this statement: it closely follows Kerouac's words about the "horrible homelessness" of French Canadians in the United States, so his suggestion is that his own deeply rooted identity, like that of his ethnic community, is permeated with rootlessness. And, of course, he has many sources of knowledge outside French-Canadian life; the context of his letter suggests that he understands his condition of exile, specific to the Franco-Americans and Québécois, as permeating his experience through and through.

In Quebec, where Kerouac is one of the most honored of U.S. authors, this is perhaps his most celebrated statement because it is a succinct formulation of a central experience of Québécois identity, that of exile.[4] In Quebec, the relatively sudden departure in the nineteenth century of a huge portion of the population, commonly known as the Exodus, was cause for great alarm among leaders who wanted to build and reinforce a francophone nation against British domination; hence, it contributed to the Québécois sense of decimated identity (Roby, *Franco-Americans* 52–53). To assure survivance in exile, members of the clergy also participated in the migration, establishing churches and parochial schools in all communities. In this fashion, the French Canadians of New England galvanized their cultural and linguistic identity, in continual awareness of the aggressions that surrounded them. In their new location, to which they were actively recruited as millworkers, they were greeted by such epithets as "the Chinese of the East" because of their reputed willingness to work for the lowest wages (Goulet 90–105).

Newspaper editorials termed them a "danger" for keeping their language and customs. In 1889 the *New York Times* cited as reasons to believe that the French Canadians would not make good citizens the fact that "for two centuries they have succeeded in retaining in Canada, the religion and the language of their ancestors, as distinctive badges of their separation from their neighbors." The editorial warns that, in the event that a great number of French-Canadians gained U.S. citizenship, "There would be a real danger that they might demand and obtain legislation favorable to their special and separate interests, and in the same degree hostile to the general interests of the community." The text finishes by declaring it a "patriotic duty for all Americans, in communities in which the French Canadian population is considerable, to insist upon maintaining American political principles against all assaults." This position, though grounded in liberal notions of inclusion through assimilation, finds strong echoes in today's xenophobic journalistic and political discourse, particularly with regard to Mexican and Muslim immigrant communities; the phrasing demonstrates to what degree such discourse is indebted to nineteenth-century, racially inflected notions of democracy. This editorial indicates the hostility and despised minority status that the Québécois faced in the United States.

Conditions and attitudes, of course, changed over the thirty-three years until Kerouac's birth in 1922, but at that time the importance of negotiating the difficult space between survivance and assimilation was still well-known to Franco Americans. At the age of twenty-eight, Kerouac makes such negotiation the overriding theme of his letter to Le Maître: He presents it as a primary purpose of his writing, even of his poetics. His mention of the "French-Canadian novel" he will one day write places the negotiation in the realm of literary representation: This book will offer an image of the "Québec d'en bas" of New England. Moreover, recent attention to several unpublished manuscripts that Kerouac wrote in French offers evidence that this future novel is part of his development of a poetics of exile that bears on the composition and style of his writing, on the ways that his texts will approach their objects of representation.

Since the Jack Kerouac Papers in the New York Public Library's Berg Collection became available to the public in 2007, the interest in these writings has been immense in Quebec: They attest to the author's quest to become a "genuine French-Canadian writer," according to Montreal journalist Gabriel Anctil ("50 ans," my translation). One of these texts, *La Nuit est ma femme* [*The Night is My Wife*], tells the story of Michel Bretagne, a French-Canadian struggling with who he is and what language is properly his own, whose surname signals the Kerouac family's French region of origin, Brittany.[5] Kerouac dated the notebook in which he wrote this story as "Winter–Spring 1951." That places the composition of the text just a few months after he wrote the letter to Le Maître and just before and perhaps overlapping with the major aesthetic breakthrough of his career, the three-week burst of writing that resulted in the scroll manuscript of *On the Road* (letter to Cassady, May 22, 1951, 315). As I will demonstrate, it is not accidental that Kerouac made this breakthrough at the time of his most sustained efforts to write in his native language, which had everything to do with trying to understand his relationship to it, as well as to English, which he continued to experience as a foreign language.

Shortly afterward, in a notebook dated December 16, 1952, Kerouac wrote more than thirty pages of a manuscript he called *Sur le chemin*, "On the Road" in French. This text does not tell the familiar story of the 1957 novel, but rather that of a convergence of two major currents of Kerouac's life: It relates the 1935 meeting in New York City between the French-Canadian Leo Duluoz, who drives from Boston, and Dean Pomeray, a drunk who drives from Denver (leaf 19). Duluoz is accompanied by his thirteen-year-old son Ti Jean ("Li'l Jean," a name Kerouac frequently used in his fiction to designate his French Canadian self), and Pomeray, by his nine-year-old son Dean, and they are greeted in the Bowery by Uncle Bull Balloon. The latter turns out to be a French-Canadian whose real name is Guillaume Bernier, a relative of Leo (leaf 28). Leo Duluoz, Dean Pomeray, and Bull Balloon are names Kerouac created for characters based on his own father, Neal Cassady, and William S. Burroughs, respectively. The continued migration of the French-Canadian father takes Ti Jean away from their homeland in Massachusetts to New York, the place where Kerouac began to discover the America that fascinated him when he made a definitive move away from his ethnic origins by accepting a football scholarship from Columbia University. The Duluoz–Pomeray meeting repeats and elaborates the opening event of *On the Road*: "I first met Neal" (in the scroll manuscript); in the 1957 version, of course, it reads "I first met Dean," in both cases, Kerouac's autobiographical character's first encounter with his guide in this discovery. *Sur le chemin* hence presents a departure from French-Canadian ancestry, which the father already initiates by taking his son on the road to New York in favor of the fascination with America that Cassady and Burroughs represented to Kerouac. Kerouac himself regarded *Sur le chemin* as a vital step in rewriting the manuscript of *On the Road* (G. Anctil, "Sur le chemin"): in a January 1953 letter to Cassady, he says of the French text, "It's the solution to the 'On the Road' plots all of em" (395).

In addition to these two novellas, another manuscript in the Berg Collection, five pages that Kerouac titled "On The Road, écrit en Francais [sic]," dates from around the same time. It is a transitional story between *The Town and the City* and *On the Road*, continuing the saga of the Martin family, who have become full-fledged French-Canadians and speak Kerouac's Massachusetts dialect of French. All three of these texts demonstrate that Kerouac followed through on his declaration to Le Maître about writing a French-Canadian novel, and that doing so was of great importance to the novel in which he mapped the America he discovered in his wanderings. His modesty to Le Maître regarding his ability to write in French, which these manuscripts belie, underscores his sense of both geographic and linguistic exile. The fact that a key part of the experimentation that led to the 1957 version of *On the Road* is in French suggests that he conceived of the road as integral to the poetics of exile, both literally and figuratively the conduit between two cultures by which one negotiates them.[6] In writing *Sur le chemin*, Kerouac was on the road to *On the Road*, traveling between French and English, between Quebec and the United States, not at home on either side of these pairs. The place he tells Le Maître he wishes to return to writing about, Franco-American New England, is a home in exile, an intercultural zone closely connected to what Mary Louise Pratt has termed a "contact zone," one of the "social spaces where cultures meet, clash, grapple with each other, often in contexts of highly asymmetrical relations of power, such as colonialism, slavery, or their aftermaths as they are lived out in many parts of the world today" (34).

The Strange American Paradise

In *On the Road*, Kerouac maps the broad contours of the United States as a series of contact zones, of mixes and clashes of unruly cultures that resist domination and homogenization. In his letter to Le Maître, he points to exactly this character of specific cultures in the broader United States when he tells her of becoming a writer in English by a path that is not that of assimilation: "The reason I handle English words so well is because it is not my own language. I re-fashion it to fit *French* images" (229, author's emphasis). He is referring to his frequent procedure of beginning with words and phrases in French in order to arrive at formulations in English—such as the lingering French that Le Maître signals in her gloss on his expression "the little Jesus" and writing other versions of *On the Road* in French as part of working on the English text. That is, his literary experiments are a nomadic voyage into English, an alteration of it into something foreign of which its ideologically conditioned nativism defers recognition. They are not his transformation of himself into a native English speaker in uniform American culture; instead they are his marking of himself as a vessel carrying foreign elements into this language and this culture in order to underscore the foreignness that they hide.

Toward the end of the letter he explains that, in writing *The Town and the City*, he was still succumbing to the pressures of assimilation. He says that he chose the family name Martin because it sounds English but could also be French—specifically

Norman, he remarks, thereby revealing his adherence to survivance in his specific knowledge of just where in France Québécois families stem from. In the future, he says, he will no longer make such concessions to assimilationism. His "On The Road, écrit en Francais" is evidently an attempt to correct this error. Interestingly, he compares the situation of French Canadians in the United States to that of other ethnic groups, attributing the assimilationism of his people less to the severity of discrimination against them but rather to ethnic features: They can pass for Anglo-Saxon, unlike "the Jews, the Italians . . . the other 'minority' races." He also suggests a kinship, by virtue of their shared non-Anglo-Saxon minority status, among these different groups that was already becoming important in his writing.

What Kerouac already knows from his understanding of the mixed nature of cultures, however, is that it is often important to relinquish the roots, the fathers, the ancestors, the integrity of the home culture, since such relinquishment is precisely what occasions the vitality of wandering. The mea culpa[7] of his letter to Le Maître, involving a longing to recover the origins that Franco-American survivance so vigorously promoted, is something to which he continually returns in his work, usually discovering that the origins are no longer there to be embraced and hence that further wandering is necessary. His awareness of this tension between trying to recover and departing from an integral notion of origins is evident in a consideration of a few of the changes he made between the scroll and the published versions of On the Road. The first of these is the opening sentence, which in the scroll reads as follows: "I first met Neal not long after my father died" (109). These words amount to a summary of the end of The Town and the City, in which the death of the father is the occasion for wandering, since in the new novel Cassady embodies the vagabondage of America. But in rewriting his manuscript, Kerouac takes more distance from the father by omitting him altogether: "I first met Dean not long after my wife and I split up" (1). By replacing the death of the father with the separation from the wife, Kerouac affirms the lack of dependency of the present-day discovery on a relationship with the father and a reverence for ancestors; he instead characterizes wandering and the close male relationship it entails as a function of an end to a conventional household. That is, in extending the migration of his people to the United States through making it a broader American vagabondage, he celebrates rather than laments the deracination that enables the multiculturalism of America.

The second emendation of On the Road that I want to signal is the change of the narrator's name from Jack Kerouac to Sal Paradise. Although this alteration underscores the fictional nature of the main character (I would call "Sal" a translation of "Jack."), Kerouac continues to hide his French Canadianness, his declarations to Le Maître notwithstanding. But he does so only partially, in such a way as to reveal the heterogeneous composition of U.S. culture that is emerging as the real lesson of his relationship to his community. The character is fairly substantially Italian American, a member of one of the more "visible" minorities that Kerouac names in his letter to Le Maître; this status allows Kerouac to shelter his French Canadianness in the broad category of "ethnic," which in U.S. ideology galvanizes the notion that all foreigners come more or less from some vague country somewhere else. In creating Sal Paradise, Kerouac plays heavily with this category. Sal's full name, Salvatore (meaning savior in Italian), is a transparent affirmation of the messianic qualities

Kerouac thought great writers had, himself included. The name Salvatore Paradiso restates Kerouac's declaration of the beatitude of his generation. But along with Italianness, he sneaks in a little French Canadianness: the last name is not Paradiso, but rather Paradise—Englishized, and at the same time approaching the French *Paradis*. This is still a common name in French Canadian areas of New England, and in some cases families have changed it to Paradise.

Especially since Kerouac tended to hear things simultaneously in English and French, as in the case of *beat* and the French *béat*, blissful, it is easy to discern in his narrator's name *sale paradis*, "dirty paradise" (Waddell 17), a notion also suggested by the words "the ragged promised land, the fantastic end of America" (*On the Road* 1957, 83) with which Sal describes Hollywood.[8] This double entendre extends that of *beat/béat*, according to which the blessed are precisely the downtrodden; it also builds on the phrase reportedly at the origin of the name Sal Paradise, the phrase "sad paradise" that Kerouac misread in a manuscript by Ginsberg (Charters, *Kerouac* 86).The dirty paradise is also the one discovered by immigrants with high hopes for their voyage to the United States. Through his cartography of it, Kerouac aims to redeem this unfortunate paradise. In addition, the very notion of a beaten down, wandering savior draws on an idea that arose in nineteenth-century Québécois Catholicism: Political and clerical leaders interpreted the very difficult migration to New England as directed by God for the purpose of bringing the Catholic faith and hence civilization itself to the "heretics" (Protestants) south of the border. In this understanding, the French Canadian people, whose land was "abandoned by its mother, conquered, invaded . . . submitted to all the regimes that were going to absorb it," on the road to New England became the "messenger [*commissionnaire*] of France and God" (Routhier 294, my translation).[9] Of course, Kerouac alters this notion considerably with his brilliantly synthetic imagination: His religious thinking is highly syncretic, distant from absolutist Catholicism, but in this Québécois source one may fully discern a version of the idea of the abused and beaten wanderer who actualizes ubiquitous holiness and beatitude.

The name Sal contains a further ambiguity in that it can function as feminine. Sal's Chicana girlfriend, Teresa or Terry, once calls him "Sallie" (100), a name far more common to women than men. Although the passage does not suggest anything else that's feminine about Sal, this nominal gender ambiguity reproduces the one that Kerouac, in *Satori in Paris*, signals in his given name, Jean-Louis. Traveling in France, the narrator explains that, although he identifies himself to people as Jean, his passport says John, to which he legally changed it, "because you can't go around America and join the Merchant Marine and be called Jean" (95). The ambiguity more broadly underscores the feminization affected by U.S. ideology on foreigners, especially those of non-Anglo-Saxon, non-Protestant origin, and above all the French, with whom many equated the French Canadians.

Kerouac brings these ambiguities to the narrative of *On the Road*, which is a search for America through its many contact zones. These occur around borders between regions, such as Mexico and the United States or different geographic divisions of the latter—"the dividing line between the East of my past and the West of my future" (15). They take place near or along rivers marking points of transition, such as the Hudson, the Mississippi, or the Rio Grande; in multiethnic, multilingual spaces, such as the African American section of Denver, the French Quarter of New Orleans, and Mexican communities in California; in shadowy underworlds and energetic jazz venues. They have to do with the mixing of immigrant and other culturally distinct communities, and frequently with signs of the U.S. legacy of slavery. In "a little Frisco nightclub," Slim Gaillard, "a tall thin Negro with big sad eyes," "grabs the bongos and plays tremendous rapid Cuban beats and beating bongos yells crazy things in Spanish, in Arabic, in Peruvian dialect, in Egyptian, in every language he knows, and he knows innumerable languages" (176–177). The notion of "beat" becomes one of nomadism, a drumbeat motion bringing ecstasy that traverses the limitations imposed by a sedentary, stratified culture. In these zones there remain few obvious traces of Kerouac's Québécois identity: In a way, then, he continues to hide himself, but at the same time the distance he takes from his origins attests to the degree to which *On the Road* is a result of his poetics of exile, an attempt to bring his writing practices to bear on a broad and encompassing vision of the United States that does not hew to one region or group.

In the picture he paints, there emerges a cartography of contact zones, which take shape through movements of migration and along the roads passing through them. These movements undermine distinctions between one zone and another and instead offer large spaces of heterogeneous culture. Kerouac conveys these spaces through his syntax: In the passage above, he links multiple actions occurring in a single space to give the impression of continual movement and geographic admixture. Elsewhere, he ties together disparate geographic zones through a cartographic syntax that conveys their contact, interaction, and permeation of each other:

> Cheyenne again, in the afternoon this time, and then west over the range; crossing the Divide at midnight at Creston, arriving at Salt Lake City at dawn—a city of sprinklers, the least likely place for Dean to have been born; then out to Nevada in the hot sun, Reno by nightfall, its twinkling Chinese streets; then up the Sierra Nevada, pines, stars, mountain lodges signifying Frisco romances. . . . (60)

This passage conveys both movement and locale. Through brief descriptive phrases the text emphasizes the differences between these places; through syntactical juxtaposition, it runs them into each other, hence presenting the trajectory through them as a series of related contact zones.

American Idyll

In Part One, the end of the road, so to speak—which is only the beginning of its next segment—is the Chicano community of California's Central Valley. In this section, Sal recounts his passionate but also mundane relationship with Terry. Although many have accused Kerouac of exoticizing marginalized populations in *On the Road*, of writing the dreams of a white boy out slumming, the clichés with which he often opens his descriptions function as a rhetorical setup in advance of a harsher look at reality. Tim Hunt points out that Kerouac deliberately created a character with limited understanding in order to throw into relief the discoveries he makes; in notes, the author compares his narrator to such figures as Boswell, Pip, and Sancho Panza (4).

The following passage is probably Kerouac's most audacious use of this strategy in *On the Road*—and it has also been the occasion of most of the accusations I just mentioned. Sal's wide-eyed enthusiasm is at its most patent here, directed toward workaday tasks no doubt regarded as unpleasant by those who engaged in them: "We bent down and started picking cotton. It was beautiful. Across the field were the tents, and beyond them the sere brown cotton fields that stretched out of sight to the brown arroyo foothills and . . . snow-capped Sierras in the blue morning air. This was so much better than washing dishes on South Main Street" (96). The rest of the paragraph details the technical aspects of cotton picking, as well as the bloody hands and aching back that it brings on. Still, Sal romantically pushes against this reality by rejoining to his own empirical observation, "But it was beautiful kneeling and hiding in that earth" (96). Sal describes the beauty of assuming a praying posture amid these rough labor conditions—here and in many other places in the book he wavers between recognizing the harshness of reality and retreating from it in a romantic, downright spiritual dream. This narrative logic is one of Kerouac's approaches to the idea of a *sale paradis*—dirty places become paradise through the utopian and beatific act of dreaming, and the dreaming takes place in the prose that links itself to the cartography of motion through the country.

Rachel Ligairi sums up the criticism of Kerouac's use of racial cliché in *On the Road*: "[H]is stereotypical idealization of people of color elides the hardship associated with minority life in pre–Civil Rights America and perhaps even reenacts colonial patterns of paternalism" (139). This is true, but only to a point, since the cotton-picking scene continues somewhat surprisingly by sharply signaling racial antagonism: Sal speaks of how the Okies, with whom things seemed otherwise peaceful, "went mad in the roadhouse and tied a man to a tree and beat him to a pulp with sticks" (97). Without stating the color of the unfortunate man, Sal indicates that the Mexicans have reason to be afraid, and that he himself "carried a big stick with me in the tent in case they got the idea that we Mexicans were fouling up their trailer camp" (98). The phrase "we Mexicans" is striking here, since it comes at the moment when Sal underscores the antagonism, as though he becomes Mexican less by virtue of working among Mexicans and loving a Mexican woman than by virtue of finding himself on one side of a looming racial conflict. He explains, "They [the Okies] thought I was Mexican, of course; and in a way I am" (98). These words are part of both Sal's and Kerouac's negotiation of identity. As someone of ostensibly Mediterranean origin, Sal is keenly aware of being racially marked by white men as an object of violence. With regard for Kerouac himself, as a member of a community that not long before was composed mainly of migrant workers living in a border zone, severely discriminated against by the white Protestant majority, his relationship to the Mexican farm workers in California is one of entirely justified sympathy and empathy. As Kerouac tells Le Maître, he is aware of being white mainly in appearance, an appearance offering a mask of whiteness to cover an identity best described as off-white.

That Kerouac regarded Mexicans as bearing a kinship to the Québécois peasants with whom he identified is evident elsewhere in his work. In *Desolation Angels*, narrator Jack Duluoz recounts his mother's revelation in Mexico when she sees peasants praying. This knowledge, coupled with Duluoz's remark that "*Içi les espanols sont marié avec les Indiens* [Here the Spanish married the Indians]," as the French did in Quebec, prompts his mother to say, "They believe in God just like us!" Duluoz explains the sense of homecoming for them both: "Now she understood Mexico and why I had come there so often even tho I'd get sick of dysentery or lose weight or get pale" (384). In the same notebook in which he wrote *Sur le chemin* in Mexico in 1951, Kerouac sketches the genealogy of the Duluoz family, referring to his Québécois lineage as fellaheen, the Arabic word he frequently uses for Mexican and other peasants. Kerouac adapts this term from Oswald Spengler, who in *The Decline of the West* uses it to designate the peoples who precede and follow the organization of civilization—hence, those who stand outside it and effectively offer nothing to it (169–170, 174–175, 184–186). However, Kerouac alters Spengler's meaning, seeing in the fellaheen—composed of groups that dominant cultures have marginalized such as Amerindians in Mexico or the Québécois—a power to exceed the limitations of organized civilization and offer vital contributions to it. To understand Sal's claim that he is Mexican "in a way" as an identification that operates "only figuratively," as Mark Richardson does (217), misses the real affinity that Kerouac's own ethnic situation induces him to affirm and the profound cultural connection that the affinity indicates. In any case, treatments of Kerouac's attitudes toward ethnicity that, like Richardson's, take no account of the author's own background, presenting him as purely and simply white, are flawed.

It is nonetheless understandable that many critics have been troubled by Kerouac's invocation of racial clichés in *On the Road*, seeing in it an affirmation of U.S. "apartheid," as Robert Holton writes (*Road* 62). In the scene among California farm workers, Kerouac dips into plantation fantasy by depicting African Americans who "picked cotton with the same God-blessed patience their grandfathers had practiced in ante-bellum Alabama" (96). Although Kerouac's fundamentally realist technique involves deploying dreamlike clichés in order to bump them against reality, hence revealing their limits and throwing the entire dream-world into relief, there is little to say about this sentence except that here the technique fails. Sal the dreamy naïf lays it on thick and comes off as too youthful.

Kerouac takes Sal deep into the utopian dream of a society in which people can overcome racial antagonisms in order to work and live happily together, while at the same time leaving him aware that in U.S. society race must continually be negotiated. Hilary Holladay assesses Sal's attitudes by writing that he "seems racially confused rather than merely racist" ("Parallel" 110). This is an accurate assessment, but I would add that Sal is also racially uncertain. When Sal says that he had white ambitions his entire life (180), he is reaffirming not his social privilege but rather his self-understanding as someone who has striven for bourgeois status only by relinquishing his identity, while seeking ways to do otherwise. In connection with a different set of texts, Nancy Grace succinctly formulates the nature of Kerouac's "ambitions" here: "[H]is denial of being an American advances his critique of the master narrative, implicitly asking whether one can be an American in a system that subverts its very belief in the essential self by forcing particular individuals into psychological or physical exile based solely on categorical signifiers" (*Kerouac* 13). Grace is commenting mainly on a letter Kerouac wrote to John Clellon Holmes in 1952 in which he reflects on issues of ethnicity in the United States and his relationship to the dominant white culture that recur in all of his work. It is striking that in *On the Road*, Sal speaks of "white ambitions" in relation to ethnic groups he encounters in Denver, a city of the U.S. heartland. Although regions on or just beyond the geographical periphery of the United States, such as California and Mexico toward the end of the novel, offer limit-experiences involving encounters with notable cultural others, Kerouac presents large parts of U.S. culture as already heterogeneous, as composed of contact zones. He maps an America made of mixed cultural fermentations at both its periphery and its center, strongly challenging the tenability of such a binary notion.

In addition to the sites of ethnic mixing to which Sal is drawn in Denver, a place to which Kerouac accords a large part of his narrative, New Orleans, a U.S. city at a geographical limit quite different from California, also has a prominent place in *On the Road* because it functions as a space of mobile cultural interaction. New Orleans gains this status partly by being the home of Old Bull Lee, the character based on Burroughs. The narrative introduces Bull as a kind of cosmopolitan bohemian, an exemplar of transnational American nomadism. Bull appears as a late, decadent aristocrat, moving among the socially and culturally marginalized sector of the international elite—some members of which have still not relinquished claims to old nobility—as well as in the seedy areas of many different cities, working the odd jobs that waning wealth necessitates (143). But Kerouac describes him as "a Kansas minister with exotic, phenomenal fires and mysteries" (145)—this man just as much embodies Middle America. The exoticism of Old Bull Lee is both offset and complemented by his heartland charisma, these two sides constituting an appeal to an earlier era.

Although Sal and Dean want Bull to show them the wildness of New Orleans, their friend responds with contempt for the city, precisely because of its social stratification or segregation: "It's against the law to go to the colored section. The bars are insufferably dreary" (146). However, Sal feels drawn to the lingering cultural heterogeneity of New Orleans, a function of its geographical situation as a port city on direct routes to quite different and distant places. In describing the ferry ride between the section of New Orleans where Bull lives, Algiers (a name already suggesting geographical alterity), Sal notes these connections, visible in "ghostly fogbound Cereno ships with Spanish balconies and ornamental poops, till you got up close and saw they were just old freighters from Sweden and Panama" (147). This spot on the Mississippi River, which like Old Bull Lee is a confluence of "mid-America" and faraway places, offers exoticism partly by being so foggy, hiding the brute character of its reality and giving way to Sal's imaginative flight. This fanciful image comes to an end by encountering reality, which turns out to be not all that hidden, composed of the real artifacts of international commerce—which might be less interesting but which nonetheless indicate cultural convergence.

Mapping Cognition

All of these contact zones prepare for the finale of the novel, the trip to Mexico that the trajectory of Part One prefigures by culminating in Mexican communities in

California. The contact zone between the United States and Mexico, which includes parts of each country, presents the greatest challenge in *On the Road* to the ideology of complacent, sedentary culture. The broadness of the zone, beginning in San Antonio with such signs as houses and streets indicating a cultural shift, is underscored by the six pages that the narrative takes to traverse it."'Ah,' sighed Dean, 'the end of Texas, the end of America, we don't know no more'" (273). Dean presents the border crossing as the terminus of all that has become familiar to him and Sal, "America," and even the end of their ability to know and recognize what's in front of them. As it has throughout the novel, the narrative continues to function by beginning with clichés that prove unable to dominate the reality that they confront. Sal describes Laredo as a "sinister town," filled with crime because of its proximity to the border and the presence of contraband. They are nearing a cultural change: "Just beyond, you could feel the enormous presence of whole great Mexico and almost smell the billion tortillas frying and smoking in the night" (273). This sentence contains an astounding contrast, that between the unfathomable size of Mexico that can be described only in the vaguest terms—"enormous," "whole great"—and the particular cultural detail of "the billion tortillas." Although it is not inaccurate to speak of tortillas as a widely prepared food in Mexico, focusing on them as an identifying marker makes the description a cliché because it ultimately conveys almost nothing about the place to which it is assigned.[10] Sal attempts to master the unknowable vastness of Mexico with the word billion, which becomes much less significant when it is attached to this detail.

The set of clichés that Kerouac deploys through Sal and Dean in this scene, building up expectations of entering another world, is in rapid, kaleidoscopic clash with reality. Despite the build-up, the physical passage from the United States to Mexican territory occurs very quickly, in a single sentence that relates nothing remarkable: "But everything changed when we crossed the mysterious bridge over the river and our wheels rolled on official Mexican soil, though it wasn't anything but car way for border inspection" (273). The clash in this description is between the words "everything changed" and "wasn't anything but." If nothing actually happens when everything changes, then the change is the result of cognitive expectation based partly on reality but that fails in the face of reality. Next, Sal's narration provides less a cliché about what Mexico looks like than an indication of the process by which a cliché is made: "Just across the street Mexico began. We looked with wonder. To our amazement, it looked exactly like Mexico" (274). It looks exactly like Mexico because it conforms to their preconceptions, and it is a surprise that the enormous change they await at the border does not come. The cliché at issue here is made in contact with the mundane details of everyday life in Mexico, which immediately become the familiar image by which Mexico is apprehended. Kerouac does not elaborate these details here, other than saying that Mexico "looked exactly like Mexico," because the point of the passage is to demonstrate the collision between preconception, which draws mainly on cliché, and reality. The surprise is that there is no surprise; although there is a cultural shift with the transit from one geographical zone to another, it takes place rather in an extended border zone in which cultures pass through each other, interweave, and continuously affect each other.

It is the in-between-ness, the hybridity of a contact zone that makes knowledge of it possible; nonetheless, those attempting to know it will often resort to clichés in order to address the ineffability of what they encounter. Dean continues to repeat the idea of a total transformation, even as he acknowledges the continuity of their quest in the contact they are making with the cultural reality of Mexico: "Now, Sal, we're leaving everything behind us and entering a new and unknown phase of things. All the years and troubles and kicks—and now *this!* so that we can safely think of nothing else and just go on ahead with our faces stuck out like this, you see, and *understand* the world as, really and genuinely speaking, other Americans haven't done before us. . . ." (276). The unknown, which they sought also in the many U.S. contact zones they visited, intensifies here and becomes a genuine challenge to their cognitive apparatus, which up to this point has remained narrowed in a mesh of clichés, though far from completely enclosed by it. Farther into Mexico, the cultural difference becomes more pronounced as the clichés are stripped away by contact with reality. But even as he combines empirical description with rhapsodic poetry to convey the ecstasy of expanding cognition, Kerouac continues to invoke certain commonplaces:

> Not like driving across Carolina, or Texas, or Arizona, or Illinois; but like driving across the world and into the places where we would finally learn ourselves among the Fellahin Indians of the world, the essential strain of the basic primitive, wailing humanity that stretches in a belt around the equatorial belly of the world from Malaya (the long fingernail of China) to India the great subcontinent to Arabia to Morocco to the selfsame deserts and jungles of Mexico and over the waves to Polynesia to mystic Siam of the Yellow Robe and on around, on around, so that you hear the same mournful wail by the rotted walls of Cádiz, Spain, that you hear 12,000 miles around in the depths of Benares the Capital of the World. (280)

Although in this passage he articulately challenges the paternalistic U.S. stereotypes of Mexicans through poetic description, Kerouac also draws blatantly on the annoyingly persistent topos of primitive indigenous peoples, a chief device by which empires exercise epistemological domination.

Nonetheless, he turns this topos against its own principal thrust: the phrase "the essential strain of the basic primitive, wailing humanity" is a designation that points to something much larger and beyond the ken of U.S.-Western cognition; especially since the "capital of the world," Benares, is the most sacred city in Hinduism and hence well beyond the sedentariness of dominant U.S. culture.[11] Kerouac communicates the experience of feeling that one's own knowledge is utterly narrow and limited, unable to apprehend the vast majority of cultural phenomena in the world without resorting to cliché and commonplace.[12] His citation of the great distances from one place to another, which dwarf the supposed expanse of the United States and even the cartography of traveling from the United States to Mexico, gives an impression of the extent of these phenomena. Rather than lumping together "the rest of the undeveloped world," in Ligairi's words (152), the list of indigenous peoples around the globe that likens them to "Fellahin Indians" functions similarly to Kerouac's syntactical linking of disparate locations in the United States: these groups are in some contact with each other, when the globe is conceived as a whole, but the contact occurs along a continuum that valorizes the difference between all of them. That is, according to Kerouac's reconfiguration of the Spenglerian notion of fellaheen, they constitute a vast and variegated cultural vitality, which contributes to the sense of enormity that runs against the imperial mask and gaze that Sal (less so Kerouac, as the orchestrator of this rhetorical technique) to a degree dons.

The passage continues with a physical description that Sal plainly offers as a critique to U.S. stereotypes, images made of a limited, determined set of signifiers: "These people were unmistakably Indians and were not at all like the Pedros and Panchos of silly civilized American lore—they had high cheekbones, and slanted eyes, and soft ways; they were not fools, were not clowns; they were great, grave Indians and they were the source of mankind and the fathers of it" (280). The antiquity that Sal attributes to the Mexicans he encounters is no doubt a variation on primitivism. However, his particular statement of it here allows something quite different to break through—a vigorous reversal of the paternalism with which imperialism deploys its primitivist notions. The effect is to convey, in the midst of clichés such that it is all the more surprising, the awareness of a U.S. cognitive apparatus that up to this point has been largely self-assured. Sal makes this discovery in the course of his own nomadism, which, though he began it in the United States, allows him to leave the confines of its culture and ideology and encounter nomads connected to a global culture. Wandering began, for both Kerouac and Sal, as a relinquishment of the quest to recover the rootedness of the father's culture; this relinquishment is ultimately accomplished in an encounter with a group of fathers whose connection to global nomadism points the way out of the cognitive strictures of rootedness and the attempts to reproduce it. These newly found but much older fathers are in effect anti-fathers with respect to the former ones, since they invite the vagabondage that affirms the vitality unavailable in rooted culture, and even less so in the attempts to reproduce it through nostalgic cliché that Sal has experienced across the United States. Although this scene somewhat depends on such cliché, its main push is against the narrow cognition that deploys cliché in the first place.

The process of cognitive disruption intensifies as Sal and Dean travel further into Mexico to the point where empirical description itself, which seems unable to escape from recourse to cliché, breaks down completely. In a passage that appears to have received little critical attention, Sal relates the experience of an encounter with reality that almost completely eludes cognition to the point where objects and persons remain scarcely intelligible:

> I saw streams of gold pouring through the sky and right across the tattered roof of the poor old car, right across my eyeballs and indeed right inside them; it was everywhere. I looked out the window at the hot, sunny streets and saw a woman in a doorway and I thought she was listening to every word we said and nodding to herself — routine paranoiac visions due to tea. But the stream of gold continued. For a long time I lost consciousness in my lower mind of what we were doing and only came around sometime later when I looked up from fire and silence like waking from sleep to the world, or waking from void into a dream. . . . (284–285)

Sal first presents the experience as perhaps a marijuana-induced hallucination, but then suggests that much more is at issue. The dreamlike series of perceptions strongly calls into question the distinction between waking and dreaming life. The normal organs of perception, the eyeballs, become less relevant as the vision bypasses them; little remains of the cognitive apparatus, which has so far been unable to apprehend any unfamiliar object or person without trying to make it familiar by some recourse to cliché.

This experience shatters cognition in a brilliant, undifferentiated visual stream. It is made of gold, the very material that initially occasioned the European imperial conquest of Mexico. But Kerouac removes gold from its narrow use, here and in other books, in order to make it function aesthetically and even spiritually,[13] hence transforming the narrow experience of U.S. tourists into a greatly expanded faculty of knowledge. This passage also bears Christian messianic connotations: among other things, it echoes the arrival of the heavenly Jerusalem of Revelation 21:18, which is "pure gold." But in his usual anti-orthodox fashion, Kerouac depicts the revelation as an earthly, secular revealing of reality, an end time only of the limitations of sedentary U.S. culture. The operations of dreaming become fully activated in a kind of "effective" dreaming: Sal Paradise's cognition is transformed, and the novel itself then works at undoing its own systems of representation in their dependence on cliché. As it does in the novel in which Ursula K. Le Guin introduced the term, *The Lathe of Heaven*, effective dreaming here has a utopian function: It can ultimately remake U.S.-Western cognition, moving it toward a capacity to admit the vastness of global cultural variety. By the end of the novel, with his apprehension of America as "raw land that rolls in one unbelievable huge bulge over the West coast, and all that road going, all the people dreaming in the immensity" (307), Sal Paradise arrives at the beginning of such an expanded cognitive disposition. *On the Road* points to the eventuality of its further realization.

Through this procedure, the novel effectively demonstrates Kerouac's poetics of exile, which maps a series of American identities that resist strict national and territorial fixity. Although Kerouac partially leaves these in place, he raises far-reaching questions about the placement of persons and groups on one side or the other of a distinction between dominant identity and its forcefully designated others. In carrying this out, Kerouac draws heavily on his Québécois, Franco-American background and the relationship to dominant U.S. culture that it offered him. He develops the colonized but in-between status of the Québécois, as well as their habitation of zones that belong to more than one nation and hence not fully to any of them, extending it to an appreciation of the vitally heterogeneous cultures of a broadly conceived America and its relation to bordering territories. At about the same time that the expression "Third World" first appeared, in a 1952 argument by economist Alfred Sauvy indicting the blindness of both capitalist and communist imperialism, Kerouac began a literary masterpiece that continues to contribute to the understanding of an internationalizing United States and its place in global culture.

Notes

While preparing this essay, I received a generous grant from the University Research Council of the University of North Carolina at Chapel Hill, for which I am grateful. I also benefitted from the sites where I conducted research, where a number of people kindly and ably assisted me. I thank the Centre de Recherche Interuniversitaire sur la Littérature et la Culture Québécoises at the University of Montreal for the position of visiting scholar that I held there during the summer of 2009; I am thankful in particular to Patrick Poirier, scientific coordinator, and Ariane Audet and Louise-Hélène Filion, documentalists. During my visit to the Henry W. and Albert A. Berg Collection of English and American Literature in the New York Public Library, I was humbled by the expertise and guidance of curator Isaac Gewirtz and librarians Ann Garner and Stephen Crook, for which I am very grateful. Leslie Choquette, director of the Institut Français at Assumption College, has shared with me her vast knowledge of Franco-American history and culture, directing me to many sources, for which I am grateful. I thank Martha Mayo of the Center for Lowell History, Tony Sampas of the Pollard Memorial Library and the Libraries of the University of Massachusetts Lowell, and Robyn Christensen of the Worcester Historical Museum for generously assisting me in gaining access to documents.

1. In the *New York Times*, Charles Poore called Keraouc a "brilliantly promising young novelist."

2. The title of a declaration by Adolphe-Basile Routhier on the divine mission of French Canadians in America is telling: "Le rôle de la race française en Amérique [The Role of the French Race in America]." The sense of the word race in the nineteenth century, in both French and English, is somewhat different from today's: it is close to "lineage" or "bloodline," and it is tied to group characteristics by which one may declare uniqueness and usually superiority.

3. I use the French adjective and noun pertaining to the persons and things from Quebec. The English equivalent, Quebecker, functions as a noun only; its limited range is a testimony to the degree to which francophone Quebec continues to be discursively marginalized in anglophone Canada.

4. Cf. Michel Lapierre's introductory comments to Kerouac's letter in Poteet: "No one could express better than Jack Kerouac that profound Franco-American identity that subsists in spite of the abandonment of the French language" (445, my translation). Albert Faucher describes the emigration to the United States as "the major event of French-Canadian History in the nineteenth century" (244, my translation). Cited in Roby, *Franco-Americans*, 1. See also Purdy 23–24.

5. Gewirtz provides quotations from and an image of the manuscript of *La Nuit est ma femme*, as well as some astute comments about its role in the writing of *On the Road* (100–101).

6. For important observations on Kerouac's use of French in his novels, see P. Anctil, "Paradise Lost" 93–103.

7. Paul Marion suggested to me this expression for Kerouac's position in this letter.

8. Robert Holton quotes these words in an essay in which he develops the idea that the recurrence of rags, trash, scum, and dirt in *On the Road* mark the novel's most direct challenge to the regularity of dominant culture ("The Tenement Castle" 71).

9. Cf. Roby, *Histoire* 38 and *Franco-Americans* 43–44.

10. Ligairi provides an insightful analysis of the way that the narrative of *On the Road* engages with reality by a retreat into simulation, a process akin to the production of clichés that I am describing.

11. I am grateful to Nancy Grace for signaling the importance of Kerouac's mention of Benares in this passage.

12. Cf. Holton, *On the Road*: "Sal's respect for these people allows him to penetrate the racist American clichés and stereotypes that so often reduce and mock them, an important accomplishment at this moment in cultural history" (117).

13. Nicosia shows that in much of Kerouac's work gold functions for Kerouac as the substance of visions and as "the symbol of ultimate spiritual hope" (401).

Chapter 3

Beat Transnationalism under Gender: Brenda Frazer's *Troia: Mexican Memoirs*

Ronna C. Johnson

"To theorize about 'women' or 'patriarchy' one must stand in some experience of commonality or political alliance, looking beyond the local or experiential to wider, comparative phenomena."

(James Clifford, "Notes on Theory and Travel")

"No need to tell the rest of Acapulco, anyone who has ever been to Acapulco knows the rest and, if not, the travel folders on Third Avenue are adequate enough information, reckless tourism."

(Bonnie Bremser, Troia: Mexican Memoirs)

Scholarship has theorized the foundational male-centeredness of the Beat Generation literary movement and its notorious obliviousness to women's literary production and legitimacy as writing subjects, but approaches to Beat transnationalism nevertheless continue to underestimate gender as a basis of the movement's construction and a relevant category for its analysis,[1] even when works inexorably foreground it. Just so, no text elucidates Beat transnationalism and its gendered specificity, and the condition of women Beats' literary purdah, as comprehensively as does Brenda Frazer's 1969 *Troia: Mexican Memoirs*. A lost classic of Beat experimental writing, out of print until its 2007 reissue by Dalkey Archive Press, *Troia* recounts the 1961 travails of Bonnie and Ray Bremser, a minor Beat poet, on the lam in Mexico with their baby Rachel, fugitives of New Jersey prison authorities pursuing Ray for parole violation. The Mexican sojourn this flight entailed, which is the manifest subject of *Troia*, is narrated in the daily two-page letters Bonnie wrote to Ray from March to November 1963,[2] during his second incarceration when she was living back in New

York (Grace and Johnson 113). Frazer, then called Bonnie Bremser, retrospectively details her life of open prostitution on the road in Mexico and the couple's desperate relinquishment of Rachel there. Recounting her often shocking and emotionally wrung-out Mexican experiences, Frazer's letters to Ray—answering his request to titillate him and standing in lieu of sexual intimacy during their separation (77)—providentially provided the neophyte writer an indispensable literary apprenticeship (Grace and Johnson 113) that resulted in a benchmark of Beat writing: a transnational female road tale rivaling Jack Kerouac in visionary mind and hipster "kicks."[3] *Troia*'s female hipster, whose sexuality and maternality tangle with and tangle up in the road's border-crossing myths and juridical procedures, makes conspicuous the unrecognized gendered premises of Beat transnationalism.

The book's complicated provenance includes material phenomena of its publication that derive from and reflect Beat movement assumptions about gender and literary agency. Brenda Frazer's metamorphosis into Bonnie Bremser, from American college girl to *gringa* hustler, engages with Beat Generation stereotypes of women and obstacles faced by its women writers. Frazer was born in Washington, D.C., in 1939, and married Ray Bremser in 1959 after knowing him for three weeks. When they took the fugitive road to Mexico in 1961, Frazer was a twenty-two-year-old mother of an infant fathered by Bremser; when he turned her out to support the family and his writing, she was twenty-three (191). In 1963, when she wrote the letters to Ray that comprise *Troia*, she was twenty-four, younger than any of the male Beat writers when they composed their classic works. However, reflecting the contingent status of women writers of the Beat Generation, Frazer's groundbreaking text came out in a furtive, proxy publication. At Ray's behest and without Frazer's oversight, the sometime poet Michael Perkins edited the letters into a four-part narrative published in 1969 by Croton Press in New York. According to Perkins, Frazer was "a woman who was innocent, for the most part, of 'literature'" (1983, 34), a creature whose writing had to be elevated to literary competence, he implies, by his and Bremser's editorial interventions. Moreover, Frazer did not authorize the salacious title under which the narrative appeared: *Troia*, said to be derived from Helen of Troy, is apparently French slang for whore or sexual adventuress or courtesan (Grace and Johnson 112; Charters, *Troia* iii; Hemmer, "Prostitute" 102). Thus *Troia* was edited into a sequential narrative, titled and published as a book outside Frazer's aegis by two male poets skeptical of her literary acumen but intrigued by her confessions of sexual hazard. The text's pedigree of appropriation, exploitation, and literary commodification;[4] its multiple authorship (Frazer, Bremser, Perkins); and its evolution from private to public, from intimate to panoptic, which typifies Beat writing, constitute its Beat mystique and lineage.[5] *Troia* is a paradigm of Beat literature, yet anomalous: It may be treated as an autonomous literary discourse, but to identify the authorial hand is a complex, gendered procedure that speaks to female Beats' struggles for literary legitimacy, and compromises or destabilizes claims of any analysis, including those of this essay.

Situated on the margins of Beat literature, *Troia* is an oppositional text. It is a woman's road tale that "insists on the possibility of resistance" to hegemonic conditions of the road, evincing what feminist geographer Gillian Rose terms a "paradoxical geography" of occupying simultaneously "both the centre [sic] and the margin, the inside and the outside" of language, culture, power (155). It conveys traditional Beat movement discourses of free sex, visionary enunciation, and existential adventure, but its experimental hybrid narrative form and gender alterity—the protagonist's female subjectivity—deconstruct "beat." Indeed, *Troia*'s gender alterity deforms the genre the text performs: the road tale, the narrative or epic representation of national and transnational (geographical) movement away from civilization to unsettled terrain, is a foundational premise of the New World Anglo-American myths with which Beat literature is concerned and identified. *Troia* subverts midcentury and Beat Generation sexual politics and archetypes of the feminine to redefine—rescript and de-script (Enevold 84)—Beat formations of the road tale, problematizing imagoes and legends of Beat transnationalism through rereadings determined by gender. *Troia*'s proto-feminist gender formations—Bonnie's simultaneous multiple subjectivities as wife, mother, daughter, sister, whore—shape the text's hipster account of sex, drugs, marriage, maternity, vision, and travel south of and across the U.S.-Mexico border, exposing aesthetics and forms of Beat writing as gendered, rather than generic, "beat." *Troia* intervenes in received Beat movement literary formations and the accepted roster of practitioners as the tale's sexual politics of location, a politics of resistance, brings gender to bear on a canonical Beat genre.

Troia is often claimed to be a female *On the Road* (McNeil; Anderson; Hemmer, "Prostitute"), which is as close as critics have come to recognizing its subversive replication of the Kerouac imago. Two critical essays on *Troia* published in 2003 approach it through optics of gender and female sexuality,[6] yet struggle with its gender difference in Beat and postwar culture. *Troia*'s graphic narrative of hustling complicates M. Christine Anderson's study of "contemporary [post-war] discourses on femininity, domesticity, and sexuality" (255) and, alternatively, in a focus on female sexuality without feminism, provokes Kurt Hemmer's attention to Frazer's "pornographic style" ("Prostitute" 103).[7] These "recovery" essays subsume the literary-aesthetic to the sociocultural, perpetuating *Troia*'s subaltern status in the nature/culture dualism that subtends patriarchy. This reception of *Troia* that emphasizes the prurient content of Frazer's story confines it to the female social body (nature), thus denying it the male literary mind (culture); derogated as female, the text is partitioned from the esteemed masculinized "beat."[8] My feminist study challenges notions of women Beats' "free" sexuality in a counterculture where, like the post-war U.S. mainstream from which it descends, female bodies and sexualities are read through the disenfranchising madonna/whore binary. This is given literal expression in *Troia*, whose literary innovations on received Beat imagoes and tropes clarify their sociopolitical sexual stereotype. In this, *Troia* is what critic Mary Louise Pratt terms an "auto-ethnographic text," a representation constructed by marginalized speakers "*in response to* or in dialogue with . . . representations others have made of them," creating by "selective collaboration with and appropriation of idioms . . . self-representations intended to intervene in" hegemonic modes defining them ("Arts" 35). *Troia*'s auto-ethnographic discourse transcends its editors' male fantasy "memoir" of a female hipster's sex exploit(ation)s; it revises Beat ethics, aesthetics, and assumptions of narrative agency, interrogating gender and genre in Beat literature with a transnational road narrative fueled by economies of the female body. *Troia* is the "lost" Beat text whose re(dis)covery reanimates what can be claimed for Beat literature's quest for spiritual regeneration and sexual liberation, what the quest can be said to be, and, finally, who can be meant to engage it.

Troia's (On the) Road Tale and the Female Beat Subject

In metaphoric, discursive ways, and in plot-driven ones, *Troia* is a road tale that clarifies the gendered character of the traditional genre it reprises. From *Moby-Dick* to *On the Road*, the road tale is an American genre notably congenial to its famous white male practitioners. Feminist cultural geographer Janet Wolff recognizes that while "narratives of travel, which are in play in the metaphoric use of the vocabulary, are gendered," the "metaphors of travel . . . [are] androcentric" ("On the Road" 232). Anthropologist James Clifford notes that the term "travel" evokes "middle class 'literary' or recreational movement . . . practices long associated with male experiences and virtues" and argues that studies of geography and travel must account for "different populations, classes, and genders [that] travel" differently and therefore construct divergent "kinds of knowledges, stories, and theories" ("Notes" 183), just as *Troia* departs from but is still a Beat road tale, differently framed, produced, expressed from its male Beat counterparts. Wolff recognizes that there is "nothing inherently or essentially masculine about travel," since women have always traveled, but agrees that "Western ideas about travel . . . have . . . transmitted, inculcated, and reinforced patriarchal values and ideology," gender biases that would implicate the female road tale. In this, the discourse of travel, which is central to Beat writing in the road tale and to transnational transit, "typically functions as a 'technology of gender'" (Abbeele 1992, xxv–xxvi; qtd. in Wolff, "On the Road" 232), in the phrase of Teresa de Lauretis. *Troia's* auto-ethnographic road tale deconstructs the hegemonic of the masculine as the dominant narrative mind. Its female focus refocuses the Beat road tale's genre and aesthetics (archetypally those of *On the Road*), socio-cultural and political expressions, and dramatic effects, elucidating how these disciplinary elements rely on gender for realization. Jessica Enevold points out that a "man in a role is, as always, not considered as a male but as a protagonist" (78), inviting consideration of the way a woman in a role is restricted to her sex, as in the female nominal *troia* by which Frazer's protagonist is objectified and marginalized. Trafficking in canonical Beat discourses, *Troia* tells them slant, merging memoir and road tale, domesticity and prostitution, fugitive desperation and adventure, rescripting their determinants to reveal the gendered genres by which the narrative constitutes itself in the troped name of its female hero.

Women writers of Beat road narratives have critiqued the genre's abandonment of the domestic sphere and thus made a literature comprised of materials that male-authored Beat writing, like "classic" male-authored American literature, has precisely defined itself in reaction against (see R. Johnson "Mapping"). Rose argues that "feminist subjectivity," energized in *Troia's* representation of a female Beat hero, negates "founding antimonies of Western geographic thought" such as domesticity and the road. Refusing "to distinguish between real and metaphorical space," this gender-conscious (feminist) subjectivity "threaten[s] the polarities which structure the dominant geographical imagination" to "allow for the possibility of a different kind of space through which difference is tolerated rather than erased" (155). This suggests that a female-centered, proto-feminist road tale such as *Troia* enacts its "politics of resistance" to female subordination and oppression (Rose 154) by refusing hierarchy and accommodating all the terms in oppositional binaries, polarities such as madonna/whore, female/male, by which males retain dominance of females in Sherry Ortner's cultural anthropology. As a woman's road tale in a hipster diaspora—where the female domestic purdah is relocated to the male road—-*Troia* also exemplifies Enevold's claim that the female road tale brings genre and gender into "a productive crisis" (75); its hybrid travel tale still speaks the Beat patois of movement, desire, and discovery. In this respect, Frazer's road tale engages and fuses with, not ignores or excludes, the domestic: Bonnie travels as Ray's wife with their baby, Rachel, in her care. This condition of the narrative, then, brings what Amy Kaplan calls the "manifest domesticity" of the feminine to the anti-domestic masculine sphere in a radical innovation on classic American and Beat narratives of the road.

I keep the nominal distinction between *Troia*'s author, Brenda Frazer, and its narrator protagonist, Bonnie Bremser, to hold the place of its literariness,[9] the experimental discourses that have unfortunately been eclipsed in reception and reputation by the gritty confessions of tarnished romantic love and sex-on-demand that make *Troia* (seem like) a woman's "natural born" road tale akin to the iconic film *Thelma and Louise* (1991). The tale signals its postmodern aesthetic by its reflexivity, a self-awareness of narrative process and composition (seen, too, in *On the Road*), as when Bonnie admits she is writing "a composed interlude [as opposed] to what I knew happened at the time . . . embellishing the facts" (44). This maneuver typifies Enevold's idea of "de-scripting," a deconstruction of genre by self-conscious reflexive rhetoric that undermines fictive illusion (84). On a diegetic level, *Troia* is a tale told by a subject-author (Brenda Frazer) about an object-protagonist (Bonnie Bremser). These positions and figures overlap and blur in *Troia*'s reflexive fusion of protagonist and narrator, as in this sequence in which the narrator's reflexive self-imprecation, "be humble, Bonnie," is followed by making explicit the implied narrative gaze: "I see me at the water's edge . . . I am conscious of my thinness in the bikini . . . I shake the water from my hands—my wedding ring flies into the sand and seafoam and I frantically pursue it, spontaneously crying" (44), a hypnotic list of declarative clauses that enact the narrator's claim to subjectivity paradoxically through her self-objectification in her own gaze. As a self-reflexive literary text, *Troia* undercuts the titillation of the male fantasy by which it was organized and commissioned, as in this discourse that, explicitly pairing Bonnie's bikini and wedding ring—signifiers of body and heteronormativity that evoke the binary of whore and matron—inscribes a complex subjectivity onto the specularized female body caught in the humanizing flung hands of Bonnie's despair.

Troia's challenge to the hipster stereotype of the "chick" in its narrativization of bohemian street life and Beat transnationalism performs, rather than represents, sexuality and gender, albeit as conducted and orchestrated by patriarchal dictate.

Its enactments affirm Judith Butler's theories of gender performativity, that not a natural original but a cultural imitation which has no original constitutes gender. Bonnie stresses prostitution's enactments and display—the act of "put[ting] on a good show forcing [the johns] to come and have done" (34); "enjoying what I am paid for . . . and when I don't[,] I put on a good enough show so that none would ever know" (50)—a transactional sexuality legible only in performance. Her prostitution is framed as a sex show for Ray, who demands to watch her with her first john (32–33) and procures other men to have sex with her for money while he observes, hidden from view (34), a voyeurism duplicated in the letters about these moments that he enjoins Bonnie to write to him. Issuing from male dictate, and conveyed under male editorial and publishing control, *Troia* is a compromised "memoir," written to Ray's "order" (53), which is spelled out in a letter to Bonnie that is itself pastiched into the narrative in its epistolary form, artfully staged with dramatic ellipses at the beginning of Book Two, presumably by the editor Perkins. Projecting a specifically erotic poetics, Ray bids Bonnie to "tell me some sexual items . . . draw up a plan, a plot, a sequence! Start alone, self-sex, then me, then he, then he or she and so on!," likening her hoped-for response to a "twelve-hour scherzo, fill[ed] with progression," a "symphony" of sexual acts played with a single proviso: "Make your flesh delirious for me, but unperformed without me!" (77). Less theatrically, Frazer says she wrote her "troia" letters to Ray to "improve the[ir] relationship" while he was in prison and she was living in New York (Grace and Johnson 121–123). Such disparities of desire and motive speak of gender and power, as in the letters' asymmetries of proprietor and petitioner that delineate the assumed patriarchal male right to commodify a female "true sex" confession.

   Troia explicitly derives from conditions of patriarchal marriage, reductive binary sex roles, and male hegemony that even hipsters perpetuated, as in Ray's 1967 epic poem about Frazer, *Angel*, which depicts Bonnie as his creation, the eponymous "angel," an objectifying trope in opposition to "troia," also of Ray's device. These two signifiers, redolent of the patriarchal mind, form a binary reminiscent of madonna/whore. Ray's directive to Bonnie dictates the terms of the text's production and textualizes its erotic poetics of a state of constant arousal; Ray's requirement that Bonnie report to him as a sexualized body perennially tumescent renders her narration the linguistic equivalent of unconsummated foreplay. Humiliated into performing her marital sexual duty to Ray by means of prostitution, Bonnie is made the family "breadwinner" (33, 55), a euphemism for provider that denotes and connotes a man's ability to support wife and family;[10] Bonnie is obliged to assume both the "Victorian ideal of the passive nurturing mother and the breadwinning father" (Rose 55), which refuses binary polarities by embodying both gender roles for the distinctive simultaneity of female subjectivity recognized by Adrienne Rich and Rose. Bonnie's ironic self-designation as breadwinner/wife recalls feminist accounts of the bourgeois marriage as the marital exchange of women's sexual favors for men's money that is identical with prostitution (and/or rape) (Gilman 1898; Dworkin 1987). Both wife and courtesan, Bonnie, unlike the namesake Helen of Troy, is turned out by her husband who hawks her like commodity goods: "Ray went off to the center of town, El Centro, armed with a picture of me in a bikini, while I sat at home waiting nervously . . . try[ing] to make the baby comfortable" (33). Bonnie's abjectness is conveyed in her reflections on her prostitution: "The first experience almost finished me . . . Ray . . . no doubt spread the news [of it] to all of his friends. . . . From then on I felt hunted, furtive" (33); "I am full of moods and bad humors, always brooking my importance as the breadwinner" (55). Her "horror of being the bread-winner" (33) is dismissed in Ray's rationalization that she is a "whore": Because Bonnie confesses to contriving a sexual encounter with "N" (31–32), Ray "fully believed I was capable of walking the streets . . . I was forced to be a con artist— pure necessity sent me into town" to hook to feed the "skinny" baby and to keep Ray writing poetry (33, 31). Ray's order that Bonnie report sex acts she performed is the linguistic, narrative equivalent of the hustle he puts her on. By its etymology in patriarchal dictate, *Troia* problematizes how, and under what circumstances, women and women's writing can be "beat": when female sexual appetites are displayed for male stimulation; when female sexual subordination proves male prowess; when female hipster sexuality serves marital obligations but surpasses "square" postwar sexual repressions and hypocrisies (McNeil; Nadel): when in the collapse of gender polarities the madonna is literally the whore.

Troia resists gender dictates through a radical "beat" sex narrative that dissolves the madonna/whore binary, a move mirrored in the fusion of the text's self-same narrating subject and narrative object. In *Sexual Politics* (1969), the groundbreaking scholarly manifesto of the second wave women's movement published the same year as *Troia*, Kate Millett anatomizes male hegemonic privilege as founded on female subordination: "One of the chief effects of class within patriarchy is to set one woman against another" in the classic "antagonism between whore and matron"; "[t]hrough the multiple advantages of the double standard . . . [the male] partici-pates in both worlds, empowered by his superior social and economic resources to play the estranged women against each other as rivals" (52) in divide-and-conquer competitiveness. *Troia's* radical move makes the narrator, Bonnie, a subject who simultaneously embodies the antithetical female archetypes of matron and whore (Ray's angel and troia), challenging female rivalries that promote female disempow-erment. As subjugated wife, desperate mother, and ambivalent prostitute, Bonnie achieves subject status by her narrativized "embrace" of these simultaneous selves, anticipating Adrienne Rich's 1976 theories of femininity in *Of Woman Born*, that the "mother is *both* subject and object at the same time"; that the feminine is "a multiple subjectivity, a nexus of various dialogical selves" (Ganser 114), as mothers are always already also daughters. The patriarchal double standard mandates that sexually versed women (whores) need not be respected; respected women (wives/ mothers) are divested of sexuality; and only men hold the privilege to partake of both types of women (Millett 52). *Troia* and Frazer undo this tidy sequence, which is the essence of the text's radical mediation in Beat genres and philosophies from the margins of the female. Frazer's troia is an agent who makes her own condi-tions: "I would like some respite for care of [the baby] to become what is necessary. I embrace my prostitution" (51). Speaking the tensions of her resistance, Bonnie's claims for the "necessary" and her "necessity" signal her lack of options, her oppres-sion. *Troia's* simultaneities of the feminine, Bonnie's maternality and adult female sexuality, inscribe a hybrid subjectivity that matches its amalgam of literary forms. Bonnie's fealty to Ray's power ("I embrace my prostitution") affirms and ironically subverts the compliance. Her assent nominally fits with his command that she prostitute herself, but it is also a seizure of, if not the means of, literary production, then of the means of marital subjugation; it manifests the troia's subjectivity. In this, the wife/prostitute—the madonna/whore—unifies polarities of her social location against the patriarchal dictate that she can have virtue or sexuality, be either wife-mother or troia, but not both. *Troia*'s challenge to the prostitute's sequestration from the wife manifests Frazer's idiosyncratic, revisionary participation in and embodiment of "beat."

Troia On the Transnational Road

Troia adapts poetics of Kerouac's road narrative, modifying the genre's terms for the female protagonist, specifying that female sexual freedom and freedom to profit by sexual self-expression are in fact coincident with, not exclusive of, matrimony and maternity. In this, Frazer makes what feminist critic Jacqueline Bobo delineates as "an alternative reading," a "subversive" or "against the grain" reaction cognizant that the "system that produced the text"—here the "boy gang" of Beat and classic American literatures—"is fundamentally at odds" with female participants (96). For Pratt, this challenge is expressed in the "parodic, oppositional representation[s]" of the dominant discourse made by the subjugated (35), here Frazer's addition of a baby to the representation of the road journey. The following run of words aesthetically and stylistically conjoining the movements of prose and the road poses a challenge to male exclusivity and anti-domesticity in Frazer's modifications to the familiar Kerouacian imago:

> A road which grows out of the solid surety of modern highway dotting in weak secrecy into the plain to Abasolo where another almost not to be seen road, goes nowhere, but goes – we want to see where all the roads go, since then, but this first trip just get us there and quick, get us there where we are going, and we don't know yet that nothing waits but the bottom waiting to be scraped in our own whimsical and full-of-love fashion—got to get there and quick—*damn the crying and wet diapers and laps full of Gerbers on the bus, of leg cramps and not much to view*—Padilla, Guemez, Ciudad Victoria, chicken salad sandwiches and the unknown feeling of a waterfall. In all of these places we stop, passing through, rushing downward, seeking our level, slowly dying, get it over, let's get there. . . . The driver announces the last lap and everyone stirs and gets excited at the news, not realizing it is more than 3 hours of approach to Mexico City. I look out and God drops from his hand the myriad stars and constellations I have never seen before, plumb to the horizon flat landed out beneath the giant horoscopic screen of Mexican heaven. (11–12; emphasis mine)

This passage owes a clear debt to the lyricism of *On the Road*.[11] But *Troia*'s accounts and contents are explicitly gendered female, as in the startling and nearly perverse reference here to the baby, Rachel, who is more Frazer's road partner than is the frequently absent Ray; the mother and child image is often "suppressed" in male-authored Beat texts even though it is archetypal (Pratt, "Arts" 35). Frazer repeatedly depicts the difficulties of being "beat" on the road with the baby, as above: "damn the crying and wet diapers and laps full of Gerbers on the bus, of leg cramps and not much to view" (12). In Kerouac (and Melville), women and babies are left behind,[12] whereas, as Bonnie recounts, on "[t]he bus ride to Mexico City, full of this, I am constantly with the baby on my lap, broken hearted at every spell of crying, the frustration of not being a very good mother really—trying to groove, trying to groove under the circumstances" (9). *Troia* shows that the Beat impetus to hit the road to escape confinement (as in Ray's imprisonment) and partake of hipster plea-sure ("groove") is compromised for the female Beat traveler with child. As women Beats' tales repeatedly evince, women's sexual freedom leads to maternity, a brake on movement that preserves male dominance in road tales: Unlike the baby's father, Ray, Bonnie is "tied down by . . . bodily realities" (Anderson 254) that under-mine movement. The female body restricts the female to the body in patriarchy, an essentialist devaluation *Troia* resists in Bonnie's "trying to groove" even while being yanked into a deflationary reality of maternal failure.

This discursive tension and resistance, exposing gender's salience to the narrative enunciation, "rescripts" the Beat road tale. For instance, Bonnie's seduction of "N" is a case study of *Troia*'s parodic, oppositional response of the subordinated:

It is decided for me that I will travel to Veracruz by bus with N and the baby. Ah bitter, I was not about to accept with grace my maidenly burdened-by-baby responsi-bility . . . [I]n rebellion . . . I decide to try my seductive powers on N . . . did indeed entice his hand where it should have by any standards stayed away from, the baby on my lap. (15)

"By any standards" of the male road tale, the female lap would be unoccupied, available, exemplified by *On the Road*, specifically Sal's sexy encounter on a bus to Los Angeles with Terry, who travels without her son. Bonnie's "rebellion" against femininity's "maidenly burdened-by-baby responsibility" is to seduce N to stimu-late her even as the baby lies on her lap, a move that rescripts and de-scripts *Troia*'s Kerouac-Melville heritage, deforming the male Beat subject's narrative genre, the road, by speaking the female Beat subject's compromised, domesticized sexual desire. Such a gender revision disrupts the "stable, centered sense of knowledge and reality" (Pratt, "Arts" 37) inscribed in dominant literary imagoes, such as male buddy pairs partaking of the road. Yet Frazer's appropriation and rescripting of the male road tale by inserting the mother and child is at least temporarily stymied by the couple's divestiture of Rachel. Ray's arrangement of an adoption for Rachel (121–122) leaves Bonnie again a "chick"; it also, paradoxically, effects her closer status to men, as she anticipates "the baby being taken care of by some rich people where she will be safe, and I will not have the immediate worry that my investiga-tions will be tampering with anyone else's life but my own" (116). Without Rachel, Bonnie would be, like men, detached from the domestic, free to live an experimental life ("investigations")—as in *On the Road*, manic geographical movement and male camaraderie are predicated on Sal's "split-up" from his wife, also a condition of male freedom in the Robert Frank film *Pull My Daisy*, and intensified in an unacknowl-edged murder of a wife that releases the Burroughs' protagonists in *Queer* and *The*

Yage Letters to flee Mexico for Peru and beyond. The baby's relinquishment registers Bonnie's new fitness for the road, but it is rendered in a near lacuna that suggests domesticity's silencing by the voluble discourses of the road—that, at least in this instance, the road halts "[manifest] domesticity's outward reach" (A. Kaplan 588).

Beyond modifying the road tale with domestic determinants, *Troia* enacts the female seizure of prerogatives of the male road hero, Beat and classic American, through Bonnie's maternality and surrender of Rachel. As Enevold notes of *Thelma and Louise*, the female road tale is "an appropriation of a set of qualities traditionally viewed as traits of masculinity . . . (here: inhabiting the road) while, at the same time, retaining traditional qualities of femininity" (81); it grafts familiar stereotypes (the wife and mother; the beat "chick") onto an unfamiliar template of the unfettered, anti-domestic road. This appropriative rescripting in Frazer's oppositional road tale renders it a reprise of Kerouac's, but in the service of the deviant empowerment of a female subject: It interrogates Beat literature in terms of who is fit to undertake the transnational road—the child-free traveler—illuminating gender's destabilizing interference with border crossing in contrast to its presumed invisibility or irrelevance. Bonnie's separations from Rachel and ensuing pressures to retrieve the baby, discussed below, evince an oscillation between maternal freedom and maternal encumberment in service of the male road discourse. This role conflict and instability suggest Pratt's "contact zone" of intercultural, transnational conflict, "social spaces where cultures meet, clash, and grapple with each other, often in contests of highly asymmetrical relations of power" ("Arts" 34). But in *Troia*, the "contact zone" of the border and the back-and-forths of Frazer's border transversals refuse "asymmetrical" intracultural grapplings by Bonnie's seizure of her means of subjugation, her prostitution, which, free of responsibility for Rachel, she puts to the service of securing her freedom of the road.

While women on the road escaping home or convention, nation or law, confront barriers and experiences that contradict the road tale's masculine hegemonic,[13] male Beat writers depict transnational travel as gender neutral or genderless, as well as politically innocent, tendencies *Troia* contends. In *On the Road*, for instance, Dean declares his global fever: "We'd dig the whole world with a car like this because, man, the road must eventually lead to the whole world" (230); "digging" is a charming euphemism for the imperialist hunger to consume a passively waiting world. *Troia* problematizes male Beat literary fantasies of transnational freedom by exposing their reactionary patriarchal politics, which have been praised for ostensibly countercultural, anti-imperialist stances (see Martinez, "Imperious"). Bonnie is "ungracious," "contemptuous" of hipster "revolutionaries" who "stop at our house [in Mexico] on their American way to Cuba . . . and idealism and here we are left to grope with the snake of time and capitalism growing; I wince every time I see a Coca-Cola sign" (55). *Troia* differentiates who can take the transnational road and who is confined to home, who is revved up by revolutionary fervor and who plagued by guilt ("wince") about global U.S. capitalism. Frazer recognizes the heedless global appetite of the "American way" that Kerouac poeticizes in *On the Road*, where the road to the "magic border" is "the route of old American outlaws who used to skip over the border to go down to old Monterrey," Mexico (276), like Ray and Burroughs, to escape pursuit. Laden with fantasies of imperialist consumption, this Beat ideal is imagined as a hemispheric body supine and awaiting congress in Sal's "vision of the entire Western Hemisphere rockribbing clear down to Tierra del Fuego and us flying down the curve of the world into other tropics and other worlds" (265–266). In *Troia*, Bonnie is the "hemispheric" "rockribbing" "curve" of road that males "take." Her subaltern status obliges her to walk the street rather than fly down the road to "other tropics and other worlds," in the gender-coded and exclusive, not universal, road tropes of conquest and consumption that Kerouac employs. Inserted into a road narrative, but relegated to the prostitute's stroll, Bonnie becomes the bait and reward for men's movement; in Laura Mulvey's much-cited formulation, she embodies to-be-looked-at-ness.

As Martinez and others note, the celebrated Beat writers are white men unmolested at borders for their legal irregularities, shielded by their race, gender, and U.S. nationality; this is the condition of their transnationality. When gender is made visible, however, factors such as class status apply. In Frazer's female optic on the road narrative, it is white male prerogatives that are contingent and transient. They are seen to dissolve as Ray is detained at the U.S.-Mexico border, unable to parlay his whiteness into passage free from legal reach because of his class and caste status as a poor poet-parolee on the lam. Unlike the patrician Burroughs, never detained at any border for extradition to face charges of killing his wife or his numerous drug law violations, Ray, proving the weight of class status, is immediately arrested at the border for parole violation and held in the Webb County Jail in Laredo, Texas, while Bonnie is stranded in Nuevo Laredo, Mexico, for being without her papers or the baby who legitimizes them (78). *Troia* witnesses the spoliation of Ray's white male privilege at the border: He is clapped "under arrest for unlawful flight" (72) on the "legality . . . that his tourist visa was expired"; he is defamed, targeted in post-HUAC (House Un-American Activities Committee) Cold War discourse as "a drug addict and a communist, those two offenses the most comprehensible to nervous Mexican officials, and most often used whether any offense exists or not" (90). Illuminating the relation of gender to class, Ray's only privilege is having Bonnie's body to spend, which his title "troia" unironically suggests. (Considered in this context, the 1971 U.K. edition title, *For Love of Ray*, implies that loving Ray costs Bonnie her body.) As it proves Beat transnationalism to be a function of gender, race, and class, *Troia* revises the male road tale to fit conditions of the female subaltern by grounding the Beat quest in the materiality of the gendered body. On the hustle, which "is only necessary in Mexico, and there unavoidable" because there is nothing (except her prostitution) "between us and starvation and the jailhouse" (33), Bonnie turns to her body to provide, which is disadvantageous because, as Ortner argues, women's associations with body "confine [them] universally to certain social contexts . . . [that are] seen as closer to nature" and distant from the valorized, cultural male "mind" (76–77). But this institutionalized denigration of the body as "female" and inferior is a ruse of power-holders that is transparent to the female subject. As Rose notes, "Skin colour [sic], class and gender are all social attributes which are inscribed onto bodies; and part of women's sense of oppression, of confinement, is their awareness of that" (145). While male Beat narratives have hoped for the road's facilitation of escape from (bodily) confinement, what Rich has called "the politics of location" (1986)—an insistence on the situated nature of experience and politics that starts with, and cannot evade, the body—is a central premise of *Troia* on the transnational road.

Troia's corporeal discourse is expressed in graphic interactions of the body and the state on the border, an impasse of gender positions and police detainment. Frazer's account does not imagine a borderless hipster subculture or untrammeled entry as in Kerouac's cavalier narratives, where "Nuevo Laredo . . . looked like Holy Lhasa to us" and Mexican border cops are indulgent: At the "border inspection . . . [t]he Mexicans looked at our baggage in a desultory way. They weren't like officials at all. They were lazy and tender" and wave Sal and Dean through with paternalistic solicitude (274–275). The thwarted flights of *Troia*'s vulnerable bodies depict the snares of official culture as nearly insoluble, an impermeable border full of jeopardy: "I am violently afraid of the United States and Texas, but I am coming to you fast, Ray, like a tornado, fast as every irregular bag of tricks I can muster will get me there" (78). *Troia*'s Mexican border cops are menacing persecutors. They always find Bonnie's "papers are out of order," forcing her to struggle to stay out of jail (90): "I could not cross the border, for my papers had expired and I didn't have the baby with me, and the immigration officials were waiting for me at the Nuevo Laredo bus stop" (78); Mexican "immigration people . . . threat[en] to arrest me because of my papers" (36); "the police on the American side would like to get me on anything"(101), such as the absence of the child in arms. Frazer never explains why Bonnie needs Rachel at the border; perhaps mother and child share visas, passports, identification photographs. The repeated insistence on Bonnie's possession of the baby, however, signifies that her (U.S.) nationality is inextricable from her maternity just as the border reduces Ray from Beat poet to petty outlaw. This fusion of nationality and maternity in the (female) body reinstates *Troia*'s corporeal politics of location over male road kicks. The crises of *Troia*'s dispossessed female traveler marked by maternity and prostitution ("irregular bag of tricks") render Bonnie's travel a displacement coerced by marriage and motherhood to "nomadism" (see Deleuze and Guattari). Deterritorialized through the material female body, Bonnie journeys endlessly with "no reterritorialization *afterward*" (Deleuze and Guattari 381), which disappoints a Beat hope typified by *On the Road* that crossing the geographical border between the United States and Mexico assures escape from the confinements of postwar middle-class life. Or, in Caren Kaplan's feminist revision of Deleuze and Guattari, rather than wandering with no reterritorialization to come, female "identities are 'both deterritorialization and reterritorialization.'"[14] In tense transversals of the U.S.-Mexico border, the perilous international crossings with which *Troia* is obsessed, the tale inscribes oscillations with no surcease, leading to no escape, a cycle that defines this transnational road tale, and to which it is confined.

Crossing the U.S.-Mexico border, Bonnie is unloosed from domesticity's sequestrations to a chancy liminality of the transnational zone exemplified by metamorphoses of subjectivity. Bonnie's daily border crossings to visit Ray, who is awaiting extradition in the Texas jail, entail a need to "differentiate Nuevo Laredo from Laredo" (101), travel/mobility (Mexico) from home/stasis (United States) in Ganser's formulations (70). But while the nearly matching signifiers for the contiguous cities (Nuevo Laredo/Laredo) divided by identical, simultaneous borders form a U.S./Mexico binary, in the feminist geography of female travel, binary distinctions do not hold. The linguistic repetition of Nuevo Laredo/Laredo that signifies the transnational cusp undermines differentiations, verifying Clifford's speculation that in "new localizations like 'the border' . . . hybridity and struggle, policing and transgression" entail "the subversion of all binarisms" ("Traveling" 109) for a liminality that increases potential for transformation. In Nuevo Laredo, Bonnie notes, "no discretion necessary in this open scene of welcome if you are an American with money or a Mexican hustler of some sort, but . . . . anything in between . . . as I was . . . [required] an official escort" (112)—for Bonnie, a john. Being "anything in between," neither American with money nor Mexican hustler, signifies a productive liminality that matches Bonnie's claims to an intercultural subjectivity: Her "necessary" and "unavoidable" Mexican prostitution (33) is said to have "broke up all the American inhibitions I ever possessed; I know that I am as much Mexican as I am New Yorker or even spade, Negro, Veracruzana, I have undergone the metamorphosis completely" (39). The broken "inhibitions" signify borderlessness, a "metamorphosis" out of gender homogeneity to simultaneity of female subjectivities. The intercultural border zone of Bonnie's "metamorpho sis," like the Nuevo Laredo/Laredo cusp, disperses binaries: "Nuevo Laredo was a mixed scene all along, a precarious one for me and Rachel, but at least more sure than that in Laredo" (112). The preferred Mexican side of the border offers a paradoxically "sure" "precarious" diversity—the "mixed scene" —syntonic with the "multiplicities of subjectivity" of *Troia*'s feminine optic. *Troia*'s claim for Bonnie's "metamorphosis" of subjectivity by the intersection of gender and genre, femininity and the road, recalls Sal's wishful and transient appropriation of Mexicaness in *On the Road* (97), which is gratuitous and superficial. Bonnie "prefer[s] to stay in Nuevo Laredo than ever put [her]self at the mercy of American ways of life again" (80). This discursive resolution of subjectivity by existential, philosophical transnationalism results from the "productive crisis" of gender and genre in a critical feminist thesis (Enevold).

Evincing its seizure of the road narrative for the female Beat protagonist, suspended on the transnational border, *Troia* disputes the public/private gender divide, the traditional polarity that opposes "home/stasis and travel/mobility" and that is gendered male/female accordingly (see Wolff, Ganser, and C. Kaplan above). For instance, when Bonnie leaves the Mexico City-Veracruz loop and, in search of Ray, crosses the U.S.-Mexico border, her movement attracts the attention of the state and multiplies the watch she attracts as a prostitute soliciting the gaze of potential johns on the border: On "the dusty streets of Nuevo Laredo," she writes, "I feel the eyes of Mexicans on me, I am paranoid . . . through the checking points of customs" (80). The penetration of the private by the public is embodied by the surveillance of the state: "My citizenship is questioned every time I cross the bridge . . . I put them on at every turning" (81). But Bonnie's innovative "put on" is her contradictory embodiment of maternity and prostitution: officially and evidently *both* madonna and whore. On the border cusp, this fusion and confusion of gender roles produces a liminal femininity akin to the "in between" of Nuevo Laredo. Border crossing specularizes Bonnie as the fallen maternal, her prostitution a juridical abjection even as its monetary compensations promise to reunite her family from the dispersals of poverty and persecution.

Border authorities, Frazer notes, "are well-trained to recognize the difference between flavor and true nationality" (80), between being a sexy mother and being a sex worker. But crossing resists such differentiation, as the liminal U.S.-Mexico border evokes Bonnie's hybrid subjectivity; both whore and Madonna, she performs the troia in the maternal body, bribing immigration officials with free sex and retrieving her forsaken baby:

> I fuck a border Mexican cop and make it across the border illegally on a bus full of Mexican shoppers—I don't care. That was the first time I ever fucked someone for something other than money or love . . . I will have to go back to get the baby in Veracruz before I can even talk to him about crossing the border . . . this was the biggest favor I ever fucked for. (78–79)

The "embrace" of sexuality's paradoxical liberation-exploitation correlates to the feminine "paradoxical pace" "simultaneously inhabiting centers and margins" (Rose 153). Bonnie's multiple simultaneous subjectivities as madonna and whore, "New Yorker or even spade, Negro, Veracruzana" (39), emerge on the transnational border, which mandates a sex performativity that, as Butler has theorized, is, rather than "nature," how gender is seen and known, exemplifying how discourses of travel are technologies of gender, how discourses of travel serve to construct gender in *Troia*.

In *Troia*'s border crossings, gender problematizes male Beats' legends of transnationalism and stymies transnational fluidity as they had conceived it. Ray is emasculated, dispatched from outlaw paterfamilias-pimp to state prisoner, his Mexican freedom exposed as an illicit patriarchal illusion of masculinity. Bonnie lingers in Mexico with new men who are made into texts in her required sex letters to Ray. Eventually returning to New York, she compliantly, automatically seeks a john, ostensibly to report on, but then writes what Ray already knows, of her unexpected encounter on the street of him, still her husband, whom she nevertheless treats as a john by requiring his deposit of ten dollars for her time (211–213). This sequence suggests prostitution's penetration of and continuation in marriage, an institutional instance of the failure of binary divisions and the triumph of feminist simultaneity and postmodern narrative hybridity. *Troia*'s hybridity of confession and literary invention motivates its resistance to patriarchy's madonna/whore binary, evidence that gender ideologies do circulate in the "*dis-location[s]* of culture" which, "in an age of accelerating globalization, . . . has become deterritorialized and diasporic" (Jay 37). Plausibly transforming female gender identifications and authority in the collapse of binaries on the transnational modern-postmodern divide, Frazer's complicated fugitive narrative bids to partake of Beat literature's liberations, but in the troia's terms of multiplicity, liminality, paradox, and the sexual empowerment derived from unifying maternality and female promiscuity. While Bonnie is no anarchist, her assertion that she "can start a revolution any time I like in my head" (37) reserves consciousness for the female artist. The *Troia* letters, their textualization of Bonnie's private mind ("head"), achieve a radical intervention in the Beat transnational road tale where, in the liminal contact zone of the border, the Beat heroine is liberated, "stubborn, wildly defiant of any discipline" (101). In this space of transculturation and potential self-invention, *Troia* clarifies the limited conditions under which, and for whom, the border can be border-less, the national, transnational.

Notes

1. See the essays collected in Schneiderman and Walsh 2004. See Belgrad 2004; Martinez 1998, 2003; Rachel Adams 2004; Saldana-Portillo 2002. These critics and scholars of either Kerouac and/or Burroughs have little to no recognition of the constitutive role played by gender in formations and understandings of Beat-hipster transnationalism. Transnationalism so represented as genderless and classless seems to occur in an ideal state of abstraction, that of the dominant culture, itself defined by its elisions of gender, race, and class specificities and alterities. Sexuality alone is accounted for in these critics' views into Beat transnationalism, doubtless because the hetero- and homosexual writers foreground it, but of course without admitting to gender. Carden opens discussion of the gendered construction of male Beat travel texts in her examinations of Kerouac and Cassady; see 1–4.

2. In both the Croton and Dalkey editions, *Troia* on its last page is dated October 11, 1964. The memoir is otherwise said to be based on letters written from March to November 1963; Frazer notes in an interview, "I wrote two pages a day for the better part of a year" which fits with that nine-month period (Grace and Johnson 122). I have no information to clarify the end-date of "October 11, 1964," which is at variance with the March-to-November 1963 dating. It is also unclear when the untitled preface on pages 1 through 5 was written—whether after the book was assembled for publication in 1969 or even earlier.

3. Transnational Beat road tales written by women include Joanne Kyger's *The Japan and India Journals, 1960–1964* (1981), accounts of Asian and South Asian religious travel with Gary Snyder, Allen Ginsberg, and Peter Orlovsky; Janine Pommy Vega's *Tracking the Serpent: Journeys to Four Continents* (1997), a memoir of transnational road travels; and Anne Waldman's *The Romance Thing: Travel Sketches* (1987), which evokes the nineteenth-century narrative staple, the sketch, which traditionally confined its gaze to village or home. The Frazer, Kyger, Vega, and Waldman texts are prose fiction/memoir; neither Kyger, Vega, nor Waldman were running from the law and none practiced prostitution.

4. Frazer seems not to have wanted publication of the letters that became *Troia*. She does not possess the original letters or a holograph version of the narrative and is uncertain how many letters were used of the "400 to 500 small pages" she wrote at "two pages a day for the better part of a year" (Grace and Johnson 122). She began a prequel and a sequel to *Troia* in the early 2000s that she has published in excerpts (see Peabody) and is calling the text "Troia: Beat Chronicles" (Hemmer, *Encyclopedia* 105).

5. *Troia* is truly a fugitive text, stolen from its author and commodified into a saleable item whose first and only original edition, Frazer notes, is making money on the rare book market for others (Hemmer, "Prostitute" 102). For more information on Frazer's ambivalent take on the composition history of *Troia*, see Nancy Grace's 1999 interview with Frazer in Grace and Johnson.

6. An essay on *Troia*, Heike Mlakar's "Jack Kerouac's and Brenda Frazer's Shared 'Romantic Primitivism': A Comparative Study of *On the Road* and *For Love of Ray*" that appeared in 2007 (*NeoAmericanist*, an online student-run journal for American studies, 1, vol. 3, notes 19 spring/summer 2007: 1–11), erroneously attributes to Kerouac a famous passage by Ralph Waldo Emerson from "Self-Reliance," and appropriates a striking argument from Hemmer's earlier essay without attribution to him (3). These problems are reproduced in Mlakar's *Merely Being There is Not Enough: Women's Roles in Autobiographical Texts by Female Beat Authors*, published in 2008 by Universal Publishers.

7. Hemmer defends the pornographic aspects of *Troia* in terms of his larger thesis about *Troia*'s challenges to post-war "containment" culture. But it is hard to find the revolutionary aspects of the "salacious" passages given that they were written as traditional wifely sexual subservience and obedience to a domineering, coercive husband.

8. See anthologies of primary source material and short biographies in *Women of the Beat Generation: The Writers, Artists, and Muses at the Heart of a Revolution* (1996), edited by Brenda Knight, and in *A Different Beat: Writings by Women of the Beat Generation* (1997), edited by Richard Peabody. Helen McNeil and Amy L. Friedman published important first essays in A. Robert Lee's *The Beat Generation Writers* (1996). Two seminal studies, Johnson and Grace's edited collection, *Girls Who Wore Black: Women Writing the Beat Generation* (2002), and Grace and Johnson's *Breaking the Rule of Cool: Interviewing and Reading Women Beat Writers* (2004), define the subfield of women Beat writers, locating them in three generations.

9. Frazer sometimes signs herself "Brenda (Bonnie) Frazer" (see Grace 2004, 109–130), and there are more arcane versions of her double name in print, such as "Bonnie Bremser Frazer," a name she herself has not taken or used, to my knowledge (see Anderson 2003). Anderson says "Brenda Frazer" is the author's "birth name [and] the name she uses now is Bonnie Frazer" (253). To my knowledge, this is accurate. Frazer has signed e-mails and letters "Bonnie Frazer."

10. Bonnie's prostitution is unpacked in terms of post-war containment culture gender roles and imagoes of the nuclear family by Hemmer ("Prostitute" 110–111) and Anderson (258–259), respectively.

11. Frazer intentionally followed Kerouac and his method of sketching, setting an object before the mind and drawing it with words in a meditation of visualization. "It was copying," she explained; "If I sound like Kerouac, it's because I tried to" (qtd. in Johnson & Grace 2002, 174–175; Grace and Johnson 115).

13. See Anderson (256) for a list of women's domestic confinements in *On the Road*.

14. Feminist studies have begun to address gender and the road tale genre, as Enevold's chapter on *Thelma and Louise* suggests. Alexandra Ganser has the most theoretically apt and original study to date (2009), while some rudimentary discussion may be found in Katie Mills's reductive study, with unacknowledged previous scholarship, *The Road Story and the Rebel: Moving Through Film, Fiction, and Television* (SIUP 2006), which focuses on mass media and popular culture.

15. See Caren Kaplan's "Deterritorializations: The Rewriting of Home and Exile in Western Feminist Discourse."

Chapter 4

The Beat Manifesto: Avant-Garde Poetics and the Worlded Circuits of African American Beat Surrealism

Jimmy Fazzino

A political art, let it be
tenderness

—Amiri Baraka ("Short Speech to My Friends")

John Clellon Holmes's essay "This Is the Beat Generation," which served as a public introduction to the notion of "Beat" when it appeared in the *New York Times Magazine* on November 16, 1952, is but the first of many published attempts at self-definition and self-assertion on the part of Beat writers. While the Beats never produced a "Beat manifesto" as such, a whole range of Beat texts contain what we might call a manifesto function as key figures such as Holmes, Jack Kerouac, and Allen Ginsberg, in addition to many "minor" Beats, believed themselves compelled to define and redefine their aesthetic and social practices, to state and restate their opposition to post–World War II American conservatism. Exploring the ways in which Beat writers have borrowed and adapted the formal and rhetorical features of the avant-garde manifesto, an initial claim of this essay will be that the Beat movement owes as much to European traditions of the historical avant-garde—futurism, Dada, and surrealism chief among them—as it does to a strictly American tradition of Whitmanian democracy and the open road mythos. But at the core of my argument lies the further assertion that to reevaluate Beat writing in terms of its engagement with European experimentalism is also to reassess the role played by African American writers in the Beat movement as a whole. The work of Amiri Baraka, Ted Joans, and Bob Kaufman evinces a particularly intense and longstanding commitment to avant-garde poetics and politics, and by illustrating their truly *worlded* conception of the history and legacy European avant-garde, I hope to shed new light on the internationalism of Beat writing.

The manifesto tactics informing such texts as Baraka's "BLACK DADA NIHILISMUS," Joans's "Proposition for a Black Power Manifesto," and Kaufman's *Abomunist Manifesto* are also operative in those that, like Holmes's *New York Times* article, seek to define the substance and significance of the Beat movement. The productive displacements and deferrals, for example, that we will see operating in Joans's and Kaufman's manifesto-texts are a persistent feature of Kerouac's many attempts at explaining just what Beat means. In one of the best-known instances, his 1959 *Playboy* essay "The Origins of the Beat Generation," Kerouac's genealogy takes on cartoonish proportions as it expands to include everyone from Count Dracula to The Three Stooges. Holmes's account is similarly expansive yet contains what now seems like a shocking exclusion: not a single artist, poet, or performer can be found among the myriad hipsters and hooligans who populate his *Times* article. As Ann Charters has noted, "Nowhere in this early article did Holmes refer to Beat Generation writers, because he did not think of himself or his friends Ginsberg and Kerouac in this way, although he shared with them the new sensibility he had described" ("Variations" xx). Such equivocations and ambivalences betray an insistent openness and a refusal of dogma that, far from sapping the strength from these texts, are a source of their lasting interest and importance to Beat studies. The conspicuous self-effacement on the part of Holmes and Kerouac reminds us that even the earliest, most canonical articulations of Beat-ness are anything but prescriptive or hegemonic and that Beat manifestoes have been written by a diverse body of constituents, each of whom has transformed the movement in his or her own way.[1] Even Ginsberg's "Howl," which for many does succeed in capturing *the* essence of the Beat Generation, registers a productive tension between the controlling vision of the poet and the absolute freedom he celebrates in his protagonists.

Holmes's *New York Times* article finds a precedent in F. T. Marinetti's 1909 "Founding and Manifesto of Futurism," which marked a direct engagement with and appropriation of the forces of bourgeois journalism and the mass press when it appeared on the front page of *Le Figaro* and in papers and journals across Europe. As the manifesto becomes a dominant mode of self-representation among the various avant-gardes, the form will become increasingly self-reflexive. Manifesto writers begin to recognize the irony of announcing the radical singularity of their aesthetic project with a manifesto form that, only a few years after Marinetti's "Futurist Manifesto," is already somewhat banal. Tristan Tzara's 1918 "Dada Manifesto" begins, "To proclaim a manifesto you have to want: A.B.C., thunder against 1,2,3, lose your patience and sharpen your wings to conquer and spread a's, b's, c's little and big, sign, scream, swear, arrange the prose in a form of absolute and irrefutable evidence" (148), drawing attention to what he sees as the tired predictability and general inconsequentiality of the form. Parodying the rabid contrarianism typical of the manifesto, Tzara soon takes to writing them on behalf of fictional characters with names such as Mr. Antipyrine and Mr. AA the Antiphilosopher. But while the Dada manifestoes practically revel in their futility, the form continues to exert its strange power. André Breton's first and second *Manifesto of Surrealism* may represent the zenith of the genre, and the richly multivalent response on the part of Baraka, Joans, and Kaufman to Breton's *révolution surréaliste* will be a primary concern throughout this essay.

Ever since Marjorie Perloff's landmark *Futurist Moment*, the manifesto form has been central to our understanding of the historical avant-garde and its hallmark claims on the radically new. Two recent studies warrant particular attention. In *Manifestoes: Provocations of the Modern*, Janet Lyon argues for a genre with rather porous boundaries (12), and her expanded conception is especially relevant when considering the manifesto function of various Beat texts. Lyon also draws our attention to the tortuous temporality of a genre that attempts simultaneously to offer a new version of history, to create the demand for action, *now*, in the present, and to project a vision of a future in which its project will have become reality (16). In *Poetry of the Revolution: Marx, Manifestos, and the Avant-Gardes*, Martin Puchner emphasizes the manifesto's performativity, both in terms of its seeking to *create* a new movement or worldview in the very act of naming it and giving voice to its demands—there were no Futurists, in other words, before Marinetti announced their birth on the front page of *Le Figaro*—and in terms of the genre's notable theatricality (22).[2] But in their desire to break with tradition, to produce an event in the strongest sense of the term, manifesto writers are often confounded by a form that, as Tzara indicates, has become utterly conditioned and conventional. The performative force that both actuates and delimits the manifesto form gives rise to the characteristic impulse among avant-garde groups to continually rewrite their foundational texts, returning to the scene of the crime in order to recapture original energies and clarify original positions.

In performing a group's aesthetic or poetic practices, the manifesto is a transgressive genre, and the mixing and denaturing of genres has been a primary concern for manifesto writers.[3] Puchner, largely following Perloff in her discussion of Marinetti's *arte di far manifesti* (art of making manifestoes), accordingly develops a concept of "manifesto art" (89) in order to read a whole series of important works of avant-garde poetry, painting, and sculpture in terms of their dual nature as manifesto and artwork. Puchner also argues most forcefully that with the *Communist Manifesto*, Marx and Engels created a model, less for the content (whether political, artistic, or the like) than for the form (the manifesto form itself), that generations of subsequent protest would take up and transform (11). Tracing such a lineage reiterates what is at stake when avant-garde writers and artists, the Beats included, strive to change the world with their art. The most cogent formulation of an avant-garde politics, however, remains that of Peter Bürger, in whose dialectical analysis of the historical avant-garde the defining move of any avant-garde group is "to reintegrate art into the praxis of life" (22), to bridge the gap between art and politics, art and the world.

Finally, in using the terms world and worlded throughout this essay, I am indebted to the authors of *The Worlding Project: Doing Cultural Studies in the Era of Globalization*, who deploy their concept of the world as a critical term aimed squarely against forces of globalization and notions of "the global," seeking out and upholding the contingent and heterogeneous in opposition to the totalizing mechanisms of global capital and cultural hegemony.[4] A worlded critical procedure will always be attuned to geographic and historical specificity and to material practices that run counter to the naturalized yet deracinated transcendence of the global. To world the Beats is to emphasize not only their trans-Atlantic linkages but also their interaction with third world and post/colonial spaces. It is to wager that the Beats are irreducible to a single, unified movement so easily assimilated into the commodity spectacle or so thoroughly depoliticized and repackaged as a globalized notion of U.S. counterculture. With regard to African American Beat surrealism, a worlded perspective would, for example, consider the profound influence of Aimé Césaire, whose distinctive images of fecundity and decay are deeply rooted in Martinican soil and history and form a kind of figurative or descriptive dialect far removed from the language of Breton and other European surrealists. Like Césaire in his Caribbean context, Baraka, Joans, and Kaufman will each argue powerfully for the African origins of surrealism as they seek to reactivate the movement's anti-colonial, anti-racist energies.[5]

Looking back over Baraka's long and varied career, one finds it tempting to mark a clean break between his early Beat period and the developments that follow. This view is well represented by Werner Sollors, whose authoritative *Amiri Baraka/LeRoi Jones: The Quest for a "Populist Modernism"* equates Baraka's Beat-inflected writing with an ineffectual, narcissistic bohemianism in contrast to the serious, engaged commitment of his more explicitly political art. I want to suggest, however, that Baraka's mid-1960s turn to the Black Arts movement signals not a repudiation of the Beat and avant-garde aesthetics that characterize his early work but rather their evolution in accordance with the scope and ambition of his Black Nationalist and Marxist writing. Aldon Nielsen, who places Baraka at the center of his study of African American postmodernism, cites one interview in which Baraka explains,

> I was always interested in Surrealism and Expressionism, and I think the reason was to really try to get below the surface of things. . . . The Civil Rights Movement, it's the same thing essentially, trying to get below the surface of things, trying to get below the norm, the everyday, the status quo, which was finally unacceptable, just unacceptable. (49, ellipsis in the original)

Nielsen concludes that for Baraka, surrealism has always involved "a political as well as an aesthetic logic" (49), and the fact that Baraka produces his most self-consciously avant-garde poetry during the headiest years of the U.S. civil rights movement should not go unremarked. Far from indicating a turn *away* from the world or a dismissal of political engagement, Baraka's avant-gardism reenacts the quintessential move to close the gap between aesthetics and politics, art and the world. And while the remarks cited by Nielsen deal specifically with a conflation of surrealism and civil rights, they also point the way to a sustained critique within African American Beat writing of institutional racism and imperialist domination across the globe.[6]

In a set of texts including "BLACK DADA NIHILISMUS" and the play *Dutchman*—William J. Harris calls them "transitional" in that they bridge the gap between Baraka's Beat years and his subsequent commitment to Black Nationalism (xxi)—Baraka's continued engagement with the European avant-garde most often hinges on Breton's infamous provocation from the *Second Manifesto of Surrealism* that "the simplest Surrealist act consists of dashing down into the street, pistol in hand, and firing blindly, as fast as you can pull the trigger, into the crowd" (125). Baraka translates Breton's dictum into specifically racialized terms, and the specter of indiscriminate murder becomes a powerful trope in Baraka's work for years to come. In an oft-cited passage from "BLACK DADA," he writes:

> Come up black dada
>
>   nihilismus. Rape the white girls. Rape
> their fathers. Cut the mothers' throats.
> Black dada nihilismus, choke my friends
> ....
> (may a lost god damballah, rest or save us
> against the murders we intend
> against his lost white children. (*Dead Lecturer* 72–73)

With "BLACK DADA," Baraka has begun addressing himself to, and speaking on behalf of, a "we"; thus the poem's deeply unsettling images of physical and sexual violence should be understood primarily in terms of their appeal to a collectivity. The scenes of racial bloodshed that appear with increasing frequency in Baraka's work of the 1960s and 1970s are never simply a matter of style or the overheated rhetoric of *épater la bourgeoisie*; they are nothing less than a call to arms and revolution. Also significant is Baraka's invocation of Damballah at the close of "BLACK DADA," which registers the subversive syncretism of worlded African slave traditions that have provided a model for his own transformations of Breton's surrealist revolt.

With his celebrated play *Dutchman*, Baraka dramatizes Breton's scene of originary surrealist violence in the highly charged interactions between Clay, protagonist and self-proclaimed "Black Baudelaire," and the white Lula. While it is Clay who, finally driven into a rage by Lula's constant goading, threatens bloody murder, in a crucial reversal of events, it is Lula who takes the decisive action in which the play culminates. In his work on Baraka, Sollors does recognize Clay to be more a "Black Breton" than a "Black Baudelaire" (127), but in Sollors's reading, Clay's death is meant to mirror Baraka's own rejection of white bohemia and its avant-garde aesthetics. However, if we instead read Clay as a fundamentally tragic figure, defeated by his own weakness and lack of commitment, his death then signals not Baraka's rejection of surrealism but rather his redoubled effort, absolutely following Breton in the *Second Manifesto*, "to make for [him]self a tenet of total revolt, complete insubordination, of sabotage according to rule" (125). Clay's death becomes a key reference point in Baraka's 1965 manifesto for "The Revolutionary Theatre," which lays the ideological, if not the formal, groundwork for what soon becomes the Black Arts movement.

Baraka's polemics in his manifesto for "The Revolutionary Theatre" follow much the same lines as those in *Dutchman* and "BLACK DADA," but what makes Baraka's manifesto especially important to the present discussion are its strongly internationalist designs and its worlded view of human oppression. When he writes, for example, "The Revolutionary Theatre is shaped by the world, and moves to reshape the world" (*Home* 212), I take him at his word as calling for a politically engaged art that indeed has the world as its proper object. In this as well, Baraka recognizes surrealist precedents, writing, "[e]ven as [Antonin] Artaud designed *The Conquest of Mexico*, so we must design *The Conquest of White Eye*, and show the missionaries and wiggly Liberals dying under blasts of concrete. For sound effects, wild screams of joy, from all the peoples of the world" (211). In a curious confluence of imagery and influence typical of the Beats' worlded vision, "dead Moctezuma" has already made an appearance in "BLACK DADA" alongside Hermes Trismegistus, Jean-Paul Sartre, and a whole range of black heroes and martyrs, and Baraka certainly has Antonin Artaud's "Theatre of Cruelty" manifestoes in mind when formulating his own "Revolutionary Theatre."

It would seem that by highlighting a set of texts that revel in threats of racial violence aimed, at least in part, at the author's Beat peers, and that are nearly con-temporaneous with Baraka's mid-1960s abjuration of Greenwich Village bohemia, I would be seeking to emphasize the *dis*-continuities between African American Beat writers and the Beat movement as a whole. The same might be said of Ted Joans's "Proposition for a Black Power Manifesto," which offers a glimpse of the poet at his most uncharacteristically polemical and makes it clear that "whiteboy, this *Ain't* your bit!!" (*Black Manifesto* 13, emphasis in the original). On the contrary, I believe that these texts, along with Bob Kaufman's *Abomunist Manifesto*, do far more to reveal their profound affinities with the Beat movement at large in a shared commitment to traditions of radical and avant-garde poetics and politics. While Breton's pronouncement that Joans was the "only African-American surrealist" (qtd. in Nicosia, "Lifelong" iv) remains dubious, Joans's life and work are clearly marked by an avant-garde ethos indeed inspired by Breton. Joans's debt to surrealism has been widely noted; what I want to stress is the case he makes for the transnational dimensions of even the most canonical French surrealism. In a 1975 interview with Henry Louis Gates Jr., Joans is insistent on the point of surrealism's international character.[7] He describes the French surrealists as "internationalist" (76) and Breton as a "man of all nationalities" (77), and in the same interview, Joans is himself described by Gates as "Afro-America's Tri-Continental Poet" (72). Joans's project is no less than one of remapping the world in accordance with the capaciousness of his poetic vision. In 1962, he had begun living off and on in Mali, and his work mirrors this geographical shift with an increasingly Pan-Africanist emphasis and a closer proximity to the aesthetic tenets of the Black Arts movement. But like Baraka, Joans never abandons his early Beat and avant-garde influences; his poetry instead becomes increasingly interested in asserting that surrealism's roots lie in African, and not European, art and culture.

The Black Nationalism at the heart of Joans's manifesto closely parallels Baraka's work in the late 1960s, but Joans remains somewhat more skeptical than Baraka of programmatic modes of resistance. This wariness is evident in the rather ironic ear-nestness of Joans's "Proposition for a Black Power Manifesto," where he writes:

Since this a piece of prose
Black Power prose
a proposal for a Black Power manifesto

and not really "the" manifesto
I wont be mad if a black cat cops-out on what I manifest. (*Black Manifesto* 34)

This sentiment is remarkable in the way it seeks to avoid the limitations of resistance based in dogma by merely "proposing" a manifesto based on spontaneity and the unconditioned promise of the future-to-come. His claiming to have written not "the" manifesto but rather the proposal for a "manifesto-to-come" prefigures an argument Jacques Derrida will later make concerning the *Communist Manifesto*, which in Derrida's reading seems to be aware of its own limitations and necessary contradictions as it enacts a series of deferrals that will never quite exhaust its utopian promise of social transformation. Joans's "Proposition" manifests the call of the unconditioned in ways very near to what Derrida sees operating in the *Communist Manifesto*. Joans declares, for instance:

> Rebellion yes, rioting no! We must remain ready to act in our revolution at all times. For a moment will come when passion has infected the air, things will be tense and uptight: the black community will be so mad that it can barely breathe, and it is then that the most extraordinary events happen independently of any of the preparations that have been made. (34)

From a pragmatic point of view, the revolution must always maintain the element of surprise; when Joans's manifesto urges, "We must be cool, even though there is a 'long hot summer'" (34), it recognizes that one must move beyond predictable, and therefore containable, forms of revolt. To be successful, any mass movement must retain a core of flexibility, creativity, and freedom. By formulating his call to vigilance, and ultimately to arms, in these terms, Joans places himself and his manifesto squarely within a tradition reaching back to Marx, adopted and adapted by countless radical movements and avant-garde groups around the world.

Like many avant-garde manifestoes, Joans's "Proposition" also raises important questions about genre and the manifesto form. Written in mixed verse, it nonetheless asserts itself as "as piece of prose / Black Power prose" (34) and actually forms part of a larger work titled *A Black Manifesto in Jazz Poetry and Prose*. While it could describe the whole of Joans's oeuvre, the "jazz poetry" of the title refers more specifically to the notes taken by Joans at the 1967 Newport Jazz Festival in Europe and included just after the "Proposition." Describing sets at the festival by performers including Miles Davis, Sarah Vaughn, and Thelonious Monk—who Joans calls "the surrealist of modern jazz—the Dadaist of traditional piano playing" (43)—Joans's notes judge performances on the basis of their "blackness" or "whiteness" and take on a strong Black Arts quality corresponding to contemporaneous work by Baraka in that direction. Joans's notes also allow the music of "our greatest black creators" to enter into his manifesto and, in a sense, answer Joans's calls for a radically self-assertive black art (12). The final section of the *Black Manifesto* comprises a set of poems themselves acting as manifestoes in their unyielding assertion of the primacy of African forms and modes of expression. Laying out Joans's vision of an empowered Africa, the manifesto poems are not qualitatively different from other work by Joans in the late 1960s—somewhat less playful but with the same Black Nationalist and Pan-Africanist concerns. In one poem, "Ego-Sippi," Joans writes:

> i've lived at TIMBUCTOO/TANGIER/HARLEM/ & HAARLEM
> HOLLAND too double crossed the Atlantic which i shall
> rename THE AFRICAN OCEAN blue
> NOW I read my poem in 'Sippi
> and all y'all know thats saying a lot. (58)

Here we have the worldliness of the speaker, the global view, the overlaying of civil rights and anti-colonial struggles, and a process of worlded remapping whereby the "double crossed" Atlantic becomes the *African* Ocean. The same forces at work on the language of these poems have also pervaded Joans's "Proposition" and the *Black Manifesto* as a whole, and the manifesto-poems that relay "messages" or provide timely "warnings" recall Diane di Prima's *Revolutionary Letters*. Published in 1971, the same year as Joans's *Black Manifesto*, di Prima's *Letters* is another highly performative piece of Beat agitprop that clearly foregrounds its manifesto functions.

Joans's surrealism is most transgressive when it resists moving into abstract notions of "global" or even "African" space. The compressed imagery and densely layered narratives of a poem like "The Statue of 1713" are properly dreamlike and hallucinatory, but they are grounded in a great deal of specificity. Written "en route Tenerife / 5 March 1967," the poem describes, according to Michel Fabre, a reverie occasioned when, "[s]hortly after Breton's death," Joans chanced upon "Paris's small Statue of Liberty lying on its side on the Left Bank, on its way to a new location" (314).[8] In Joans's poem, however, we encounter the statue (now the figure of Breton himself) not in Europe but in Africa, making it explicit that surrealism is of African provenance. The revered statue of Breton has been meticulously crafted and lavishly adorned with the soil and spirit of the continent. And while elsewhere Joans is more likely to address a unified, undifferentiated Africa, in "The Statue of 1713" he describes "owl wings from Mali," "Tuareg war shots," and a pedestal of "rock that / tumbled up from Adrar des Iforhas" (*Teducation* 220). Here, Joans's Africanist vision gives way to a worlded conception of Black Power, rooted in local soils but open to unforeseen crossings and connections. Far from enclosing or isolating, the worlded view, by recognizing local histories and terrains, allows them to be in even more direct and intimate contact with one another. Hence the intimacy of the "ancient poster from Montmartre" that "serves as a rug for the chief fetisher" who carves Breton's statue (221). On the shifting sands of the Sahara—"The desert like the metropolis is full of mirages" (221)—the poem must constantly re-orient itself, and as in all of Joans's worlded poetry, here he directs a process of geographic and linguistic mapping:

> The statue of André Breton
> leans toward the East ignoring the West
> both thumbs pointing outward
> signifying faith in the South and North. (221)

Meanwhile, other "fetish brothers" have been "entrusted to / translate the surrealist manifestos into / Tamachek thus enabling one to read them / backwards as well as forwards" (221). The appearance of Lautréamont's Maldoror midway through the poem—"I pull my mosquito net up to allow / Maldoror a chance to enter my bed / He is a hairy tarantula tonight" (221)—points to the multiplicity of Joans's surrealist influences and acknowledges a longer lineage of avant-garde forebears. The Uruguayan-born Lautréamont allows Joans to cast perhaps a wider net spatially as well, while drawing attention to Joans's ever-present erotics of influence and inspiration.

In *The Practice of Everyday Life*, Michel de Certeau makes a crucial distinction between "strategies" and "tactics." Strategies—hierarchical, top-down, totalizing— Certeau opposes to tactics, which involve fleeting alliances, unexpected juxtapositions, and what Certeau calls "making do" (27). Joans's manifesto-texts, and African American Beat writing more generally in its engagement with the European avant-garde, operate within the realm of tactics. Joans's *Black Manifesto* puts forward a vision of collective revolt and liberation based on spontaneity and pragmatics rather than a programmatic party platform; understood in terms of Certeau's strategy-tactics paradigm, the seeming contradictions that run through Joans's manifesto become vital to his larger poetico-political project. He can express a general aim: "To free our black selves with our own Black Power / and by any means necessary!!" He adds, "Black Power is not an ideology of Western thought" (*Black Manifesto* 13). However, Breton has not entirely left the picture. In "Proposition," Joans also writes:

> Black Power is dreams that are carried over into reality. Black Power has the real and beyond the real in which to move. Our African ancestry has enriched us with this marvelous surreality. Black Power warriors can change into invisible animals that can spring out of the electric wiring inside of whitey's house. (16)

The electric presence of African surreality recalls a similar pattern of imagery from "The Statue of 1713," where "the pedestal on which it stands / made of marvelous owl wings from Mali / gives off artificial lighting / accompanied by Tuareg war shouts," and "[t]he pedestal of Malian owl wings is weeping / causing showers of electric sparks to fall / on the sand" (220). These sparks scare away bandits and carry "the truth of the poet" (220). Certeau would say that Joans's manifesto makes use of Breton, and without irony he can employ manifesto tactics to decry the entire "Western ideology" within which the manifesto form itself developed. The circuitry in which Joans's "Black Power warriors" carry out their maneuvers becomes the image of worlded currents of resistance and revolution.

In line with both Joans's "The Statue of 1713" as well as Baraka's "BLACK DADA NIHILISMUS," avant-garde strains in Kaufman's writing are borne out in a web of allusions asserting the continuity, often invisible or submerged, of the Beat movement with not only the various groups of the historical European avant-garde but also with a longer history of radical and antinomian art. He writes poignantly of an "Ancient Rain," which is the presencing of that history within the U.S. civil rights movement, America's Cold War dread, and Kaufman's own struggle to come to terms with the meaning of his art. The challenge facing the poet is how to transform avant-garde texts and traditions in order to respond to a specific historical moment, and this remains something of an open question in Kaufman's work. In "Sullen Bakeries of Total Recall," which appears in *Solitudes Crowded with Loneliness* alongside a reprinted *Abomunist Manifesto*, he sorrowfully remarks:

> I acknowledge the demands of Surrealist realization. I challenge Apollinaire to stagger drunk from his grave and write a poem about the Rosenbergs' last days in a housing project . . . speeding to the voltage mass of St. Sing Sing. . . . And yet when I think of those ovens, I turn my head in any other direction. (42)[9]

The "demands" of surrealism can be understood as yet another iteration of Breton's "tenet of complete insubordination"—in a late interview with Gerard Nicosia, Joans too will refer to surrealist "demands" ("Lifelong" iv)—but Kaufman's poem goes a step farther and interrogates the relevance, even the possibility, of using what amount to anachronistic avant-garde models to process the horrors of the Holocaust and the threat of nuclear war. At the same time, Kaufman acknowledges the perilous debt placed upon later generations of writers who would presume to speak for and with the victims and martyrs of the past. A way beyond this very real impasse, however, is already suggested by the worldly and worlded nature of Kaufman's commitment to "Surrealist realization." This recognition of the heterogeneity, multiplicity, and historical and geographic specificity of influence and inspiration, rather than distancing or isolating us from other times and places, serves to bind us ever more tightly to them and their persistent demands on us here in the present.

In a number of Kaufman's poems, we have the familiar world-as-body conceit, but one in which the poet's mapping procedures—Kaufman refers to them as "memory worlds" in the poem "African Dream" (*Solitudes* 4)—are radically generative because they are always being conjured in conjunction with other moments and spaces (civil rights, the Cold War, surrealism). The multiplicity of Kaufman's "memory worlds" is both a testament to multiple surrealisms and an uncanny artifact of the dense folds of revision and repetition that perfuse Kaufman's corpus. An untitled poem collected in *The Ancient Rain* fleshes out the dream of "African Dream" in a sequence that begins, "I dreamed I dreamed an African dream. My head was a / bony guitar, strung with tongues" (22). The poem continues along these lines, its oneiric, synesthetic imagery echoing that of "African Dream." Another poem, "Blues for Hal Waters," further reworks this dream content, beginning, "My head, my secret cranial guitar, strung with myths plucked from / Yesterday's straits" (*Ancient Rain* 28). The easy internal rhyme of "strung with tongues" has been replaced with the somewhat headier "myths plucked with / Yesterday's straits." But the most significant substitution in "Blues for Hal Waters" is this: the entire history of Kaufman's "African Dream"—its echoes, repetitions, and surrealist transmutations—becomes the poet's *secret* song. The last version of the poem/dream contains a hidden assemblage, the secret of its own making. This and other hidden continuities will eventually become the image of the "Ancient Rain" in that long poem, which "falls silently and secretly" from "a distant secret sky" (*Ancient Rain* 75–76) and describes in the most expansive terms possible Kaufman's worlded vision of connectivity and transformation.

However evocative these examples may be, nothing by Kaufman compares to his *Abomunist Manifesto* in terms of its foregrounding the multiplicity of sources and contexts for avant-garde Beat writing. Through all its wordplay and willful inanity, the *Abomunist Manifesto* remains seriously engaged with the history and rhetoric of the manifesto form as Kaufman performs the very linguistic and semantic experimentation he calls for and forth from the world, seeming to insist more than anyone since Breton himself that an absolute poetic and artistic freedom is a prerequisite for social transformation. The *Abomunist Manifesto* shares many characteristics of the avant-garde manifesto while also critiquing the manifesto form itself. It is in large part a parody of hipsterdom, and its very name indicates Kaufman's ironic, neo-Dada stance toward the manifesto. Part of the burden of the manifesto is to name a group, and the name Kaufman gives his, Abomunists (which, of course, do not exist), is based on nonsense and a bizarre assemblage of terms (abominable, communist—-ists of any persuasion—read also "beatnik"). The overall form of the *Abomunist Manifesto* is also very much a pastiche composed of self-contained sections with headings such as "Lexicon Abomunon" and "Abomnewcasts," each of which cannily point to a specific aspect of the manifesto form.[10] Here, the former speaks to the need for a new language to match the aesthetic or social project of a group claiming to be radically new—while also referencing the increasingly commodified, popularized "hipster speak" of the late 1950s—and the latter to the avant-garde manifesto's appropriations of mass media forms. Fifty years after Marinetti's "Founding and Manifesto of Futurism" was printed on the front page of *Le Figaro*, Kaufman's mimeographed manifesto began circulating up and down San Francisco's Columbus Avenue announcing the demands of the Abomunists. With echoes of the revolutionary pamphlet or religious tract, Kaufman scrambles the European avant-garde into a longer history reaching back to the "Founding Fathers," Barabbas and Christ, and Hindu scripture—complete with "music composed by Schroeder" (*Solitudes* 85). Kaufman's manifesto is at once incendiary and risible; the Abomunists dare us to take them seriously, dare us to ignore their demands.

After a brief opening salvo titled, appropriately enough, "Abomunist Manifesto," Kaufman continues with nearly a dozen addenda, postscripts, and clarifications. Out of this mélange is created a document that reenacts in one gesture the early history of the futurists or Dadaists, where an originary manifesto—Marinetti's "Founding and Manifesto of Futurism"; Tzara's "Dada Manifesto"—is quickly followed by a flurry of subsequent ones defining various aspects of the movement or reasserting its founding ethos. Kaufman's manifesto playfully but cogently performs this avant-garde drama, a defining aspect of the manifesto genre and the movements it has launched. Its very form recognizes the necessary multiplicity of the avant-garde manifesto: not just multiple manifestoes from each group but also the past and future transmutations the manifesto always carries within itself. So in the *Abomunist Manifesto* we get "Notes Dis- and Re- Garding Abomunism," an immediate equivocation or negation of the platform just presented. In essence, Kaufman's is a self-negating manifesto as "dis-garding" becomes "discarding." Faint echoes of avant-*garde* can also be heard in the "dis-" and "re-" *garding* of the manifesto. Later on, we get "Further Notes (*taken from* 'Abomunismus und Religion' *by Tom Man*)," and, later yet, "Still Further Notes Dis- and Re- Garding Abomunism."

The selective history put forward by the manifesto is written in terms of its projected future as it describes a past that *will have been*, and the vast, imagined history of the Abomunists is a clear concern of Kaufman's manifesto: not only the history of the Abomunists but also history as itself abomunist. "Abomunism," according to Kaufman, "was founded by Barabbas, inspired by his dying words: 'I wanted to be in the middle, but I went too far out'" (78). Past Abomunists have included Krishnamurti, Edgar Cayce, John Hancock, and Benedict Arnold, these last two implicating the very founding of the United States as somehow "Abomunist" (i.e., an abomination). Kaufman's crazed namedropping in these sections is reminiscent of the far-reaching and often unexpected Beat genealogies provided by Kerouac and Ginsberg, while early Abomunist history has been recorded in "the Live Sea Scrolls. . . one of the oldest Abomunist documents ever discovered" (82).

"$$ Abomunus Craxioms $$" skewers the axioms upon which party platforms, whether hip/avant-garde or square, are erected; Kaufman's wise-*cracks* reveal the cracks that inevitably appear in any group's doxa. The "Abomunist Election Manifesto" is one of the more parochial sections with its calls for "the abolition of Oakland" and "statehood for North Beach" (81), and as it calls to mind the long history of disenfranchisement not just in the Jim Crow South but across the United States, the "Election Manifesto" leaves us wondering about what faith Kaufman places in electoral politics. "Boms," a brief series of word sketches, evokes the martial origins of the term "avant-garde" and foregrounds its composition by "Bomkauf" (Kaufman's Abomunist *nom de guerre*), and the sketches share in the poem-as-weapon thinking of Joans's "hand grenade poems" (Nicosia, "Lifelong" v) and Césaire's *armes miraculeuses*. The aural and syntactic deformations at work throughout the *Abomunist Manifesto* make Kaufman's text performative in the manner of Marinetti's sound poem *Zang Tumb Tuuum*, where the creation of a new poetics (in Marinetti's case, the poetics of war) is at once demanded and fulfilled by avant-garde manifesto art (Perloff 90; Puchner 90–91).

"Excerpts from the Lexicon Abomunon" and "Abomunist Rational Anthem" pile layer upon layer of verbal irony and constitute the deadly playful core of the text's lasting significance and appeal. From the early days of the Beat movement, hipster slang was easily identifiable and the beatnik argot soon appropriated by a wider public. Kaufman seems eager to disassociate himself from the Beat vernacular even as he codifies it in his "Lexicon Abomunon." He writes, "At election time, Abomunists frink more, and naturally, as hard-core Abo's, we feel the need to express ourselves somewhat more abomunably than others. We do this simply by not expressing ourselves (abomunization). We do not express ourselves in the following terms . . ." (80). Kaufman's simultaneous avowal and disavowal of the very movement it is attempting to define—"we do not express ourselves"—is typical of Beat manifestoes, from Holmes to Kerouac and beyond. Read as an avant-garde poetics, the "Abomunist Rational Anthem" engages even further in a productive deformation of language. "Derrat slegelations, flo goof babereo," it begins. "Sorash sho dubies, wago, wailo, wailo" (85). Its "rationality" is an appeal, not to the kind of instrumental reason decried by Breton in the first *Manifesto of Surrealism* but rather to the distinctly surrealist "unreason" of what Césaire will call "my logics" (91). Maria Damon, in her chapter on Kaufman in *The Dark End of the Street*, points to the language games of the *Abomunist Manifesto* as prime examples of "unmeaning jargon" in Kaufman's work, which, Damon argues, "differs sharply from meaning-lessness. His unmeaning—as in unnaming—aims to destroy actively the comfort of meaning in service of the furious, spasmodic play of jazz energy. His jargon is both the special code of initiated hipsters and . . . the bubbling up and over of untamable sound" (41). Damon underscores the political implications (and avant-garde origins) of Kaufman's "nonsense poetry" when she relates it to Césaire's surrealist project of "breaking the oppressor's language" (40–41).

Nothing in this essay has been meant to suggest that the phenomenon of Beat surrealism is exclusive to Baraka, Joans, and Kaufman. In fact, the most compel-ling *material* link between the Beats and the European vanguard has to be Philip Lamantia, who Breton called "a voice that rises once in a hundred years" (qtd. in Charters, *Portable* 317) and who, as a teenager, spent time in New York with Charles Henri Ford and Parker Tyler's circle of surrealists-in-exile during the Second World War. Avant-garde martyrs Vladimir Mayakovsky and Frederico Garcia Lorca become important reference points in Ginsberg's life and work, and a poem such as "At Apollinaire's Grave" makes it clear that Ginsberg counted the French sur-realists among his poetic forebears as well. William S. Burroughs's postmodern-ist approaches to narrative and authorship build on earlier Dadaist and surrealist techniques and share in their commitment to the processes of chance. Cases have even been made for Kerouac's "spontaneous prose" as taking part in the great sur-realist tradition of automatic writing. What sets Baraka, Joans, and Kaufman apart is the much greater insistence with which an avant-garde poetics is linked to both oppositional and community-forming practices in their writing, to how they see themselves and their role as writers, and to how they understand the connection between radical art, political struggle, and social change. Even Baraka's aesthetic pragmatism, characteristic of his work in the Black Arts movement and often read as a disavowal of his earlier Beat experimentalism, cannot be fully appreciated with-out a serious consideration of its avant-garde origins. Writing, in a sense, from the "margins" of the Beat Generation (to use Damon's term), Baraka, no less than Joans or Kaufman, reminds us of the centrality of the international avant-garde—in par-ticular, the tactics of the avant-garde manifesto—to Beat writing. This signal con-tribution to the Beat movement, with its corresponding insistence on the worlded dimensions of the European avant-garde, forms the core of their rich and enduring legacy among the Beats.

Notes

1. My work in this essay is very much in line with what I call "The New Beat Studies," exemplified by the volumes *Reconstructing the Beats* (edited by Jennie Skerl), *Girls Who Wore Black: Women Writing the Beat Generation* (edited by Ronna C. Johnson and Nancy

M. Grace), and by a host of recent publications that seek to expand and reconfigure the Beat canon and introduce a more capacious set of historical and theoretical paradigms for understanding the Beat movement.

2. The "seeking to create a new movement" is the performativity of J. L. Austin's *How to Do Things with Words*, where "constative utterances," statements of fact, are contrasted with "performative utterances," statements that effect some action or change in the world. The classic example of Austin's performativity is the wedding vow that, in its very utterance, *makes the marriage happen*. My essay will also draw from Derrida's critique of Austin in *Limited Inc*, *Rogues*, and elsewhere.

3. In fact, the manifesto as a distinctly modernist form has had much to do with notions of the avant-garde manifesto as collage or découpage. See, for example, Carlo Carrà's *Manifestazione Interventista*, Wyndham Lewis's *Blast*, or any number of futurist, Dadaist, or Lettrist works.

4. In developing their notion of worlding, editors Christopher Connery and Rob Wilson draw from a range of thinkers including Heidegger, Jameson, Said, and Spivak, and from Hardt and Negri's analysis of Empire's post-national hegemony.

5. These currents of influence are always multidirectional. In his recent book, *A Transnational Poetics*, Jahan Ramazani places Baraka within a network of criss-crossing trans-Atlantic energies, traveling from Whitman to Lawrence to Olson to Baraka to the "Black British poets," who "complete a parallel transatlantic loop by drawing on the example of the militant, vernacular poetics of the Black Arts Movement, which in turn owed debts to the Beats and Black Mountain poets . . . and to Harlem Renaissance poets such as Hughes" (33). Ramazani, arguing for a "*translocal*" approach (43)—a term he borrows from *Worlding Project* contributor James Clifford—and a "particularized" understanding of literary internationalism (44), articulates yet another way to remap the sources and legacies of African American Beat writing.

6. Todd Tietchen locates Baraka's initial break with both white bohemia and the mainstream civil rights movement a few years earlier in another transnational crossing: Baraka's 1960 trip to revolutionary Cuba with a delegation of African American writers and artists. Tietchen further argues that revisions Baraka made for the second version of his "Cuba Libre" essay (published in 1966 in *Home: Social Essays*) reflect Baraka's growing radicalism in their new emphasis on "proto-Black Power activist" and fellow traveler Robert Williams (87). The revised "Cuba Libre" sets Williams and Castro together as "transnationally aligned" revolutionaries (96) taking part in a long tradition of armed insurrection.

7. Joans's interview is reprinted in the 1998 issue of *Discourse* titled *The Silent Beat* (after Bob Kaufman), which serves as a valuable compendium of primary texts and criticism focused on minority voices within the Beat movement.

8. Fabre writes that "Joans was happy to learn that, during the 1931 Exposition Coloniale, the Paris surrealists had opened an anticolonial exhibit displaying European 'tribal fetishes' like bibles, crucifixes, and stereotyped images of blacks of the kind found on Banania cocoa boxes" (314). Breton and the surrealists remained emphatically opposed to European imperialism, a stance registered, however obliquely, in Baraka's reference to Artaud's play *The Conquest of Mexico* in "The Revolutionary Theatre."

9. James Smethurst writes in capacious terms about the nexus of Jewishness, blackness, and leftism in Kaufman's life and work in "Remembering When Indians Were Red: Bob Kaufman, the Popular Front, and the Black Arts Movement," which appeared in *Callaloo* in the 2002 special section on Kaufman edited by Maria Damon.

10. Breton's first *Manifesto of Surrealism* also comprises several discrete sections with competing voices, demands, and even typographies. After the polemical rhetoric of the first section denouncing realism and its attendant logic and epistemology, introducing Apollinaire's term *surréalisme* as a countermeasure, and praising Freud's systematized exploration of the unconscious, Breton includes a list of quotations from his surrealist colleagues before moving on to quote a seemingly random list of facsimiles of newspaper headlines. By juxtaposing these disparate items, Breton's manifesto introduces the element of chance that lies at the heart of the surrealist movement.

Chapter 5

The Beat Fairy Tale and Transnational Spectacle Culture: Diane di Prima and William S. Burroughs

Nancy M. Grace

Part I

In 1967, French philosopher Guy Debord (1931–1994) provocatively decreed that everything directly lived has become a representation. In this world, which he laid out in *The Society of the Spectacle* and later in *Comments on The Society of the Spectacle* (1988), "the tangible world is replaced by a selection of images which exist above it, and which simultaneously impose themselves as the tangible par excellence" (*Society* Point 36). The spectacle created is the image-mediated social relationship among people. Jean Baudrillard, Max Horkheimer, Theodor Adorno, and others have posited similarly, prophesying our current youth-culture obsession with zombies: mirror forms of what the Internet generation subconsciously fears it has become. Their world, a legacy of twentieth-century power exercised predominantly by commodification of freedom through material consumption, perpetuates the spectacle, which spreads virally, globally, as a fluid funhouse of signifiers without a signified. Within this time/space continuum, writers of the Beat Generation have struggled with their own versions of the zombie-walking death that spectacle generates, and as a result, Beat textual representation frets with itself, discursively puncturing and repairing the deigetic membrane of material and spectacle unity. The "frets" of this project are multiple, so it should come as no surprise that border-crossing spectacle developed as an intertextual characteristic of the Beat aesthetic, many writers intentionally blurring high and low cultural artifacts—often freely, sometimes perversely—to replicate, repudiate, and revise representations of nationhood, self, identify, and history. To these ends, a genre that has garnered an unexpected degree of Beat popularity is the fairy tale, a genre that, as I will discuss below, participates in the very spectacle culture that Debord and his fellow Situationists resisted.

Not surprisingly, Beat scholarship has paid the fairy tale scant attention, perhaps because it has been simplistically marginalized as children's or girls' literature. But the tale makes sense as a form that might attract Beat writers, many of whom were philosophically committed to the concept of childhood as a pure state of being and also identified magic and wonder as counters to the horrors of the nationally and globally focused Cold War. One need look no further than Jack Kerouac's *On the Road* and Allen Ginsberg's "Howl" to find these themes. Many of Diane di Prima's poems reflect this same impulse, which has long grounded her poetics in what she calls "Magick," the use of vision and trance to reach transnational and trans-human dimensionalities, or what she describes as "light and time and the movement of the mind . . . Some way to play with reality, bend it to your will" (*Recollections* 83). Poetry and plays by Helen Adam, Madeline Gleason, ruth weiss, and Anne Waldman also draw upon architexture of the genre, as does Kerouac's *Doctor Sax: Faust Part Three* (1959), the peritextual title of which explicitly references the Faust tale; distinct genre elements, most noticeably a castle, magical helpers, monsters, and a happy ending, mark Kerouac's landscape as homage to the "Fairie" realm.

The insistence on fantasy in childhood *and* adulthood in these texts fits smoothly within the history of the fairytale, essentially a narrative of magic or wonder, known as *les contes des fees* in French and *zaubermarchen* in German. As folk narrative, the fairy tale subsumes fables, parables, animal stories, and ghost stories—many fairy tales, ironically, contain no fairies at all, a fact that led J. R. Tolkien to conclude that the genre resides most accurately in "the Perilous Realm itself, and the air that blows in that country." In this particular kind of place, as Tolkein envisioned it, magic is taken seriously "to survey the depths of space and time" and "to hold communion with other living things" (34–35). These threads are by no means limited to Tolkien's hobbits, but speak directly to important themes in Beat art, much of which is deeply rooted in American interpretations of libertarianism and romanticism.

Scholars recognize the fairy tale as a polygenetic artifact, originating in oral culture, intended for adult audiences, and dating back thousands of years, some of the earliest examples found in China and India (Zipes xiv). Western versions have been disseminated as material products of culture through globalization, with the oral form developing into the literary fairy tale associated with adult female literate court life in seventeenth-century France, where through the bawdy and scatological it expressed personal desires as well as social and political concerns. In industrialized cultures, the fairy tale has become a stock form appropriate for teaching children moral lessons, a quality scholars attribute to Charles Perrault's collection in France in the seventeenth century and the Grimm brothers' German collections in the eighteenth and early nineteenth centuries. In the United States, the tale's pedagogical role became entrenched through Bruno Bettelheim's *The Uses of Enchantment*, a compelling psychoanalytic treatment of the genre that mistakenly assumes fairy tales were historically directed at children. However, the fairy tale retains its power to express adult themes, and, in this respect, it is a fitting genre for Beat writers, who often saturated their art with righteous moralism and didacticism.

Scholars of the fairy tale recognize that taletellers have long claimed the tales for national and local purposes, plagiarizing and rewriting plot and character, while unabashedly presenting the altered narratives as the folk or literary original. Di Prima, in her collection of world fables titled *Various Fables from Various Places* (1960), called such projects "propaganda, either religious or political" (183). The Grimm brothers remain the most notorious of "propagandists," intending their collection to preserve a German past and German values (McGlathery 6). Similarly, Italo Calvino found elements of Italian nationalism as he explored various folk stories (Bacchilega 20). Consequently, the provenance of the tales is so complicated that they often escape national and cultural boundaries. In fact, Cristina Bacchilega calls the contemporary fairy tale a borderline, hybrid, or transitional genre that "bears the traces of orality, folkloric tradition, and sociocultural performance" (3). In this condition, it has become a most malleable genre, frequently duplicated and revised.

Revisionists generally premise their work on the belief that the precursor form is flawed and requires revision aimed at improvement or at least critical commentary. Perrault certainly did. So too did di Prima, who, despite her laudable disdain of propagandists, states in *Fables* that she rewrote the tales by modernizing spellings and omitting many of the morals to create a "lovely [or 'delightful'] ambiguity" (183). (Not all readers will interpret "lovely" and "delightful" as positively as did di Prima.) Yet readers and authors of fairy tales have at least since Victorian times been led to believe that the tale exists beyond human artifice. Charles Dickens, for instance, opposed his friend George Cruickshank's overt rewriting of some tales, stating that tales "must be as much preserved in their simplicity, and purity, and innocent extravagance, as if they were actual fact. Whosoever alters them to suit his own opinions . . . appropriates to himself what does not belong to him" (Victorianweb.org). Scholar Jack Zipes concluded that this kind of thinking renders the tale "harmless, natural, eternal, ahistorical, therapeutic," something that "[w]e are to live and breathe . . . as fresh, free air . . . [that] has not been contaminated and polluted by a social class that will not name itself" (7).

Translated into the discourse of spectacle theory, Zipe's insight situates the fairy tale within the stream of representations that nullifies the lived realities of human existence. What many consider a transitional or hybrid genre with visible textual markers of its origin now primarily exists as image supplanting the tangible with the nonliving illusion of eternal freshness and purity, as Zipe contends: "[o]nce a fairy tale has gelled . . . it seeks to perpetuate itself indiscriminately" (15). Like a coloring book illustration, then, the fairy tale invites transformation while resisting extermination.

In spectacle culture, the fairy tale flourishes globally as children's entertainment commodified through Disney films such as *Beauty and the Beast*, *The Little Mermaid*, *Cinderella*, and *Snow White and the Seven Dwarfs*. The Disney tale began with the release of the animated film *Snow White and the Seven Dwarfs* in 1934, just when the major writers of the Beat Generation were coming of age and when cinema as technological innovation was seeking a broader popular audience. Since then, the spectacle impetus to act upon technological advances has led to a proliferation of consumables from interactive games to videos to Web-based portals on which users can create their own fairy avatar—as Debord wrote, "[w]hen an instrument has been perfected, it must be used" (*Comments* point 29). The fairy tale has even been transformed into the legal Disney Princess brand, consolidating characters such as Cinderella, Pocahontas, Sleeping Beauty, and Snow White as a marketing engine aimed specifically at little girls. The brand has earned $4 billion in global retail sales since its inception in 2000, selling, as the Disney Website proclaims, images that "touch every aspect of girls' lives *around the world*" (emphasis mine). Disney (truly a signifier without a signified) justifies *as a global reality* the proliferation of the static image of a white-to-faintly-brown female ideal (and the identically colored male ideal). Boldly claiming authorship—"It is a world 'Disney' has created" (disney-consumerproducts.com)—Disney paradoxically obliterates the "purity" of the fairy tale as beyond authorship *and* the uncountable number of tale tellers who have left their marks upon the tale. By so doing, one of the world's largest media conglomerates reproduces for the sole purpose of generating capital a homogenous vision of heterosexual humanity, and the social world thus produced becomes a flatland upon which individuals reside in passive isolation.[1]

If Debord had written about the fairy tale, and Disney's in particular, he might have contemptuously presented it as a force that "demands in principle . . . passive acceptance which . . . it already [has] obtained by its manner of appearing without reply, by its *monopoly of appearance*" (*Society* point 2, emphasis mine). He might also have ridiculed attempts to critique the spectacular condition of the tale, arguing that spectacle "escapes the activity of men" such that "wherever this is independent representation, the spectacle reconstitutes itself" (*Society* Point 18). This last point suggests the impossibility of escaping spectacle culture. Situationists resisted this logic, however, presenting as a tactic of resistance *detournement*, or the mingling of familiar spectacle images with alien and thus subversive contexts, much as Marcel Duchamp did when he placed a mustache on DaVinci's Mona Lisa or as Debord did in the eponymously named film adaption (1973) of his book. By the late 1980s, though, Debord had come to recognize that efforts to expose spectacle actually depend upon spectacle itself, and that what he perceived as the obliteration of history transformed contemporary events into "a remote and fabulous realm of unverifiable stories" (*Comments* point10). This is exactly what we see today in the way instantiations of the fairy tale address global struggles for freedom, selfhood, desire, and the body.

What interests me about the Beat response to the fairy tale is that those who turned to it did not blindly accept what Debord called the monopoly of appearance or the stultifying logic of imprisonment in spectacle, turning to the very "turning" of images that would reveal the dystopian nature of spectacle. Even those who applied little criticality exhibit some awareness of the problems inherent in spectacle. However, what they are not equally aware of is how their use of the form perpetuates the annihilating process they resist. To illustrate, I discuss in the second part of this essay two complicated forms of Beat detournement: Diane di Prima's late-Beat-era text *Dinners and Nightmares* (1961) and William S. Burroughs's early cyber-era theatrical production *The Black Rider* (1990). Both illustrate how the supposedly simple fairy tale encodes intricate chronotopes that critique spectacle culture. Both, although to different degrees, also demonstrate that if those who engage in this challenge wish to be recognized, they cannot help but join the very spectacle they profess to destroy (*Comments* point 3).

Part II

Dinners and Nightmares, Diane di Prima's first mature work, generates a personal mythopoeia and a modern syncretistic explication of mid-twentieth-century life that embraces recognizable American entelechies and eschatologies—specifically, self-identity intricately bound to a creative community as an antidote for a monstrous universe. This community emerges in the linear compilation of poems, conversations, short stories, lists, recipes, dreams, jokes, and diary entries, lending *Dinners* a collage-like appearance defying assignment to any particular genre. Its focus on female-centered sexualities, domesticity, rebellion, and other experiences diverges from literature written by first-generation male Beat authors. However, consistent with Beat writing in general, *Dinners* performs modernist and post-modernist self-fragmentation and obliteration, while embracing memory and self-representation.

Unlike di Prima's *Various Fables*, *Dinners* does not reproduce well-known tales. Nor does it explicitly transform well-known tales for purposes of cultural critique, as does, for example, Anne Sexton's *Transformations*. Instead, *Dinners* maneuvers an amalgamation of fairy tale architextures as one of several devices to construct a New World/Old World configuration in which the New World is predicated on the Old but cannot destroy the Old—and the Old World cannot rule the New. New spaces develop, as self and history are distorted by the shape of the other, proposing that one should question to what extent the precursor forms are benign and the subsequent forms inferior.

This epistemological enterprise begins in the short prose text "What Morning Is" that opens the collection. The text, what one might today call flash fiction, acts as a contemporary revision of the Genesis creation story, in Judaic-Christian culture the ultimate "once upon a time" narrative. Consider, for instance, the opening of the King James Version, with its soaring, sermonic language: "In the beginning God created the heaven and the earth. And the earth was without form, and void; and darkness was upon the face of the deep. And the Spirit of God moved upon the face of the waters. And God said, Let there be light: and there was light" (Gen. 1:1–3). Unabashedly obliterating divine scripture, and in effect the myth of humans as divinely created, di Prima's story strikes a cut-to-the-chase American attitude: "First you wake up and it is daylight" (13). The "you" is a "she" named "di" instead of a "he" and awakens not to "dominion" over "every living thing that moveth upon the earth" (Gen. 1:28) but to everyday urban misery. She senses that something is amiss because someone is honking a horn in the street, agitating her to the point that she considers smashing his head with a rock (13). However, instead of doing bodily harm to others, she turns to the pragmatism and hedonism of food, friendship, writing, and a hot bath, so that on this first morning she stands clean and naked, wearing nothing but the sun, and thinking, "Yes OK I'll swing it"—a secular and fifties "hip" revision of "replenish the earth, and subdue it" (Gen. 1:28).

To understand what di Prima accomplishes here, let's return to Bettelheim, despite my earlier caveat regarding his uncritical stance. Bettelheim argued that myths and fairy tales speak in symbolic language about the unconscious content of the human psyche but that myths focus on a particular hero, often divine in nature, often national in scope, and help develop the superego. Mythic heroes have names and individual personalities, but "the demands they embody are so rigorous as to discourage the child [or adult] in his [or her] fledging striving to achieve personality integration" (39). The fairy tale, which often names only its main character or employs ultra-common names, Bettelheim sees as a cautionary tale focused on the ego and id, promoting an earthy, sensual, and secular sense of wonder and hope, congruent with Zipes' claim "that it tells about everyman, people very much like us" (40) in a world that defies Westphalian nation-state boundaries. Since *Dinners* intermingles dreams and fairy tale texts, Bettelheim's distinction between the two is also useful. Defining dreams as problems to which a person knows no solution and to which the dream finds none," he discerned in fairy tales "the relief of all pressures" which "not only offers ways to solve problems but promises that a 'happy' solution will be found" (36). One does not have to accept Bettelheim's Freudian paradigm to see that "What Morning Is" presents a clever allusion to a major Western creation myth and then quickly fills that shell with a second-person tale of the sensual, earthy, and secular in which the "you" delightfully effects a delicately magical transformation of mundane human anger into sun-bathed self-resolve. The text resists the perpetuation of national or theocratic mythologizing to hint instead at a critique of such texts by foregrounding the female "everywoman" who with hope-filled wonder narrates from the Beat margins of American culture her own future—at least she's ready to "swing."

While the blurring of myth, dream, and fairy tales distinguishes *Dinners*, it is the collection's explicit fragmentation of fairy-tale architexture that emerges consistently throughout, creating a tension between myth and fairy tale, modern narrative and fairy tale, and image and materiality. For instance, the dominant voice of the text, created by the lack of prescribed commas and periods, produces a paratactic style, suggesting a wonder-filled, Huckleberry-Finn perspective on the world. The episodic quality of the fairy tale is established through passages that begin with "So I said," "So my mother was," "So we went," and "Now to understand" or "now, now, one night": two short stories even begin with "Once upon a time." Magical creatures including a unicorn, giant, troll, and gnarled chess players scamper throughout. Many characters are simply called "boy" or "two girls"; others carry a generic animal or human name. Fairy tale–like actions occur, as in "What I Ate Where," which features the story of a young woman who lives in a garret-like room and magically acquires the talent to paint. Allusions to specific fairy tales also emerge, as in "Daughters of Evening: Scenario for a Proposed Movie" in which three sleeping women and a mysterious black coffin obliquely allude to "Sleeping Beauty" and "The Glass Coffin." Even the acts of reading and creating such tales are metafictively addressed: the first in "What Do Frogs Say?," which centers on the act of reading animal tales to a child, and the second in the poem "Songs for Babio,

Unborn," which stops mid-point so the speaker can announce that she will "[n]ow tell the tale" of the exotic world of poetry that her child will encounter when it meets its mother (126).

The key here, as I noted with respect to the historical propagation of fairy tales, is revision. Di Prima does not revise tales such that one encounters the full hypotext but relies upon fairy tale elements to deftly forge an intertextual world leading readers to think more about the genre itself than any specific tale. Similar to what Keven Paul Smith found in his study of the postmodern fairy tale in contemporary fiction, these forms "defamilari[ze] narrative as we are used to experiencing it and refamiliariz[e] the reader with storytelling in an oral context" (112). A reader is encouraged to consider the text as something other than literary and recognize the foregrounded storyteller as a self-generated meta-fictional presence. The fairy tale fragments disrupt a representation of post–World War II U. S. culture as a seamless, timeless land of wealth, happiness, and security, leading readers to persistently question the world they have entered and consider how literary practices establish and undermine reality.

Four short prose texts accept this role head-on, establishing a larger discursive frame with which to interpret other devices of *detournement* in *Dinners*. The first, titled "The Very Happy Couple" and dated 1954, begins like a classic fairy tale: "Once upon a time there was a very happy couple"; it also employs the classic episodic fairy tale structure in which something catastrophic disrupts happiness. However, the tale makes *no* pretense whatsoever of being a children's story. Within the Perrault/Grimm/Disney spectacle of marriage as heterosexual bliss void of sex, di Prima inserts a new tale about prescribed heterosexual courting and marriage practices, including dating, kissing, abstaining from sex until marriage, getting married, and then having sex. In a twist of fairy tale convention, magic or wonder does not exist external to the couple (for example, as a fairy god mother or magic spell), but *within* them as natural awareness of their sexual attraction to each other. However, as in many fairy tales, they do not recognize the power. At each step along their sexual journey, they dutifully follow the customs, even using contraceptives once they are married, but find the experiences disturbing, so they deny the attraction, coded repeatedly as the phrase "turned their backs on each other," and move to the next stage. The story ends with them in bed sleeping back-to-back, a barren/nonliving union in which male and female are estranged from each other, their own bodies, and, most disturbingly, the generative principle of life itself (140).

On one level, the tale suggests that the material body as the site of creativity, especially the female body, is severely constrained through dehistoricized representations. Di Prima's new fairy tale disrupts the New World space of timeless homogeneity by forcing into it realistic responses of physical bodies to culturally determined practices that control the sexual body. Interestingly, however, the fairy tale simultaneously reifies features of the very spectacle representation that it disrupts, promoting a biologically based morality to replace modern family planning practices and female reproductive rights. Patriarchal dominance, encoded in the generic fairy tale's prince-and-princess happy ending, depends upon belief in the primacy of the biological imperative to reproduce. Even though "The Very Happy Couple" rejects that paradigm by rejecting the happy ending, any tale warning against processes to stymie the imperative affirms, to some degree, the myth of patriarchal supremacy through ownership of the female body.

Two other short stories in the collection, both dated 1955, intimate that at this early stage in di Prima's maturation as an artist she wrestled with the difficulty of connecting intimate relationships to human reproductive capacities and to artistic reproduction. This configuration emerges through elements of the animal-groom tale, which typically features three motifs: marriage to (or cohabitation with) a mysterious nonhuman figure; a transgression that results in the magical lover leaving; and a journey to find the beloved and secure a lasting union (Windling 1). The first story, "Tale for a Unicorn," begins with "Once upon a time" and introduces a female protagonist simply called "a poet" and her good friend the unicorn who live in a "horrible city" (145). The same female poet appears in the second tale, "The Trouble with Unicorns," but this one depicts multiple male unicorns, implicitly presented as lovers. The magic other is transgressively *many* others, a significant revision on the dominant Perrault/Grimm/Disney paradigm of white, heterosexual monogamy, suggesting that female sexual desire can be satisfied in many ways and that the taboo against such deviance deserves eradication.

In the first story, the unicorn is depicted as in many folk narratives: as a "noble, chaste, fierce yet beneficent" other-worldly male creature (Shepard 273). Not exactly a Christ-figure, however, this unicorn resides in the material world and possesses special powers to see members of the animal kingdom (that is, humans) and other magical figures. The unicorn clearly signifies the marginalized and oppressed human "Other" whose goodness and autonomy have been quashed but who nonetheless develops strategies of resistance that remain cloaked yet potent. The female poet, in contrast, is flawed by self-righteous egotism: she gets "Kinks" in the brain, the severity of which the narrator signals by capitalizing the initial "k." Likewise, in the second story, "The Trouble with a Unicorn," the unicorns remain "othered," but they are careless and thoughtless, refusing to appear on time for dinner, showing up "because they're hungry, or they forgot where they were going," their magic powers of vision reduced to false sensitivity (147). The female poet in this tale is bewildered and frustrated, impotent to understand unicorn nature. The representations of the unicorns/female poet dyad in both stories depict the difficulties of sustaining interpersonal relationships, as well inter-group relationships, which deteriorate rapidly if even one party is unwilling to or cannot translate the experience of the other.

Both stories develop this theme through the tale motif of separation. "Tale for a Unicorn" explains separation as a quarrel between the poet and the unicorn caused by two events: the poet develops a brain Kink—a hip version of fairy tale avarice—and they subsequently leave the safety of home for the "Land of Adventure," where she encounters the unicorn's friends, described as hybrids belonging to both the human and magic worlds. Greedy for the full attention of her friend and in a zone where she becomes the outsider, the poet makes fun of the others of the Other, angering the unicorn, who consequently leaps away into the night, leaving the poet to realize her foolishness. The narrative concludes with somewhat of a happy ending— "she knew that poets were proud and unicorns were proud and that apologies just wouldn't do at all. / And so she wrote this tale" (146)—expressed as meta-fictional discourse. The lines create a circling effect as the poet takes pen in hand to write

"Once upon a time," storytelling going beyond apology, the performance of which by social dictum should heal a breached relationship. This story, instead, moralizes that reconciliation and atonement come from one person's willingness to imagine the life of the Other, to relinquish the needs of the ego to save the magic of the relationship, even if one cannot fully participate in the magic of the Other. However, while the ending affirms bridging of human differences and asserts female artistic autonomy, it exists as a representation of representation—not human connection in a lived material world: the poet and the unicorn remain estranged. In fact, narrative as dehistorizied fairy tale suggests that the Other and the Not Other can never integrate and that art thus produced is imprisoned in exclusivity (145–146).

In contrast, "The Trouble with Unicorns" begins in the middle of separation, discarding the literary lie of dehistoricized origin and existence. Waiting in frustration for her unicorns, knowing that something has happened to separate them but not knowing what, the poet in Beat argot is "Very Bugged": "You never know . . . when they'll turn Up. Or how," she says (147). The problem lies within the unicorns, now more human than superhuman in their apparent selfishness. But instead of following the tale type and sending her poet on a journey to seek the lovers, di Prima's poet chews her finger and pops pills, impotently shaking her fist at cockroaches under the sofa. Even in such a transgressive Beat state, fairy tale magic fails, especially for the female, whose ego imprisons her in a domestic world of her own making where she finds herself "starving to death Waiting" (147). Like the satirically titled "Very Happy Couple," the poet and the unicorns, bound by internalized and gendered images of how one should and can act, turn their backs on each other and on life. The force of the tale does not counter the hegemonic anti-miscegenation image but instead vilifies the Other as ubiquitously uncaring and thoughtless, reason enough to refuse the possibility of reunion, that is, the obliteration of inter-group separation, for eternity. The poet and the unicorns remain locked in radically separate states of being.

These states of being, in the happy couple and the unicorn stories, allude not only to individuals but also to actual nation/states and the many states-within-states, the boundaries of which open and close depending on one's sex, class, gender, sexuality, and other spectacle markers of similarity and difference. At the macro level, all three tales are set in an urban/U.S. space. The first unicorn story explicitly takes place in the Land of Adventure, which is Greenwich Village (146); the second is set in a bohemian pad, also evoking Greenwich Village. The national character of "The Very Happy Couple" is more difficult to discern since the tale contains almost no descriptions of setting, but the precise plotting of conventional dating practices speaks directly to Western, especially U.S., middle-class mores. This story, then, represents the way in which image culture naturalizes and thereby destroys individuality and life within a national ethos. The unicorn stories, in response, reveal pockets of resistance to such destructive mediation within the larger state-imposed identity. The fairy tale features establish all three of the settings as hybrid spaces, not fully Tolkien's "Perilous Realm," but not fully the historical materialism of 1950s Greenwich Village or the United States. The ahistorical quality of this in-between zone challenges readers to recognize the magic in everyday American life, along with the impossibility of integrating magic into either regional spaces or the larger national space, fast subsuming the world through military, technological, and spectacle dominance.

The latter theme di Prima directly addresses in "Memories of Childhood," a tale about a young unnamed boy who sees a giant holding a hydrogen bomb over the little boy's house. Eschewing the coupling of impersonal fairy tale architexture with the personal (no "female poet" thinly veils di Prima herself), the tale disrupts spectacle culture's relentless Cold War representation of U.S. military power as the omniscient, benevolent ruler who saves the world. The hypotext upon which it rests is most likely "Jack and the Beanstalk," a fairy tale of English origins in which a young man named Jack, whose family lives in poverty, defeats a wealthy giant who resides in a magic space above them, accessible via Jack's magic beanstalk. Some scholars read the tale as cautionary, seeing Jack's victory as pyrrhic in that he becomes a mirror image of the giant. Others interpret his actions as nation-building allegories representing the development of the British Empire, as Jack subdues the uncivilized giant (Tatar 138). "Memories" retains few "Jack and the Beanstalk" plot details, but its depiction of the giant as a crude presence reflects the hypotale. Di Prima's giant is supernatural (like a god, he holds the power to destroy everything), human-like (the little boy describes him as "a big tall man"), strong (he can hold a bomb), and, finally, unpredictable and stupid (he tells the boy to leave him alone or he might become nervous and drop the bomb [53]; later he falls asleep, becoming an even greater threat) (von Franz 89–90). The giant, a menace to humanity, looms over a world in which borders do not exist and if they did would not provide protection. This characterization is reinforced by the absence of two textual features of the classic fairy tale: the third-person narrator and the "Once upon a time" introduction. "Memories" is told by the young boy as a first-person narrator, who begins his story in *media res*: "So I said to him Hey mister what're your doing with that H bomb how come you waving it around like that?" (53). Both techniques firmly establish the immanent destruction of all life in the ever-present present, and the rejection of the artifice of the prime mover, in particular, opens the way for consideration of realistic human causes.

In the face of total annihilation, the little boy is not an allegory for individual greed or pride; neither is he a pawn set out by his family to help save them; nor is he an image of the beginnings of global empire. Instead, he represents the voice of truth emanating from the child, much like the young boy in Hans Christian Anderson's "The Emperor's New Clothes."[2] The little boy and his friend can see the giant, and they try to divest him of the bomb, but fail, as do the boy's efforts to warn his parents, who patronizingly tell him that the giant is only a tree, that god will not let the world be blown up, and that he should go play. They then smack him and send him to bed—a very unhappy ending indeed! The parents may experience resolution of the conflict, having expressed their frustration, but the boy is left alone, bereft and worried that the stupid, sleeping giant will accidentally drop the bomb while having a bad dream. The little boy's hope that the man and the bomb are simply a "Noptical Delusionment" (53)—a playful mix-up that can be sorted out by looking at things differently—is exposed as itself a "delusionment." The bomb and its human agents, spreading the lie of national security by threatening global destruction, are all too real.

Di Prima's fairy tale fictions communicate a profound belief in the power of communal and individualistic narrative, one that does not shy away from either the horrors of the atomic age or the falsity of the American Puritan ethos. Confronted with both—where spectacle culture reifies as truth the fallacies of "duck-and-cover" and the "Ozzie and Harriet" nuclear family—fairy tale architexture in *Dinners* disrupts the image of U. S. security, heteronormativity, white supremacy, and masculine power with the discourse of a single and sexual Beat woman, alongside a prepubescent child, as the centers and carriers of human knowledge and being. Without the fantasy of a personal god, magical unicorn, or benevolent governmental authority, the individual woman artist and the child are left to reclaim from the land of the nonliving the human body as a site of creation. The adult female and the child are not always happy or successful in their roles, since fairy tale architexture in *Dinners* frequently relegates them to a disempowering domestic sphere. But simultaneously, architexture proclaims their power real and capable of saving humanity rather than destroying it. In *Dinners and Nightmares*, then, the realm of "Fairie" as the union of spectacle and *detournement* remains a dangerous terrain.

*   *   *

Williams S. Burroughs, who died in 1997, lived into the historical moment that Debord described as one in which spectacle culture exists as accepted fact, as something that goes without saying. Burroughs was highly cognizant of the pervasiveness of spectacle fetish, as well as the general public's blind acceptance of it, and, as Timothy Murphy has shown, attempted to actualize Situationist *detournement* through the cut-up method developed by Bryon Gysin.[3] Here, we think most obviously of the *Nova* trilogy or the films *The Cup-ups* and *Towers Open Fire*. However, a more contemporary example of Burroughsian *detournement* is *The Black Rider*: *Casting of the Magic Bullets*, the comic opera that he composed with singer-songwriter Tom Waits and playwright Robert Wilson. The opera premiered in Hamburg, Germany, in 1990. Burroughs was approached by Wilson to write the libretto, although Burroughs has said publicly that the story is not his (*Burroughs Live* 720). In fact, the title, an explicit intertextual reference, alludes to Carl Maria von Weber's opera *Der Freishütz*, which premiered in 1821 in Berlin and has remained one of Germany's most popular operas. This intertextual relationship suggests that *The Black Rider* speaks directly, as both parody and praise, to the nationalistic dominance of the tale type, which can be traced back to the Bohemian-German wonder tale also known as *Der Freishütz*, loosely translated as the free shooter, a Faust variant in which a dark rider representing the devil dispenses magic bullets to men seeking egoistic power. Contemporaneous with Weber's opera, Thomas de Quincey's short story titled "The Fatal Marksman" (1823) appeared, and one can trace its genesis to a tale in *The Book of Ghosts*, a collection of ghost stories by Johann August Apel and Friedrich Laun, published between 1811 and 1815; the collection was first published by Ludwig Lavater and printed in Zurich in 1569.[4]

In one version of the tale, a greedy young clerk named Georg Schmid makes a deal with the devil for sixty-three magic bullets with which to become a rich hunter: he is told that sixty of the bullets will hit their mark but three will fail, and he must cast them in a wooden glen between 11 p.m. and midnight on a particular day without interruption or he will belong to the devil; he fails, consequently losing his wealth and freedom. Other versions, including *The Black Rider*, feature a young clerk named Wilhelm who desires to marry the Head Ranger's daughter (Katchen in *The Black Rider*). But since Wilhelm is a mere clerk, the father refuses to sanction the match unless Wilhelm becomes a ranger who can enrich the family with fresh game. Despite multiple warnings, Wilhelm makes a pact with a demon huntsman and then casts magic bullets, but at the final demonstration of his newly acquired hunting skills, he fires one of the bullets destined to miss its mark, shooting his betrothed. The devil, a pirate figure called Peg Leg in *The Black Rider*, claims her corpse, and Wilhelm dies of madness in an asylum. As Burroughs has remarked, "A devil's bargain is always a fool's bargain" (*Burroughs Live* 719, 750, 793).

The composition and publication trail appears to end around the fourteenth century when folk references to magic arrows emerge in medieval treatises on witchcraft. So the story remains rooted in the world of "Fairie," free of authorship, a status replicated by the composition history of the contemporary version. The opera is billed as a collaboration amongst Burroughs who wrote the libretto; Tom Waits who wrote the lyrics; and Robert Wilson who created, staged, and directed it.[5] But from what Burroughs has said, Wilson exercised considerable authority over the direction of the writing. In a 1996 interview, Burroughs explained that he would write something and then show it to Wilson, who would "decide whether he wanted it or not—what he wanted changed, what he wanted for it. So [Burroughs] endeavored to write what [Wilson] wanted" (*Burroughs Live* 771). Others were also involved. For instance, Waits, who has acknowledged his own romance with Beat writers when he began his career (Feinsilber), said that Burroughs would send him material that their dramaturge, Wolfgang Wiens, would then edit and arrange. Waits would occasionally use some of Burroughs's material in the lyrics, and sometimes they'd collaborate: "like in [the song] 'Just the Right Bullet.' 'To hit the tattered clouds you have to have the right bullets'—that's all Burroughs. 'The first bullet is free' – that's me" (Hodgins, "Strange"). Waits has likened this process to working with bottle caps: "you can glue 'em down wherever you want. And mix them with your own macaroni" (Feinsilber). Although traces of Burroughs's "colors" can be discerned in the themes of guns and drugs as well as Dutch Shultz–type language and some dystopian imagery, without a line-by-line analysis such as the brief ones Waits provides, the dozens of productions of the opera subvert interpretations of authorial intent and authenticity. The opera operates like the fairy tale genre itself in that its origin remains fundamentally murky, despite the presence of the author function in *Black Rider* literary and intellectual property discourse.

On the level of plot, *The Black Rider* is extremely faithful to its older tale type. But it is by no means a simplistic duplication. Through a set of literary and theatrical devices, the opera twists the tale into a hybrid contact zone—a stunning representation of postmodern multimedia intertextuality—where Germanic wonder tale meets 1920s American tough guys, rubes, and chumps; American literary heroes; folk balladeers; gospel singers; and carnival barkers. The first productions were produced in two languages, bits of English sprinkled amongst the German. The opera's bilingual character lends it a cosmopolitan air. However, viewers limited to only one of the languages find themselves trapped in a liminal zone where identity repeatedly shifts from being in to being out, neither here nor there. The challenge becomes one of persistent translation, which as a metonym for human existence encourages one to accept, as Judith Butler maintains, the mode of translation as the only process leading toward a viable multicultural understanding of society (*Undoing Gender* 229).

Simultaneously, the bilingual dialogue addresses etymological similarities and differences between English and German, both of Indo-European origin. The linguistic twinning ironically highlights the sharp political and historical differences between British and German cultures, stylizing the opera as a white Anglo-critique of white Germany and contemporary fascist revivals.[6] The twinning also negates superficial demarcations of national, falsely race-based boundaries codified as official languages, intimating the fallacy of nationalistic domination, be it the Germany of Hitler, the England of Victoria, or the United States of Reagan. The message that addiction to power and immortality leads to disappointment and doom is encoded throughout the opera, which, as Wilhelm's dilemma about whether to stick with the clerk's pen or take up the hunter's gun illustrates, also questions the patriarchal hierarchy in which physical and technological prowess dominates linguistic craft. *The Black Rider* hints that, in fact, cultural representations of individual manhood and cultural dominance signify the pervasive "fool's bargain" that, on a large scale, has eradicated individual identity and agency. This concept is encrypted, not only in *The Black Rider* but also in earlier folk versions, in the trope of the father's "ownership" of the daughter, aligning the female with nature, that which the males, aligned in binary opposition as culture, indiscriminately claim "dominion over" and persistently destroy, to the disadvantage of all human life. In other words, individual liberty always rides on the back of someone else's servitude or slavery—a fascinating twisting of a construct that generally functions to oppress women and "the other."

This theme is further developed through the motif of doomed love, expressed poignantly in the song "The Briar and the Rose," a contemporary version of the Scottish folk song "Barbara Allen." In many collected forms of the old song, two lovers are tragically united only in death, a rose growing out of the young man's grave and a briar out of Barbara Allen's. "The Briar and the Rose" echoes these, as Wilhelm and Katchen, singing a duet in which they prophesy their own doom, acknowledge that only human tears will unite the briar and the rose. The trope also appears in "The Flash Pan Hunter," sung by Wilhelm's devilish uncle and a hunting boy, attributing the tragic love affair to Wilhelm's pact with the devil; since Wilhelm cannot wait to become part of the devil's clan, "The briar is strangling the rose . . . back . . . down" (Wilson, Thalia unpaginated). These lines demonize the briar, just as the Grimm brothers do in their "Sleeping Beauty" tale in which briars strangle the castle in which the princess, named Briar Rose, lies asleep until awakened by the prince. *The Black Rider*, however, mingles the fairy tales and the folk song to halt the Grimm/Disney tale at the point of the curse that sends the innocent princess into a hundred years of sleep—or in Katchen's case, death at the hands of her beloved: the natural process of death overtaking life continues unabated, an accurate description of natural organic processes (it is all nature after all, the briar and the rose) *and* a warning against the trans-spatial destruction of nature by the false human ego.

The opera achieves even more explicit detournement through Wilson's irreverent staging. As Jackie Wullschlager writes, the opera presents "graceful, cold artifice"; its actors evoke a silent movie, and Wilson's staging transforms "children's drawings into three-dimensional monstrosities. Crooked chairs, two meters high, dangle at odd angles . . . pine trees are scissor cut-outs which collapse and grow again like cartoons" (Tom Waits Library). Video clips of numerous productions, readily available on YouTube, reveal that, like the fairy tale, *The Black Rider* productions have little use for psychological character development through dialogue. The language favors the bizarrely incantational and magical more than the conventionally logical and linear, with lighting, shapes, and sounds flourishing as hieroglyphs actualizing Artaudian and German expressionist ideals that undermine proportion and harmony. "The story is told visually," Wilson said, "so Burroughs' [sic] text can be more abstract and Tom's songs are poetic and complement the story. *The Black Rider* [is] expressionistic, quick and colorful, and highly exaggerated" (Linders). Stagings overall create an exceedingly jagged, disorienting twist of the sanitized Perrault/Grimm/Disney tales, forcing recognition of the pernicious consequences of the fairy tale image—which may explain why a number of reviews of the opera in the United States report theatre goers exiting at intermission: in a nation still defined through the fantasy of individual wealth and freedom, Beat-European detournement faces a tough crowd.

A similar twisting effect is created by many of the lyrics. The opera is relentless in this respect, beginning with "The Lucky Day Overture," squawked in a guttural mockery of a carnival barker hawking a sideshow of "human oddities," including a three-headed baby, a monkey woman, and a seal boy with flippers for arms (Waits). The barker warns the faint-of-heart to stay away and then encourages everyone to visit the snack bar! These characters do not appear in the opera, but the lyrics create an immediate visual artifact of the grotesque fringes of human existence. Audience members find themselves in the center of the production where they become part of the sideshow itself and, in a disturbing doubling effect, members of *the sideshow's audience*, selves so immune to human suffering that they gaily watch themselves watching, before blithely heading to the snack bar to purchase toxic hamburgers, hotdogs, and French fries.

The overture signals the hidden grotesque nature of all that follows, none the least of which is the opera's theme song, "Black Rider," sung by the devil who invites the audience to "[c]ome along with the Black Rider / We'll have a gay old time." Whether intentional or the result of language drift, the song evokes the chorus of Irving Berlin's "Alexander's Ragtime Band" with the catchy "Come on and hear! Come on and hear!"; Berlin's lyrics include the claim that the band's bugle call is so magical that it will make one want to go to war. "Black Rider" transforms the superficially innocuous Louis Armstrong or Andrews Sisters covers into a vampirish proclamation that he will drink the audience's blood like wine. In effect, the song becomes a medieval moridat, or murder song, akin to Berthold Brecht and Kurt Weill's "Mac the Knife" from *A Three Penny Opera*, the devil's turning of the song laying bare "Alexander's" jingoistic, militaristic heart.

Fascinatingly, a second alien text evoked by "Black Rider" that interrupts hegemonic spectacle authority is the theme song to the 1960s cartoon *The Flintstones*. The song's catchy child-like babble ("yabba dabba doo!") entices young viewers with the claim that if they watch the show, they will "have a gay old time." Subliminally, these lyrics reinforce the cartoon's imposition of one fantastic consumption image (the co-existence of humans and dinosaurs[7]) over another fantastic consumption image (the post–World War II nuclear family), the two merged into a single monstrous product of mass culture. "Black Rider," by activating this silly yet enormously popular distortion of human history, exposes the deadly vacuity of what spectacle advertises worldwide as harmless children's entertainment.

Other songs continue this process, although Waits has said that he did not want to give too much away, preferring to credit the audience with interpretative intelligence (Hodgins, "Strange"). Sometimes the voices blend with those of the fairy tale characters, but many reinforce the opera's greater theme as well. "Tain't No Sin," for instance, which can be traced back to 1920s and 1930s vaudeville, jocularly encourages all to "take off your skin / and dance around in your bones," lines which also appear in "Black Rider"; at one point the audience even hears Burroughs on tape chanting the lines. Waits identifies them as Burroughs's reference point for the entire opera (Dansby), and, if that is the case, they may be Burroughs's cut-up revelation of the travesty of superficial conformity: the homogeneous material nakedness that conjoins us all as an ironic antidote to the false homogeneity of spectacle passivity.

It is at the level of character types, however, that *The Black Rider* finally shows its detournement cards, so to speak. Toward the end of the opera, and with delicious postmodern humor, Ernest Hemingway, Hemingway's agent, and Burroughs inexplicably emerge as transworld characters, that is, names that a reader or audience easily recognizes from another discourse, such as history or fiction, and that function in an intertextal zone questioning one's reality (Smith 22). Building on Umberto Eco's concept of transworld identity, Brian McHale finds such borrowed characters to abound in postmodern fiction, where they often "spectacularly violate, and thereby foreground, the ontological boundaries between fictional worlds" (58). Crossing from the narrative constructions of historical discourse (the kind Hayden White makes transparent) to fantasy discourse, Hemingway et al. momentarily reify the contemporary ontological significance of the narrative, while also illustrating Debord's claim that in spectacle the celebrity represents a living human being filling "the image of a possible role" (*Society* Point 60). Debord had little use for the celebrity who, "embod[ies] the inaccessible result of social labor by dramatizing its byproducts magically projected above it as its goal: power and vacations, decision and consumption, which are the beginning and end of an undiscussed process" (*Society* Point 60). The celebrity, he declares, identifies only with "the general law of obedience to the course of things" (*Society* Point 61). With deadly comic *dis*obedience, *The Black Rider* disembowels Hemingway's celebrity status as the great machismo writer and hunter, inserting within it the image of an old man who sells his soul (art) to Hollywood to propagate the fantasy Hemingway. Burroughs's own spectacle representation then interjects a contemporary adaptation of a "Confucius Say" maxim: "He who hang happy ending on story about death, shall likewise take a hangman's rope," calling out not only Hemingway's spectacle identity but also Burroughs's own Beat-mediated identity as that which threatens the autonomy of the individual. Perhaps what *The Black Rider* collaborators are suggesting is that even they recognize the dangers in their own participation in spectacle. The banality of their roles, the threat of becoming merely an image with no tangible existence, lurks all too close as a destructive, yet intoxicating, presence.[8]

Unfortunately, the post-premier history of the opera actualizes this very threat. First, quickly hacked out mass-culture reviews endlessly produce static images of Burroughs as a demonic Beat bad boy simplistically defined by guns and drugs. A few of these even make the erroneous claim that Burroughs chose the free shooter plot because it replicated his killing of his common-law wife, Joan Volmer Adams,[9] thus allowing him to engage in his own media fantasy of justifying the killing as the reason why he became a writer. Secondly, many people have come to know *The Black Rider* only through the collection of lyrics that Waits released commercially in 1993. When excised from the foundation text, the music stands as another stark appendage of the great image-driven machine that replaces a complex theatrical production with a pseudo-avant-garde brand—here, the face of Tom Waits—enabling anyone who acquires the music, legally or illegally, to assume the image of the marginalized neo/pseudo–Beat hipster.

Part III

What is it about our current era of capitalism that propels our need to remind readers of previous forms of storytelling in order to reveal the artificiality of contemporary narrative (Smith 119)? Debord would answer that it is commodity culture, which through spectacle mediates relationships among peoples. In this space above space, spectacle erases history, replacing it with unified time based on the market (*Society* Point 145) and an endless desire for pseudo-needs. Writing itself becomes suspect, since it exists outside individual consciousness and thus time. All the arts, effectively bundled into urban museums or cybernetic Websites, lose their connection to real communal human action. Might the purpose of storytelling, then, be to expose via artifice (storytelling) the lies (artifice) thus perpetuated? If we accept this possibility, the Beat adaptation of fairy tale architexture puts "a practical force into action," Debord's answer to how to destroy spectacle culture (*Society* Point 203). Certainly, *Dinners and Nightmares* and *The Black Rider* are authentic efforts to resurrect the plasticity of time and space, the power of individual human agency within a material world. However, that same fairy tale material, from the height of the Beat era when di Prima wrote to the end of the twentieth-century when Burroughs was still writing, produces a static world outside of history and memory—a "Perilous Realm" that erases individuality in service to the global diffusion of spectacle. In this context, our need to be reminded of the artificial nature of storytelling may, dangerously, feed the artificial spectacle that erases materiality and authenticity.

Ultimately, all we can know is that Beat appropriations of the fairy tale paradoxically enable the analysis and reproduction of the transnational autonomous movement of the nonliving. While we should never be satisfied with this ending (hardly the classic fairy tale conclusion, but then perhaps we should distrust it as well), writers such as di Prima and Burroughs, even while complicit in the perpetuation of the spectacle they persistently resist, signify the essential place of both the artist and the arts community in any culture seeking to translate, transmit, and transform.

Notes

The genesis of this essay was a paper written by Kat Brausch in my "Literature of the Beat Generation" course at The College of Wooster in fall 2006. Zane Shetler, a 2009 graduate of The College of Wooster, directed me to *The Black Rider*. I am grateful for their visions.

1. The power of Disney commodification in spectacle culture cannot be underestimated, especially in light of the fact that Disney earned in excess of $38 billion in revenues in 2010 alone. See *CNN Money: A Service of CNN, Forbes & Money*. 23 May 2011. Web. 26 June 2011.

2. Anderson's tale was based on a German translation of a medieval Spanish tale in a collection of tales, *El Conde Lucanor*, that have Arab and Jewish roots.

3. Andrew Hussey also addresses the connection between Burroughs, the Situationists, and the Lettrist movement. See "'Paris is about the last place. . .': William Burroughs In and Out of Paris and Tangier, 1958–1960."

4. Mary and Percey Shelley, Lord Byron, Claire Clermont, and William Polidori were reading the Apel & Laun text the evening in 1816 when they decided to see who could write the best supernatural story: Mary Shelley produced *Frankenstein*.

5. Wilson also collaborated with Allen Ginsberg on *Cosmopolitan Greetings* at the Hamburg State Opera House in 1988. Wilson directed, George Gruntz wrote the music, and Ginsberg wrote the libretto.

6. The Thalia Theater program for the first production includes illustrations that look much like the Nazi swastika. A 2004 British production also employed Nazi set design, including the double use of s, as in SS; birds resembling Nazi eagles; and the colors of the German flag: red, black, and yellow. Pia Conte-Gemes. "The Black Rider by William S. Burroughs." *Times Literary Supplement*. 4 June 2004. Web. 23 May 2011.

7. The cartoon represents what is now called *Flintstonization*, the projection of contemporary human beliefs, actions, and values onto the extremely distant past.

8. Ronna C. Johnson addresses this issue with respect to Kerouac in her essay "'You're putting me on': Jack Kerouac and the Postmodern Emergence" (see Skerl, Spec. *College Literature*). Ginsberg also addresses it in a 1991 interview conducted by Lewis MacAdams (see Allen Ginsberg Project blogspot). Anne Waldman's most recent operatic production, *Cyborg on the Zaterre*, a collaboration with musician Steve Taylor, also uses Ezra Pound as a transworld character to comment on the sins of the past (e.g., Pound's anti-Semitism) and the need for poetry (e.g., Pound's language manifesting the imagination through time and space) to reinvent our present moment; *Cyborg*, however, is not self-conscious of its potential participation in spectacle, and Pound functions more as an allegory of poetic resurrection than as awareness of an artist's own participation in the vacuous stealth of image.

9. Marianne Faithfull, who played Peg Leg in a 2004 London production, suggests as much: "By using an old folk tale, William was really able to write about himself. The main character, who takes the Devil's deal that ultimately results in the death of his sweetheart and bride, is called Wilhelm. So it's not very disguised, but disguised enough for William to have done it" (Cumming).

Chapter 6

Two Takes on Japan: Joanne Kyger's *The Japan and India Journals* and Philip Whalen's *Scenes of Life at the Capital*

Jane Falk

Critics have noted the importance of Japan as a pilgrimage site for several writers associated with the Beat Generation, most notably Gary Snyder whose extended stay there in the 1950s and 1960s was spent primarily in the study of Zen. He shared his knowledge with those at home—Allen Ginsberg, Joanne Kyger, Lew Welch, and Philip Whalen, among others—but of these, only Kyger and Whalen spent prolonged periods of time in Japan. In 1957, Kyger left Santa Barbara and came to San Francisco where she became part of the group of writers around Robert Duncan and Jack Spicer, meeting Snyder soon thereafter. They subsequently married in Kyoto and lived there together from 1961 to 1964, during which time Snyder was affiliated with the First Zen Institute of America in Japan. *The Japan and India Journals* chronicle this time, including an excursion the couple made to India. Whalen, a graduate of Reed College along with Snyder and Welch and one of the group of poets who read at the seminal 6 Gallery reading, had a slightly different Japanese experience, one not totally centered on Zen Buddhism. In fact, one might consider official Zen to be somewhat peripheral to Whalen's life in Kyoto in the late 1960s, especially as evidenced by his long poem *Scenes of Life at the Capital*. Although Kyger and Whalen had different takes on Japan and related their experience via different genres, their writing demonstrates not only the influence of Japanese culture on their work, but also Japan as a place against which they wrote, a site of resistance and contested identity. More importantly, their transnational experience occasioned the production of hybrid practices, forms, and identities.

Hybridity, a term first used to indicate the mixing of species, is often associated by cultural critics with transcultural forms within contact zones produced by colonization.[1] Even though Japan was never an American colony, it had a close and dependent relationship with the United States during Japan's Meiji Era (late nineteenth and early twentieth centuries).[2] Many Japanophiles, such as Ernest Fenellosa, helped Japan Westernize, but ironically, they were as much interested in learning from and about Japan as imposing Western modernity, an attitude replicated by Kyger and Whalen post–World War II. Consider, for example, Kyger's comments on Japan as cultural mecca at that time: "The . . . late fifties was very much reveling . . . in what Japan had to offer in the way of its cultural history: its gardening, tea ceremonies, beautiful folk craft, sense of nature . . ." ("Joanne Kyger" 127). In these cases, dominant modernizing culture was itself hybridized.

Jahan Ramazani, in *A Transnational Poetics*, claims that "interstitial concepts of culture" such as hybridization are "well suited to modern and contemporary poetry's translocal conjunctures and intercultural circuits" (28). Hybrid practices are especially evident in Kyger's relationship with Zen Buddhism, and both Kyger and Whalen's journals and poems show hybridization of Japanese literary and artistic forms and styles, what Susan Friedman in *Mappings* labels generic hybridity (95).[3] Kyger and Whalen also play out various roles or personae associated with the transnational, such as the cosmopolitan, tourist, and flaneur, exemplifying Jonathan Friedman's claim that cultural globalization creates new combinations or hybrids, one result of which is a new kind of postmodern cosmopolitan who identifies with the "world's variety and its subsequent mixtures" (74).

Beat expatriates were less tourist than cosmopolitan, or saw themselves as such, depending on how deeply they chose to enter into another culture. Expatriates such as William S. Burroughs may be seen as interfacing between cosmopolitan and tourist in their extended visits and stays in Latin America and Morocco, depending on length of stay and degree of immersion. Burroughs tellingly named this space between the interzone. Whalen inhabits another interzone, urban Kyoto, as well as exhibiting aspects of the flaneur, a term for the nineteenth-century Parisian arcade walker that Frankfurt School critic Walter Benjamin used to describe Baudelaire in "On Some Motifs in Baudelaire." Baudelaire as "man of leisure" could indulge in the "perambulations of the flaneur only if as such he is already out of place." Benjamin goes on to contrast the flaneur who "demanded elbow room and was unwilling to forgo the life of a gentleman of leisure" with the "pedestrian who would let himself be jostled by the crowd" (172).[4] The flaneur was drawn to the crowd, yet remained separate. Whether Kyger could be considered to exhibit these characteristics is less evident, as her journal is primarily located in the domesticity of house and garden.[5] But both Kyger's and Whalen's fascination with Kyoto confirms the essentially humanistic and aesthetic aspects of this Japanese urban other, in contrast and as alternative to the American scene at mid-century.

Kyger, for example, chose to immerse herself in Japan for both spiritual and personal reasons: "the impetus for going to Japan was to study Zen and to be with Gary [Snyder] and see what was happening in terms of historical Buddhism and see its history" ("Places To Go" 148). In a 1982 interview, Kyger is more specific about her interests, stating, "I wanted to go to Japan because I needed to control my mind. . . ." Furthermore, "Zen offered a practice. It was structure, guiding towards one mind that gets open" ("Congratulatory Poetics" 114–115).

Kyger's study of Zen in Kyoto at this time demonstrates hybrid aspects of Zen practice, especially in relation to gender roles. Ruth Fuller Sasaki had established the Kyoto branch of the First Zen Institute of America in Japan in 1956, and in 1958 she became abbot of a historical Zen temple, Ryosen-an, the physical home of the Institute on the grounds of the Daitokuji temple and monastery.[6] According to Sasaki in "Rinzai Zen Study for Foreigners," "The Institute was specifically designed to assist foreigners who came to Japan to study Zen to orient and prepare themselves for their study" (232). She stressed mastery of the Japanese language, especially "special Zen words and terms" (228).[7] Snyder, for example, had first come to Ryosen-an in 1956 to help with the Institute's translation projects and to study Zen at Daitokuji.[8] Sasaki's First Zen Institute also allowed for study by women, the majority of Zen monks and priests traditionally being male. Authentic Zen instruction for Westerners was still not widely available in the United States in the 1950s, hence the American interest in travelling to Japan to practice Zen.[9]

Another example of Zen's adaptation to Western needs is Kyger and Snyder's marriage ceremony. Of Sasaki's requirement that the two marry to preserve Eastern as well as Western mores, Kyger quotes a letter from Sasaki to Snyder in the Author's Note at the beginning of her journals: "'But living together in the little house *before* marriage won't do. There are certain fixed social customs that the Institute expects its members to respect.' Thus I was married almost immediately after my arrival and entered into the domain of housewife in Japan" (vii).[10] Traditionally, Japanese marriage ceremonies took place in Shinto shrines, while Buddhism provided last rites for the dead. The ceremony performed by the Chief Abbot of Daitokji was one he had devised for Western practitioners of Zen. Sasaki described the ceremony for *Zen Notes*, April 1960, a monthly publication of the First Zen Institute, after which she held a "traditional" American-style wedding reception and meal at Ryosen an with a wedding cake "four stories high and topped with a miniature bride and groom" ("Letter from Kyoto").[11]

Kyger went on to enter the life of the Institute, practicing Zen sitting meditation or zazen at the Ryosen-an Zendo in the evening. Later she sat at Daitokuji's Honzan or reception hall where "[she] was sitting six hours a time. . . ." ("Congratulatory Poetics" 115); however, there she could not sit in the main meditation hall, which was reserved for men only. She also studied flower arranging or Ikebana with the Ikenobo school, the oldest and most traditional Japanese school. At the same time, she rebelled against taking the role of traditional Japanese wife and never learned enough Japanese to participate in sanzen or personal study with a Zen master. Kyger's journals document both attitudes and are as much about integration into Japanese life as about feelings of alienation and failure to acculturate.

Her journals begin with departure from California in January 1960 and end with her return there in February of 1964. Journal entries exist for most days, though of varying lengths with date, day, daily activities of domestic life, record of weather and specifics of her garden, food eaten or prepared for guests, and trips made to tourist sites in Japan and India. She also includes dreams, excerpts from letters, lists, poems, and quotes from books read as well as self-reflections on her relations with Snyder, her Zen practice, her career as a poet, and her theories about poetry. A record of Zen sitting dominates the early years; social activities and reflection on writing, often amidst the more masculine Beat milieu, dominate the later years.

The journals, themselves, can be considered a kind of hybrid of Eastern and Western forms, as they take on the appearance of the Japanese poetic diary. Entries combine a narrative of her life with free verse, haiku, or senryu, what she considers "a way of putting a short lined sketch into the text."[12] According to Earl Miner's preface to *Japanese Poetic Diaries*, the literary diary has been a continuous Japanese tradition (vii) and one dominated by women from the time the form was brought to Japan from China up to the fourteenth century (11).[13] Distinguishing between natural and art diaries, he defines natural as a "record of fact," while art diaries include a "literary element," often the addition of poems (8–9). Early diarists interspersed prose with the tanka or waka form, while later diarists, most notably Basho, included haiku.[14]

The poem sketches, elegant, moving, or satirically clever, juxtapose with or comment on the events of Kyger's day. For example in an entry of November 4, 1960, the senryu "Gary Snyder you'd better / Admit me! / Besides I'm your wife" follows an entry reflecting on her failure to do zazen, Snyder's haircut, and thoughts on their relationship (62). A few days later, following comments on a letter from a friend, a series of three linked haiku describe scenes from her garden. The first on flowers, contrasts with the latter two on the subject of vegetables, in the process juxtaposing Snyder's and Kyger's attitudes:

> Use our Garden in a beneficial manner
> says Gary this morning
> —referring to the 6 rows of turnips
> I am.
> The green tops as feathers decorate
> The patch outside the kitchen door. (65)

Her witty take on life in Japan also recalls *The Pillow Book of Sei Shonagon*, a factual account of life at the tenth-century Heian court (a natural diary in Miner's terms). Kyger mentions this work in an entry from September 16, 1962, and an early translation by Arthur Waley would have been available to her. In his introduction, Waley characterizes the *Pillow Book* as consisting "partly of entries in diary-form. The book is arranged not chronologically, but under a series of headings such as 'Disagreeable Things,' 'Amusing Things' . . ." (21). Sei Shonagon's sometimes barbed comments as she narrates her daily life at court are at times similar to Kyger's tone.

In journal entries used to record her experiences with zazen, Kyger experiments with another Japanese form, the Zen meditation poem. Here practitioners write poetry with allusions to poems or teachings of past Zen masters to express their own experience or realization. As Charles Egan puts it in *Clouds Thick, Whereabouts Unknown: Poems by Zen Monks of China*, these poets created their own "'Chan [Zen] code' of poetic language. Images as simple as the moon, clouds, boats, reflections in water, plum and lotus . . . took on complex connotations based in Chan ideas, famous verbal exchanges, and Chan and Buddhist texts" (37).[15] A poem included in an entry for September 1963 toward the end of her stay is an example of the way she plays with this form; evidence of her perseverance in practicing zazen more consistently, it also refers to a poem by Hui Neng, Zen's sixth patriarch:

> Below us and above us lie the words
>   take away the blanket
> and there is dust
> Words built the world
>   and between us is the great icy silence of breath.
>   This simple mass of elements
>   which various causes have
>   brought together and which other
>   causes will separate.
>   And how does the phantom
>   disappear and why did he appear (261)

The allusion to dust in the first five lines recalls the Platform Sutra's famous verse exchange between two historic Zen figures, Hui Neng and Shen-hsiu, which established Hui Neng as the successor to the fifth patriarch.[16] Kyger may thus be using her poem to recall Hui Neng's, as she expresses her understanding of Zen and its attitude toward language.

Kyger further hybridizes this genre as she subtly adapts the form. Traditionally, according to Egan, these poems are written in couplets often four to eight lines in total length.[17] Instead of three couplets, Kyger breaks up her lines so that the first couplet extends over four lines and the second over five. The poem's form is thus an extension of its content, as she describes the interaction of the word and the breath in meditation, the give-and-take mirrored by the movement of the lines. Line breaks indicate units of breath. Only the last two lines maintain the traditional couplet form as they somewhat enigmatically conclude the poem.

Kyger's journals are not only a place for formal experimentation, but also a site where the cosmopolitan versus tourist dichotomy plays out, with one or the other predominating at various times.[18] Kyger attempts to adjust to Japanese life with the journal acting as borderland or transitional space between two worlds, what Susan Friedman might consider a "feminist-hybridic quest text" (259). Her journals can also be seen as what anthropologist Victor Turner terms a liminal space in which "entities are neither here not there; they are betwixt and between the positions assigned . . . by law, custom, convention, and ceremonial" (95).[19] Cultural theorist Homi Bhabha associates this liminal or interstitial space with hybridity, claiming that it "opens up the possibility of a cultural hybridity that entertains difference without an assumed or imposed hierarchy . . ." (4).

The poems that grow out of her journal entries are evidence of some of the conflicts attendant on the transnational experience.[20] One such poem, "They are constructing a craft," is an example of how Kyger, in a cosmopolitan move, layers cultures one on top of the other. The poem grows out of a journal entry dated March 28, 1960, on a trip Snyder and Kyger made to the fishing village Wakanoura shortly after her arrival. The poem is primarily a snapshot of the village where the men are building a wooden boat, while the women dry seaweed. To Kyger, the boat builders appear as part of a distant past, recalling ancient Greece, a specific allusion that she includes in the journal, but not in the finished poem: ". . . at fishing village enormous craft / being constructed solely of wood. (Ulysses)" (18). While romanticizing Japanese village life, this poem has some of the same mythic overtones of Kyger's earlier poems written before her arrival in Japan. It is thus a transcultural mapping of ancient Greece on a Japanese village from which Kyger may feel estranged, indicated by a line not in the journal: "Watching us go by, we are strange" (15).

However, despite Kyger's apparent adaptation to Japan and Zen practice, her journals give evidence of her frustration with her position as foreigner or *gaijin*. The possibility for cosmopolitan hybridity and ability to adapt successfully to the transnational experience breaks down. This can partly be attributed to sexist aspects of Japanese life, especially Zen's male-dominated practice. In a 1995 interview, Kyger mentions "how difficult it was to study Zen in Japan . . . and how you had to learn Japanese and the whole structure of koan study" ("Crooked Cucumber"). In a later interview, Kyger adds that it was "too isolating for me . . . I was taller than everybody else and the manners were so different. I was capable of disagreeing. No Japanese woman would ever do that ever" ("Particularizing People's Lives").

Historically, Japanese Buddhism had not been welcoming to women as monks or nuns. Haruko Okano, in "Women's Image and Place in Japanese Buddhism," discusses the persistence of "female exclusion" in Buddhism and specifically Zen (22). Grace Schireson in *Zen Women* notes the "scarcity of women in classical Zen literature" (38), while Isabel Stirling, Sasaki's biographer, comments that "Ruth Sasaki was a unique exception in a Zen world/environment that was primarily male. Her being there did not change that environment significantly." Kyger, herself, did not meet "any Japanese women who were lay practitioners."[21] Along with this, Kyger's lack of motivation to learn Japanese to deepen her practice may also have been an issue. Snyder, for instance, chides her on this issue in a letter included in one of her last journal entries from Japan, that of December 31, 1963: "Someday you ought to really try . . . to learn Japanese. Or give up planning to live in Japan" (269). Certainly, Kyger would have had to better learn the language if she were to continue her Zen practice in Japan.

Basic survival of a domestic nature, getting food, carrying water, or washing clothes, is a recurring theme throughout the journals, whether in Japan or India, and may also have played a part in her feelings of frustration. A poem that presents Kyger's conflicted attitude toward Japanese domestic life grows out of her journal of April 27, 1960. It begins with no mean domestic feat:

> It is lonely
> I must draw water from the well 75 buckets for the bath (1–2)

Here Kyger includes her sense of alienation, then continues to move by association from domestic duties of making the bath to those of putting away her winter clothes, at which point she begins to reflect on her Zen practice with the following lines: "Have I lost all values I wonder / the world is slippery to hold on to / When you begin to deny it" (8–10). Putting away clothes may have led to thoughts of putting away the ego and an allusion to Zen Buddhist meditation. In this case alienation turns to reflection, but such is not always the case for Kyger.

Her anger is palpable in a journal entry of April 1961 during a trip to the Japan Sea: "At train station millions of students surround and stare at us. Almost unbearable, I want to slug one of them" (97). Travel woes continue in India, especially in regard to crowding on trains. Frustration at being a foreigner or tourist relates to various personae of the transnational experience discussed by Ulf Hannerz in his study *Transnational Connections*, in which he distinguishes between the cosmopolitan and the tourist. Cosmopolitans "want to immerse themselves in other cultures, or . . . be free to do so. They want to be participants. . . . Tourists are not participants . . ." (105). Her frustration with travel in India may have been due to the fact that she was more of a tourist in India and more of a cosmopolitan in Japan.[22]

An added sense of alienation may have come from her exclusion from the male-dominated Beat poetry scene, evident even in its expatriate incarnation. In an entry of April 11, 1962, she states that Donald Allen took some of her poems for an anthology, complaining that he communicates with her via Snyder "and absolutely no word to me" (195).[23] On March 5, 1963, she writes of the "*exhaustion* of living here" (240). Less than a year later, on January 20, 1964, Kyger would return to the United States; she and Snyder would divorce soon thereafter.[24] Despite Kyger's seeming frustration with life in Japan, her experiences there as recorded in her journals were the basis for a number of poems in her first collection, *The Tapestry and the Web* (1965), published soon after her return to the states.

In contrast to Kyger, Whalen came to Japan not to study Zen but to teach English. In an interview with Yves Le Pellec, Whalen explains that Snyder asked if he wanted to teach English at a YMCA school in Japan. Whalen, needing a job, "thought it would be a nice chance to get out of San Francisco and work abroad. So [he] said all right" ("Zen Poet" 58). On the first of Whalen's two trips to Japan, he stayed sixteen months (from early 1966 to late 1967), returning to the United States to correct the proofs for his first book of collected poems, *On Bear's Head*. Although he often felt himself a foreigner, Whalen found Kyoto to be a more positive experience than did Kyger, an alternative to the bourgeois reality of American culture, his past and his Oregon roots, or the present, a government controlled by what he considered Christian war mongers during the Vietnam era. This may also have been because he did not try to accommodate his life to the Zen scene, while his status as a male may have afforded him a greater degree of invisibility.

Scenes of Life at the Capital was primarily written during Whalen's second trip to Japan, from March of 1969 to June of 1971, the capital referring to Kyoto.[25] It is a public and political poem written by an American abroad. In considering the greater significance of this work, seemingly overlooked in the history of the modernist long poem, we can read Whalen as one more poet with a political and social commentary on the American scene, that of the late 1960s. However, instead of writing about Americans abroad in the tradition of the expatriate author, he writes about America from abroad. If, as Ezra Pound believed, the purpose of the study of the past is to determine "what sort of things endure" (*Patria Mia* 68), for Whalen his own epic long poem shows what has endured in Japan, what should endure, or what the United States can learn from its World War II foe; hence it may seem natural for Whalen to borrow from or allude to Japanese culture.[26]

The poem follows in the modernist tradition, a verse epic or "poem including history," according to Pound ("Date Line" 86). Written in collage style, it is similar to Pound's *Cantos,* Charles Olson's *Maximus,* or William Carlos Williams's *Paterson,* with juxtaposed images, quotations, found sounds, and self-reflections linked by Whalen's stream of consciousness. These shifts in perspective are similar to the ideogrammic method of Pound's *Cantos.* Similarly to Olson and Williams, Whalen's poem is situated in and imbued with the history and ambiance of a particular, albeit exotic, locale—in this case Kyoto. Whalen noted in an interview that "I'll write this book . . . about the barroom and palace life in modern and ancient Kyoto," adding that he did not want "another creepy version of *Maximus* or *Paterson . . .* 'cause those things have already been done and done by experts" ("Tiger Whiskers" 36).

However, even though the poem as published fits the long poem genre, it was actually written as journal entries. Whalen first recorded details of his walks around Kyoto in notebooks and journals, then later typed and collaged the "scenes" into the finished poem. He took lines and passages verbatim from his Japanese notebooks, rearranging, cutting, and only in rare cases changing them to remove references to specific persons or incidents. In an interview with Anne Waldman, he remarked that the "original material from which it's written is spontaneous writing . . ." ("Tiger Whiskers" 37). Some of the sections were written in Whalen's house in Kyoto; some from coffee houses, bars, or restaurants; some seemingly composed as he walked the streets of Kyoto. One can imagine Whalen stopping somewhere to jot down impressions.

From an examination of his notebooks kept at the time, the poem moves roughly from summer 1969 through fall, winter, and spring of 1970 in roughly chronological order, although some rearranging has been done so that the student protests at Kent State and Jackson State in May 1970 are at the poem's center. Most of the scenes and reflections are undated, however, so that it seems to unfold in continuous time. Whalen begins *Scenes of Life at the Capital* seated in his Kyoto house, preparing to take a bath. As a wasp buzzes around his bookshelf, he recalls his Berkeley days with Jack Kerouac. From there, the poem moves back and forth between his house and scenes of Kyoto life: Takano River dye vats; coffee shops or beer halls; famous temples, shrines, or pilgrimage spots; Kyoto Municipal Museum; a Noh performance; tombs of various emperors; and the surrounding mountains and gardens.

Each scene is interspersed with or juxtaposed in Whalen's recollections of his past or reflections on the present, either his life as an American poet in Kyoto, or the political situation in the United States during the Vietnam War. He even includes the process of writing the poem itself: "To my horror and chagrin, I see I've suppressed / Lots of goody in the process of copying from ms. to typewriter . . ." (10). Various voices and themes enter and leave the poem, almost in a fugal manner, but the whole is seemingly anchored and kept moving by shifts of locale.

Thus the poem demonstrates the significance of Japan as transcultural pilgrimage site for Whalen and a reason why he chose to exoticize the modernist long poem. In an early version, published as a first section in 1970 (the Maya Quarto edition), Kyoto is characterized in an author's note as "a secret capital of art and wisdom and love scarcely known to the outside world."[27] In fact, Whalen's pilgrimage spots are cultural and aesthetic, as much as spiritual and religious: the Kitano Shrine, dedicated to Michizane Sugawara, incarnation of the deity who presides over calligraphy and scholarship; Ishiyamadera, where Lady Murasaki was said to have written *The Tale of Genji*; and the Rakushisha, haiku poet Basho's hut.

Other features of the poem demonstrate hybridization. Whalen's use of the term the Capital itself recalls the way Arthur Waley refers to Kyoto in his translation of *The Tale of Genji*, a book much admired by Whalen.[28] In the poem's last section, written from the cherry and plum viewing gardens, Whalen even includes an imaginary scene with himself as a Heian character, perhaps Genji himself, an homage to Murasaki's novel, *The Tale of Genji*:

> Lady West Gate and Lady Plum spent an hour
> Quarreling over my hair, setting lacquer cap with
> Horse-hair blinkers will it be a sprig of
> Cherry bloom or twig of spirea / Lady Plum in tears. . . . (71)

In addition, the title of the poem recalls the series of woodblock prints of Japanese landscape or urban life created by artists such as Hokusai and Hiroshige, the most well-known Japanese *ukiyo-e* artists, who took the landscape as subject matter to a high level in the nineteenth century. *Ukiyo-e* or woodblock prints developed in the Edo period in Japan, from the seventeenth century, with the newly rich class of merchants as patrons. Yoko Woodson, in an essay on Hokusai and Hiroshige, compares the Japanese classical sumi landscape painting, with its depictions of idealized scenes of mountains, rivers, and the natural world, to *ukiyo-e* prints with their "specific sites" famous for aesthetic or historic reasons. She adds that *ukiyo-e* artists depicted these sites as "personal mementos and souvenirs of these famous places" (32). Some of the most famous series include Hokusai's *Thirty-Six Views of Mt. Fuji* and Hiroshige's *One Hundred Famous Views of Edo*.

Whalen alludes to Hokusai by name early in the poem as he describes a friend drunk at Sanjo Station: "End of the Tokaido Road / Kamogawa sluicing fast under Sanjo Bridge / The wooden posts and railings shown by Hokusai" (12). Although it was Hiroshige who created prints of the fifty-three stations of the Tokaido (the main thoroughfare from Edo to Kyoto in Edo Japan; one print depicts the Sanjo Bridge), this passage indicates Whalen's familiarity with *ukiyo-e* artists and a possible influence on his title and content. Other scenes from *Scenes of Life at the Capital* are similar to Hiroshige's series *One Hundred Famous Views of Edo*, especially the scene at the end with the Kitano shrine plum blossom, which recalls one of the most famous of Hiroshige's prints, "The Plum Orchard in Kameido," featuring a celebrated plum tree named Reclining Dragon.[29]

However, Whalen's claim that the poem is about Kyoto is not really accurate. Although the poem takes place in Kyoto, it is as much about the United States during the last years of the Vietnam War. What Whalen actually does with these Japanese scenes of temples, shrines, tombs, rivers, and coffee houses is to contrast them with scenes in the United States to the country's detriment, especially its lack of culture and the violent responses to the political protests of the late 1960s and early 1970s. The comparison is between the cultured and civilized East and the uncivilized West, a reverse Orientalism. For instance, just before his visit to the plum blossoms at the Kitano Shrine, Whalen notes that Japan is a "civilization based upon / an inarticulate response to cherry blossoms / So much for Western Civilization" (73). He implies that this aesthetic appreciation is lacking in the United States, where "'Calliope' [the muse of epic poetry] is a steam piano" (74).

The Vietnam War is proof of the West's problem, a theme that appears near the beginning of the poem, soon after Whalen leaves his house to go to the Shinshindo coffee shop. At this point, he remembers friends from the past "yarded off to Viet Nam / Translated into Rugged American Fighting Men / Defending The Free World Against Godless Atheistic Communism" (15). Each word in this line begins with a capital letter for better emphasis. A few scenes further on, shortly after discovering the tomb of Emperor Murakami, he returns to the theme of the bellicose American spirit, stating, "In America we've been fighting each other 100 years" (22). In addition,

> The real shame of America is the lack of an anticlerical
> Movement or party. All parties try to compound
> With invisible State Protestant Church that theoretically
> Doesn't exist. (22)

These thoughts are juxtaposed in the announcement in bold lettering: "30 MORE SHOPPING DAYS UNTIL CHRISTMAS!" (23), suggesting the global and consumer character of this Christian holiday. He later shows the church as an outright aggressor: "Christ now returns under the name U.S.A. / Rages wild across the earth to avenge himself / Napalm and nuclear bombs for every insult" (47–48).

He reiterates these critiques, making a more direct comparison of West to East later in the poem as he questions why he should go to Europe with "several million nervous white folks . . . Totally uncivilized, fingering and puzzling over / The ruins of Western Civilization. . . ." In comparison, "In this capital we also fumble with ruins of high culture / But feelings of antique propriety keep heavy sway" (32). Juxtaposed against a description of a celebration at Daitokuji Zen temple is the claim that "Almost all Americans . . . Have the spiritual natures of Chicago policemen" (34). This was written a year after the 1968 Democratic National Convention in Chicago with its infamous acts of police brutality toward protesters at the convention, Ginsberg being one of them.

Shortly after this passage and toward the heart of the poem, Whalen brings up the Kent State killings: "This year the National Guard, weeping with pity and fright / Kill four students, firing 'into the mob' / Nobody cared" (39). He adds in an aside that "(The soldiers are also our children, we've lied to them too . . . Then put them into uniform and turn them loose with guns . . .)." This line is followed by the somewhat hopeless statement that "[n]obody cares because nothing really happened / It was on the TV . . ." (40). He then continues to move back and forth between scenes from a Noh performance and communism in Asia, the Federal Court, then a scene of Nara (the ancient capital before Kyoto) juxtaposed to more on Kent State and Jackson State and the line "There was no reason to kill them" (42).

As impassioned and significant as his protest of America and American politics and aggression is, the personae associated with the transnational that Whalen takes on in this poem somewhat compromise his message. Whalen as flaneur haunts the Kyoto coffeehouses, taking notes on the urban scene in his journals. He can be considered an outsider, a tourist, a sightseer, or an expatriate. In one scene, he feels self-conscious drinking wine in a café where customers have been "[e]dified by the spectacle of a certified FOREIGNER" (61). He observes as a *gaijin*, without command of the Japanese language, appropriating it for his own purposes, perhaps misunderstanding in the process. Similarly to Kyger, he can be seen as a cosmopolitan, manifestation of both positive and negative aspects of the global and transnational society.

According to Hannerz, cosmopolitanism entails "a greater involvement with a plurality of contrasting cultures to some degree on their own terms"; in addition, it is "a willingness to engage with the Other." However, Hannerz problematizes this attitude:

> ... the concern with achieving competence in cultures which are initially alien, relate to considerations of self as well. Cosmopolitanism often has a narcissistic streak; the self is constructed in the space where cultures mirror one another. Competence with regard to alien cultures itself entails a sense of mastery, as an aspect of the self. (103)

This narcissism can also relate to Benjamin's flaneur, who sees himself reflected in the arcade windows. We can see this, too, as Whalen tries to make sense of his country and his literary calling, yet feels unappreciated, misunderstood, or undervalued by American society while being a resident alien in a society that does value the arts. He is also trying to master his own past. In one passage he finds himself "[f]ree of that poor-ass Oregon down-home history" and then quotes his father: "'Get up out of there,' my father used to say, / 'You can't sleep your life away. / People die in bed'" (50).

Unlike Kyger, however, who leaves Japan feeling somewhat alienated, Whalen, toward the end of the poem, imagines himself as a more integrated outsider, thus partly resolving his Eastern and Western identities. He sees himself as a "representation" of Tanuki, the name for the Japanese raccoon dog as well as a character in Japanese myth and folklore associated with lewd behavior, drinking and eating. For instance, during his viewing of family outings at the cherry blossom festival, he watches young men dancing. One performs a "Tanuki prick-dance with big *sake* bottle / Sometimes held out before his crotch" (72). Whalen describes Tanuki as

Spirit of mischief, wine and lechery
Long bushy tail, thick fur, nocturnal habits
'Badger' is a feeble translation . . . much more like
Big raccoon/bear
Fat breathless popeyed manifestation
Of the Divine Spirit . . . not a bad representation
Of the present writer (73)

Not only can Whalen integrate with Japanese culture through his identification with Tanuki, but here he also identifies with a hybridized version of his bear personae, recalling the title of his collected poems, *On Bear's Head*, 1969, and "The end, of a month of Sundays," 1959, his doodle poem with bear as Bodhisattva.

In spite of this attempt at integration, however, Whalen, like Kyger, attempts to reach back to the premodern Japan beloved of the Japanophiles of the nineteenth century, rather than merge with post–World War II Japan. This regressive aspect of American interest is made evident in journalist Ken-Ichi Takemura's newspaper article "Foreigners in Japan," written for *The Mainichi*, in which he specifically refers to Kyger, Snyder, and other Kyoto expatriates, claiming that "many foreigners in Kyoto seem to be trying to live in a nineteenth-century Japan shutting themselves off from the material world. . . . On the other hand, most Japanese seek the so-called 'modern life'" (7). However, despite Takamura's critique, for these twentieth-century Japanophiles, a kind of cultural hybridization went on through literary transnationalism, enabling them to overcome some degree of alienation, evoking what Ramazani calls "non-coercive and nonatavistic forms of transnational imaginative belonging" (31).

Thus, Japan is more than Roland Barthes's "situation for writing," as noted in *Empire of Signs*, in which he sees Japan as an empty signifier on which can be projected various ideas or values: "I am not lovingly gazing toward an Oriental essence—to me the Orient is a matter of indifference, merely providing a reserve of features whose manipulation—whose invented interplay—allows me to 'entertain' the idea of an unheard-of symbolic system, one altogether detached from our own" (3). Instead, Japan for Kyger and Whalen is a standard of culture, aesthetics, and spirituality to be emulated, appreciated, and hybridized by those in search of an alternative to American values at the mid-point of the twentieth century. As part of the transnational Beat experience, Kyger and Whalen demonstrate both the importance of Japanese culture to this group of writers and the complexity of the expatriate's identity and culturation. The writing they did in Japan was also significant in each poet's artistic development: Kyger would go on to publish a number of her travel journals, and *Scenes of Life at the* Capital may be considered the culminating long poem of Whalen's career.

Notes

1. See Mary Louise Pratt's *Imperial Eyes*.
2. See H. Paul Varley's *Japanese Culture*.
3. See this study for a discussion of the "contradictory" meanings of hybridity.
4. Urban Beats often assumed aspects of the flaneur. East Coast Beat writers had a fascination with Times Square and 42nd Street and the Beat culture of hustlers and junkies they found there. In his crisscrossing of the United States, fictionalized in *On the Road*, Jack Kerouac can be seen as an automated/mobile flaneur.
5. See Janet Wolff's essay on the *flaneuse*.
6. Sasaki's husband, Sokei-an, established the First Zen Institute in New York in 1930; Sasaki's temple in Japan was an offshoot. See Isabel Stirling's *Zen Pioneer* for more on her life.
7. Kyger proofread this text early in her stay in Japan, according to her journals.

8. Buddhist scholar Jan Nattier considers such study as transmission via "import" requiring both "money and leisure," characterizing it as "Elite Buddhism" or a "Buddhism of the privileged" (189). Such study could also be considered a cosmopolitan experience.

9. Zen's transmission to the West and subsequent hybridization actually started in the century before with Zen priest Shaku Soen's appearance at the Parliament of Religions held in conjunction with the Columbian Exposition of 1893 in Chicago. In addition, the transmission of Zen from China to Japan beginning in the twelfth century was also a transnational phenomenon.

10. Page numbers in this essay refer to *The Japan and India Journals* published by Tombouctou in 1981. The reprint, *Strange Big Moon* (2000), has kept the same pagination, adding only a Foreword and Introduction.

11. Kyger does not include an entry in her journals for her Buddhist wedding, except for the statement "My name is changed" (7). The couple had been officially married at the American consulate earlier that week.

12. Quote from her letter to the author of August 10, 2010. Anne Waldman also makes this comparison in her Foreword to *Strange Big Moon*.

13. For more on feminine and Beat associations with the journal as genre, see Jane Falk's essay "Journal as Genre and Published Text."

14. Steven Carter in *Traditional Japanese Poetry* describes the classical waka or tanka form as the 31-syllable poem, with 5-7-5-7-7-syllable lines. The haiku and senryu consist of three lines of 5-7-5 syllables (xiii). Kyger defines senryu in her journals as a form that "elicits laughter by depicting truth of humanity" (111).

15. This form, as well as Zen itself, originated in China; hence, Egan's use of Chan, the Chinese term for Zen.

16. In Philip Yampolsky's translation, Shen hsiu's poem likens the mind to a "clear mirror" that needs to be polished continually so as to "not let the dust collect" (130). Hui-neng's response was that "Buddha nature" is always "clean and pure," so "where is there room for dust?" (132).

17. Egan also notes that Chinese poetry is usually written in lines of four, five, or seven syllables with a caesura in the middle before the final di- or trisyllable (40).

18. In contrast, Jonathan Skinner claims that Kyger moves beyond "'Beatnik' vagabondage" to "generous attention" to details of everyday life in her journals and poems (par. 3–4).

19. Turner was interested in connecting the state of communitas which grows out of the liminal space to the Beats and hippies in his book *The Ritual Process*. Thanks to the editors for their suggestions about liminality.

20. Most often, poems begin with an experience from the day, then move in stream of consciousness fashion. For example, "My Sister Evelyne," begins with an image of a naughty child seen at Sarnath and concludes with stanzas about Kyger's sister. Other poems build from her dreams; some describe domestic scenes. The fact that most of her references to daily life are somewhat oblique may be due to an effort on Kyger's part to avoid the confessional, which in her "Places to Go" interview, she considers "so limiting" (144).

21. Isabel Stirling from an e-mail of July 27, 2010, and Kyger from a letter of August 10, 2010.

22. The emphasis in Kyger's journals, especially the Indian portion, is on her feelings and reactions to foreign culture, not on an objective description of sights seen. Contrast this approach with Snyder's record of the Indian trip, *Passage Through India*. Kyger acknowledges this in her Introduction to *Strange Big Moon*.

23. Though she may feel frustrated at times, she is often quick to point out masculine shortcomings. See her acerbic comments on Ginsberg in an entry the previous day (190).

24. James Clifford in *Routes*, his study of transnational movements, notes that women are often "impeded from serious travel. Some of them go to distant places, but largely as companions, or as 'exceptions'" (31).
25. References to this poem are from the first publication in 1971 by Grey Fox Press in Bolinas; parenthetical citations refer to page numbers from this edition.
26. Susan Friedman comments on the often "hybridic" nature of the twentieth-century long poem (96).
27. Whalen published several versions of this poem in the early 1970s. See Acknowledgments of the Grey Fox edition for specifics.
28. Kyger notes in a letter of August 10, 2010, that "the [Kyoto] landscape seemed redolent of Genji's time."
29. This print was also an influence on and inspiration to Vincent Van Gogh, his painting *Japonaiserie: tree in bloom*, for example.

Chapter 7

"If the Writers of the World Get Together": Allen Ginsberg, Lawrence Ferlinghetti, and Literary Solidarity in Sandinista Nicaragua

Michele Hardesty

In Managua in January 1982, Allen Ginsberg joined two other poets—Ernesto Cardenal of Nicaragua and Yevgeny Yevtushenko of the Soviet Union—to draft a declaration that would invite the world's writers to visit revolutionary Nicaragua. Their "Declaration of Three" was one of several invitations to Nicaragua in this period that targeted writers, artists, and intellectuals, and it drew on the attractive image of Nicaragua as a place that had made literacy and literature central to its revolution. Nicaragua has often been called "the nation of poets," but after the Sandinista victory in 1979, this title might have been changed to "the nation-*state* of poets." Before 1979, as John Beverley and Marc Zimmerman have argued, poetry and *testimonios* written by members of the Frente Sandinista de Liberación Nacional (FSLN) created a culture of opposition to the tyrannical rule of Anastasio Somoza Debayle. After Somoza's departure, many poets and novelists who survived the revolution shifted their energies from opposing the government to building a new nation. "[T]he revolution was primary," said poet Gioconda Belli, "the dream we had to make reality, the most urgent poem all Nicaraguans had to help write in order that we could begin building a more just society" (qtd. in Randall, *Risking* 146). Not only did prominent writers such as Cardenal and novelist Sergio Ramírez enter top political posts, but the Sandinistas also made literacy and literature key elements of the "Sandinista experiment." Cardenal's Ministry of Culture (founded one day after the FSLN entered Managua on July 19, 1979) created an elaborate system of cultural institutions, policies, and programs—such as nationwide poetry workshops—intended to democratize culture in the wake of the large-scale literacy campaign of 1980 (Whisnant 200). In the early years of reconstruction, before the *contra* war reconfigured national priorities, literary culture constituted a vital—but controversial—part of the post-revolutionary reconstruction.[1]

That Sandinista Nicaragua appeared as a regime of poets and novelists, of literacy campaigns and poetry workshops, and of debate rather than dogmatism, was part of what made the revolution compelling to writers outside of Nicaragua. The government hosted writers from several different countries, among them Ginsberg, Lawrence Ferlinghetti, Julio Cortázar, Eduardo Galeano, Günter Grass, Salman Rushdie, and Margaret Randall, all of whom wrote about their experiences in Nicaragua. "I did not think I had ever seen a people, even in India and Pakistan where poets were revered, who valued poetry as much as the Nicaraguans," remarked Rushdie, who traveled to Nicaragua in 1986 (40). But if international writers were drawn to the importance of poetry in Nicaragua, many of them—like Nicaraguan writers themselves—also debated the relationship between politics and literature, as well as the danger (or necessity) of censorship. However, neither visiting writers nor subsequent scholars have addressed in depth two questions raised by these visits to Nicaragua: how and why did Sandinista leaders seek to enlist international literary writers to their national cause, and what does solidarity, on the basis of literature itself, signify for the cultural politics of the Sandinista Revolution, or for literature as a basis for transnationalism?

I use the term "literary solidarity" to categorize not only efforts by literary writers, both practical and symbolic, to support a cause, a struggle, or a nation, but also efforts of writers to affiliate with one another as a distinct group. Manifestations of literary solidarity ranged from the mainstream to the margins, from an official invitation from the Nicaraguan Ministry of Culture inviting a writer to the Rubén Darío literary festival, to a petition issued by the International PEN Club, to a "poet's exchange" organized by the grassroots Lower East Side/Bluefields Sister City Project. Visiting Nicaragua and writing about it in order to correct misconceptions (even with the limitations of the visitor's ability to find out "what's really going on" with a brief official visit) might constitute literary solidarity on the practical level. Then there is the symbolic significance of "the writers of the world" coming together, which itself raises questions about the role of literature and of the writer. To whom is a writer responsible, and whom does the writer represent? Does the writer speak for him- or herself, not beholden to nation? Should literature serve national politics? Is literature a universal force? Why *should* writers come together? While these questions are not specific to Sandinista Nicaragua and its campaigns of literary solidarity, they are nevertheless the unstated—and unresolved—questions that undergirded those campaigns.

In order to address these questions, this essay focuses on visits by Ferlinghetti and Ginsberg to Sandinista Nicaragua. For their part, these two poets were more interested in national and international politics than many of the other Beat writers with whom they are associated,[2] but both poets held a vision of literature (and poetry in particular) as a transcendent force and of writers as permanent outsiders, visionaries, or prophets—or to take a line from one of the original Romantic poets, the "unacknowledged legislators of the world."[3] Additionally, these poets both expressed, in various ways, the conviction that poetry was an inherently libratory force and that the state was, ultimately, a repressive force. When Ferlinghetti and Ginsberg went to the nation-state of poets, then, they supported the Sandinistas and participated amply in their campaigns of literary solidarity, but their travel-related writings expressed the conviction that state power and poetry remained incompatible. At the same time, however, the experience challenged their own imagination of poets and poetry. Ferlinghetti's 1984 account of traveling to Nicaragua, *Seven Days in Nicaragua Libre*, adopts an attitude of deliberate naïveté to confront Sandinista Nicaragua, a place that challenges the imagined opposition of the liberating power of poetry and the ensnaring power of the state. In Ginsberg's writings from his 1982 and 1986 trips to Nicaragua, he insists on speaking only for himself and speaking the truth, expecting others to do the same, but his poetry from those trips takes up the challenge of representing a reality that did not conform to those expectations. In both cases, their travel writings complicate what it would mean for "the writers of the world [to] get together," as "Declaration of Three" proclaims.

Ferlinghetti's and Ginsberg's connection to Nicaragua and Nicaraguan poetry did not begin in the 1980s. This connection can be traced back to two pre-FSLN projects of Cardenal and his mentor José Coronel Urtecho: their efforts to translate North American poetry and introduce it as a resource for Nicaraguan national literature, and their contributions to the Mexico City-based journal *El Corno Emplumado/The Plumed Horn*, which championed the extrapolitical, transnational power of poets. These projects were the venues through which Cardenal and Coronel Urtecho first came into contact with Ferlinghetti and Ginsberg, and the principles behind these projects would later inform the "Declaration of Three" and other Nicaraguan appeals to literary solidarity.

"Poets are the true Panamerican Union"

In the 1960s, there were various threads that would serve to connect Nicaraguan literature and Beat poetry, including translated works and direct contacts. Translation of North American poetry in Nicaragua goes back at least to the *Vanguardia* movement. *Vanguardia* poets, while resisting the United States's neoimperial control of Nicaragua (U.S. Marines occupied Nicaragua from 1912 to 1933 [LaFeber 11]), turned explicitly to North American poetic models in order to break free from the European influences they saw guiding poet José Darío's *modernismo* (Schulman ii). Coronel Urtecho's 1949 *Panorama y antología de la poesía norteamericana*, in which he translated and introduced U.S. poets from William Cullen Bryant to Muriel Rukeyser, suggested that the poetry from the United States could serve as a "guide" (*guía*) for the "liberation from that which is European and the adaptation to the American medium" (9).[4]

Coronel Urtecho's first North American anthology led to another, which he co-edited and co-translated with the younger Cardenal. According to Cardenal, "Coronel introduced a whole generation to U.S. poetry"; inspired by this poetry, Cardenal went to New York to study English language and literature at Columbia University (K. Johnson 16–17). Upon Cardenal's return to Nicaragua, he and

Coronel Urtecho began a much more ambitious anthology, which they did not complete until 1963. "We made a book that was over 400 pages long and begins with the North American Indians and concludes with the Beat poets," Cardenal explained (17). Other translations followed: in 1979, Coronel Urtecho and Cardenal brought out a volume of Ezra Pound's poems, which, notably, includes an Afterword written by Ferlinghetti; in 1985, they completed a book-length volume of William Carlos Williams's poems in translation.[5] By the 1960s, then, both U.S. Beat poetry and some of Ferlinghetti's and Ginsberg's poetic precursors had found their way to Nicaragua through Coronel Urtecho and Cardenal. These projects were predicated on the principle that U.S. poetry was not a force of cultural imperialism, but rather that poets and poetry were forces that could transcend political borders and that poets were the true representatives of a people.[6]

Nicaraguan poets and U.S. Beat poets came into more active contact in a journal whose goals were transnational: *El Corno Emplumado/The Plumed Horn,* a multilingual literary journal from Mexico City that North American poet Margaret Randall and Mexican poet Sergio Mondragón founded in 1962. With a name that combined the jazz horn of North America with the Plumed Serpent of the Aztecs, *Corno* featured poets from the Americas and beyond, with the heaviest representation from Mexico, Cuba, and the United States. Poems from North American Beat poets were prominent. Cardenal, then a novice at a monastery in Colombia, supplied *Corno* with his own poems, as well as his and Coronel Urtecho's translations; he also encouraged young Nicaraguan poets to send work to the journal. In a letter to the journal, Cardenal declared, "[P]oets are the true Panamerican Union" ("Letter to the Editor" 146).

The journal sought to bridge the political divide between North America and Latin America by means of poetry: "[N]ow, when relations between the Americas have never been worse, we hope EL CORNO EMPLUMADO will be a showcase (*outside politics*) for the fact that WE ARE ALL BROTHERS" (Mondragón et al. 5). Both the editors' statement that *Corno* would be a "showcase (*outside politics*)" and Cardenal's assertion that "poets are the real Panamerican Union" point to a notion that poetry is not only separate from politics but also a "true" force that constitutes a nation *and* connects peoples across borders. *Corno*'s editors go further in the Editor's Note for July 1963, comparing Cardenal's statement to a letter from Ginsberg about the "underlying universality of people's scenes" (Mondragón et al. 5).[7] Their admittedly bombastic editorial is notable for placing together these statements of Cardenal and Ginsberg about the extranational powers of poets. On one hand, Ginsberg posits poetry "scenes" as universal rather than culturally or nationally specific; Cardenal, who *was* committed to national specificity, imagines something closer to an internationalism of poets, delinked from governmental and commercial power but also more *true*. These competing but complementary visions remain apparent in these poets' 1982 "Declaration of Three."

The cultural influence of the United States—particularly the Beats—was not uncontested in Nicaragua, or even in *Corno* itself. Randall (who later described herself as having brought "the new Beat consciousness of North America" to *Corno*) moved away from what she came to consider a naïve literary rebellion and toward a national political revolution during the years she edited *Corno;* she went on to work directly with the revolutionary governments of Cuba and Nicaragua (Randall, *Coming Home* 5).[8] For other Nicaraguan writers, the problem with the Beats was that their influence was in fact a form of cultural imperialism. Ramírez, who co-founded the Sandinista-affiliated *Frente Ventana* literary group when he was a university student, saw a reflection of the Beat Generation in an early 1960s Nicaraguan poetry movement called the *Generación Traicionada* (Betrayed Generation). He rejected this group for being "nothing more than the old dependence on foreign cultural models (however justifiable those models were in their own countries)." The motto of *Frente Ventana*, then, became, "We are not the Betrayed Generation. We are the generation that will not betray Nicaragua" (White 80–81).

However, it was Coronel Urtecho and Cardenal's projects that established a basis for a literary solidarity between Sandinista poets and U.S. Beats. These connections—including translations and shared participation in *El Corno Emplumado*'s transnational project, which related variously to the construction of a Nicaraguan literary nationalism and an inter- or transnational "union" of poets—were predicated upon a *delinking* of literature and state power, as well as the conviction that poets represent not just a separate power but a "truer" power. When turning to Cardenal's later appeals to international literary solidarity, one can observe a clear continuity between his 1963 assertion that "poets are the true Panamerican Union" and his 1982 call, with Ginsberg and Yevtushenko, for "the writers of the world [to] get together" to defend Nicaragua, and finally to his 1985 invitation asking writers in the United States to attend the 1986 Rubén Darío festival: "We believe that the most important event [of the festival], for that which it can contribute to ending United States aggression against the people of Nicaragua, will be the encounter of North American and Nicaraguan poets" ("Invitación").[9] By continuing to use a discourse of literary internationalism/universalism that envisions the writer as a kind of *counter*-power, Cardenal's appeals made Nicaragua attractive to writers abroad, such as Ferlinghetti and Ginsberg.

"A Naïveté Worth Saving"

Ferlinghetti's trip to Nicaragua in 1984 was not his first experience of politically interested travel. During the 1950s and 1960s, Ferlinghetti found in revolutions abroad an excitement that he felt was absent at home during that same period: "It seems that in most revolutions there's a stage of euphoria," he explained in a 1988 interview. "I was in Cuba during that period of euphoria, about the second year of the revolution, and it was an astounding spirit that makes me feel like we're leading such dull lives over here . . . that we didn't have these great exciting things to live for, which were happening in Cuba in 1960, 61" (Ferlinghetti and Lykiard n.p.). He imagined that such euphoria was part of the spirit of 1936 in Barcelona, and he personally found it in France and Mexico in 1968. Such revolutionary euphoria, he recognized, was temporary and would be followed inevitably by police control and bureaucratization. For Ferlinghetti, the question of whether Nicaragua would go down the same path was a foregone conclusion: "Nicaragua is now the focus of passions of the Left, fifty years after such passion and hope were concentrated in Republican Spain—and disappointed; twenty-five years after the same hopes were concentrated on Cuba," he writes in *Seven Days*. "Everyone dreams their ideal of a perfect society—and are disappointed or disillusioned" (*Seven Days* Preface).[10]

His disillusionment strikes a chord common amongst Leftist and liberal intellectuals of the 1980s.[11] However, revolutionary euphoria is not for Ferlinghetti merely an illusory ideal; rather, he associates such euphoria with the real powers of poetry. Thus, while the slim and impressionistic travelogue Ferlinghetti published upon his return (*Seven Days in Nicaragua Libre*, with photographs by his traveling partner, Chris Felver) expresses support of the Sandinista Revolution, it does so in terms of poetry's centrality in Nicaragua—imagining poetry as something akin to a preserver of revolutionary euphoria. Such an imagination is doubtlessly naïve; however, Ferlinghetti claims naïveté itself as something positive in *Seven Days*.

In the Preface to this travelogue, Ferlinghetti relays an anecdote that both puts his relationship with Nicaragua and Cardenal in the context of poetry, and puts poetry in opposition to repressive political power:

> I went to Nicaragua in the last week of January, 1984, to give poet and Minister of Culture, Father Ernesto Cardenal, a seed from a flower at Boris Pasternak's grave which had been given to me by the Russian poet Andrei Voznesenski at a poetry reading against war at UNESCO in Paris. When I presented the seed to Cardenal in an open-air amphitheater in Managua, I felt I did not have to point out to him nor the audience that the seed was a symbol not only of the power of poetry to transcend all the boundaries of the world dividing people from each other, but also a symbol (from the grave of that great Russian writer who survived the most repressive period of Soviet life) of resistance to Stalinism. The theater was in the Plaza Pedro Joaquín Chamorro, who was murdered near the end of Somoza's dictatorship, the outrage over it in fact hastening the end of the regime. (*Seven Days* Preface)

The image implies an analogy. The poet Voznesenski ferried the seed from the grave of his mentor Boris Pasternak (who was expelled from the Soviet Writers Union for his *Doctor Zhivago* and refused the Nobel Prize in 1958 to avoid exile, dying in disgrace two years later) to Paris, and from Paris, Ferlinghetti delivered the seed to Cardenal in an amphitheater named for Pedro Joaquín Chamorro, the writer and former editor of the Nicaraguan daily newspaper *La Prensa* who led the pre-FSLN opposition to the Somoza dynasty and was assassinated in 1978. From poets alive and dead in the Soviet Union, the seed not only symbolizes the connective power of poetry but also warns of the dangers posed by state power. The image is also an *index* of correspondences whose complicating details (Chamorro was assassinated in a dictatorial regime; Pasternak was disgraced by a bureaucratized, authoritarian state) are not explored.

Instead, Ferlinghetti's perspective is one that is more interested in these surface connections than in depth. He was explicit about such spatial metaphors in the 1975 poem "Populist Manifesto." The poem is a rallying cry for a public, visionary poetry, whose key lines describe such poetry in spatial terms:

[. . .] [S]peak out
with a new wide-open poetry
with a new commonsensual 'public surface'
with other subjective levels
or other subversive levels
a tuning fork in the inner ear
to strike below the surface. (*Who Are We Now?* 63–64)

This "wide-open," "public surface" poetry would not preclude depth; these lines suggest that the public poetry would strike a pitch with a "tuning fork in the inner ear" that would also "strike below the surface." The image of a tuning fork implies a shared pitch between surface correspondences and complicated depths, so that the surface becomes an index of the "other levels." Ferlinghetti's work is invested in symbolic surfaces; he is a messenger making connections across networks and building an index of the depths below each network node. However, his metaphoric vocabulary has not always accounted for occasions when surface and depth are out of tune, when connections could only be made in very superficial terms. Brought back out of the abstract language of spatial form, in Nicaragua Ferlinghetti's interest in surfaces arguably made him, in the words of Pablo Antonio Cuadra, commenting on *Seven Days*, "a man of surpassing naïveté" (250).

Indeed, Ferlinghetti's travelogue questions not how *far* but rather how *deep* a writer's political commitments should go. In *Seven Days* Ferlinghetti narrated his trip as one spent on the surface, circulating among poets and circulating poems. He delivered copies of *Volcán* (the bilingual anthology of Central American poetry edited by Alejandro Murguía and Barbara Paschke and published by City Lights) to his hosts; he exchanged inscribed editions of poetry with both Cardenal and Sandinista opponent Cuadra; and Interior Minister and *testimonio* author Tomás Borge presented Ferlinghetti with a "fine edition" of Nicaraguan poet Urtecho's *Paneles de Infierno*. These exchanges make literal the boundary-crossing capacities of poetry. Yet these poets and their volumes of poetry pass through the narrative like allusions: rarely, if ever, does poetry itself become a matter for discussion. Focusing on these exchanges allows Ferlinghetti to skim over the intricacies of the literary debates raging in Nicaragua and to focus on the "euphoric" side of Sandinista reconstruction as a deliberate act of naïveté.

This deliberate naïveté is most clear in his Introduction to a poem entitled "La Bruja: Flower of Revolution," which he composed during the trip:

> Fernando Silva, the poet and doctor whom I met on our Sunday excursion, was another with whom I felt an immediate humane rapport (and it was in fact he who stimulated it by exclaiming within an hour of our meeting, "We're brothers!"). He gave me a flower after a while, saying *La Bruja* grew where nothing else would, in the most unexpected places. . . . I wrote the following poem out of a certain "revolutionary euphoria" and presented it at the reading—one can put it down as naïve agitprop—but perhaps it is a naïveté worth saving. And it related well to the seed I brought from Pasternak's grave. (*Seven Days* 1/31)

Not only does Ferlinghetti heap this passage with markers of his credulity, but he also claims his naïveté as something valuable, "a naïveté worth saving." His naïveté is something positive because it allows him to maintain his desire for a literary solidarity based in "humane rapport" and revolutionary euphoria rather than in the disillusioning complexities of state-building.

With the notion of "saving" his naïveté comes the suggestion that his naïve apprehension of *la bruja*—a symbol of a revolutionary audacity—might be "saved," valued, and circulated like the seed from Pasternak's grave. His poem, "La Bruja," travels from place to place "collecting" the seed of the *flor bruja*, making Ferlinghetti a kind of figurative Johnny Appleseed whose poem distributes the spirit of revolution. The images of the poem override the borders of Nicaragua, presenting a catalog of inhospitable climes—both physical and mental—where the flower might bloom: "Wherever there is nothing / wherever there is no sign of green," and also

> in the Sierra Maestra on [sic] our imagination
> ....
> in workshops of the mind
> in churches full of dead popes
> And in the shacks in the dirt streets of Monimbó
> sprouts this foolhardy flower[.] (*Seven Days* 1/31)

Following this catalog of images, the flor bruja, then, while originally rooted in Nicaragua (where the first decisive popular uprising against Somoza took place in Monimbó in 1978) might spread its seeds of revolution anywhere. The image can also easily traverse the distance between actual political revolutions in places like Nicaragua and the metaphoric "revolutions" within superpowers like the United States, or between revolution and the poetic imagination. The legendary birthplace of the Cuban revolution, the Sierra Maestra—despite being seen by Ferlinghetti as a failed experiment—becomes in the poem the "Sierra Maestra on [sic] our imagination." Ferlinghetti seals this transnational connection with an image that recalls the famous photograph from the U.S. antiwar movement of the 1960s: "And [la bruja] will even sprout up / out of the barrels of rifles."

With "La Bruja," Ferlinghetti presents a striking metaphor for his utopian imagination. One aspect of this metaphor relates to the idea of a "public surface." All the settings in which the seed might "sprout" are linked across a single "surface"; although these settings are different, such differences do not matter for the seed's viability. However, while the poem seems to be about the ability of the seed to grow wherever it is planted, Ferlinghetti complicates this idea by associating la bruja with the seed from Pasternak's grave. Ferlinghetti points out that the grave's seed represented the "power of poetry to transcend all the boundaries of the world dividing people from each other," but it was *circulated* from one poet to another rather than being *cultivated*. Ferlinghetti's phrase that describes the poem's gesture "a naïveté worth saving" likewise presents an image of seed-*saving* rather than cultivation. The saved, circulated seed itself could be a symbol for the power of poetry and the power of resistance; the sprouted seed (or "foolhardy flower") could represent a revolutionary euphoria that one might likewise save and circulate in the form of a *poem*. While poetry and revolution provide the means for Ferlinghetti to support revolutionary

Nicaragua, then, his deliberately naïve imagination of poetry and revolution save him from confronting the connections of poetry and state power in that country.

"You Don't Know It"

A constant traveler who kept close tabs on world politics, Ginsberg believed that it was his role to be an independent, critical voice wherever he went, and he rarely avoided controversy. His outspokenness led to his expulsion from Cuba and Czechoslovakia in 1965, yet those experiences did not stop him from organizing and taking part in collective forms of solidarity with Nicaragua nearly two decades later. In the early 1980s, Ginsberg expended considerable energy supporting revolutionary Nicaragua and protesting U.S. policy, and much of his activity involved poetry. In addition to collaborating on the "Declaration of Three" with Cardenal and Yevtushenko, he attended the Rubén Darío literary festival in Nicaragua in 1982 and 1986, participating in the latter as part of a delegation of U.S. poets dubbed the "Poets' Encounter for Peace" or the "Invasion of Poets." He also worked with grassroots organizations and initiated statements and petitions with the PEN American Center, where he served on the Freedom to Write Committee. These efforts are documented in his poetry, in a rich archive of personal papers, and in an unpublished travelogue, compiled with traveling partner Patrick Warner, which details his 1986 trip.

Despite his defense of Nicaragua in the face of U.S. power, Ginsberg maintained a position of independence that was, for him, a prerequisite for telling the truth. Likewise, he advocated free expression and spurned the notion that he had any political allegiances during his two trips. In 1982, he selected poems to read that would demonstrate his independence by, as he explained to Daniel Ortega, "mixing my criticism of U.S. aggression with my criticism of Russia and Cuba" (qtd. in Estridge 6). "Capitol Air," one of the poems he read during his 1982 visit, does just that: "No hope Communism no hope Capitalism yeah," reads one representative line, "Everybody's lying on both sides" (*Collected Poems* 754). His preoccupation with independence appears also in his notebook where, among his ideas for the "Declaration of Three," Ginsberg wrote, "Can we all speak privately or as representatives? or representatives of our own mind? myself representative of what I see & think. I have no allegiances other than that" ("Nicaragua Notebook"). During his later trip, in 1986, Ginsberg scorned his fellow U.S. poets who flattered the Sandinistas and instead hammered his hosts with critical questions (Ginsberg and Warner). In each of these instances, Ginsberg created an opposition between independent free expression and falsehoods associated with allegiances. For him, the hope for positive change in this bipolar Cold War world was necessarily based in a unified but unallied expression, as expressed by another line from "Capitol Air": "Arise Arise you citizens of the world use your lungs / Talk back to the Tyrants all they're afraid of is your tongues" (*Collected Poems* 753).

His support of revolutionary Nicaragua, then, would seem to strain his commitment to the writer's independence. However, the "Declaration of Three" itself, which Ginsberg wrote with Cardenal and Yevtushenko, emphasizes independence and truth-telling—visitors "see[ing]" the revolution "with their own eyes"—the very qualities of the writerly vocation that Ginsberg valued (Cardenal, Ginsberg, and Yevtushenko 53). Another passage downplays Nicaragua's status as a nation-state by describing it as an "experimental workshop for new forms of get-together wherein art plays a primordial role." Likewise, the declaration represents Nicaraguan citizens— intellectuals, *campesinos*, workers, and soldiers—*as writers* who participate in poetry workshops and who "write verse" (52). Imagined this way, Nicaragua's myriad writers and the "writers of the world" formed a single unity, one that could take the place of "citizens" in the previously quoted line from "Capitol Air": "Arise Arise you [writers] of the world use your lungs / Talk back to the Tyrants all they're afraid of is your tongues." Understood in the language of the "Declaration of Three," Ginsberg's solidarity with Nicaragua does not strain his commitment to writers' independence at all; instead, the declaration imagines Nicaragua primarily as a nation of writers. Ginsberg's solidarity here is with *writers as a distinct group*.

However, the very possibility of "all the writers of the world get[ting] together," which the declaration works so hard to construct, comes into question in two poems Ginsberg wrote during his trips to Nicaragua: "The Little Fish Devours the Big Fish" in 1982, and "You Don't Know It" in 1986. These poems raise doubts not only about other poets' (and politicians') independence of mind but also about that very notion that the writer is without allegiances and capable of apprehending the truth. These questions about the poet's authority arise first in a set of lyrics entitled "The Little Fish Devours the Big Fish," which Ginsberg wrote in Managua in January 1982. The second verse in particular provides a subtly satirical supplement to the optimistic "Declaration of Three." Calling Yevtushenko, Cardenal, and himself "sentimental / & reliable" as well as "poetical & prophetical," the speaker advocates that the U.S. administration and "Havana men" realize that their stranglehold on Nicaragua should be lifted, since it is a "big error / of war fever" (*Collected Poems* 866). While preserving a division between poets and governments, this verse playfully questions the legitimacy of the poets' appeal. By identifying Cardenal, Yevtushenko, and himself "sentimental / & reliable," the poem slyly deprecates the basis of the three poets' advocacy of the revolution: they are sentimentally attached and therefore can be relied upon to issue declarations in its favor. The poem suggests that these poets are neither true poets nor true prophets, throwing the poets' authority into question. Without abandoning the declaration's idea of "all the world's writers" getting together—or even acknowledging Cardenal's status as Nicaraguan Minister of Culture and thereby complicating the conceptual separation of poetry and political power—the poem opens itself to a critique of the writers' solidarity.

Four years later, during his second trip to Nicaragua, Ginsberg composed another "supplementary" poem, "You Don't Know It," which takes the international affiliation of writers as a starting place but relentlessly tests its limits. Such affiliations were a starting place for the 1986 trip. Just before his departure from the United States, Ginsberg circulated an unofficial "Statement on Nicaragua" at the International PEN Congress in New York City, which held that the U.S. government's involvement in the contra war was responsible for the hyper-militarization of the Sandinista government and its restriction of civil liberties; 163 writers signed the statement, despite their range of political beliefs ("Statement on Nicaragua").[12]

After bringing those writers together, he left for Managua with an invited delegation of U.S. poets who were answering Cardenal's call for poets to "invade" Nicaragua (Ginsberg, "U.S. Poets"). Despite these acts of affiliation, Ginsberg's 1986 trip was one of frustration for the poet; in Nicaragua he encountered a country that had militarized in the face of the escalated contra war, and he found that both his hosts and his fellow delegation members had less patience with discussions about free expression and censorship (Ginsberg and Warner).

If "Little Fish" satirically supplements the "Declaration of Three," then "You Don't Know It" amplifies a contentious debate that took place among Ginsberg and others at a gathering hosted by the Sandinista Writers Union.[13] The poem he wrote in the wake of this debate invokes a fractious world of dissident and revolutionary writers whose testimonies remain unacknowledged or misunderstood by writers on the other side of the world. In other words, this poem figuratively brings the "writers of the world" together not as independent figures capable of discerning the truth but as deeply aligned, situated figures whose experiences determine their always-partial understanding of "the reality of Nicaragua."

In the poem, the characterization of writers as situated rather than independent can be traced in the way who "doesn't know it" shifts in the poem from one set of experiences to another. In one stanza, the "you" refers to the Nicaraguans, and the poem borrows the point-of-view of Eastern European dissidents: "you say you don't know these exiles from East Europe complaining / about someday Nicaragua Gulag" (944). Later, the poem shifts to an ostensibly Central American point-of-view, and the "you" becomes a "they," referring to the Europeans:

And they don't know it, Aksionov Skvorecky Romain Rolland Ehren
burg Fedorenko Markov Yevtushenko—
....
Don't know the 40,000 bellies ripped open by the d'Aubuisson hit-men for
    Born Again neoconservative Texans (945)

In these lines, the speaker directs an accusatory voice at these European dissident writers, or those who would project experiences detailed by Eastern European dissidents onto another continent, but who do not or cannot account for the particularities of Central America's conflicts.

Another way in which the poem situates its writers is to emphasize their political positionality. For example, unlike "Little Fish," this poem emphasizes Cardenal's position as a politician rather than as a poet without allegiances. In one part of the poem, Cardenal is sandwiched within a cabinet of ministers and executives: "Nor you General Borge Father Cardenal Vice President Rodríguez you / say you don't know it" (944). Cardenal appears here as part of a list of politicians: the Interior Minister Tomás Borge, Minister of Culture Father Ernesto Cardenal, and Vice President Sergio Ramírez (whose name he mistakenly wrote as Rodríguez)—rather than as part of a collective of poets. While previously Ginsberg had characterized Cardenal primarily as a poet, here his poem is unforgiving in its criticism of Cardenal and his fellow writer-politicians *as politicians*.

There is a way in which "You Don't Know It" is Ginsberg's frustrated response to hosts who would not acknowledge facts and dangers facing Nicaragua that seemed clear to him. Yet Ginsberg cannot characterize *himself* as a truth-teller in this poem; he can only *situate* himself in terms of how he imagines his hosts see him: he describes himself near the end of the poem as just another stupid American peddling copies of *Reader's Digest* and the Moravian Bible (945–946).[14] In other words, he is another cultural imperialist who claims to "know it" and who exports his knowledge abroad. Yet if this self-characterization is facetious, the poem nevertheless does not insist on the validity of a single point-of-view. Instead, the poem insists on the importance of reading and listening as well as writing—against the specter of the cultural imperialist's *Reader's Digest* and the missionary's Moravian Bible, both of which are, significantly, abridgments. This poem holds up "Madame Mandelstam's thick book's gossip" instead, alluding to Nadezhda Mandelstam's memoir *Hope Against Hope*, about life and death in Stalinist Russia (945). And finally, the poem represents an alternative to the idea of the poet or writer as independent truth-teller, one that acknowledges writers' allegiances and their partial and situated access to "truth."

In an exchange recorded by the Sandinista-affiliated newspaper *Barricada* in 1986, delegation member Zoë Angelsey noted that "poets don't have power and they need more power." Urtecho replied, "But here the poets are in power" (*"Aquí los poetas están en el poder"* 9). The existence in Nicaragua of poets in political power deeply challenged the conception of poetry and poets regularly expressed by Ferlinghetti and Ginsberg, not to mention Angelsey, while also attracting them to revolutionary Nicaragua. This challenge was made even greater by an idea of literary solidarity (with roots in older national and transnational literary projects that involved Cardenal and Coronel Urtecho in Nicaragua and Ferlinghetti and Ginsberg in the United States) that often affirmed an idea of poetry's extrapolitical power. Ferlinghetti responded to this challenge with a deliberate naïveté that would allow him to engage in Nicaragua's revolutionary euphoria (which he associated with poetry) without associating with the powers of the state. Yet if his "naïveté worth saving" allowed him to preserve his romantic idea of the poet as independent, it did so in exchange for such a poet's insight. Ginsberg, on the other hand, responded to the challenge with two poems that question the poet's independence and insight, reckoning instead—even if in frustration—with poets who are always situated, never free of allegiances, and with only partial insight: a realistic image of what it would mean for the "writers of the world [to] get together."

The notion of literature as a force that transcends borders, and of literary writers as having an elevated role, remains current. For example, the International PEN charter reads, "Literature knows no frontiers and must remain common currency among people in spite of political or international upheavals," and asks that its members "use what influence they have in favour of good understanding and mutual respect between nations; they pledge themselves to do their utmost to dispel race, class and national hatreds, and to champion the ideal of one humanity living in peace in one world" ("PEN Charter"). In these affirmations there is a suggestion that literature, as "common currency," can itself "dispel . . . hatreds." However, what this charter does not account for is the difficult practice of literary and political solidarity, which involves reckoning with the inevitable political and social constraints on free expression as well as issues of travel and translation, reading and listening. Likewise with revolutionary Nicaragua, while hosts and supporters often used an idealized language to discuss the power of poetry and the status of Nicaragua as a "nation of poets," the reality was much messier.

Notes

1. For a fuller account of these controversies as they played out in Nicaragua, see Beverley and Zimmerman, and Whisnant.
2. While Ferlinghetti has always distanced himself from the Beat Generation, it is difficult to disassociate him from it. This essay does associate Ferlinghetti with the Beats, but it does not argue that he was politically *disengaged*—such disengagement being one of his major reasons for refusing the Beat label. See Silesky 80–83.
3. Percy Bysshe Shelley, "A Defense of Poetry" (1821).
4. My translation. "American" refers here to the Americas, not to the United States.
5. Ezra Pound, *Antología*, trans. Ernesto Cardenal and José Coronel Urtecho, Colección Visor De Poesía (Madrid: Visor, 1979); William Carlos Williams, *Poemas*, trans. Ernesto Cardenal and José Coronel Urtecho (Madrid: Visor, 1985).
6. See K. Johnson 17; White 10.
7. In his letter, Ginsberg is specifically comparing the Indian "saddhu scene" to Beat sub-culture in the United States.
8. Cynthia Young discusses a similar political turn made by LeRoi Jones (Amiri Baraka) in her chapter "Havana Up in Harlem and Down in Monroe: Armed Revolt and the Making of a Cultural Revolution" (Young 18–53).
9. My translation.
10. *Seven Days in Nicaragua Libre* is not paginated. I will instead refer to section or entry date in my in-text citations.
11. For example, in 1979 (the same year that the Sandinistas seized Managua), Communist Vietnam faced accusations that it was torturing its political opponents, causing many of the activists who had traveled to Hanoi during the war (notably Joan Baez) to publicly reconsider their support of the regime (jumping on the "disassociation bandwagon," to use a phrase from a letter to *The Nation*). Joseph H. Crown, Letter, *The Nation* (14–21 July 1979): 40–41.
12. Signatories of the "Statement on Nicaragua" included everyone from Günter Grass to Arthur Schlesinger, though some signatories included caveats: Amos Oz added "a protest over Sandinista support of Arab terrorism," Bernard Malamud and Ronald Radosh signed a statement that excluded approval of the Sandinista government, and a hand-ful of signatories (including Alfred Kazin and Mario Vargas Llosa) signed a version of the statement that excluded support for Nicaragua *and* included disapproval of Soviet intervention in Central America. In this statement, then, one can see beginnings of the differences that become fractures in "You Don't Know It." Ginsberg's discussion of these writers' caveats, as well as the overall popularity of the statement at the Congress, are detailed in the unpublished manuscript *Nicaragua Express*. See Ginsberg and Warner 22–27.
13. This debate also involved some of his fellow delegates, such as Chicano poets Alurista and Alejandro Murguía (the co-editor of *Volcán*). A significant absence in "You Don't Know It" is an acknowledgement of these poets, whose allegiance with Sandinista

Nicaragua was considerably different than his own, bearing primarily on a shared experience of colonization and oppression rather than on the writerly vocation. For more about the relationship between Latino poets and artists in San Francisco and Nicaragua in this period, see Cordova.

14. In his interview with Steven White, Sergio Ramírez commented on the exportation from the United States of such reading material in the 1950s under Somoza: "The United States wanted to give us the gift of tons of *Reader's Digest* magazines to make us thoroughly anti-Communist. But worse than that, they wanted to turn us into mediocre thinkers." See White 83.

Part 2

Reflections on the
Transnational Beat

Chapter 8

Interview with Anne Waldman

Nancy M. Grace and Jennie Skerl

In Outrider, *Anne Waldman reflects on the concept of hybridity, employing an associative structure to move from hybrid cars, such as the Toyota Prius and Honda Civic, to genetically altered rice to the possibility of hybrid cosmologies to circuits observing Mars—before lighting upon "linguistic cross-breeding as well as imagined cross-breeding." These, she muses, might produce a clash of civilizations or gradual assimilation or exchange. Poetry, she decides, "is the rival government that can make sense or perhaps more importantly reflect and ponder the strange hybrid mirror" (57).*

In the following interview, Waldman extends this theory into the current universe of transnational and national Beat influences and alliances, discussing not only how her own work has been influenced by a global environment but also the importance of Beat poetics to all those worldwide who value free speech, tolerance for diversity, and honesty. The interview was conducted over telephone and through e-mail by Nancy Grace and Jennie Skerl in May and June of 2011.

Nancy Grace: Let's start with definitions. Since they are used differently in different disciplines and other contexts, what are your working definitions of "transnational" and "global"?

Anne Waldman: I'll go to the Sanskrit and Buddhist term *"Pratitya samutpada,"* the co-arising and interconnectedness of all beings, which is something we invoke at the Kerouac School at Naropa University in Boulder, Colorado, which has been a nexus for poetics study and various writing practices. William S. Burroughs, a frequent faculty member in the early days, invoked "time and space travel" as an imaginative practice for the writer, and notions of auspicious coincidence—and presented lectures on the telekinetic experiments of Konstantīns Raudive, the Latvian writer (1909–1974) behind the "iron curtain." One could see the cut-up practice as a possibility for global "message." On a more mundane plane, poets, writers, scholars, and students come from other parts of the world to visit and participate here, and the dialogue often becomes transnational, and exchange ensues: USA-India, USA-Mexico, and the like.

Then you have the quantum physics "entanglement," referring to the fact that particles can be in two places at once and instantly coordinate their properties. A long-distance romance. Going beyond national boundaries, simply, would be the classic definition. But what we have in these terms is the more radical philosophical idea of how our high-speed technologies have heightened the possibilities for human interaction on such a massive scale, and perhaps dangerous scale. You have the unleashing of toxicity as in the Fukushima tragedy, or the BP Macondo disaster, which is affecting generations of flora and fauna, and sea life.[1] Horrible. Yes, global. Plutonium and oil slicks have no boundaries. This fundamental change in the temporal and spatial contours of our social reality and existence has huge implications for the future, which in a way has already arrived. The deeply troubling side of all this is the fascist potential as we see more and more decisions made by the "executive," where we have the high-speed imperative of modern warfare. And global positioning and the cruel, long-distance killing of people through drones and the like. Now "they"—this hydra monster—are developing "weather weaponry" to create earthquakes and floods on enemy turf. It's the large corporations and arms industry that run the show, and they will stop at nothing, including murder of the planet and all its denizens. Interesting and toxic times for the "global."

NG: In that troubling context, then, what's your understanding of the ways in which poetry and other forms of literature are being transmitted and translated across state boundaries?

AW: I think any global citizen, writer or otherwise, would share the concerns I've just mentioned. But I am interested in how this "translates" both ways. The current state or awareness of global poetics—albeit among a privileged few—seems healthier than it's been in the past here in the United States. There would seem to be greater knowledge and scholarship and appreciation of the contemporary literature of other countries and cultures—again, among a certain modest population of writers and readers—and of hybridity and diasporas in my own culture as well. And that the Beat Literary Movement and all of its cultural iconic implications—and by extension the New American Poetry— continue to magnetize scholars and translators in much of the world. To some extent, an exchange is sustained. This was always important, certainly to Allen Ginsberg, and one thinks of the way he sought out Bengali poets in Calcutta in the 1960s and stayed connected to the Hungry Generation of poets, promoting their work and literary history.[2]

There was a "French connection" to writers and translators in Paris, which was enhanced through John Ashbery and Kenneth Koch and others living or visiting in the 1960s, and keeping up those literary associations and projects. Janine Pommy Vega, who taught prison workshops for decades, had lived in Bolivia, wrote of it, and traveled the world until her recent death,[3] so there's a precedent for many of us involved in the *Outrider* culture.[4]

Jennie Skerl: Why do poets, Beat poets, you, in particular, travel, and what is the value or purpose of travel for the poet and poetry?

AW: I travel to study and extend a sense of community through my work and the work of others. I also travel to Asia as pilgrimage. I certainly attend more literary festivals abroad, traveling and returning to India and China, sites beyond the literary nexus of Europe, which was not the case forty years ago. I remember how excited Allen Ginsberg was when he first traveled to China in the 1980s. He perceived it as a further "opening of the field," as China had essentially missed modernism, the New American Poetry, and beyond. Now scholars are tackling Frank O'Hara, as well as watching Fred Astaire and Ginger Rogers movies. I have lectured and presented my own work recently in unusual places, including Kerala, India, where I visited three Muslim colleges. At an American [U.S.] literature festival in Wuhan, China, in 2009, scholars were dissecting Charles Reznikoff and Lorine Niedecker, translating Langston Hughes and Language Poetry. There were papers on Philip Whalen and Gary Snyder. All this is salutary in terms of the current generations of poets crossing and trans-migrating borders. Poets continue to be fluid in this way, and many I know are active translators—and also curious about Zen Buddhism and Tibetan Buddhism, a normally verboten subject, because of the influence of those spiritual philosophies on Snyder, Philip Whalen, and Ginsberg. If you are going to study the Beats, it's imperative to look at gender, race, black culture, drugs, Buddhism, the fellaheen worlds of Tangier, Mexico, India, the influence of jazz, the historical post–World War II framework, the doldrums of the Eisenhower years, and more. All this is salutary in terms of the current generations of poets crossing and trans-migrating borders.

Significantly, however, although contemporary foreign literature is taught in the United States, what is most experimental and exploratory may fall between the cracks as the publishing record continues to be somewhat embarrassing here. We have the exceptions of the New Directions, Dalkey Archive, Archipelago Books, and City Lights, and certain university presses. But I published my Beat anthology with Mondatori in Milan, and most of my own work is published by small presses abroad, such as the One Woman Press in the Czech Republic, which has since closed down—or Maelstrom in Brussels. *Manatee/Humanity* is being translated into French.[5] And a book in China will be from a university press in Wuhan.

NG: What is it about non-U.S. presses that make them more amenable to the exploratory/experimental?
AW: We live in a conservative and corporate business culture in the United States. There is a longer tradition of intelligent literary and philosophical discourse, certainly in Europe and parts of Asian, at least in my experience. However, the next anthology from The Kerouac School is tentatively entitled *Cultural Rhizomes at Naropa* and is being published by Coffee House Press in 2012. I'm editing it with Laura Wright.

NG: What's the specific focus?
AW: The anthology focuses on lectures, talks, and forums in the field of cross-cultural poetics that have been presented at the Summer Writing Program. The kinds of pieces include "The State of Romania" by Andrei Codrescu; "Hidden Female Shamanic Traditions," Barbara Tedlock; "Hip-Hop Culture," Alexs Pate; "Cross-Cultural Themes in Fiction," Bhanu Kapil and Renee Gladman; "Night Fish and Charlie Parker: Contemporary Vietnamese Poetry," Linh Dinh; "Moving Across Languages, Borders, and Cultures," Heriberto Yepez, Myung Mi Kim, C.S. Giscombe, and Sherwin Bitsui; "Savoring Death in Mexico," Alberto Ruy-Sanchez; "Cultural Activism," a panel with

Akilah Oliver, Joanne Kyger, and Eleni Sikelianos; "Seven Minutes in Translation" by Pierre Joris; and Allen Ginsberg on Fiji song sticks,

NG: Definitely a global focus and a fascinating re-mix of Beat and other poetic movements, which leads me to ask about the effects of a global economy on arts production today. How have you seen this reality change over the past several decades?

AW: The Internet. Huge reality shift of interconnectedness. The literary discourses that go on have greater facility, fewer boundaries. Speed. It all happens more quickly. Correspondence, exchange, many other "global" projects. I worked on an arts project with schoolgirls in Marrakech in June 2011, and I designed the pedagogy from my desk in New York, a plan working with poetry, visual arts, video, and music. Two of the other artists also came from the U.S., the cellist Ha-Yang Kim and videographer/documentarian Alystyre Julian. The project was sponsored by a Paris-based American poet and her husband, who is from Morocco, and their Tamaas Foundation, which is involved with small educational and literary arts and translations projects.

Virtual publishing is also growing. E-books. Kindle and other technologies. A lot remains to be seen about how this affects/enhances literature. My Penguin contracts, though, request that I give rights for "forms not even invented yet." I am not sure how this affects the individual artist/writer's economy directly, but one's "profile" is available everywhere. More exposure, a larger audience perhaps. There is also the question of intellectual property rights. We've seen the music industry go virtual. Who shops in stores for records or CDs anymore? Whenever I perform, there's an almost immediate accessibility to the work a few hours later on YouTube.

NG: An as artist, how do you feel about signing away rights to forms that don't even exist and having your work almost immediately posted on YouTube?!

AW: Sometimes I don't sign those fine print clauses. I'd like to know more about these projected new forms for literature; could they travel to Mars in 300 years? If we are thinking globally, and especially if the work has an immediacy in terms of political and ecological issues, I'm interested in the communication and response. Often a dialogue ensues. And one finds many like-minded and curious individuals out there, who might navigate to the Naropa Website. We decided some years back to make many of the early taped recordings of lectures, readings, and colloquy from the Kerouac School available free of charge. The Naropa Audio Archive, with thirty-eight years of lectures and readings, continues to demand care and attention. We hope to have everything digitized and up and running in several years. You could take a whole online course, or a full degree, based on the holdings of The Jack Kerouac School at Naropa. The archive is our inscription against time, in time, beyond time. In this case, a significant cultural legacy and a memory bank. We need to preserve these major literary histories because the dominant culture will erase them.

JS: Do you think bohemia can exist in cyberspace?

AW: Sure. It's a state of mind. Here, in the U.S. belly of the beast—"inside"—I still think it possible—if you're curious—to find an engaged and progressive artistic community. And much has moved into the academy, the archive as it were—one of the viable places economically for artists. I am not in traditional academia, but it seems a space artists have to negotiate. It's heartening to see what has been built on that more experimental, and in most cases, progressive ethos. The intelligence on the street is that there will be a Beat scholar housed at many colleges and universities in the coming years. The Neuyrican Café, the Bowery Poetry Club—they're also still going. There's a HOWL festival in downtown New York City each fall.[6]

NG: But what about the significance of Beat Generation writers transporting key American values around the globe?

AW: The values continue to reflect issues of candor, or Whitman's "adhesiveness," empathy, free speech, first amendment rights, tolerance on matters of gender orientation, investigative poetics, an awareness of the primary influence of black culture, the interest in the "fellaheen" worlds or what goes on below the borders or crossing borders, psychological and paranormal and neurological investigations. An interest in Zen and Tibetan Buddhist psychology and spiritual practice. Matters of ecology. I am still actively involved with the Rocky Flats Guardianship project[7] and talk about this extensively here and abroad. Many film documentaries and portraits of the Beats travel the world over. Even the recent *Howl*, which is a fictionalized movie of the poem, attests to a continued popular interest.[8] Over the years, these values have affected radical shifts in consciousness and progressive thinking, which is extremely significant politically. I think of writers and activists in Prague during their Velvet Revolution, having *samizdat* copies of *Naked Lunch*, "Howl," and Diane di Prima's *Revolutionary Letters*.[9] There was direct access to Václav Havel, himself an intellectual and playwright. He attended my reading there with Allen in 1991. The Sandanistas also had links to Beat work and writers.[10] An entrepreneurial friend of mine in Florence started his own City Lights bookstore and press for a time.

NG: How then does literature as a vehicle of social protest connect to transnational movements?

AW: Like-minded individuals find their adhesiveness on a range of issues. I was involved with Italian poet friends in protests in support of Tibet when I was on a residency in Venice a few years ago. Buddhist artists and activists all over the world stay in touch. Our Naropa program in Bali did some local ecology work, and a community of Balinese artists and teachers helped develop our program there, which sadly ended in 2002 after some terrorist incidents in the region. I have been asked to present talks on the Beat Literary Generation and their legacy in terms of social protest everywhere I migrate, from Japan to India to Indonesia.

JS: What about your relationship with the Schule für Dichtung in Vienna? How is it related to Naropa's Jack Kerouac School for Disembodied Poetics?

AW: The founders of the Schule für Dictung—Ide Hintze, who is the director; Christian Loidl; and Christina Huber—attended the Summer Writing Program in the mid-1980s and founded a poetry school based on many of Naropa's principles and, in particular, the structure of our summer program. It was not an academic institution, more of an arts project, but it held roster workshops, which were conducted in German, Spanish, and English. The accompanying festivals brought poets from Viet Nam, Siberia, many far-flung places.

The emphasis was on orality and performance. They also had the participation of great Austrian writers, such as Ernst Jandl, Friederike Mayrocker, and Hantel Hartmann. The sessions were usually just a month. I worked there one fall as a guest director. Students were attracted from other parts of Europe, and an ex-pat community writing in English was quite involved. The Schule still has some programming, an online component, and a fascinating archive. I visited there a few years ago, taught a weekend workshop, and gave a reading, and I also keep in touch with dear friends there.[11]

NG: What about the ways in which Beat writers incorporated values from outside the continental United States? Certainly, we know about how they revitalized Western interest in Eastern religions.
AW: As for the other way around, Allen brought India into the activist consciousness and juxtaposed chanting mantra with political activism, with a nod to Gandhi. There's also impressive scientific neurological work examining meditative practices of Buddhism and consciousness. My apprenticeships in Indonesia and studies in Tibetan Buddhism have informed my work and teaching and poetics at Naropa and elsewhere. Gary Snyder travels to Asia for eco-conferences and brings back tangible "field notes" information. I've met scholars and feminists the world over whose work often inflects my own thinking on these issues. Hearing a talk by Helene Cixious in England in the '80s was important—on new methods of exchange for women: gift economy, linguistic changes, the woman's body as container and contained. I spent time in Umbria with Mexican photographer Graciella Iturbide whose photographs of women are extremely powerful, with their social and political implications. Many of the festivals of late are run by women—"Le voix d'Amerique" in Montreal, some events in Sarajevo. Giada Daino, a translator of Ferlinghetti and others, has organized festivals in Calabria. I've never met Gaytri Spivak, but, having visited Benares's burning ghats and looked into "sati," I appreciate her book *Can The Subaltern Speak?*, an engrossing text on women's repression and identity.

Mexico also has an extraordinary literary tradition, and Octavio Paz was forging connections between his own culture and India from his stint as ambassador there.[12] It was wonderful to see Mexican novelists and poets featured at a recent book fair in Calcutta in 2010. Joanne Kyger continues to bring back diaristic accounts of time spent in Mexico. The cross-cultural fertilizations are numerous. I was reading to a small community of young poets at an eco-park close to the border with Bangladesh recently, traveling the long Jessore Road, site of terrible suffering immortalized in Ginsberg's poem of the same name.[13] I am experiencing a continuity in Allen's wake and try to pass on these legacies as well.

NG: No doubt there's a particular way in which Beat writers are significant in the post-9/11 global terrain.
AW: The link to Arab culture is fascinating through Paul Bowles and William S. Burroughs. Burroughs in his invocation of the Muslim Hassan i Sabbah, "the Old Man of the mountain," was prescient in terms of the internecine warfare going on in the Arab world, fanned by U.S. intervention and hegemony, these past decades. The historical Sabbah was one of the leaders of a militant Shi'a sect, a leader of subversive

assassins. One thinks of the Taliban. Al Qaeda. In *The Ticket That Exploded*, Burroughs's Sabbah in "operation rewrite" takes on the Nova Mob. There's the sense of the total abolition of the law. "Nothing is forbidden, everything is permitted" is Hassan i Sabbah's mantra.

NG: Literary studies has begun to recognize how American literature has long reflected hybrid forms of identity, even under the guise of nationalism, so I'm curious about your perception of how Beat poetics promoted or stymied such identities.

AW: There's Kerouac's *Tristessa*, the story of the impoverished Mexican prostitute who is addicted to heroin, which perhaps reifies certain stereotypes. But this is based on a personal encounter, and she's also portrayed as a saintly beauty. Perhaps more relevant here are Homi Bhabha's "takes" on the sense of a nation being an "imagined community," on cultural hybridity, the blur between boundaries; how the West needs to listen to its migrants and refugees, how its own national identities have shifted. These are issues beyond class and gender. And there's more literature from mixed identities now. The compression of time and space produces and allows patterns that go beyond national and personal identity.

I was also able to see, coming after, how Kerouac was not such an isolated loner but part of a radical milieu of hybridity and experimentation. And Burroughs was—par excellence—exploring consciousness and language and time travel and the deep "fix" of power and the state in his montages, in his dream work and "travel." He explored global addictions on a major scale and went deep inside his own demonic landscapes. This work with montage, cut-up, exploring consciousness through language has been immensely influential to many writers.[14] And that's not to forget the psychological implications of the lives of these writers as evidenced in the work, the poetics, the correspondence. Male bonding, homoerotic fixation. And exploring the relationship to the women in their lives, powerful figures in their own right. I think the critical work and scholarship on this literary community is just beginning. It's interesting, for instance, to see how Burroughs has been taken up by critical theorists/philosophers abroad—as in the work of Deleuze and Guattari, who also address Kerouac's writing.

Then we have scientific explorations into deep space and deep biology to draw on as well. For instance, my last book, *Manatee/Humanity*, attempts to get into the mind of a nonhuman elemental, catching other nuanced rhythms of mammalian "mind": "The manatee has more grey matter in the brain than man" and is "perhaps thinking archivally deeper than man / man with his boats and plastic and attitude."[15] The hybrid of identity switching through dream and linguistic invention, and seeing the identity as challenging social constructs seems a backdrop to this and recent work and performance. My long epic *The Iovis Trilogy: Colors in the Mechanism of Concealment* has myriad voices, including that of the child, embedded in its enormous epic weave.

I can't really describe with real depth all of what American poetry and literature is doing in these areas, as I am primarily focused on my own projects. But suffice it to say, in my experience, it's vast and exciting, and more and more women are creating radical texts in hybrid areas. I have been working in collaboration with Judith Malina of the Living Theatre, Steven Taylor as composer for the libretto for *Cyborg on the Zattere*, which includes twelve performers—musicians, singers, dancers—and with my son Ambrose Bye, whose meticulously composed music and soundscapes are featured in the recent CD "The Milk of Universal Kindness" [Fast Speaking Music 2011]. And I've co-written film scripts with my husband, filmmaker Ed Bowes ["Entanglement" 2009], as well as worked with the painter Pat Steir, who is inspired by the chance operations of John Cage and Buddhist philosophy. The libretto for *Cyborg* includes some of Ezra Pound's history and lines from the *Pisans* and was written in Venice.[16] I write a good deal on my travels; sections of *Iovis* originate in Vietnam, Japan, Indonesia.

NG: How does *Cyborg,* your most recent work, reflect transnational/global themes, especially with respect to the cyborg as a post-human or trans-human being that replicates natural systems? I'm thinking of Donna Haraway's provocative statement in "A Cyborg Manifesto" that she'd rather be a cyborg than a goddess.

AW: I see Ezra Pound in his cage at Pisa typing his cantos as a cyborg. I see his decline—the fascist broadcasts—as cyborgian, in that his anti-Semitic views were abetted by the power of the radio; although we use some of the transcripts in the piece, his hideous anti-Semitism, his "suburban prejudice," is weird and exposed. He might have been executed for his "crimes," his treason, against the state. Then you have the contrasted beauty and exploratory nature of the *Pisans*. Both, both, the knot of this problem everywhere. The poem is also a kind of cyborg, in terms of how it travels. Performance as cyborgian. The fascination for many of fascism— note the resonance of these words, its martial empire zone. Fascism from the Latin *fasces*, a bundle of rods tied around a bronze axe, a Roman symbol of power, of "strength through unity." The axe a cyborg. I think of Emily Dickinson's fascicles here as anti-fascistic—those bound beribboned handwritten gems, cutting though space and time.

We open the oratorio in a casino, a not so subtle nudge toward usury. Goldman Sachs, Morgan Stanley, etc., etc. I also see the war culture, implicated in this text, as cyborgian with its monstrous drones, or the new intercept systems that were played out in the capture of Osama bin Laden. I see myself a cyborg as I jet through the sky. The problems of Venice, where part of the oratorio is set, come into play—the *aqua alta*, the sinking island, the ecological degradation.

Another thought: Conceptual Poetics posits that nothing is newly interestingly originated, and we might as well just appropriate and spew out the same texts in new forms. Robotic poetics. The cyborg gives a frame to our racing technology. It's not a time for gods and goddesses. The old male heroes are in question and decline, doddering. The goddess seems a new-age trope, although I know the history better, and honor the female deities of the Buddhist pantheon, and the view of prajna—highest wisdom—environment—manifesting as a female precept.

I also continue to work overtime to make up for the paucity of male Beat sensitivity to the female experience and body, except as—for the most part—sexual object. There was neglect, yes; they stymied identity, knee-jerk sexism to some extent, although I never felt that personally, coming on the scene a bit later and established as "Mother Naropa," as Burroughs called me. I was also able to "get the goods" from these elders, which fueled my infrastructure work as an editor and curator. I would include them in my projects to "keep the world safe for poetry," tame them for women perhaps? Part of my alchemical practice?

NG: How can art be used to make the world a more humane place for women?

AW: I think it's a long process, making the world more humane for women, but I can only speak in a limited way as an artist who travels and presents my work and views of equality in varying contexts. I was recently working, as I noted, with teenage Berber girls in Marrakech. Women have only recently been granted certain rights in Morocco, since 2006: divorce, custody of children, property, and the like. The king just decreed a few weeks ago that the Berber language could be officially acceptable as a lingua franca. This is welcome news, but it's also an ancient language, and one wonders at the implications of such a tardy response.

NG: What about the impact of race and ethnicity related to transnational/global hybridity?

AW: My family is now a hybrid. I have several white/African American nephews and nieces—a mixed race grandchild. The mongrel and second generation Brit and Greek, plus the older Euro-Irish Italian-Jewish are also in the mix. My Greek mixed relatives are learning the language, traveling back. It's a huge subject. As Amiri Baraka says, you'd have to be "beyond the Van Allen belt" not to have African in you as a human.

NG: You're clearly a global traveler, that cyborg in a jet plane, so from your experiences, what is the legacy of the Beat literary movement inside and outside the United States?

AW: I think I've spoken of some of the "outside" legacy, the persistence of the power of that ethos, and there's the fact that these figures—Ginsberg, Kerouac, Burroughs, and others—were culturally iconic, holding a status that went beyond their writing. They were cultural heroes, affecting popular culture on an enormous scale abroad as well. Rock music, advertising, film, spirituality, the rucksack revolution. It's a different time now. The male "hero" is almost an endangered species, which is salutary from a feminist perspective.

NG: I'm not seeing a lot of female protagonists that carry much cultural weight these days either.

AW: But who are your male protagonists with cultural weight? Please name some. Females are woefully absent in the serious political discourse, agreed. However, creative people generally, both men and women, who have accomplished something, who shift the consciousness of a generation and beyond, are rarely visible now.

JS: Why do you think that is?

AW: There's great activity below the radar, and online, and there are remnants of bohemian lifestyle and deep quality and commitment to the creative work, of course, but much of what's visible is celebrity culture. It plays, it's economically lucrative, the idiot rogues of the political machine who never have anything intelligent to say. That's why the Occupy Wall Street "temporary autonomous zone"[17] is refreshing and stirring: There's no alignment with a political organization and no celebrity hierarchy.

JS: Are there specific ways, then, that avant-garde, outrider, alternative literary communities ultimately connect with each other across national borders?

AW: Through familiarity with the work and practices of one another. Through gift economy and mutual concerns about peace, the environment. Through intellectual discourse and the terms of the writing itself. Art may be the only antidote to the dystopic hegemonic monolithic death drive of empire and war. As I have said many times, there's something in humanity's consciousness that wires them for a practice that can reflect back something of the mystery of our consciousness, while we still have time.

Notes

1. The Fukushima Daiichi nuclear disaster is a series of equipment failures, nuclear meltdowns, and releases of radioactive materials at the Fukushima I Nuclear Power Plant, following the 9.0 magnitude Tōhoku earthquake and tsunami on March 11, 2011. It is considered the second worst nuclear disaster after Chernobyl. The BP Macondo disaster is also known as the Deepwater Horizon disaster. Deepwater was drilling on the Macondo Prospect; on April 20, 2010, an explosion at the site killed eleven men who worked on the platform.
2. The Hungry Generation or Hungryalist Movement was an Indian literary movement in the Bengali language that focused primarily on poetry and lasted from 1961 to 1965. It was led by Malay Roychoudhury, Samir Roychoudhury, Shakti Chattopadhyay, and Debi Roy (Haradhon Dhara). The poetry, which exemplified their belief in the physical pleasures of life and their mission to represent an impoverished, betrayed people, so disturbed the Indian establishment that they arrested several of the poets on obscenity charges. The movement has also been credited with significantly changing the language and vocabulary of contemporary Indian literature. Ginsberg traveled in India in 1962, spending quite a bit of time in Calcutta; he met and became friends with this group of young Bengali poets and kept it touch with them for years. They were aware of the Beat literary movement and published some Beat poetry in their journal, *Krittikas*; in turn, some of them were published in the United States and travelled to the United States.
3. Janine Pommy Vega: February 5, 1942–December 23, 2010.
4. In *Outrider*, Waldman presents the following explication of the term: "'OUTRIDER' was a term some of us adopted early on at the inception of The Jack Kerouac School of Disembodied Poetics. . . . I felt the need to define the lineage pedagogy and view of a burgeoning poetics program that was increasingly seeing itself outside the official verse literati culture academic mainstream. And capture, poetically, impetuously, the *zeitgeist* of that program" (39).
5. *Manatee/Humanity* was published in 2009 by Penguin.
6. The festival is sponsored by HOWL! Arts Inc., a not-for-profit organization inspired by the late poet Allen Ginsberg. Founded in 2003, the organization celebrates the artistic diversity of the East Village. See http://www.howlfestival.com/about/howlartsinc.
7. The Rocky Mountain Peace and Justice Center was founded in 1983 by a group of individuals involved in nonviolent resistance to the Rocky Flats nuclear weapons production plant. See http://rmpjc.org/. In July 2007, the U.S. Department of Energy transferred almost 4,000 acres of the site to the U.S. Fish and Wildlife Service, which created the Rocky Flats National Wildlife Refuge. Activists, however, remain concerned about the degree to which the site may still be contaminated.

8. *Howl* (2010), directed by Bob Epstein and Jeffrey Friedman, explores the genesis of Allen Ginsberg's poem "Howl" and the obscenity trial against Lawrence Ferlinghetti and City Lights, which published it.

9. The Velvet Revolution was the six-week period of November 17–December 29, 1989, which brought about the bloodless overthrow of the Czechoslovakian communist government.

10. See Hardesty's essay in this volume. The Sandanistas National Liberation Front overthrew the Somaza regime in Nicaragua in 1979, remaining in power until 1990.

11. The Schule was founded as an independent artists' project in 1991. See http://sfd.at /english/english-summary.

12. Paz served as Mexico's ambassador to India from 1962 to 1968.

13. According to the Allen Ginsberg Project (Web), "Jessore Road is the main road from Jessore, Bangladesh, into India, which hundreds of thousands of refugees used to flee the war of independence (Bangladesh Liberation War [March-Dec. 1971]) between West Pakistan and East Pakistan (soon to become Bangladesh). Allen was so distraught by what he saw that he wrote one of his more important poems, 'September on Jessore Road,' after he returned to New York."

14. See, for example, *Shift Linguals* by Edward S. Robinson (Rodopi 2011), which traces the literary legacy of the cut-up method.

15. The book is structured as a Tibetan Buddhist initiation called *wang* (empowerment), in which the enlightenment sought is empathy with other beings.

16. *Cyborg on the Zattere* is a two-act opera, recital format, by Waldman and musician/ composer Steven Taylor and is set in a casino on Wall Street; Pound's cage in Pisa, May 1945; St. Elizabeth's "madhouse"; and Venice, the Zattere (near where Ezra Pound lived and died). In the premier of the opera (April 20–30, 2011), Waldman played the cyborg character.

17. The term "temporary autonomous zone" originates with Hakim Bey's important manifesto *T.A.Z. The Temporary Autonomous Zone, Ontological Anarchy, Poetic Terrorism.* Brooklyn, NY: Autonomedia, 1985, 1991. n.d. Web. 13 Oct. 2011.

Part 3

Global Circulation

Chapter 9

"They . . . took their time over the coming": The Postwar British/Beat, 1957–1965

R. J. Ellis

A 1960 encounter between John Lennon and a Beat poet, Royston Ellis (Turner, *Hard* 20–21), a meeting which led to "The Beetles" being respelled "The Beatles," stands as one of the more visible signs of a complex postwar Atlantic cultural crossing—the Beats' arrival in the United Kingdom—that remains largely unelucidated. Adopting Robert von Hallberg's contention that "minor poetry" should be regarded as "one of the more reliable indices of the cultural level of a nation" (19–23), this essay considers how British Beat poetry might be recuperated to stand as an "index" of postwar British culture. However, a problem is created by the fact that, as Allen Fisher observes, the term beat "is weak."[1] So I have sought to consolidate it by approaching poets associated with the British Beat to discover their perspectives. Most refused to accept the label, a resistance signaled in this essay by separating the words *British* and *Beat* with a slash: British/Beat. An unease accompanies the term's Atlantic crossings that needs explicating.

To help me on my way, in 1999 and again in 2010, I asked almost forty poets questions about the British/Beat. Only a few identified themselves as Beats: Michael Horovitz, Pete Brown, Dave Cunliffe, Libby Houston, Steve Sneyd, and, from a younger generation, Ian McMillan.[2] Such lack of enthusiasm is predictable: writers mostly dislike compartmentalization (the "Angry Young Men" as much as the Beats), but another reason for rejecting the label rests in transatlantic tensions. On the one hand, mistrust over the quality of American Beat writing surfaces in the United Kingdom: Ginsberg's and Kerouac's occasional embrace of the confessional was unattractive;[3] Kerouac's unevenness was criticized and his Buddhistic leanings were uncongenial ("Kerouac is a spiritual simpleton" was one anonymous verdict in *Migrant*); Ginsberg fared better, but his advocacy of transcendental meditation and his "dodgy advocacy of LSD" were mistrusted (Brown II), while some found him "strident and loud" (McGough I); Corso was sometimes praised but also identified as limited and a "shit" when encountered.[4] Indeed, even Brown judged that other U.S. writers, such as Robert Creeley and Lawrence Ferlinghetti, were "more important than the [core] Beats" (Brown II). Such reservations were part of a larger U.K. hostility. Thurairajah Tambimuttu's *Poetry London*'s summer 1960 issue, retitled *Poetry London New York*, may have featured Ginsberg's "Poem Rocket," Corso's "Frightening Difference," and Kerouac's 215th Chorus from *Mexico City Blues*, but it also carried a fierce attack. The Beats, for Tambimuttu, were too "imprecis[e]," with "few . . . even worthy of print" (3–4, 10).

Though most British/Beats remained less condemnatory, stressing instead how the Beats provided a way into other U.S. writing, such as Kenneth Patchen's and Kenneth Rexroth's (Brown II; Burns II), such ambivalence makes British poets unlikely to subscribe to the appellation Beat. Reciprocally, Ferlinghetti, in 1963, "expressed unfavorable opinions of the English poetry he'd heard" during a visit in 1963, while Ginsberg disliked sharing the stage with a succession of bad "local" poets "monopolizing" the time at the 1965 Albert Hall "First International Poetry Incarnation." Ginsberg even covertly laid out part of his fee prior to a 1984 recreation of the event to hire Basil Bunting, Tom Pickard, and Roy Fisher "as balance for what he didn't enjoy about the other Brits" (A. Fisher I).[5]

So reasons exist for mutual antagonism and explain why writers such as Adrian Mitchell, one of Ginsberg's "bad local poets," reject any British Beat labeling: "Forget about British 'beats,'" he urges, "none of us were that" (Mitchell I). Mitchell's intransigence can introduce a chorus, aroused by my 1990 correspondence. Alexis Lykiard: "I don't think there were . . . any British Beats, except for Alex Trocchi"; George Cairncross: "I was never aware of a British Beat Movement"; Alan Dent: "I don't think such a thing exists"; Tom Pickard: "I don't think the term [is] very useful"; Gael Turnbull: "I don't find it very useful"; Roger McGough: "I'm not sure what it means"; Jim Burns: "I've always had a problem with it"; Tom Leonard: "the Beats didn't actually interest me"; Jeff Nuttall: "the best of us were not so much Beats as modernists"; Allen Fisher: "It's never occurred to me to use it"; Barry Cole: "MEANINGLESS." Barry Edgar Pilcher, whose self-stylization as "Britain's only beat poet" gains legitimacy faced with this chorus, anticipated its burden: "most poets . . . never seem to want to be associated with anything beat" (Pilcher I). Cole even suggests that Beat writing, when first encountered in the United Kingdom, seemed an "alien growth," albeit one very attractive to him (Cole II).

All this lends piquancy to Brown's 1959 poem, "Few":

Alone tired halfdrunk hopeful
I staggered into the bogs
at Green Park station
and found 30 written on the wall
Appalled I lurched out
[. . .]
thinking surely,
Surely there must be more of us than that [. . .] ("Few" 1)

Brown's sense of isolation in "Few," at least in part, relates to this antipathy toward the British/Beat label, not least because he had appeared in the "Bible of the Beats," the *Evergreen Review*, in 1959 (Brown, "Africa" 53). Understanding its sources, however, soon becomes not only a literary issue but also a matter of complex, hybrid cultural transnationalisms. Though substantially U.S. molded, both by U.S. writing and U.S. popular culture, multiple Atlantic crossings are involved. Beats drew promiscuously upon wider influences: Mexican, Mayan, and Aztec culture; British, European, Chinese, and Japanese literature and art—this list can lengthen. For Steve Sneyd, U.S. Beats were significant guides: their approach to Shelley, Blake, and Japanese poets "set these writers free from safe/defused boxes" (I), offering interpretations running against those of the New Critics in the States and the British academy. Yet plainly, other avenues exist as well: Arthur Waley, for example, provides another such avenue for British and U.S. Beats' far Eastern engagements.

However, the U.S. Beats were certainly catalysts. The euphoria of VE day and VJ day was quickly replaced by war-weariness and, for the left, memories of defeat in Spain and betrayal by Stalin (Hewison, *Siege* 3–72). In the United Kingdom, postwar austerity and rationing, made particularly necessary by U.S. insistence that Britain repay its war loans, made living conditions almost as harsh as during the war (Hewison, *Siege* 185; Hewison, *Anger* 14). Radical thought was marginalized, as the universities, dominated by Oxford and Cambridge ("Oxcam"), tended "to promote the ethics of the Cold War" (Hewison, *Anger* xii). The United Kingdom's futile invasion of Egypt after Nasser's 1956 Suez Canal nationalization and the USSR's brutal suppression that same year of the Hungarian uprising, which largely destroyed British Communist party membership, accentuated this. Cyril Connolly described the sociocultural climate as "bureaucratized and war-weary," so conformist that, in Burns's words, "it is difficult to convey just how square the square world was" (Connolly 305–306; Burns, *Beats* 81).

This period of austerity, encapsulated in the predominance of black and white in photography and film and the emergence of "kitchen-sink" realism, was typified by the quotidian privations of rationing—captured by Libby Houston's 1961 poem, "Post-War":

>   I remember
>   my mother
> talking about bananas
> in 1944
>   . . .
> they came in paper bags
>   in neighbours' hands
>   when they came
>   and took their time
>   over the coming (7)

The arrival of bright yellow transatlantic bananas, when finally de-rationed in 1954, clashed with austerity's drabness and metonymically foreshadowed the Beats' brazen upsetting of postwar U.K. culture's reticence: "The rawness and energy . . . was like

. . . a sunrise in a vault occupied by the dull Movement poets" (Patten I). As Tom Lowenstein puts it, "Snyder & G[insberg] challenge[d] the Brit-educated sensibility to imaginative travel" (I). Writing became not a means of recording black-and-white provincial austerity but a liberating space;[6] Ginsberg's trenchant "America . . . / Go fuck yourself with your atom bomb" signaled a colourful literary arrival (*Howl* 32).

For Horovitz, the Beat became a breaking out into celebration (I)—a contention borne out by the brightly colored covers of three British/Beat anthologies: Roche's 1967 *Love, Love, Love: The New Love Poetry*; Horovitz's 1969 *Children of Albion*; and Morgan's 1971 *C'mon Everybody*. These anthologies, along with Cunliffe's significantly earlier *Poetmeat* 8 (n.d.; c. 1964) and Allnutt, d'Aguiar, and Mottram's later *The New British Poetry* (1988), together constitute one picture of the scene I am tentatively mapping. Many of their poets were born in the early 1940s, so were teenagers when Andre Deutsch published *On the Road* in Britain in 1958. Interest before then was limited more to word of mouth; Yann Lovelock contends that the beginning of the British/Beat is linked to *On the Road*'s success—even though "Howl"'s censorship or sheer chance (such as Cairncross's accidental discovery of *Gasoline*) had led to earlier "pioneer" encounters (2). Though *The Town and City* was read by Dave Cunliffe in 1954 and David Tipton in 1955, and Tipton consumed both *On the Road* and Roy Fisher's copy of *Howl* in 1957 (Tipton I),[7] such early contacts were rare. The Beats broke through relatively late in the United Kingdom—during 1958/59—even if a few had already dug deeper (Tipton read *Evergreen Review* from its 1957 inception).[8] Symptomatically, Burns recalls reading "Jazz of the Beat Generation" in *New World Writing* in 1957 not realizing who "Jean-Louis" was, while Tipton claims he read the Beats without knowing that was what they were called. The Beat phenomenon only broke in the wake of *On the Road*'s reception and the repercussions of the censorship of "Howl."

This stirring of interest led to more exposure, and the adoption of new ways of speaking about society and the individual. Awareness rapidly blossomed: the renaming of the Beetles occurred within two years. Lee Harwood's account of encountering Beat writing is representative: "1958/9 Ferlinghetti—*Coney Island of the Mind* via a US student at Queen Mary College . . . 1959/60 Jack Kerouac's *On the Road* (via friends with U.S. contacts) and . . . City Lights pocket poets [. . .]—Corso's *Gasoline*, Ginsberg's *Howl*" (I). To this needs to be added Gene Feldman's and Max Gartenberg's 1959 transatlantic anthology *Protest: The Beat Generation and the Angry Young Men*, which also encapsulated in this juxtaposition how the U.S. Beat's protest writing was more colorful and often more alluring than the British Angry Young Men's, just as U.S. film's bright Technicolor dazzled British audiences.

This chronology, however, means the British/Beat had little contact with the first wave of U.S. Beat activity, instead catching the peak of Beat's second wave—a broader cultural phenomenon: "the Beat Generation," generated by the late 1950s hype around *Howl* and *On the Road*, and the rapid media takeover within which "beatnik" often became the slightly dismissive soubriquet of choice and "Beat" became both an international cultural and celebrity signifier.

The British/Beat's inspiration fed off this second wave; other origins, such as contacts with the "homeless men, misfits, tramps, ex-Servicemen & the rest who swarmed on bombsites and derries or shivered and coughed and spat . . . just generally drifting around," whom Chris Torrance regards as "the original" British Beats, were less significant.[9] The Beat that the British/Beats were attracted to was, in Nuttall's telling phrase, "Ginsberg's generation," implicitly recognizing how Kerouac and Corso were by the late 1950s in drug-dependent decline and how the Beats, already by then comprehensively media-processed, had acquired celebrity allure, a shift explaining how Nuttall can refer to the Beat movement as "middle-class" ("Bomb" 107).[10]

My term "allure" is intended to convey the glamour the U.S. Beats possessed: the glamour of the literary rebel, meshing with a contemporary fascination with the existential rebel, evident in the acclaim Colin Wilson's uneven *The Outsider* attracted in 1956.[11] The censorship of "Howl" and later *Naked Lunch* granted Beat writing an aura: hard to get hold of, it promised a quasi-existential authenticity. This aura was enhanced by a publishing time-lag between the United Stated and the United Kingdom: "Fifties' British editions of USA publications were usually officially released a couple of years after American publication . . . original imprints [were] . . . smuggled in . . . by servicemen" (Cunliffe, "Nomadic" n.p.). To this extent, Nuttall's claim that the Beat phenomenon was "a literary thing" is correct,[12] although Libby Houston suggests it is better to think of the Beat influence as deriving from a "Beat *mode*" featuring performance, accessibility, openness, freshness—"direct address" (I). David Miller urges that the British/Beat be related to the freight of "social rebelliousness" and "life attitudes associated with it" (I). What Miller means can be illustrated by the impact on Roger McGough of the interplay between Beat writing and photographs of Beat life taken by Fred McDarrah in Elias Wilentz's *Beat Scene* in 1960 (when McGough was 23): "How I longed to escape from Liverpool & read at the Gaslight Café with Diane di Prima and hang out with Ted Joans in his Astor Place Studio" (II). So Steve Sneyd regards the British/Beat as a "lifestyle choice"; Cairncross calls it "an attitude of mind" (Sneyd I; Cairncross I).

The Beats, then, might be best thought of not as a "literary" but a "cultural thing"—if, that is, one can recover the sense extant in the late 1950s and early 1960s that culture as a concept was inextricably linked to art—enshrined in Nuttall's 1968 proposal, "Culture [is] . . . the broad effect of art" (*Bomb*, 8). The arrival of the Beat is the reason why the Beetles became the Beatles, but it is also part of the reason why the Beatles became a legitimate object of cultural study—and such an astonishing success.

Quite simply, the British/Beats' American encounters reconstituted for them the category "art" and redefined what being a poet entailed: "To Be a Poet" as Libby Houston suggests, was decapitalized. Poetry's former exclusivity was, in the eyes of the British/Beats, shattered by the U.S. Beats' impact and their excoriating dismissal of the New Criticism, crystallizing British/Beat discontent with the Movement's and Group's dominance of U.K. poetry. Eric Mottram's vituperative assault on the Movement as "a boring . . . establishment clique" ("The Establishment," significantly, being a 1953 coinage), part of his general attack upon what he saw as the conservatism of postwar British literary culture and his advocacy of U.S. and British "new writing" (conspicuously including William S. Burroughs and Ginsberg as well as the poets of the British Poetry Revival),[13] introduces another chorus. Consider, for example, Burns: "I didn't want to know about Kingsley Amis/Philip Larkin/

The Movement and that whole Little England thing" (I); Nuttall: "I . . . despised bourgeois qualities of Movement and Group" ("British Beats"); and Dom Sylvester Houedard: "the Movement . . . [was] depthless and unoriginal" (151). For Nuttall, the Movement and Group generated an "insular provincialism [in] British poetry" (*Bomb* 105). Insofar as the Movement can be regarded as a "skeptical" reaction against what J. D. Scott described as the "lush" apocalyptic and new romantic poetry confronting the "despair of the forties," it did not prove inspirational for postwar youths finding no more comfort in the Group, which, for my purposes, can be seen as a relatively "local affair" (Scott 400; Powell 201). Tom Pickard sums it up: "a diet of Larkin and the Movement . . . and the usual dreary offerings from the Oxcam Literary Mafia . . . made me despair" (156). But, as forties despair was followed by 1950s austerity, a return to the 1940s apocalyptic and new romantic modes (however much Dylan Thomas might be admired) rarely resulted. Instead, interest in British modernists (such as Bunting, Roy Fisher, and Norman MacCaig) revived, while the British/Beats' trail led away from the Movement's and Group's relatively formal diction and metrics into an exploration of the "New American Poetics," even within the heart of the academy: Lykiard in 1960, for example, held poetry and jazz sessions in Cambridge, and under his editorship, *Granta* started "publish[ing] stuff on the Beats, Nouvelle Vague & c." (II).

At the center of this lies the issue of accessibility and how a redefinition of writing and its relation to culture could be effected: Roy Fisher said, "I was glad to see someone had kicked out one of the side walls of the jail" (I). Harwood believed that

> [i]t was an immense release. . . . poetry seemed the territory of a particular social group (middle class, academic, etc.) and talked in a remote and artificial and passionless language . . . [in] rigid forms . . . the Beats somehow were a green light to write directly how one felt with spontaneity & wildness (I).

As Lovelock records, the Beats licensed an "escape [from] . . . a stifling home environment . . . the social climate was . . . appalling" (4-5). It was an opening-up, as a web of people more-or-less simultaneously discovered the release promised by the Beats: a London/Oxford University axis that mixed promiscuously with others (such as Johnny Byrne) and took to widespread travelling (involving Horovitz, Brown, Houston, and Byrne); a Carshalton group (Chris Torrance calls it "the Mob": Torrance, William Wyatt, Dave James, Don Bodie); an anarcho-cultural group (Jeff Cloves, Dennis Gould—who were decidedly less Technicolor); an Edinburgh/ Glasgow nexus; informal groups in Newcastle and Liverpool; and individuals energetically networking (Burns, Cunliffe, and Vine) or taking up "insider/outsider" positions, passionate about U.S. films, jazz, and writing, such as Lykiard (II).

A strongly regional, often northern dimension emerges, centered on Edinburgh, Glasgow, the north-east, Liverpool, the north-west—plus Bristol, where Vine was based. It is in this regional, predominantly northern, aspect to the British/Beat that a class dimension exists—its northern accent suited disaffiliated protest. Cunliffe starts "Some British Beat History" with the words, "Grim cobbled Northern industrial streets & chill pavement slabs" (17). But the British/Beat did not typically return to affectionately critical but relatively conservative portraits of gray, class-bound lives, like those found in much of the writing by postwar Angry Young Men (see Feldman and Gartenberg 192-242). The British/Beat instead took up, often in reading-performances, the Beats' egalitarian search for vibrant cultural variety.

However, different nodes of British/Beat performance evolved different empha-ses. Lykiard sees north-east British/Beat writing as "closer in spirit to the Beat sen-sibility" than Merseyside's "naive (mis)appropriation" (I)—perhaps because of the overwhelming vitality of the Merseyside pop-music scene and because contact with the London-based Horovitz/Brown axis lent a gentle performance-oriented play-fulness to the Mersey poets' sound. Indeed, variations somewhat center upon the degree of intimacy established with Horovitz's caravanserai. When Houston views Cunliffe's poetry as "heavy, very heavy" (Int), this is perhaps because what might be called a "Cunliffe ambit" (his "British Beat" articles featured Ted Andrews, Harold Learey, Neal Oram, Burns, Gould, Reg Bridges, Harwood, Jeff Cloves, Pilcher, Torrance, and Sneyd) was more left-political and more working-class than Horovitz's generally more "middle-class" group,[14] which unsurprisingly possessed the entrepreneurial *nous* to harness the Atlantic Beats' commercial potential.

Though such schematizations founder on the fluidity that characterizes all Beat exchanges, they help identify how the British/Beat's celebratory break-out allowed some British/Beats to hone dexterous, free, often short, even *slight,* performance-oriented poetry possessing a relevant immediacy that is far from easy to achieve or sustain (Houston Int). It was also shocking. Indicative of this is both Brown's enthu-siasm over how Ginsberg, during a largely overlooked first U.K. visit in 1956, took George Melly to task ("No, man, you've got to shoot come all over the audience" [qtd. by Brown Int]), and how Ginsberg explicitly brought the issue of the atomic bomb into his verse. "Howl" is the crucial model here, conjoining portraits of "mad-men" "fucked in the ass by saintly motorcyclists and scream[ing] with joy" with denunciation of "the scholars of war" (*Howl* 9, 12). The importance of generating shock can be indicated both by Houston's anecdote of how at one 1961 reading an attempt to recite an expurgated version of Ginsberg's poem was shouted down and by her recognition of how the strident directness of the U.S. Beats' attacks on Cold War mind-sets gave British/Beats more confidence in their own CND (Campaign for Nuclear Disarmament), anti-war allegiances (Int).

Though the alienation of the British/Beats generally took softer forms, they do repeatedly project a sense of standing outside both political and poetry establish-ments and often relate this to issues of class. Instructively, the more metropoli-tan—and potentially more comfortably placed—British/Beats were the ones who could take to the road; Horovitz, Houston, Brown, and Johnny Byrne lived and read together, even for a while attempting at one Edinburgh Festival to live off their gigs' takings—an enterprise abandoned when they became "dangerously malnour-ished" (Houston Int, II). Most other (largely northern) British/Beats rested more confidently in a location within or coeval to the working class, and for these there is something in Horovitz's idea that the British/Beat represented a break from the "received ideas" of what forms working-class writing could assume (Int). But com-mon to both Britain's Metropolitan Beats and Northern Beats is an opening-up of possibilities—of circulating and being heard and published—as the habits of mind of the age of austerity faded.

I now want to explore the cultural relations of this British/Beat field. The British/ Beats' keen interest in things American needs to be carefully identified as an extension of growing popular interest in the United States, but of a particular kind, oriented toward aspects of its culture—"rebellion," youth, African American culture, jazz, sexual frankness—an enthusiasm that conflicted with a quite widespread, contrasting, anti-Americanism in this period. A source of this antipathy seems to be the seductiveness of U.S. culture, which even caused Richard Hoggart, founding father of British cultural studies because of his advocacy of defining far more broadly what is significant in British cultural history, to be uneasy about the way his "Juke-Box Boys" in 1957

> [spend] their evening listening . . . to the 'nickelodeons' . . . girls [and] . . . boys aged between fifteen and twenty with . . . an American slouch . . . almost all [the tunes] are American . . . [with] the kind of beat which is currently popular . . . [and] liv[e] to a large extent in a myth-world compounded of a few simple elements which they take to be . . . American. (282–283)

Such anti-Americanism, however, simultaneously defined what could be alluring about U.S. culture (that which the academy and/or the establishment rejected), and there the Beats seemed to be located.

The British/Beats' embrace of American culture was skeptical, partial, discriminative, and strategic, but always rooted in an attraction to the idea of open, egalitarian access and based upon a cultural disaffiliation founded upon a mistrust of what British/Beats saw as elitist discourses of education in the United Kingdom, offering constrictive definitions of culture and literature that neglected contemporary writing. Barry Miles claims that as a sixteen-year-old in 1959, the most contemporary poet he had encountered in school had been "Siegfried Sassoon" (I), while Adrian Mitchell satirically writes that between 1952 and 1955 he spent three years at Oxford studying "Modern English Literature (500–1815)" (I). A strong "anti-academia" line runs through the British/Beat, a trait displayed perhaps more fiercely than that found in the core American Beat writers. Horovitz's 1962 *New Departures* editorial is representative: "universities are out of the question for experimental and adventurous spirits" ("Editorial" 41).

Generally, a youthful desire to evade cultural foreclosure exists. Lovelock suggests that the term "generation gap" became common at this time, and I relate this to how turning to the United States as a "way out West" could be set against what Keith Tuma describes as a "mainstream . . . wounded rhetoric about American boorishness and cultural imperialism . . . sustaining . . . profoundly anti-intellectual and insular poetries" (5, 15). The British/Beat broke away from this vicious, colorless, and compliant insularity, as when Mitchell celebrated Barry Bondhus's 1966 Vietnam protest (dumping "buckets of human excrement" in his draft board's files) with terms linking him to American comic-book superheroes: "Look, look at Barry Bondhus— / That boy can fly" ("Moon" 27). Such popular U.S. cultural references enabled British/Beat disaffiliation to articulate itself accessibly, and though what resulted was sometimes a partial interpolation into America's Western myth of escape, what also emerges is an almost studied, selective avoidance of indiscriminate pro-Americanism.

The partialness of the British/Beats' embrace of U.S. culture stems from the way that their contacts with the United States repeatedly encountered a hybridity that disturbed any representation of a U.S. "dominant": the U.S. Beats themselves, the bohemian and avant-garde nexus they made visible, and U.S. servicemen—white, black, Mexican, immigrant—offered a mix of cultural influences and identities, which the British/Beats picked up on—with jazz clubs a particular focus, since import restrictions made U.S. jazz records hard to obtain at this time. Given the preponderance of Americans in the United Kingdom whose stake in the dominant was often uncertain, complex Atlantic exchanges result, which can readily understand Ginsberg's "America, I'm putting my queer shoulder to the wheel" as not a call to resume America's national duty but as a complex dialectical proposal—partly knowingly subsumed, yet ironically recognizing this subsumption, and resisting it, pushing the wagon in a queer direction ("America," *Howl* 23). Ginsberg's phrase recognizes that complex negotiations are possible when confronting mainstream cultural maxims, especially when projected in popular mass-cultural productions that can be taken up in a variety of ways. The British/Beat adopted this species of subtle positioning, refusing to view popular mass-culture as solely the preserve of cultural dopes. Nuttall's seamless slides across the Atlantic when adumbrating the emergence of his uneasy opposition in his *Bomb Culture* in 1968 is enabled by this alteration, and by the attendant nationwide presence of American arts in these years. For example, certain films had a huge impact: Kazan's *On the Waterfront* in 1954 (with Marlon Brando's acting), *A Face in the Crowd* (1957), *Death of a Salesman* (1957), *Rebel without a Cause* (1955), and *The Wild One* (1953). U.K. audiences were startled by these films and attracted to them. Television's introduction in 1955 (Gardiner 102) and especially music, both jazz and popular music, were other fields of re-negotiation. American artists—Patti Paige, Frankie Lane, Guy Mitchell—alongside key iconic figures of the 1950s, such as Doris Day and Frank Sinatra and his 1955 "Songs for Swinging Lovers," had a huge impact. These must be set beside the growth of R&B and rock (Bill Haley and the Comets in 1954, followed by Elvis Presley, Little Richard, and Fats Domino) meshing with a surging interest in big bands, swing jazz, and the blues.[15]

Cataloguing these examples makes it easy to see both their sheer variety and prolixity. It is symptomatic that Kenneth Allsop's 1957 "free-associations set off . . . by the phrase 'The Fifties'" is riddled with American elements (Louis Armstrong, the Actor's Studio, James Dean, Brando, jeans, jukeboxes, Monroe, Presley, TV advertising jingles, horror comics), even though Allsop himself is appalled by the "picture it gives of a sick and meretricious society" (40). Such fears both buttressed representations of Presley and rock music as the threatening face of U.S. culture (stoking up "Rock Around the Clock" and "Presley" riots in U.K. cinemas) and ensured that embracing the U.S. Beats and other imported cultural transatlantic productions was more radical than now seems likely.

I am of course *not* claiming that a desire to watch American films or listen to jazz or Bill Haley somehow made one a proto-British/Beat. The Atlantic constituted a political arena in which the furor over the Beats must be regarded as only part of a larger series of cultural exchanges between the United Kingdom and the United States. The British/Beats intervened in all this, however, by taking up and promoting U.S. popular cultural images of rebelliousness and disaffiliation.

This promotion depended most upon their Beat-derived accent on performance, which led to a further counter-hegemonic populist widening-out—a democratization drawing people into the arena of poetry via their overlapping waves of activity—with "readings," jazz collaborations, and "Liverpool types" (McMillan Int) offering audiences an integrated interlace of performance, energy, "fun," protest, and disaffiliation. It would be simplistic to portray the British/Beat as a concerted force for social revolution, however minor: Sneyd cautions cogently that "illusions that it wd break the control of an Establishment elite at the 'top end' were just that, because of . . . the skill of such people at capturing/taming/absorbing into their 'control structures'" (I). Symptomatically, in this respect, one fount of British/Beat performance was Oxford, within the golden triangle (London/Oxford/Cambridge): Lovelock went to Oxford, where he met Ian Hamilton, whose *Tomorrow* published Horovitz's first Beat-influenced writing; Houston was at Oxford; and Lykiard edited *Granta* in Cambridge. This scene was predominantly made up of writers from "middle class background[s]" (Lovelock 4), though Brown, a frequent visitor, is one exception (Houston II). Yet, nevertheless, the British/Beats were visibly both offering and *doing* something different: "this went far beyond poetry and fiction. It all connected with the 'radical' spirit of the time and the hoped-for collapse of the old system" (Harwood I); "I liked the idea of poetry engaging with a movement for social change" (Dent I). In this sense, the British/Beat "kicked out the walls"—for not only working-class but also the middle-class youth in an increasingly mobile social context.

What this disparate group achieved in common via networking and/or reading tours was a breakout into "the life of the country" to find different, new poetry constituencies and communities.[16] For the Oxford/London axis, reading performances were indeed the starting point. Houston sees performance as British/Beat's inaugural phase, as Edinburgh sub-Fringe readings (1959/60/61) rapidly spawned other enterprises: "Live New Departures," "inspiring . . . newly higher-educated working class young men and women" as it toured round Britain out of London (I); Brown's "Goings On" readings in the Soho Club and poetry readings in the Partisan Coffee Bar in London; "Henri's Hope Street Poets at Liverpool's Everyman Theatre"; readings at the Grove Pub in Leeds; Newcastle-upon-Tyne's Morden Tower readings (where the inaugural guest was Brown and where Ginsberg and Burroughs read); and bookshops such as Ultima Thule (in Newcastle) and Trent Bridge Bookshop (in Nottingham). These and other endeavors played a key role in the 1960s "British Poetry Revival," to which the pop connections forged in Liverpool by Henri, McGough, and Patten (via his magazine, *Underdog*) were crucial, enabled by the Beatles' star status at the time (Mottram, "Revival" 86–117).

Through the influence of this "Performance Beat," "what we [British/Beats] did took root," Horovitz maintains (I). "Took root" to the extent that even poets such as Tom Leonard, despite having a clear sense of his difference from the British/Beat, concedes that the British/Beats aided him "tangentially," since usually it was they who "organized readings" which in turn had an impact on his poetics: his participation contributed to his poetry's accessibility and pace (I). Leonard's concession is a sign of how performance became crucial, influencing form, content, and phrasing. Brown and Horovitz's evolving poetry performance co-operation, *Blues for the Hitchhiking Dead*—defined as "neither poetry nor jazz but jazzpoetry" by Jerry Hooker—stands as one benchmark. The idea of poetry performance was to become a key British/Beat legacy: "the Beat goes on" in both punk ranting (John Cooper Clarke, Joolz, Seething Wells, Attila the Stockbroker) and pop. The complex relationship between performance poetry and pop lyrics is signaled as early as 1960, when Lennon regarded Royston Ellis as at "the converging point of rock 'n' roll and literature."[17]

Thinking through how to build upon oral phrasing was crucial. Consider, for example, William Wyatt's poem "monk theme":

> . . . the progress
>   he makes
>
> skipping from note to note
>   he tumbles
>   like a waterfall
>
> over sad &
>   gentle rocks (314)

Horovitz contends that one can value the poem for its "sound effects . . . rather like Thelonius Monk, with his wonderful dynamics and yet his steadiness . . . the play of vowels and consonants and the way the poem is laid out." For Horovitz, these "anti-formal things" signaled the difference (Int). The British/Beats, however, may not always have taken up their jazz inspirations accurately; as Roy Fisher puts it, "as a musician, I found the jazz link a little specious and touristic" (I). Brown accepts this: "Horovitz and I were poor musicians, really, at the time" ("Riding"). Yet aurally a paradigm shift was affected.

This signals another central element to the British/Beat: it's partly Ginsberg-inspired enthusiasm for searching out new poetic modalities (in the case of Wyatt, surely, William Carlos Williams—one of Ginsberg's own models), a search above all promoted through networking. Since U.S.-published books were thinly available and word of mouth important, the British/Beats needed to become enthusiastic literary detectives, a reflex leading them to both largely neglected U.K. poets (like MacDiarmid and Bunting [Brown, Int]) and the wider U.S. avant-garde scene, via outlets such as City Lights, *Evergreen Review*, and Donald Allen's *New American Poetry*. America's poetry map was quickly quartered, since reading contemporary American writing possessed an illicit allure: obtaining one book became a clue about how to obtain others. The Pocket Poets (PP) listed on the back cover of *Howl*, the fourth Pocket Poets chapbook, led readers to the poetry of Ferlinghetti (PP 1), Rexroth (PP 2), Patchen (PP 3), and William Carlos Williams (PP 7). Even when U.K. poets name writers other than the core U.S. Beat figures as influences (and Ferlinghetti, Rexroth, O'Hara, and Patchen are often nominated), the Beats are still implicated in U.S./British poetry's Atlantic circulations. Pickard's account of a Beat-inspired initiation is typical: "I came across the Beat movement and first got a sniff of the Americans, discovering a punchy, taut and tender language. Following through some of the Beat's major sources I came to e.e. cummings, Whitman and Pound" (156).

So, when U.K. poets mention how tracking down Beat writing led them to the work of others, superseding the Beats as influences, a British/Beat circulation becomes involved. Harwood, for instance, says that "maybe more important than the Beats . . . were the writers they associated with or who they made one aware of for the first time" (I); according to Burns, it was avant-garde writing and painting that introduced him to the Beats, Black Mountain poets, and the San Francisco Renaissance (I). Through this contact with other, related strands of American activity, such as *Migrant's* interest in Black Mountain, promoted by Michael Shayer in the United Kingdom and Turnbull in the States, poets opened up—or as Lockwood maintains, "it was thru such editorial enthusiasms that we of a Beat persuasion had our perspectives widened" (11).

A widening of the idea of what poetry constituted and how it could speak more accessibly occurred. The adoption of new transatlantic types of hybrid poetic practice promoted the deployment of different language-registers, distinct from "received" BBC English, which Tom Leonard felt had dominated but which now swiftly caved in (100–102). The British/Beats' performance tours also promoted multi-racial links, stemming not only from involvement with musicians but also from contact with U.S. servicemen, West Indian communities, and other subcultures, including drug subcultures (Brown Int). In this process, new language-registers and rhythms—nonstandard English modes—were absorbed, seasoning the British/Beats' embrace of the U.S. Beats' vibrant demotic practices. Houedard, paraphrasing Ginsberg, sums this up as "dropping any fixed language habit" (146). This also ties in with the issue of class: the "lower" classes' language, rhythms, and modes were brought into poetry; Tipton, for example, arguing that "in the 1950s . . . most English literature was written by upper middle class writers . . . American was more democratic therefore closer in spirit" (I). Though there are ideological ramifications to Tipton's invocations of a democratizing American spirit, British/Beats were aware of how they always risked over-immersion in mainstream U.S. ideological discourses. Tipton urges attention to the prevailing "ideological . . . significations": "An interest in American poets [of] . . . the Allen anthology roster . . . was a sign . . . that poetry, no less than jazz and America painting, did not signify U.S. ideology or global politics to us then, for if it had it would have been an object of revulsion" (I). Both U.S. Beats and British/Beats had an understanding of the potency of diversity and dissent, enabling them to distinguish their tactical engagement with mainstream ideology from simple-minded complicity: for the U.S. Beats, in order to generate emotional assent for their disaffiliation; for the British/Beats, to attack the suffocating complacencies of 1950s Britain's classifications through, in Horovitz's words, a new "accessibility" to a significant degree also "coming up naturally because . . . [of] growth of TV & other media" (I). Signaling this British/Beat awareness was the advent in 1960 of *Coronation Street*, a television soap opera set in a working-class part of the north-west of England and featuring for about the first time broad Lancashire accents.

The U.S. Beats also illuminated how open communication might be done— *afresh*—to create a "generous, inclusive" atmosphere (Houston I). Alan Dent felt it offered an "emotional openness . . . rare . . . among the English, especially the edu-cated English" (I), while for Cairncross, "it opened up a new world" (I). As poetry's boundaries changed, and the line between it and other cultural changes and develop-ments wore paper-thin, the British/Beat contributed to rising anti-Bomb, anti-war sentiments and helped shape the alternative culture that followed. Miles's account of how he "began to connect to the nascent counter-culture" in 1961 begins, almost iconically, with visits to "Pete Brown's home in Oppidans Road, Primrose Hill . . . shared by designer Mal Dean . . . [while] further west . . . John Hoppy [Hopkins's] . . . place was cool . . . there was always a copy of *Naked Lunch* on the table . . . still illegal at the time" (Fountain 8).[18] Thus the founder-editor of *International Times*; biographer of Ginsberg, Kerouac, and Burroughs; publicist and bookseller for the U.S. Beats (via his Indica bookshop); and central organizer of the 7,000-strong 1965 International Poetry Incarnation portrays the United Kingdom's "nascent counter-culture" as ges-tating in British/Beats' homes.

British/Beat, then, plays a key role in a post-war disabling of notions of any unitary national culture. Exploring the British/Beat inevitably widens out to map broader cultural interactions bridging the Atlantic divide on a level other than that established by global capital's exchanges—fundamentally contributing to a breaking-down of the stranglehold of the golden triangle in a "challenge to the largely Oxford/London establishment scene" (Burns I). The British/Beat net-work's inclusive transatlantic openness aided its concerted take-up of Bunting's, MacDiarmid's, and Fisher's concerns for their locales, permanently adjusting the United Kingdom's poetic registers. Fisher's *City*, focusing on Birmingham, marks this: "Wharves, the old parts of factories, tarred gable ends rearing to take the sun over lower roofs. Soot, sunlight, brick-dust; and the breath that tastes of them" (20). As Burns puts it, "much early activity had a non-metropolitan basis—Newcastle, Liverpool, Edinburgh, etc., with magazines and presses across the provinces" (I). Perhaps it can be described as a fundamental demetropolitanization. Even if metro-politan centering did come to "reassert itself" to a degree (Burns I), Hugh Kenner still could claim in 1987 that "London is no longer the center of poetry" (254).

The British/Beat contribution to the rapidity and reach of this relocation was fundamental, through its reading-tours and its promotion of little magazines and small presses. Mentioning a few of these gives a sense of this centrifugal process: *New Departures,* especially the anthology-sized *New Departures* 2/3 (1960) featuring Kerouac, Corso, Ginsberg, and Creeley alongside (from Europe) Ionesco and Queneau and (from the United Kingdom) Silkin, Donald Davie, Michael Hamburger, and Adrian Mitchell; Cunliffe and Tina Morris's *Poetmeat* (1962–1967); Burns's *Move* (1964–1968); Nuttall's *My Own Mag* (1963–1966), which featured, beside such poets as Anselm Hollo, Tom McGrath, and Nuttall himself, considerable cut-up work by Burroughs, especially during the times that he was living in London in the 1960s;[19] Chris Torrance and Michael J. Dyke's *Origins/Diversions* (1963); Patten's *Underdog* (1963–1966), with issue 6 (1965) featuring McGough, Patten, and Henri alongside Trocchi, Hollo, and Creeley; and Tom Raworth's *Outburst* (1961–63).

All these little magazines show a propensity to reach outward and draw in others, a "bridging" reflex matched by the way the British/Beats themselves crossed over into other magazines. Consider the following three: (1) Ian Hamilton Finlay's *Poor.*

Old. Tired. Horse. (1962–1967), which Houston sees as "reveal[ing] an international brother/sisterhood" by featuring European and Latin American poetry, and which, in issue 1, featured Brown and Hollo alongside Edwin Morgan, Hamilton Finlay, and Turnbull (I); (2) Lee Harwood's *Soho,* whose first issue (1964) featured Tristan Tzara beside Hollo, Hawkins, Brown, and Cunliffe; and (3) Jon Silkin's *Stand* (1962 ff.). As importantly, there were street-level attempts at outreach, an explosion of mimeographed little magazines and related endeavors, such as *Bean Train* and the Bean Train Press readings (Roger Jones, Spike Hawkins, and Johnny Byrne, 1963), "steer[ing] a middle course between—on the one hand poetry written by professors of poetry ensconced in universities, making rules first and poems after;—& on the other hand . . . lunacies of English hipsterism with its false borrowed language" ("Bean Train Press Readings" n.d. [1963?]). Similarly noteworthy are Jeff Cloves's *Poetsdoos* (1966–1969), featuring, for example, in issue 7 (1969) Arthur Moyse, Dennis Gould, Cobbing, Cunliffe, and Morris; and, in the mid-1960s, *Yahahbibi,* featuring small, leaflet-style productions, such as "Occasional Word Ensemble," a large sheet of paper, 45 by 71 centimeters in size, folded in half and crammed with poems: Houston, Hawkins, Horovitz jammed alongside Larry Eigner.[20] Such outlets offered on-the-street immediacy.

The British/Beats also crossed over into the mainstream, usually via sympathetic editors (the Cambridge/London-based *Circuit 2* and *Aylesford Review* being cases in point). More significantly, however, they helped establish alternative outlets and audiences. As Cunliffe puts it, the British/Beat was "the taproot" of Mottram's 1960s "British Poetry Revival" ("Forgotten"). Cunliffe sees the Beats as fundamental to the founding of a "by-pass" of "traditional distribution networks . . . free[ing] poetry from university control and government approval" ("Forgotten"). Beat readings, and the little magazines and small presses their enthusiasm generated, helped open the field, sometimes substantially—as with the first Albert Hall gathering or by way of the 1965 obscenity trial of *The Golden Convolvulus*—which occurred after this erotic anthology (featuring work by Cunliffe, Vine, George Dowden, and Tuli Kupferberg) had been seized by the postal authorities—during which the defense forced the prosecution to accept that Arthur Moyse's anthology, like all serious literature, should, in the famous phrase from Roth v. United States (1957), be "taken as a whole." This made the trial, in the *Times Literary Supplement*'s estimate, "important for the future of [all] the little magazines and the poets contributing to them" (qtd. by Cunliffe, "Convulsions" 19). A verdict of indecency, if not obscenity, was nevertheless returned.[21]

The establishment of what might be termed a dissemination-nexus occurred, promoting the circulation of first a literature, and then, inextricably, an accompanying counter-culture, which, as the 1960s Beat moved into a final "hippy" phase (in Houston's dry labeling), was increasingly characterized by hype, commercialization, rip-offs, and "heavier" drugs (Houston Int).[22] This "second generation" was for Dent just "too commercial, too opportunistic" (I). The Technicolor covers of *Love, Love, Love*; *C'mon Everybody*; and *Children of Albion* plainly have this other, mass-market-oriented side to them, appealing to a mid-1960s psychedelics-aware audience. But I want to urge the need to preserve some sense of origins. Pop culture did encapsulate processes of commercialized globalization, but the phenomenon does not solely subsist in processes of late-capitalist exploitation. The Atlantic Beat that helped shape it was also disseminating disaffiliation and protest in what might be termed a "counter-globalization." Of course this, too, was never pure and simple; it, too, was implicated. But the Atlantic Beat did contain artistic discourses of disaffiliation to set against the dominant, globalizing commercialism of the mass culture-industries. It did deploy cultural counter-readings of mass culture, establishing alliances—albeit uneasy ones—with oppressed minorities by way of jazz, drugs, dissident sexualities, and sexual liberation, though sexism infused this last element. As Houston notes: "I think men called the tune . . . women did get a raw deal from the so-called freedom of the 60s" (I). Indeed, Allen Fisher lambasts the "British Beat" as "sexist . . . male and boring" (I), though Cairncross counters by recalling that in his little magazine, *Bogg*, he "used many women poets" (I). These traces in the British/Beat remain a sign of its compromised identity but should not be allowed to becloud other, radical allegiances or how it drew together transatlantic disaffiliations. And this is why its poetry is more consistently political than it at first appears. It declines to adopt the common sense "voice of the nation" that the Movement so often adopts as a norm, and so its politics must be complex. Take, for example, Alan Jackson's 1964 poem, "Edinburgh Scene":

> we used to be typists
> but the hell wi that
> now we live with these boys
> in a two room flat
>
> ....
>
> the boys are a' big beardies
> they think we're awfy sweet
> we never know which one we're with
> that's what it means to be beat (55)

On one level, this is designed to shock norms. Its deployment of "beat" as the poem's last word, emphasizing the term's American connotations, confronts head-on the constrictive, often anti-American undertones of early 1960s polite society. More disconcertingly, it is also laced with irony—with a sense of how sexual politics creates issues of exploitation, but ones that can be negotiated: the poem inverts the stereotypical masculine failure to know *her* name. The politics is not being reduced to simple black-and-white positions. Neither a lightly ironized Beat-ness nor sexism is endorsed, but no quarter is conceded to the work ethic or austerity. In this light, revisiting Brown's "Few," discussed much earlier in this essay, reveals unexpectedly political implications. Beyond the ironic connotations of the title (echoing both Churchill's description of Battle of Britain fighter-pilots and Christ's words to the chief priests and Pharisees), the sense of embattlement the poem projects can be related to the way the British/Beat performatively sets itself against both pervasive anti-Americanism and the Cold War's nuclear escalations.

It is as important to assess the British/Beat in this terrain as to read it in terms of its stylistic importance for British poetry. "Minor poetry" (if this phrase means anything other than poetry resolutely neglected by major publishers) always can be part of a significant cultural re-mapping. The British/Beat, I therefore contend, did exist, in a cultural process of redefinition: transgressing literary boundaries to become more culturally engaged, often via protest, always via open accessibility, founded upon a fundamental inclusiveness and a concern with the popular.

The British/Beat is "social poetry" in this particular sense. Some recuperation is necessary, or sight may be lost of this socio-cultural dimension to the British/Beat—its pivotal transgressive complexity. As Allen Fisher wrote,

> Late '50s and early '60s over the back fence from school to "Swing Shop" Streatham (blues and jazz), coffee bars, juke boxes, snooker halls. Large collections of blues and eventually R&B, rock 'n roll, jazz. . . . almost everything Burroughs published in small press (this is before *Naked Lunch* trial) all that wonderful collage material . . . Ferlinghetti, later *Fuck You* Ed Sanders *Peace Eye,* Bungies Coffee House, Better Books . . .coffee and happenings and readings, Bill Butler, Bob Cobbing then Lee Harwood and Miles. Then early ICA in Dover Street and "beat" blur into everything.
> . . . well it's to do with "beatitude" and not drop out as such. It's whack box. It's the horror in 1968, not celebration, but pissed off. It's Aldermaston marches joined at Streatham against the bomb. It's anarchist meetings and rooms full of books and paper around a bed and a printing press. It's Brighton beach and Cornwall and sometimes a jazz festival or folk or blues and then Rock was normalised. It includes lifting the seats up in Odeon Streatham at *King Creole* to dance. (I)

The British/Beat does indeed "blur into everything" through its hybrid identity as a transnational Atlantic cultural circulation: (e)migrant Atlantic, black Atlantic, antinuclear Atlantic, anarchic Atlantic—blurred together in a Beat Atlantic. So when the "Beetles," named originally as an oblique homage to Buddy Holly's Crickets, was re-spelled as "Beatles," it not only made plain a U.S. lineage but also offered up a wholly justifiable if likely unconscious tribute to the British/Beat's post-war cultural significance.

Notes

This essay, reprinted by kind permission of Maney Publishing (http://www.maney.co.UK/), is a highly substantial reworking of "From 'The Beetles' to 'The Beatles': The British/Beat 1955-1965" that appeared in *Symbiosis* 4.1 (April 2000): 67–98. Print.

1. Allen Fisher, correspondence with R. J. Ellis, January 30, 1999. This essay depends heavily on research carried out in 1999 and 2010. Future references to such correspondence and interviews will appear in the text, followed by "Int" if an interview is the source, by the Roman numeral I if the source is the 1999 round of letters, and by the Roman numeral II if the source is the 2010 round of letters. See also note 2.

2. The 1999 respondents included Jim Burns, I, January 14; Barry Cole, I, January 13; Dave Cunliffe, I, February 2; Alan Dent, I, January 17; Allen Fisher, I, January 30; Roy Fisher, I, January 12; Lee Harwood, I, January 14; Michael Horovitz, I, January 23; Libby Houston, I, March 10; Tom Leonard, I, February 13; Tom Lowenstein, I, February 7; Alexis Lykiard, I, January 27; Roger McGough, I, May 1; David Miller, I, March 8; Ian McMillan, I, February 14; Adrian Mitchell, I, May 2 and June 4; Jeff

Nuttall, I, July 4; Brian Patten, I, May 12; Tom Pickard, I, January 28; Barry Edgar Pilcher, I, April 27; Steve Sneyd, I, February 11; David Tipton, I, February 14; Gael Turnbull, I, April 7; Michael Wilding, I, January 30; Tom Leonard, I, March 29; Pete Brown, Int, February 25; Houston, Int, May 13; McMillan, Int, April 21; Horovitz, Int/talk, May 4. The 2010 respondents were George Cairncross, I, May 9; Barry Tebb, I. March 29; John Seed, I, May 2; Chris Torrance, I, September 6. The 2010 second round received second replies from Roger McGough, II, May 10; Pilcher, II, May 1; Cole, II, April 30; Cunliffe, II, May 11; Tipton, II, May 18; Harwood, II, April 29; Burns, II, May 11; Brown, II, May 8; Sneyd, II, May 9; Lykiard, II, May 10; Houston, II, July 15. The poets selected are all those who were active at the time, who survive, and whom I identified as in any way more or less closely associated with the British/Beat, but the selection ultimately depends on whether I could trace and contact them and whether they replied. This sampling is therefore not scientific.

3. Libby Houston comically describes encountering this very British distaste for public confession: when reading out a "Howl"-indebted poem, ironically entitled "Small Call," laced with autobiographical detail, her frankness stunned the room into silence (Int; see also Tuma 47).

4. Brown, Int. See also: "Corso . . . was originally my favourite [but] . . . his poems don't wear so well" (Brown, "Albion" 17). Cairncross, however, noted his admiration for *Gasoline*.

5. Brown, "Albion" 16; Miles, *Ginsberg* 123. British poets did not monopolize the Albert Hall reading. Peter Whitehead's film *Wholly Communion* (1965) shows Ferlinghetti, Corso, and Ginsberg reading for longer, although the U.K. poets' generally shorter poems won more audience response. As McGough puts it: "I was always disappointed at Beat readings (Albert Hall, etc.)" (McGough).

6. Conran suggests that the 1950s saw Britain "like photography, change from black-and-white to colour" (6).

7. Roy Fisher and Turnbull were important early disseminators. Turnbull gave Fisher "Howl" in September 1956 and, later, "a few other pieces, possibly by Kerouac & c." (Fisher).

8. Tipton also, "about this time," read John Clellon Holmes's *Go* (1952) and obtained Donald M. Allen's anthology *The New American Poetry* (1960) immediately upon publication (I). Allen's anthology only slowly rose into prominence in the United Kingdom, although Eric Mottram was to review it early on in *The London Magazine* in 1962, and its title inspired the much later, and similarly wide ranging, 1988 anthology *The New British Poetry* (Allnutt, D'Aguiar, and Mottram). This featured some of the poets on the edges of the British/Beat, such as Tom Raworth, Jeff Nuttall, Roy Fisher, and Tom Leonard, but the only British/Beat it published in the fuller sense of this phrase was Frances Horovitz (married to Michael Horovitz). Its 1988 date makes this almost inevitable, but also none of the editors were much in sympathy with the work of the most central British/Beat poets, such as Brown, Houston, Horovitz, McGough, and Cunliffe.

9. Chris Torrance, 1985, qtd. in Cunliffe, "Nomadic," n.p. Cunliffe contends that, before the U.S. Beats reached the United Kingdom, a British/Beat existed, part of an international Beat community of which the first U.S. Beats were only a New York bohemian part. My research does not support this idea, unless we are to understand that just as, for example, Kerouac witnessed in the immediate post-war period "beat[en]" hoboes traversing America, so tramps wandered across postwar Britain and over war-blighted Europe.

10. This also tempts Nuttall to assert that "Corso . . . and . . . Bremser . . . were both adopted . . . largely for their delinquency and the special frisson it created" (*Bomb* 107). Despite an element of truth in this account, Kerouac must and does simply disappear from this account.

11. Gardiner, 119–120, quotes eulogies by Cyril Connolly and Philip Toynbee. See also Nuttall, *Bomb* 41 ff. Whatever its shortcomings, Wilson's *The Outsiders* is recurrently mentioned, for example, by McGough. See also Allsop 156–190.

12. Nuttall, "The British Beats."

13. Mottram, "The British Beats"; Mottram, *Burroughs* 1971; Mottram, *Ginsberg* 1972; "in the *Spectator* in September 1953 . . . Henry Fairlie first used the words 'the Establishment'" (Gardiner 70).

14. As typified, Nuttall claims, by its involvement with "skiffle" and its unconvincing downward bridging of social groups (*Bomb* 44).

15. John Lennon describes this: "You start off with, say, rock & roll in just the late fifties and the sixties when all the kids including me were on James Dean and Elvis" (Lennon).

16. Ferlinghetti, qtd. by Horovitz, in "Poetry in Motion," n. p. [6]. The short-lived "Poetry in Motion" poetry co-operative included Brown, Hawkins, Henri, Hollo, Horovitz, Houston, Alan Jackson, McGough, Ted Milton, Mitchell, Nuttall, Patten, and Pickard.

17. See Turner (*Hard Day's* 196) and passim; McMillan 415. Horovitz's suggestion that British/Beats were "the new oral poets" and their poems "truly popular songs" ("Poetry in Motion" n. d. [6]) is borne out by Pete Brown's transmogrification into a pop lyricist, writing for *Cream* and his own bands, *The Battered Ornaments* (1968/9) and *Piblokto!* (1969–71). However, if the Beats' role in developing performance is over-pressed, a species of imperialism creeps in: the British black, Benjamin Zephaniah, has even been kidnapped, as has Lynton Kwesi Johnson (McMillan Int). Rap and poetry slams should be more complexly located, with important roots in black oral culture and music, such as reggae, West Indian forms (calypso), and jazz scatting. Yet it is not completely gestural to detect Beat connections, for other sets of crossings exist, ones connecting these black writers—and Edward Braithwaite—to religious, oracular, and bardic traditions that also gave rise to Ginsberg's performances (see Tuma 258, 264): complex Atlantic exchanges (Black Atlantic Beat/U.S. American Beat) have an impact upon both U.S. Beat practices and the British/Beats (see Jerry Hooker, qtd. in "Poetry in Motion" n. d. [7]).

18. Houston, married to Mal Dean, is left out of this account, replicating early 1960s sexism.

19. For a complete run of *My Own Mag*, fully revealing the extent to which Burroughs was championed by Nuttall, see http://realitystudio.org/bibliographic-bunker /my-own-mag/.

20. Gray, n.d.: n.p. I have been unable to track down bibliographic information on *Yahahbibi*. It seems to date to the mid- to late 1960s.

21. Lykiard (II) suggests that this trial has been airbrushed out of the accounts of postwar U.K. censorship battles because the "posh literati" at the time did nothing to help. Almost the only defence of Moyse at that time can be found in Cunliffe's *Poetmeat* 11 (summer 1966).

22. Changes to the meaning of underground between 1946 and 1969 illuminate this process. In 1946, John Hampson uses the word to refer not to any counterculture but to an underworld "of crime, of have-nots, of abnormal desires and inclinations" (133). By 1969, however, in Horovitz's *Children of Albion: Poetry from the Underground*,

the term had assumed countercultural connotations. Nuttall dates this change to 1964 (*Bomb* 175). Again, Atlantic Beat circulations are implicated, promoted by a late 1950s "cultural nucleus that looked mainly towards America and the Beats," identified by Nuttall as the "beginning of the Underground" (*Bomb* 191) as the term "the Beat Generation" transmogrified into one applied to a transnational generation inspired by Vietnam protest as much or more than anti-bomb sentiments.

Chapter 10

Beating Them to It? The Vienna Group and the Beat Generation

Jaap van der Bent

When the global features of the Beat Generation are discussed, the basis of those discussions is usually the life and work of one or more of the Beats, which is then brought to bear on social or literary developments that were taking place outside the United States. However, in a recent publication which places the Beats in a transnational context, "The Transnational Counterculture: Beat-Mexican Intersections," Daniel Belgrad is especially concerned with a "give and take from both sides" and consequently with the ways in which "the Beats' literary project intersected with the major currents of Mexican cultural and intellectual life" (29). Even though Belgrad's essay suggests that the Beats "took" much more from Mexico than they "gave," he ultimately argues successfully that there was a "shared cultural vision" (39) between the Beats and Octavio Paz, the writer whose life and work Belgrad uses in particular to establish a connection between the Beats and Mexico.

The following essay will show how a similar "shared cultural vision" existed between the Beat Generation and a group of Austrian writers, the so-called Wiener Gruppe (in English often referred to as the Vienna Group), whose emergence in the 1950s was due to social and cultural similarities between the United States and Austria in the years following World War II. A comparison between the Beat Generation and the Vienna Group reveals that shared social and cultural conditions are likely to lead to literary developments that to a large extent are also similar. Even though initially there was no direct contact between the two movements, both the Beat Generation and the Vienna Group reacted to restraining post-war conditions by opposing them. While spirituality and transcendence are relevant in varying degrees to both movements, the Beat Generation and the Vienna Group are both strongly concerned with the liberation of language and consequently also of the self. The desire of the Beats to open up language, illustrated by the spontaneous quality of much of their writing, is mirrored by the fervor with which the Vienna Group engaged in various montage techniques.

In contrast to the interaction that took place between the Beats and Mexico, it is clear that the Austrians "took" more from America than they "gave." Looking for ways in which the Beats benefitted from Austria, one could think of a figure such as Wilhelm Reich, whose theories influenced Beats as diverse as William S. Burroughs and Diane di Prima, or of Mozart, who occasionally appears in the work of Jack Kerouac. More concrete and personal connections between the Beats and Austria can be found in the emigration to the United States—in 1938 and 1950, respectively—of the poet and artist ruth weiss and of the photographer Harry Redl. However, in spite of the social and cultural similarities between the two countries, the United States obviously had a stronger influence on Austria than the other way around. Therefore, and also because some of the experiments of the Vienna Group seem to prefigure those of the Beats, it seems logical to use post–World War II Austria as a starting point.

Austria and the United States

In *Coca-Colanization and the Cold War: The Cultural Mission of the United States in Austria after the Second World War*, Reinhold Wagnleitner describes how in the years following World War II, especially in the late 1940s and early 1950s, Austria increasingly felt and gave in to the impact of U.S. culture. In convincing and personal detail, Wagnleitner points out how, partly because of the "massive direct and indirect support that the export of [U.S.] culture received from the government of the United States" (2), in post–World War II Austria the press, theater, film, and music were affected by the United States, the country where, in the eyes of many Austrians and other Europeans, "everything was better, fresher, younger, more colorful, more glowing, sassier, more technically perfect . . . " (296). However, even if the State Department had not gone out of its way to employ U.S. culture as an anti-Communist deterrent, there would still have been a number of striking similarities between the postwar United States and postwar Austria (as well as other European countries). Of course, the United States and its allies had won the war, which led to an economic boom in the United States that has been the subject of numerous books and essays. Those same books and essays usually point out that the flourishing economy not only brought prosperity and comfort, but that the postwar years in the United Sates were also associated with the Cold War, the fear of communism, the rise of large corporations, and, as a result of these and other factors, a strong tendency among Americans to play it safe and to conform.

Even though Austria, as part of the German Reich (into which it had been incorporated in 1938) had lost the war, in some essential ways Austrian society after the war resembled U.S. society. It is true that, unlike the United States, the country had been badly damaged by the war, but the U.S. Marshall Plan quickly helped to strengthen the Austrian economy. However, as was also the case with the United States and its citizens, material wealth was not the final answer to the problems that confronted Austrians after the war. Many Austrians felt ashamed by the role which Austria, and in many cases they themselves, had played during the war. They tried to repress their feelings of guilt, together with their fear of communism and the Cold War that had broken out between the United States and the Soviet Union, both of which (together with France and Great Britain) were occupying presences in Austria until 1955. As a consequence, many Austrians harkened back to the imperial greatness of the Austrian-Hungarian Empire, which had come to an end in 1918. This tendency to prefer the past to the present gave rise to powerful conservative forces which not only determined post–World War II Austrian society but also its cultural life.

In fact, as far as literature is concerned, the same tendency to play it safe and to conform that was found in both U.S. and Austrian society at large also character-ized the literary scene of the two countries. While in the United States, with few exceptions, poets adhered to the rules put down by the New Critics and novelists shirked experimentation, Austrian writing after the war was marked by "bourgeois conventions and restorative tendencies" (M. Butler 237): novelists and poets were expected to produce work that would have been appreciated in a glorified past and to avoid any subject or literary style that could shock or offend. Not surprisingly, both in the United States and in Austria (and other European countries), writers and other artists who could not adjust soon began to rebel. In the United States, a number of groups emerged that attempted to bring in some fresh air, and something similar happened in Austria. While the United States witnessed the emergence of, among others, Black Mountain writing, the San Francisco poetry scene, and the Beat Generation, in post-war Vienna young artists and writers also grouped together to make a new beginning. In Vienna, one of the earliest and most important meeting places for those in favour of renewal was the Art Club, founded in February 1947 by the author and painter Albert Paris Gütersloh, the art historian Otto Demus, and the painter Gustav Kurt Bech.

Initially, the Art Club was a stomping ground for visual artists, in whose lives the club played a role that can be compared to that of the Cedar Bar in the lives of the abstract expressionist painters in New York. However, as was the case in New York when painters and poets began to mingle, at a certain moment the Art Club also became an important meeting place for the new generation of Austrian writ-ers, especially after December 1951, when the cellar of the Art Club was opened for literary activities. Gütersloh once referred to the club as a "haven for those who have been officially suppressed and scorned" (Strasser 21). Here photographer Harry Redl, who in 1950 would emigrate to Canada and the United States to take iconic pictures of the San Francisco Beats, got together with the young Austrian poet Hertha Kräftner, whose work has become increasingly appreciated since her suicide in 1951. Here, also, a number of budding writers first met who would later form the Vienna Group.

At first, the writers in this group, as well as other Austrians, were unaware of the new developments that were taking place on the U.S. artistic and literary scene. This was partly due to the policy of the so-called America Houses in Austria: U.S. Information Centers which were set up by the U.S. government in various parts of the world after the war had ended. They were meant to project "democratic ideals and the American way of life" (Wagnleitner 129), something which could not be achieved by paying too much attention to artistic expression that was overly critical of U.S. society. As a consequence, U.S. librarians abroad tended to introduce authors such as Louis Bromfield, John Steinbeck, John P. Marquand, and Pearl S. Buck. The America Houses in Austria, some of which functioned throughout the 1950s and early 1960s, were definitely not the place where Austrian readers, including the members of the Vienna Group, could become acquainted with recent U.S. writing of a more experimental nature, for instance, that of the Beat Generation. Still, a closer look at the Vienna Group will reveal striking similarities between its aims and achievements and those of the Beats.

The Vienna Group

As was also true for the Beats, the Vienna Group consisted of a number of writers who were united by friendship and a desire to liven up the literary scene, but who were all highly individual artists. In the same way that Gregory Corso's poetry is strikingly different from that of Allen Ginsberg, the work of, for instance, Oswald Wiener can hardly be confused with that of other Vienna Group members such as Gerhard Rühm and Hans Carl Artmann. Rühm (b. 1930) and Artmann (1921–2000) were the first of the five core members of the Vienna Group to cross paths. Their initial meeting took place at the Art Club in 1952, and they were soon on friendly terms. As Rühm himself wrote, using only the lower-case letters that the Vienna Group tended to prefer: "by 1953 my contact to h.c. artmann had turned into a friendship-like relationship. we met more and more frequently, had a lot to discuss – also as we walked a stretch together on our way home to breitensee when we had missed the last tram, or spent our last groschen on a small espresso rather than saving it for the ticket" (Weibel 16). One thing that must have struck the two men during their walks and talks is that, while they shared some basic feelings about life and literature, their attitudes toward writing were rather divergent. While both admired the work of Gertrude Stein and that of German Expressionist and French Surrealist poets (work that had been largely unavailable in Austria before and during the war), Artmann's poetic stance seemed more traditional. As Rühm put it: "while my own interests focused on the 'constructivists,' who, unlike the surrealists, worked with the language and not just in the language (perhaps also because music had taught me to think in formal disciplines), artmann drew on black romanticism and surrealism, which apparently could be combined surprisingly well with austrian traditions" (Weibel 18). And while the three members who joined the group subsequently (Konrad Bayer, Oswald Wiener, and Friedrich Achleitner) shared most of Rühm's and Artmann's literary preferences, in some ways they were also worlds apart. Bayer (1932–1964) combined a fascination for dandyism with a love of jazz, which is how he got to know jazz trumpeter Oswald Wiener (b. 1935), who at first (like Burroughs) had hardly any literary aspirations. However, while Bayer "toyed with guns, black magic, séances" (Green in Bayer, *Selected* 4), Wiener was much more disciplined: after having contributed substantially to the Vienna Group for a number of years, he pursued a career in mathematics and computer science. That same sense of discipline characterized the life of Friedrich Achleitner (b. 1930), who in 1955 become the last member to join the group. During his time in the Vienna Group, Achleitner wrote less than the others; he studied architecture, published a number of books on the subject, and has been described as "seemingly the most modest and unassuming of the five," who, as an architect, "brought a great constructivist clarity to their methods" (Green in Bayer, *Selected* 6)

In spite of the individual differences among the members of the Vienna Group, they shared a number of interests that were sometimes strikingly similar to those of the Beats. First, the lives and works of both groups were informed by a strong sense of social criticism. In the case of the Austrian writers, this perspective comes out in their rejection of many social developments that were taking place in postwar Austria. They opposed the staid materialism and sense of comfort that seemed to satisfy most of their compatriots in the late forties and early fifties. And while it is true that at first sight the Vienna Group as a whole seemed less concerned with spirituality and matters of the soul than were the Beats, it cannot be denied that especially Bayer's life and work are marked by an all-encompassing urge toward transcendence. Like the Beats (especially poets such as Lawrence Ferlinghetti and Ginsberg), the members of the Vienna Group also strongly disapproved of anything related to war and the war industry. When the allied occupation of Austria came to an end in 1955 and the government almost immediately began to consider the possibility of rearming the country, Artmann wrote, in May of that year, a "manifesto" against rearmament, which contains the following lines:

> It is an infamous impudence
> an incomparable impertinence
> to run antimilitaristic propaganda
> through ten long years
> hypocritically howling filth and obscenity
> declaring tin soldiers and indian movies
> to be amoral
> (the posters are up on the walls yet . . .)
> and then
> in the first breath of a so-called
> final freedom
> to press dirty guns in the hands of
> mere babes barely out of school!!
>
> (Weibel 60)

Artmann's pamphlet was signed by twenty-five people, including Wiener and Bayer. Artmann, Bayer, and Wiener, together with four other people who had signed, then staged a protest walk through the center of Vienna on May 20, which ended before the Vienna Dom. There they were first escorted off the church grounds by the parish priest and then told by the police to disperse.

Another obvious connection between the Beats and the Vienna Group is the interest in jazz that both groups had. While Austria was part of the German Reich, from 1938 until 1945, jazz could only be played in secret. However, as Wagnleitner has pointed out, "[s]hortly after the liberation of Vienna through the Red Army, the jazz musicians crawled out of their basements, and in spite of the sorry state of the material situation, there was a surprising renaissance of the jazz scene" (207). The Art Club and its literary basement played an essential role in that renaissance. There, visiting U.S. musicians such as Gerry Mulligan and Oscar Peterson got together with Austrian jazz musicians, prominent among whom were the classically trained Friedrich Gulda and pianist Joe Zawinul, who, after moving to the United States, became famous for his work with Miles Davis and the group he founded with Wayne Shorter, Weather Report. There were evenings at the Art Club when "Cab Calloway would play Mozart, after which Friedrich Gulda would sit down at the piano and play jazz" (Fialik 79). For some time after the war, most jazz played in Austria—as suggested by Konrad Bayer's playing the banjo—was rather traditional. However, after the arrival of some of the more progressive U.S. jazz musicians in Vienna, bebop and cool jazz also caught on. The Austrian film-maker Ferry Radax remembers how in the cellar of the Art Club at a certain moment Dizzy Gillespie's "How High the Moon" had almost become the "national hymn," which was played every night on the piano: "Or 'All the things you are.' In my film *Am Rand*, which I made between 1961 and 1963, Bayer plays a beatnik who only listens to these tunes, which was meant to be a reference to Jack Kerouac's *On the Road*" (Fialik 48).

Music, though not necessarily jazz, also played a role in the public performances that were staged by the Vienna Group, which made the group known to a larger public. After having organized a group reading of their poetry that took place in a small theater in Vienna on June 20, 1957, four members of the group (Artmann by then no longer took part in all the group's activities) felt the need for a kind of contact with their audience that would demand more from both the performers and the spectators. Consequently, the Vienna Group produced two evenings of a form of literary cabaret that somewhat resembled the Dadaists' "Cabaret Voltaire" in Zürich during World War I. The two performances of the group's "Literarisches Cabaret" took place in Vienna on December 6, 1958, and on April 15, 1959, and both sessions consisted of an "anarchic farrago of sound poems, polemical chansons, mini-happenings, inspired (and at times infantile) clowning, together with some abuse of the audience itself, aimed at provoking the latter into new modes of participation and perception" (M. Butler 243). The performances of the Vienna Group clearly illustrate the extent to which its members, like the Beats, were interested in the use of voice and physicality to get meaning across and to establish a connection with the audience.

Still, the emphasis on the spoken word had a different outcome in the work of the Beats from that of the Vienna Group. While the Beats and some of the Black Mountain poets (Olson immediately comes to mind) were especially interested in the connection between poetic language and the use of the breath, for the Vienna Group an important area of literary practice was that of the dialect poem: poetry that reflects local speech. This poetic genre had always been popular in Austria, but, as Michael Butler points out: "Far from continuing the folklore tradition of dialect literature, Artmann, Rühm and Achleitner were attracted to dialect initially by the plasticity and directness of local (especially Viennese) speech and the visual 'alienation effect' of such language when transcribed phonetically" (241). Although Artmann was the first of the Vienna Group to explore the vernacular and to write *dialekt-gedichte*, his example was soon followed by Rühm and somewhat later by Achleitner. Rühm remembers how "artmann and i attempted to agree on a uniform and binding phonetic spelling, which for the sake of simplicity should make do with the normal alphabet" (Weibel 18). In the end, their spellings "deviated in some minor respects" (Rühm in Weibel 18), but this attempt at consistency is already quite suggestive of the systematic approach to language that was shared by all members of the group. In fact, their dialect poetry soon "became part of the 'Wiener Gruppe's' increasingly methodical reflection on the nature of language itself" (M. Butler 241).

Language and Philosophy

At first sight the difference between the Beats' more-or-less spontaneous poetry and the Vienna Group's carefully crafted dialect poems seems to suggest a major rift between the two groups. It is true that, from time to time, Bayer experimented with automatic and drug-induced writing, following in the footsteps of Henri Michaux, the French poet whose work was also admired by some of the Beats. And one of the first literary statements of the group, Artmann's "Acht-Punkte-Proklamation des poetischen Actes" (Eight-Point Proclamation of the Poetical Act) (1953), claims that art "was to be spontaneous and independent of public acclaim or critcism" (M. Butler 237). What the Vienna Group was especially concerned with, however, is not spontaneity in writing, but the connection between language and reality. This is why they were very much interested in language philosophy and, some more than others, avid readers of the works of language philosophers such as Fritz Mauthner, Ludwig Wittgenstein, and Max Stirner. In various ways, these philosophers all claimed that humans are conditioned by language, and that our thoughts and even our acts—in short: our way of life and looking at the world—is determined by the language that we use. Inspired by these philosophers, as well as by the experiments of the Dadaist and surrealist poets of the early twentieth century, the writers of the Vienna Group believed that it is only possible to change one's way of life if one changes, opens up, and liberates one's language. While not all the Beats developed ideas that were as drastic as these, the way in which the Vienna Group looked upon the connection between life and language is highly reminiscent of how Burroughs viewed the determining role of language, and at the same time shared the Austrian group's interest in both Wittgenstein and the Dadaist poets. It is therefore no coincidence that, when the Vienna Group eventually was exposed to the work of the Beats, they felt a special affinity with Burroughs. This affinity is clearly to be found in Wiener's only novel, *Die Verbesserung von Mitteleuropa* (The Betterment of Central Europe); striking similarities with some of Burroughs's theories and experiments can also be found in Bayer's work, especially in his novel *Der Sechste Sinn* (1966), published in English as *The Sixth Sense*.

In fact, many of the experiments with text, image, and sound that the Vienna Group engaged in beginning in the early 1950s seem to prefigure the experiments that were carried out by Burroughs and a close circle of friends at the Beat Hotel

in Paris in the late 1950s and early 1960s. Rühm, for instance, has become famous
for photographic collages full of striking and shocking contrasts, which he began
to make in the 1950s. And the first group reading of the Vienna Group, in June
1957, consisted not only of "individual and simultaneous readings" but also of "tape
recordings and projections, interspersed with some theory" (Rühm in Weibel 24).
However, what the Beats usually referred to as cut-up and collage, the Austrians
called methodic inventionism and montage. The former of these two methods was
first applied in 1954, when the group was rapidly getting up steam. One of the
group's friends, the sculptor Marc Adrian, was "raving about the golden mean"
(Bayer in Weibel 34) in mathematics and suggested that it could be applied to literature. (Strikingly enough, it was also a visual artist, Brion Gysin, who introduced
Burroughs to the cut-up method.) Bayer was the first to pick up on Adrian's suggestion and was very "proud" and enthusiastic because now "everyone can be a poet"
(Weibel 34). Bayer has described methodic inventionism in a way that seems to
foreshadow Burroughs's decription of the cut-up method: "take a number of words
(your so-called verbarium), draw up equations which reflect the golden mean (later
any type of mathematical series at all was taken, everything was permitted) and
begin to order the words accordingly until the supply of words is exhausted, or
select by counting until all the words have been used (etc. ad libitum . . .)" (Weibel
34). Methodic inventionism appealed to the other members of the group as well,
and soon not only Artmann and Bayer but also Adrian and Artmann's girlfriend,
Erni Wobik, were writing "until smoke [was] coming out of our pencils: poetry as
a participation sport, in other words" (Bayer in Weibel 34). In this case, Bayer's
description is clearly reminiscent of accounts of Burroughs and his friends who,
after the discovery of the cut-up method, almost could not stop cutting up any texts
or images in sight.

    Like the cut-up, the other method often used by the Vienna Group, montage,
had already been used in the arts, both in writing and in painting. Like methodic
inventionism, it appealed to the Vienna Group because it, too, could be used to
contest the control exerted by language and linguistic structures. The method was
introduced in the group by Artmann, as Rühm has pointed out:

> 1956 we wrote our first joint pieces of work. artmann was browsing his dictionaries
> (books on foreign grammar and encyclopaedias were among his favourite literature),
> rummaged up a textbook on the bohemian language from 1853, by a person called
> terebelski; there he came across a collection of simple sentences that, given their arbi-
> trary sequence, were bound to catch his attention – his eye well-trained by invention-
> ism – as poetic alienation. artmann and bayer selected the most appealing sentences,
> regrouping them somewhat – the first "montage" was completed. (Weibel 20)

Montage, the conscious or arbitrary rearranging of sentences or sentence parts,
clearly has more in common with the cut-up method than methodic inventionism.
Both methods attracted the Vienna Group because their potential to contest language control implied a de-individualization of language. While Bayer was happy
that methodic inventionism brought poetry to the disposal of all, Artmann in his
"Eight-Point-Proclamation of the Poetical Act" had even claimed that "one can be

a poet without having so much as written or spoken a single word" (Weibel 54). Another important manifesto, Wiener's "Coole Manifest" (1954), which was signed by the entire group (except Achleitner, who had yet to join) but later destroyed by Wiener, also attempted to redefine the concept of literature:

> puns, deliberately pointless jokes, the language of business signs and bureaucracy, the vocabulary of crossword puzzles and advertisements, fragments of used blotting paper, random illustrations from books and medical treatises, combined with suitably shocking texts etc., were all potential literary material in the struggle to unmask the pretentious falsity and crippling restrictions of bourgeois aesthetics. (Best 238)

Paradoxically, however, as is also true for the cut-up method, the use of "methodic inventionism" and "montage" does not necessarily create a completely "unpersonal" kind of writing. In the same way that it is almost always possible to immediately distinguish a cut-up made by Burroughs from one made by Gysin, Beiles, or Corso, even the most "de-indivualized" pieces of writing by single members of the Vienna Group can in general be traced back to their originators. As far as montage is concerned, each member of the Vienna Group applied the method in his own way. Rühm used the elements that were singled out by Wiener in his "Coole Manifest" (autographed public announcements, obituaries, etc.), but as a composer he also collaborated with the pianist Hans Kann; together they performed their "geräusch-symphonie," "a montage consisting of nothing but noises on sound wire" (Rühm in Weibel 16). The "remarkable montages" (Rühm in Weibel 24) that Achleitner produced from 1957 on stood out because in them he took words and phrases literally, thus creating new meanings and demonstrating the arbitrariness of language. Artmann, especially after he became disgruntled with the montage technique, "sometimes even faked the montage or mixed the original sentences with sentences of his own" (Rühm in Weibel 24). Bayer, who had helped to introduce the montage technique, sometimes used texts written by others, but ended up using montage in a highly personal and immediately recognizable manner in his novel *Der Sechste Sinn*. Because Wiener in 1959 destroyed virtually all the writing he did as a member of the Vienna Group, it is hard to tell what his montages looked like exactly. However, he still relied on the technique when he composed *Die Verbesserung von Mitteleuropa* between 1962 and 1967.

Wiener and Bayer

Like *Naked Lunch* and other work by Burroughs, Wiener's *Die Verbesserung von Mitteleuropa* soon after publication became a cult book that seems to be referred to and talked about more frequently than it is actually read. It is, again like *Naked Lunch*, a difficult novel (or anti-novel) that combines fiction and theory, although in *Die Verbesserung von Mitteleuropa* the theoretical parts are much more prominent than in *Naked Lunch*. Both the fictional and the theoretical parts in Wiener's book illustrate the views on the connections between language and reality that had earlier been established by the Vienna Group as a whole, and the fictional parts (such as aphorisms, diary entries, and anecdotes) lead up to the introduction and discussion of an imaginary but conceivable machine called the Bio-Adapter. The "invention" of this machine is the outcome of Wiener's interest in computers, cybernetics, artificial intelligence, and related subjects. After having studied law, music, African languages, and mathematics (and after having left the Wiener Gruppe), Wiener started a career in data processing and later became a director of a data processing company. He was also politically active and, together with the artists Günter Brus and Otto Mühl, during the student movement of 1968 took part in a manifestation called *Kunst und Revolution* (Art and Revolution), staged by a notorious art movement usually referred to as Viennese Actionism. Because Brus during the manifestation "had defecated and masturbated in public while singing the national anthem" (Rebhandl), he was handed a jail sentence, which he avoided by moving to Berlin. Wiener's contribution to the event consisted only of a talk about cybernetics, so the charges against him were quickly dropped. Still, he decided to follow Brus's example, and in 1969 he also settled in Berlin, where he ran a pub and later studied mathematics and computer science. In the work he has been engaged in since then, he has managed to combine his interests in cognitive sciences, philosophy, and literature.

Wiener's interests to some extent resemble similar or comparable concerns that play a role both in Burroughs's life and in his work. While Burroughs apparently was not enthusiastic about computers (as far as writing was concerned, his typewriter satisfied his needs), and while the adding machine to him was a symbol of control, he was aware of the possibilities of machines to improve man's situation and well-being. He spent long periods experimenting not only with tape recorders (which could be used to contest the strictures of time and language) but also with, for instance, Wilhelm Reich's Orgone Accumulator, L. Ron Hubbard's E-meter, and Gysin's Dream Machine. Wiener's Bio-Adapter is meant to have similar beneficial effects. Put into practice, it would be able to bring about ultimate freedom, not only from the constraints of language but also from those of the body. According to Wiener, the Bio-Adapter offered "the first discussable sketch of a complete solution for all world-problems" (Weibel 690). In the course of his discussion of the device he claims that

> the human being to be adapted is uninterruptly probed for his needs, until they can themselves be produced by the adapter itself for the purpose of increased pleasure gains. namely, the adapter's learning structure carefully leads the whole unit out of the initial stage, which immediately takes effect after starting, and into the successive phases, during which ever more comprehensive sensual and intellectual abilities can be enjoyed, finally culminating in an expansion of consciousness, to be achieved by variously coupling the adapter's structures according to grade. (Weibel 690)

In view of statements like these, and with an eye to some of Wiener's other concerns, one should not find it surprising that Burroughs's work appealed to him. As *Die Verbesserung von Mitteleuropa* makes clear, by the time Wiener was writing the book, works by the Beats had actually begun to affect the Vienna Group. In a long list of sources and influences at the end of the novel, Wiener refers (along with dozens of other books) not only to Burroughs's *junkie, naked lunch, nova express*, and *the soft machine* (all of which he referenced in lower case) but also to Kerouac's *gammler, zen und hohe berge*, the German translation of *The Dharma Bums*. The influence of these books is visible in particular in those sections of Wiener's novel that are less theoretical and of a more autobiographical nature. Then Wiener's use of language becomes highly associative and spontaneous as he tries to capture the excitement of music and the impact of drugs. In one of those sections, intriguingly titled "ajo ajo / ajo mi re," Wiener also explicitly refers to the Beats. Moreover, as has already been suggested, the structure (or lack of structure) of *Die Verbesserung von Mitteleuropa* is to a large extent due to Burroughs's cut-up technique.

A combination of Burroughs's experiments with language and Kerouac's auto-biographical method also seems to mark Bayer's most extensive piece of fiction, *Der Sechste Sinn*. The book came out two years after Bayer's death, and in some ways the genesis of the novel echoes that of Burroughs's *Naked Lunch*, as well as that of Bonnie (Bremser) Frazer's memoir *Troia*. Having begun the book around 1960, in the summer of 1964 Bayer was still working on it, trying to meet a deadline he had arranged with his German publisher. At the time he and a number of friends had retreated to a tumbledown castle in the Austrian provinces. There, Bayer's girl-friend recalls, the manuscript "lay around largely untouched on the floor" (Green in Bayer, *Sixth* 6) and people sometimes even stepped on it, a state reminiscent of that Burroughs's found himself in when writing *Naked Lunch* in Tangier in the mid-1950s: "When Paul Bowles visited [Burroughs's] room in the Muneria, the floor was covered with hundreds of yellow foolscap pages. Many of them had been stepped on; you could see sole and heel marks on them. They were covered with rat droppings and bits of cheese sandwiches" (Morgan 261–262). Moreover, neither in the case of *Naked Lunch* and *Troia* nor in that of *Der Sechste Sinn* was the final editing done by the author him- or herself. Frazer has stated that she was not involved in the organization of her book, which was basically assembled by her publisher, Michael Perkins: "He put it together. I have notes. I have no idea where those sections were in the original manuscript. He picked and chose among the pieces" (Grace and Johnson 120). It is an equally well-documented fact that some of Burroughs's friends and literary acquaintances, including Gysin and Sinclair Beiles, established the final order in which the chapters of *Naked Lunch* were published. In the case of Bayer, it was his friend and literary executor Rühm who put the manuscript of the novel into shape:

> at first sight the manuscript . . . created a fairly chaotic impression, although num-
> bered almost throughout, many of the pages had additional sequences of numbers
> that produced divergent groupings. it turned out that these numbers represented
> major groups, secondary groups and inserts, which allowed the pages to be brought
> into a meaningful sequence (Green in Bayer, *Sixth* 5).

The first few pages of *Der Sechste Sinn* consist of a montage of a number of scenes and sentences that have a surreal quality and do not immediately make sense:

the farmer's wife remained unmoved in the style of the fin de siècle, although it was only a few minutes until her dinner. A distinguished-looking man observes us. he clatters about the room. she gives an almost perceptible smile. . . . nina, who was lying on the dressing-table, had bags under her eyes and was covered in hair. (17)

From the beginning, there is, as in *Naked Lunch*, the feeling of being oppressed by outside forces: "when life and property are threatened all distinctions come to an end" (17). Out of this dream-like muddle emerges the story of a number of characters who are easily recognizable as Bayer himself (franz goldenberg in the novel), his girlfriend (mirjam), and his ex-wife (the nina referred to above), as well as friends from the Vienna Group and others. These characters all lead more or less bohemian lives and take part in a number of "adventures" both in Vienna and in the Austrian countryside. Central to these adventures and to the characters' many discussions are the contingencies of language, time, and the body. Time and again and in various ways, they try to rise above these and to reach the transcendental state of being that is implied by the title of Bayer's novel.

For Bayer, the manipulation of language was one way of attaining transcendence. This is again reminiscent of Burroughs, who not only considered cut-ups as a way to contest control, but also as a way to achieve Rimbaud's "systematic derangement of the senses" (Calder, "Burroughs" 269). There is, in fact, a spiritual quality to Bayer's life and writing that distinguishes him from the other members of the Vienna Group and aligns him to some extent with the Beats. Like some of them, he was very much interested in Zen Buddhism and even meddled in magic, and like them he also experimented with drugs. However, because drugs were expensive and difficult to get hold of in postwar Vienna, in his spiritual quests he sometimes had to make do with ether and even with gas. Even Bayer's death at the age of thirty-one, usually cited as a case of suicide, according to Kurt Strasser, may very well have been the result of an experiment with gas that got out of control (Strasser 33–34). To give his argument more strength, Strasser convincingly quotes the following passage from *Der Sechste Sinn*:

> when goldenberg returned to his room he turned on both taps, closed the window and made himself comfy on the sofa. the smell was not unpleasant and he waited for sleep to come. he didn't see his life passing before his eyes and wondered whether he should turn the taps off again, but as he was about to get up and snuff the taps' breath he changed his mind and remained on the sofa, and once he had decided to remain lying on the sofa he decided to get up, and once he was resolved to do so he decided to remain on the sofa. the smell was not unpleasant and goldenberg breathed in the gas quite effortlessly. He was about to leave the sofa – he had remembered his six senses – when he fell asleep without having seen his life pass before his eyes. (36–37)

Referring to this same passage, Michael Green also points out that, while "many reviewers have been led to conclude that his suicide was the logical consequence of his literary theory," Bayer's close friends "tended more to the opinion that his death was simple foolishness, a stupid mistake, or an irrational act peformed under stress" (Green in Bayer, "Selected" 3–4).

Conclusion

After Bayer's death and the disintegration of the Vienna Group, the influence of the Beats on Austrian writers only seemed to grow. This was partly due to the fact that it took some time before some of Kerouac's major novels were published in German; the German translation of *On the Road* (*Unterwegs*) came out in 1959 and that of *The Dharma Bums* in 1963, after which it took another two years before *Tristessa* was published in German; strikingly enough the German translation of *The Subterraneans* (*Bebop, Bars und Weisses Pulver*) only came out in 1979. And although the German translation of Ginsberg's "Howl" had already been published in 1959, it took a few more years before more Beat poetry was published in German. In fact, it was only in the early 1960s that the Beats gradually became a fixed point in Europe's literary landscape as a whole.

A good example of an Austrian poet who was influenced by the Beats, but quite differently from the Vienna Group, is Walter Buchebner (1929–1964). Having started out as a rather romantic and conventional poet who rejected the—in his eyes rather sterile—experimentation of the Vienna Group, Buchebner's life and work were strongly influenced by his discovery of the work of Ginsberg and other Beat writers. Ginsberg, in particular, is referred to frequently in his later poetry and, together with Burroughs and Kerouac, also in the statements on poetry that he put on paper in the early 1960s. By then Buchebner had developed a kind of writing he called "active poetry," which in many ways is reminiscent of Kerouac's spontaneous prose and Beat writing in general. As Buchebner's diary entries make clear, "active poetry" was meant to liven up Austrian literature, which in his view was "dead"; it would only come alive again if it would acquire some of the spontaneous and rhythmical qualities of jazz, as well as the "high speed" (96) of some of Kerouac's prose and the "metal-hard diction" (91) of Burroughs's *Naked Lunch*. In Buchebner's view all of these qualities come together in Ginsberg's writing.

While Buchebner's work did bring some fresh air to Austrian poetry, it did not affect the staid and formal quality of Austrian society. In the eyes of many, Austrian society today is still as conventional as it was in the post–World War II period. Therefore it is not surprising that Austrian artists and writers still find inspiration in the work of the Beats. In recent years in Austria, the spirit of the Beats is especially to be found in the work that is being done at the Vienna Poetry School. This Schule für Dichtung was established in 1991 by the Austrian poet Ide Hintze, who had come into contact with Ginsberg the year before. The school was partly a result of their meeting; Hintze and a number of other Austrian poets and performance artists decided to embark on a project that in some ways resembles the Jack Kerouac School of Disembodied Poetics in Boulder, Colorado, founded by Ginsberg and Anne Waldman, with input from Diane di Prima. One of the aims of the Poetry School is "the development and refinement of spontaneous-mind poetic activity for purposes of teaching, enlightenment and beauty, or aesthetic pleasure" (Hintze). In order to achieve this, many Austrian and foreign writers and artists have taught at the school, including not only Ginsberg and Waldman and other Beats, but also the rock musician and writer Nick Cave, and many Austrian poets and performers.

Among the school's documents on the Internet, which is used extensively for teaching, there is a picture (taken at the school in September 1993) of Ginsberg in a kneeling position, in the process of photographing H. C. Artmann. If one should so desire, the picture can be read as a belated tribute of the Beat Generation to the accomplishments of the Vienna Group, who in some instances were ahead of what the Beats were doing.

Note

Translations from texts not (yet) translated into English are the author's.

Chapter 11

Prague Connection

Josef Rauvolf

It didn't take long—after the 6 Gallery reading, after the publication of "Howl," *On the Road*, and other works—for the glory (or, depending on one's point of view, the contamination) of the Beat Generation to cross the Atlantic and land in the fertile soil of the Socialist Republic of Czechoslovakia. Former Czech president Václav Havel put it aptly in his foreword to Allen Ginsberg's book of interviews. He speaks about how the general revolt of the Beats resonated in Czechoslovakia's "unfree conditions as even more rebellious than in the land of their origin" because it was perceived "not only as a denouncement of the social establishment and as a quest for new attitudes and a new lifestyle," but also, and more importantly, "as a potential instrument for resistance to the totalitarian system that had been imposed in our existence" (*Spontaneous* ix).

The Czech reception of Beat writers, and of Ginsberg in particular, may be viewed in two different ways: we can seek how and to what extent Beat influence is visible in Czech writing, and, more broadly, what influence it had on the lifestyle and ideas of the young generation of Czechs. As for the latter, which is easier to detect, the first regular information about the Beat Generation came in the years preceding Ginsberg's visit to Prague in 1965 through books[1] and the bi-monthly journal *Světová literatura*,[2] in which the essay "American Bohemia" by Igor Hájek was published in November 1959.

However, we should not forget: while Beat texts were published in Czech, with commentaries and essays, that did not mean it was easy for Czechs to follow the Beat example. This was especially true for lifestyles and attitudes, which young Czech readers were unable to fully embrace. It was simply impossible in a totalitarian state where secret police, informers, and the general public were offended by Beat lifestyles.[3] As Havel wrote: "If those who knew the literature and, by fostering it, created through this common knowledge a brotherhood, a community of nonconformists, when they expressed their views, it was, understandably, more

hazardous in our situation than it could have been in the United States of America"
(Ginsberg, *Spontaneous* ix).[4] This sentiment could be clearly applied to the group
of Czech authors associated with Edice Půlnoc (Midnight Edition) who, in tight
isolation, wrote at the same time as their American counterparts, in the late 1940s
and early 1950s, and whose work, lifestyles, and attitudes present many similarities
to the Beats.

In this respect, Hájek's essay deserves a closer look. In a mere twenty-four pages, it
offers long excerpts from "Howl," including the William Carlos Williams foreword;[5]
parts of "Sunflower Sutra"; the complete "America" and "At Apollinaire's Grave";
extensive portions of *On the Road*; and excerpts from John Clellon Holmes's *The
Horn*. This selection may seem narrow by today's standards, but keep in mind that
Hájek's sources were limited: the Iron Curtain kept out anything that might have
disrupted the building of socialism. The regime did not hesitate to clamp down on
anything it perceived as a threat—and the concept of culture as an ideological weapon
and tool in pushing the party line advanced by Stalin's theoretician and henchman
Andrei Alexandrovich Zhdanov was still officially praised and practiced.

Hájek introduced a wealth of information, writing about other works by Ginsberg
and Kerouac as well, analyzing reactions to the Beats, positive and negative alike.
He pointed out the Beat Generation's connections to, and roots in, European traditions. Hájek was critical: "There wasn't much positive in this revolt. . . . The
Beats couldn't tell the difference between the progressive avant-garde and mislead-
ing, empty pranks and freaking. The Beat generation gave up in a way" ("Americká
bohéma" 229, 227). He underlined the nihilism, the lack of perspective or positive
attitudes toward society. But did he really mean it? It seems likely that he bowed to
the censor, inserting just enough critique for the essay to receive the needed impri-
matur. This hypothesis is supported by his inclusion of otherwise useless citations
of Soviet literary critics, which was a typical tactic for bypassing censors. The translated books were published along with fake "literary" essays that placed the work in
the context of the Marxist class struggle and declared it a harsh critique of capitalism
and imperialism. The quotations from Soviet critics made it even better. And the
readers knew how to read it.

As for "Howl," the excerpts selected for publication are revealing in this respect. The
first one finishes with "who disappeared into the volcanoes of Mexico," leaving out the
verses about "super communist pamphlets" (What would the authorities have thought
of that?!) as well as the ones about sexual pleasure and insanity. The translation continues with Part II, but without any footnote (again, probably due to its content merging
the holy asshole and cock with holy Moscow and the fifth International).

When Hájek's essay, thanks to the already mentioned tactical critical approach,
passed the censors, the Beat writers became "acceptable," and their works could be
published and read in public. It is interesting to observe that the regime did not use
the works' critical attitude toward U.S. politics as it did with other (extreme leftist) U.S. writers such as Albert Maltz, Benjamin Appel, Alexander Saxton, Victor
J. Jerome, and Philip Bonosky—all of them published in Czech translations in
huge numbers. The Beats were useless for the purposes of Communist propaganda
because of their suspect anarchist recklessness.

Beat Midnight

Parallels with the Beats emerge in the lives and works of the above-mentioned Czech authors grouped around Midnight Edition.[6] The *samizdat* (from Russian for "self-publishing," usually carbon-copied and illegally distributed texts in the Soviet bloc) edition was founded in 1949. From 1949 to 1953, it published poets Egon Bondy (b. Zbyněk Fišer, 1930–2007), Ivo Vodseďálek (b. 1931), Jana Krejcarová (1928–1981), as well as the now world-famous novelist Bohumil Hrabal (1914–1997) and others. There were forty-four "books" edited, mostly of poetry, a few of prose, and some of art collages.

Despite the fact that the Beats and Czech writers could not have known about each other—not only because the Iron Curtain kept them from disseminating their work to the West but also because, at least at first, the U.S. writers' works existed in only a handful of carbon copies—the parallels persisted through the 1960s, and in some cases even longer. As contemporary Czech philosopher Miroslav Petříček wrote: "Despite the isolation it's not only possible but indispensable to recognize the art development parallels that run simultaneously in another place" (14). There are many points of intersection, and it is worthwhile to note the connection, even if it was not a case of direct influence but rather of synchronicity.

What were the roots of this synchronicity? The experiences on both sides of the Cold War and the Iron Curtain were strong and inescapable: the shattering experience of the war, the world's postwar order, and the threat of World War III, this time nuclear. John Tytell wrote that "[t]he postwar era was a time of extraordinary insecurity, of profound powerlessness" and that "[f]ew periods in our history have presented as much of an ordeal for artists and intellectuals" (5). Norman Mailer, in *Prisoner of Sex*, "wondered how he survived these years without losing his mind" (Tytell 5), reminding us of Bondy's recollection that "the whole nation at least went in fears[,] in massive insecurity, the good half of [the] population in pure horror" (*Prvních deset* 64). The political purges and trials in communist Czechoslovakia found their counterparts in U.S. McCarthyism. The "nakedness" Tytell speaks of finds a parallel in Bondy's self-exposing verses about his sexual problems and troubles with excretion. Like William S. Burroughs, Bondy did not hesitate to write without emotion about his addiction to pills and alcohol. Speaking about lifestyle, Bondy remarked that "all this was just a manifestation and way of instinctive defense against totalitarian establishment" (*Haňťa* 8). Tytell's statement sounds similar: "The Beat movement was a crystallization of a sweeping discontent with American 'virtues' of progress and power" (4). If we look at more positive similarities, both groups were strongly intellectual, well read, and culturally educated. The Beats, for example, intimately knew the European avant-garde, which was also true of Middle-European poets. Synchronicity leads to many common artistic starting points and attitudes, and we may assume that the same goes for the later resonance of Beat in Czechoslovakia before and after Ginsberg's visit to Prague in 1965.

Martin Pilař described the Midnight Edition circle as follows (*Underground* 25),[7] and these characteristics can be applied to the Beat Generation as well:

1. creation of an independent culture without any contact with the establishment;
2. radical rejection of any pressure;
3. abandonment of an obligatory program;
4. emphasis on an authentic lifestyle;
5. emphasis on authenticity in artistic work (e.g., realism, slang, defiance of social, and cultural taboos);
6. critical attitude towards the establishment and its frozen value system; and
7. deflection from social norms.

Other characteristics typical of the Midnights (we can say almost the same about the Beats) were conscious outsiderdom; sympathy with the insulted and humiliated; fascination with the dregs of society; life on the edge of the law and often over the edge; embrace of extreme psychological experiences, including use of psychedelic drugs; hospitalization in psychiatric institutes, viewed as important experiences or as refuge from a hostile universe; refusal of military duty; rejection of "success" and "career"; emphasis on individual freedom; and negation and transcendence of sexual taboos. Added to these is an interest in "regular" people; the avoidance of art with a capital "A"; the rejection of *l'art pour l'art* of elitism; and, as noted historian and editor of these writers Martin Machovec expressed it, "the deestheticization and drastic purification of poetic language" (qtd. in Alan 159).

Půlnoc writers tried, Machovec continues, "not to shrink under the enormous pressure of mass psychosis and the offered myths, but on the contrary to take hold of them, to uncloak them by specific persiflage and so 'paralyze' them in a way" (qtd. in Alan 163). Of course their critical attitude toward the regime was limited, since any open action would have resulted in the regime sending them either to prison or the gallows.[8] To what extent these writers' activities were monitored by the StB (the official abbreviation for Státní bezpečnost, the political secret police) is unknown, since Bondy's files were destroyed or may have ended up in the KGB vaults. In any case, the StB knew about the publishing, as we see from long "protocolary testimony about Trotskyites" given in jail by Milan Herda sometime between 1950 and 1952. About Bondy he disclosed, "I heard that he publishes some kind of edition, maybe 'midnight,' in four copies that bring manifestations of his and of the people circled around him" (qtd. in Alan 525). Why the police let them be in a time of omnipresent paranoia and oppression is still a mystery.

As Petříček notes, "It's clear that authenticity was neither a catchword nor a program but a necessity. . . . Authenticity is something irreducible in a man" (13). The "different" social norms involved, as Bondy stated, were "vagabondage, theft, beggary and antisocial activity of all kinds.[9] From this lifestyle also follows expression on an artistic level as open as in 'Howl' or *On the Road*. It is easy to prove with texts" (*Haňťa* 8). As Machovec put it, "These were works that often depicted, in a very specific, drastic, authentic and real way the time of their origin, the Stalinist pandemonium of early-1950s Czechoslovakia" (qtd. in Alan 66).

We can take as an example Bondy's *samizdat* book *Total Realism* (*Totální realismus*, 1950), actually the term he used for his early 1950s work in which his autobiographical texts looked like mere transcriptions of mental notes or observations without any visible input by the poet: "I was reading the news about the traitors' trial / when you arrived / After a while you undressed / and when I laid down with you / you were fine as usual / When you left / I finished the news of their execution" (*Totální realismus* 10), or "I sit in my cell / and watch the poster / glued to the opposite wall / it says / The Jailguards Corps / the crushing fist of working class / or look out the window / behind the bars there's a tower / and the sky miraculously / blue (*Totální realismus* 10). The picture of the time is correct and chilling: "The street loudspeakers announce exact time / the hours when the power will be shut off / the results of the newest trials / and of matches" (*Totální realismus* 9). As in the following poem, Bondy's form is clearly reminiscent of Burroughs's "no-emotions" factualism: "My love died today / She performed an abortion on herself / the child she had from the other one" (*Totální realismus* 17). As Bondy later explained, "In this poetics there was strictly omitted any didacticism or moralization" (*Haňťa* 7). We may find similar stances in Beat writers. Consider, for instance, Kerouac's "Belief and Technique for Modern Prose," in which he states, "Remove literary, grammatical and syntactical inhibition" (Parkinson 67)—or Burroughs's laconic reaction to the Ginsberg-Carr dispute that art is "a three-letter word" (Watson 35).

Other examples can be drawn from Bohumil Hrabal. In his long epics such as "Beautiful Poldi" and "Bambino di Praga" (both 1950), we see dread, agitation, and outsiderdom: "... the road to paradise is open all day here / only these acts of craziness keep the mechanism / of our orderly lives in balance" (*Poupata* 140) or

[. . .] Christ in white sneakers
will sit with head thrown back
will be tried for aphorisms about revolt
when he traveled around the lake
now I see his grenade exploded too
as he walked among men without a basket
that he could walk his way to the furnace's edge
now I see that it was him who
dyed his hair green and went to the opera house
it was him who strolled down the boulevard
and walked a lobster on a leash
....
it was him who danced naked in the theatre
just a cone on his head
he was everywhere
where there was scandal
where they cut the cloth for freedom flags" (*Poupata* 148)

The long poem "Beautiful Poldi," drawing on Hrabal's raw experience in the steel mills, anticipates the enumerative form of the first two parts of "Howl," finding beauty in the "dirty" reality of the everyday in a manner strikingly similar to Ginsberg's "In Back of the Real" and "Sunflower Sutra":

Considering all these poems, it is difficult to oppose Bondy's claim in 1990 that [u]n-doubtedly because the Czech art kept pace with the contemporary art abroad something really remarkable happened in the Midnight Edition group in 1949–1953. It created practically a downright analogy of works by [the] American Beat generation—and a few years in advance. The authors of Midnight Edition lived with [the] background of a much more dangerous and crueler time than the one we know from the autobiographies and books of the Beat generation. [We lived] permanently in the shadow of war, and in the shadow of labor camps and mass political persecution as well. . . ." (*Haňťa* 7)

The fact that at that time neither he nor any other Midnight author knew anything about Beat writers supports this statement. Thus, the Midnight writers, despite being almost completely unknown in their own country and abroad as well,[10] were full-fledged philosophical companions of the Beats.

Viola: Beat Haven

Igor Hájek's article not only called attention to the Beat phenomenon but it also served as an inspiration. It was no coincidence that there was a massive increase in hitchhiking in Czechoslovakia in the early 1960s, and not only because of the popularity of Kerouac. There were articles published about this way of hip travelling and the word spread. Hitchhiking was suddenly simply normal. Other indirect results of the popularity of Beat texts were public poetry readings and the establishment of poetry theaters, despite the fact that historically there had not been much of a Czech tradition of public poetry readings. Small poetry theaters sprang up not only in Prague but also in smaller towns as well.

The most important poetry theater was Viola, a wine bar in Prague. Its beginnings were closely tied to the Beat writers, and its importance cannot be overestimated.[11] Viola opened on July 22, 1963, despite a government ban on the opening of new stages. Its first program was titled, provocatively, "Who Owns Jazz?" and presented work of Czech poets alongside poems by Gregory Corso and Lawrence Ferlinghetti. Viola's program confirms its status as a bastion of Beat: of the first sixteen performances (from its 1963 opening until Ginsberg's visit to Prague in spring of 1965), we find no fewer than six evenings devoted to Corso, Ferlinghetti, and Ginsberg (who himself read "Howl" there). Quickly, the poets who would later be called Beat formed a tight circle around Viola along with a loyal audience. This proved that it was possible—in a limited way, for a short time—to establish what were known as "islands of positive deviation." As one of the insiders, the poet Vladimíra Čerepková, recalls,

There was [a] completely unrepeatable and specific atmosphere, bohemian life, jazz, great program[s], meeting[s] with fabulous musicians, painters, directors, with other poets' poems. There were artists and journalists from the whole world coming in. And all this was happening in the Communist grayness, under constant police interrogations, in omnipresent censorship and in [an] overall unfree state. This paradox is now almost impossible to imagine." (Riedlbauchová 40)

However, as another Viola poet, Inka Machulková, points out, "Everything published or read at our shows must pass the censor" ("Já, beatnička" 7). According to actor Radim Vašinka, who recited Ginsberg's works, "Originally it wasn't snobbish at all. It attracted a certain kind of audience—not admirers of poetry, but people who sensed a certain social intensity in the poetry. And that was what drew young people to the Beats" (Müllerová 15).

Hail the King

On February 18, 1965,[12] as the Czechoslovak Airlines's regular flight from Havana touched down on the runway, Ginsberg, freshly expelled from Castro's Cuba, had no way to anticipate the dramatic months that awaited him in Prague. Nor could he have had any idea to what extent his visit would influence not only himself but also the country to which he had escaped. At any rate, the poet was landing on fertile soil. His poems had already been published in magazines, and a collection of his poems was being readied for publication as a book. Although Ginsberg had not considered visiting Prague before and had not been invited, fate would have it that, when he was forced to leave Cuba, he could not fly directly to the United States via Mexico because of a ban on such travel. He was escorted to the airport where the police put him on the Czechoslovak airplane they had booked for him. Knowing he had contacts in Prague, he did not object.[13] Thanks to these contacts, Ginsberg was an official guest of the Writers Union (receiving $75 in Czech crowns, or about ten weeks' wages). He had royalties waiting for him,[14] and he stayed at a luxurious hotel in the center of town. His visa was valid until May 15, 1965.

Witnesses' memories of his arrival on the Prague scene differ. For poet Čerepková, it was a revelation "to see the American poet with my own eyes. We didn't miss a thing. He arrived in winter and walked around in his tennis shoes. Everybody imitated him, walking around outside in the snow in brand-new sneakers. Inka Machálková and I took him to U Nováků for a taste of Czech cuisine. He didn't like Czech dumplings, just pecked at it" (Müllerová 26). Painter Karel Chaba's memory is more reserved: "Ginsberg came to Viola in white sneakers,[15] looking pretty ragged. Not too tall, running around. This was a non-communist intellectual twenty-something crowd. Everybody pissed him off, following him around like pricks" (Müllerová 30).

In these two attitudes, we can find roots of the reception he received in Prague. Was it ready for him? As it turns out, the answer is both yes and no. After the show trials of the Stalinist 1950s, with almost 300 sentenced to death and tens of thousands sentenced to many years in prison, after all the censorship and spying, there seemed to be a slight thaw, a loosening up, in public life and culture alike, but Ginsberg's visit proved these hopes to be but an illusion. For the first time since the Nazi occupation of World War II, Czechoslovakia's Communist regime allowed the student celebration of May Day (Majáles),[16] but it did not hesitate to take strong action against the students—or foreign visitors, even if they were official guests of the Writers Union.

Ginsberg, as was his wont, found his bearings immediately and perfectly, leaping into Prague cultural life, both official and unofficial, meeting people, talking, reading poems. He did not neglect his private life either; while there he had sexual adventures, which were exactly what the regime eventually used as an excuse to expel him and what was also wielded extensively in later propaganda. As for Ginsberg's "unofficial" welcome, he became a legend in the streets of Prague, a real celebrity. Everything about him and his image, including the sneakers, deviated from the norm. And yet everywhere he went he received a positive welcome. He frequented Viola, installing himself on the unofficial cultural scene with the literati and the translators, and having long discussions with students.[17] Balling. Reading. And writing poems.[18] The poet was "officially" welcomed as well, with encomiums even published in the Party's daily *Rudé právo*, of course with the almighty censor's blessing. "I came to find out about your reality, and from Prague I will continue my research of the socialist universe," the March 3 edition of *Rudé právo* quoted Ginsberg as saying. Besides praising his poetry, it said: "Soon our readers will have a chance to better acquaint themselves with his poetry in a planned translation of 'Howl.'" Under the headline "A. Ginsberg discovers ČSSR," the *Svobodné slovo* newspaper wrote: "Allen Ginsberg has [a] small discovery for him[self]. And Czechoslovakia has discovered a personality very important in American progressive writing" (*Poláčková*). This was March 20. The poet himself was soon to discover the extent of his discovery.

Apart from these shallow phrases, *Literární noviny* published Hájek's essay "From a Bradbury-like World into the Prague of Early Spring" ("Z bradburyovského světa"), emphasizing the Beats' political side while posing the rhetorical question of whether these writers would be accepted in socialist Czechoslovakia. Hájek writes about Ginsberg's imitators and his mastery of craft, letting him talk at large about the poets who influenced him, about intuition and total openness. Ginsberg speaks about how the modern state "cuts people off, building dams between them, inoculating them with fear of expressing love's desire" ("Z bradburyovského" 8). Hájek's essay later invoked harsh criticism from the highest Party levels, and it is easy to understand why sentences like these would make the rigid post-Stalinist ideologues angry. Hájek's inspirational view can be seen as the voice of one group. The other remained silent. It was March 21. All was calm. But the calm was just an illusion.

Beat (the) Mephistopheles

Official hostility began after Ginsberg was elected King of May on May 1 during the Majáles in a staged ritual in which he was to govern over the students (and to spend the night with the Queen of May, something that did not materialize). Over the next few days, Ginsberg was arrested three times, beaten on the street, driven to an alcohol treatment center, and lost his diary. The climax came on May 7 when he was escorted to the airport and put on a flight to London,[19] officially expelled from the country. In the air, he wrote the poem "Kral Majales," describing his nearly three-month stay in "realsocialism," presenting it in counterpoint to the beauty of

Old Town. The poem was so strong that he published it with only minor revisions, confirming the inspirational power of Prague. And he read it in public for the remainder of his life.

The background to the incident described in the poem ("knocked down on the midnight pavement by a moustached agent who screamed out BOUZERANT") has never before been revealed. But we can clearly see the hand of the StB at work. As Ginsberg recalled years later, he suspected that it was set up. StB files confirm his account. Ginsberg's attacker claimed that Ginsberg had his fly open and his hand between the legs of a female while a man was stroking Ginsberg's penis, that he was attacked and had to defend himself. Both Ginsberg and the witnesses (the young lady and her boyfriend) strongly refuted this account. Strangely, the mysterious "homophobic" attacker was released—until I discovered his name listed in the archives of the StB as its agent. Of course he did not reveal his identity to the policemen. Nor did he tell them of his secret mission to fray the poet's nerves to the point that he would leave the country. Actually, for "undermining a foreigner," he received a "bonus" of 500 crowns, or two-thirds of the average Czech monthly income at that time.

The StB's interest in Ginsberg is clear from a note in a police memo dated May 3: "7. section, note: get tape recording or other document about G's impact or influence, medical record. Accomplish operation E-4" (i.e., phone-tapping in StB terminology). This and other documents reveal that Ginsberg was being watched (in an operation called May Bug), photographed, and bugged. The police stole his diary. How this happened is still a mystery, and there are at least four Rashomon-like versions about its loss and location.

Ginsberg was reproached by his biographers for having (sexual) contacts with dubious characters, thus giving the regime arguments against himself. For example, Barry Miles states that "he mixed with people in Prague that most individuals in literary circles would have avoided" (*Ginsberg* 366). The police files do not mention any such dregs of society. These young men wrote poems, adored Ginsberg, and since some of them had already had homosexual experiences, there was no "corruption of youth" as the propaganda alleged. Michael Schumacher, too, writes that "[i]n Czechoslovakia and the Soviet Union, he had been much more cautious [than in Cuba], yet he had still been more provocative than the citizens of those countries would have ever dared to be. Just because he was [a] guest of these countries did not mean that he was immune from their laws or customs" (444). On the other hand, Schumacher quotes Ginsberg's 1969 letter to Corso: "'complaints' by parents were manipulated and phoney like Kafka" (444). No, the files show that the parents, perhaps surprisingly, were not manipulated.

Ginsberg actually did not violate any Czech law. Homosexuality, then as now, was legal for anyone over the age of eighteen, and he claimed in the letter to his father that he had not taken any drugs (although, according to Jan Samohel, Ginsberg did take the legal prescription drug Fenmetrazin, a Czech amphetamine, with himself, other friends, and lovers.). And Jan Zábrana quotes in his diary a note Ginsberg left for one Czech friend: "I want to blast some shit with you. Do you have any pot? Are you carrying? Can you turn me on??? Say Allen Ginsberg on the Eve of his departure for Moscow gave you this sign Al" (*Celý život* 237). He did talk about drugs, but that was not a criminal act. Did he speak openly against the regime? No. He was as cautious in his public words as he was in his diary. All evidence indicates the regime had it in for him.

Why an American Poet Was Expelled From Czechoslovakia

The change from adoration in the media to condemnation was swift, almost overnight. On May 2, the daily *Mladá fronta* published a long article about Majales with a funny passage about Ginsberg on the truck with a big sign saying "Voting for Ginsberg you prove your proletarian internationalism" (and a young child asking his father, "Who's that Ginsberg?" and the father answering, "It must be some candidate . . ."). The passage ends with "American poet Ginsberg was elected as King of May. However, there were rumors about the revolution and overthrowing this crowned head" ("Šťastná" 4). Did the journalists already know about the action against "the candidate"?

In March, Ginsberg wrote enthusiastically to his father that "[e]verybody here adores the Beatniks, & there's a whole generation of Prague teenagers who listen to jazz &wear long hair & say shit on communism & read *Howl*. . . . and I run around with teenage gangs & have orgies & then rush up to Writer's [sic] Union & give lectures. . ." (*Family* 231). Two months later he wrote from London in a different tone: "Czech police stole my journals, notebook & later expelled me for anti-state orgies" (*Family* 234).

A full-page article titled "Allen Ginsberg and Morale" (subtitled "Why an American poet was expelled from Czechoslovakia") was published in *Mladá fronta*, the Communist Youth daily, on May 16. In typical newspeak, the anonymous author (according to different witnesses, his name is Josef Schnabel, the newspaper's culture section editor)[20] summed up the sins that Ginsberg had supposedly committed: alcoholism, drug use, sexual perversion, contempt for the authorities, and corrupting Czechoslovakia's youth—all supported with quotations from the stolen diary, psychiatrists' records, and letters from resentful parents of the poet's friends or lovers, denouncing their sons (supposedly unscripted, although at least one was written at the direct request of the police). This loyalty is "understandable" as these fathers belonged to the communist elite: one worked at the Party Central Committee, the other as deputy minister. All these quotations are, given the usual praxis of the StB, real and still exist in the secret police archives, which illustrates to what extent the StB was running the show and how confident they were. Piquant is the fact that a translation of this article surfaced in Ginsberg's FBI files. (According to Schumacher, on April 26, while Ginsberg was in Prague, J. Edgar Hoover, the first director of the U.S. Federal Bureau of Investigation, signed a document portraying Ginsberg as potentially dangerous because of his anti-establishment statements [449]). The *Mladá fronta* article attacked not only Ginsberg but also everyone who met him or wrote about him, that is, intellectuals and writers.

Let us pause to consider—the true targets of the article, the intended audience, were not ordinary people, whose opinion did not matter to the StB (and who could not have cared less whether some freakish American homosexual got expelled or not). No. This article, strategically published in the "more liberal" *Mladá fronta* (as opposed to the "hardline" *Rudé právo*, which published only a very short article titled "Hangover with Ginsberg" ["Kocovina s Ginsbergem"], condensing the *Mladá fronta* piece on the next day, May 17), was aimed at the intellectuals: the artists, writers, art union members, and magazine staffers—all those who needed a slap on the wrist to be shown who was in charge and to be put in their place. The journalist Viktor Šlajchrt, who came to the same conclusion, rightly notes that, unlike in the 1950s, it was no longer possible to string intellectuals up or toss them in jail for twenty years. Into this situation, like wishful thinking, rode America's poet of nonconformist thinking and behavior. The Czech literary magazines welcomed and applauded him, giving the powers that be one more argument for a crackdown. While the poet was living it up and writing it all down in his diary,[21] the StB was silently at work. In other words, Ginsberg was manufacturing ammunition for the barrage. His observations of Czechoslovak reality were both biting and true. Unknowingly, however, he helped the regime to strengthen its totalitarian roots—at least for the next three years.

Czechoslovakia's president and Communist Party head Antonín Novotný, who in collaboration with the StB must have been the architect of Operation May Bug, had to have been satisfied. Not only did he succeed in frightening intellectuals but two important magazines were also abolished: the literary/philosophy monthly *Tvář*, which Václav Havel worked for, and the monthly *Knižní kultura*, in which under the guise of "book culture" contemporary art and literature were published. The day after Ginsberg's expulsion, in a speech marking the twentieth anniversary of liberation, Novotný warned:

> Again we emphasize that those who would speculate, who would spread, whether directly or indirectly, bourgeois morals and send over "cultural" and other personalities to influence our youth; those whose moral profile is a disgrace to bourgeois society itself; they will fail. Unfortunately there are some individuals here who laid the ground for these people in the media, covering for them and calling themselves their friends. The next time we will think more carefully about such a guest. (Šlajchrt 11)

Everyone got the message: mission accomplished.[22] Ginsberg's visit served a purpose, although he knew nothing about it.

Aftermath

Culture in Czechoslovakia took a long time to recover from the blow it suffered at the hands of Novotný and the StB—until spring 1968, in fact, when the Stalinist president fell. In any case, Ginsberg's visit was not forgotten. Publication of all other translations of his work was prohibited, with production stopped on several planned selections of poems; the same held true for other Beat writers.[23] But their works lived on and, indeed, continued to circulate (especially "Howl") in countless carbon copies, which were even read in public, albeit semi-legally.[24] Ginsberg's name was not permitted to be printed or mentioned; he became persona non grata.[25] A Jan Zábrana poem, written in 1960, presents ramifications of this reality: "As I read Ginsberg / I don't think about America / but about how they / just for nothing / destroyed the generation / the war spared / (even it!) . . ." (*Básně* 100). The poem not only connects Ginsberg's name (note the "destroyed generation" phrase) with Zábrana's general "waste land" feeling of the late 1950s and early 1960s when the poem was written but also indirectly speaks about Ginsberg being eradicated ("just for nothing") from official Czech culture as well.

In spite of all the defamation campaigns and censorship, Ginsberg's trip remained alive in memory, as he discovered for himself in 1993 when he returned to lecture for a few weeks at Olomouc University and experienced the following encounter at a local cafe:

> A man came up to me, shook my hand and asked me to sit down at the table. He said that he'd been in jail and had read my poetry and it had given him encouragement while he was in jail. So I asked which poem, and he said "Sunflower Sutra," so he actually remembered which it was. I hear it had a psychological impact that was useful to people in Czechoslovakia. Maybe the same impact that it had on me, because those poems were like discoveries of my own nature.[26]

The place where the man read his poem is significant for all of Ginsberg's Czech readers, and not only them—everyone was in some kind of jail, and art and writing offered a way to slip through the bars into freedom. It may sound like a pathetic cliché, but it is the truth.

Czech Beat

Given how many Beat translations were published in Czechoslovakia, even before 1989, and how legendary Ginsberg's visit became,[27] it is no wonder the Beats served as inspiration to so many young poets, even if most of them simply copied the formula. Probably the most famous Czech "Beat" poet is Václav Hrabě (1940–1965), who wrote over eighty poems and some prose works as well. He died of gas poisoning on March 15, 1965, during Ginsberg's visit, arousing all sorts of speculation, including StB murder, but all the evidence suggests that the death was an accident. His short life was connected to Viola, poetry, and jazz. These facts, along with his poems, made him a legend—and a Beat poet. But if it is true that Hrabě lived like his American counterparts, uprooted and hitchhiking around the country, his poetry grew out of Czech pre- and postwar poets Jiří Orten, Jiří Šotola, and Nobel Prize laureate Jaroslav Seifert, along with French medieval *poète maudit* François Villon. Hrabě, though, was familiar with the Beats, and we can identify some points where they aligned: his emphasis on everyday life, candidness, craft, simplicity, his respectful treatment of ordinary people and workers, and his lack of intellectualizing. He even named Ginsberg in one of his poems, and there are echoes of Ferlinghetti in his work, namely "Sometime during eternity / some guys show up" from *A Coney Island of the Mind*:

And there was jazz caroling its twelve bars
in the wet sand in honor of this guy
who finally should've come to this world
and who is said /?/ to gentlemanly play all
our trials for us ("untitled," *Stop-time* 63)

Ferlinghetti's influence can be found in other Hrabě poems as well, exemplified by his "Monk in Blues" about jazz musician Thelonious Monk, which also manifests the inspiration of Kerouac's jazz poetry. Hrabě wrote a few blues poems as well.

Vladimíra Čerepková (b. 1946) was also part of the Viola inner circle; she too lived a Beat life, and, like Hrabě's, her name is inextricably tied to the near-obligatory epithet "Beat." Again, like Hrabě she was a Beat poet more because of the way she lived her life than because of her work. Her childhood and adolescence were strikingly similar to Corso's: born nine months after the war ended, she never knew her father (legend makes him a Red Army officer) or motherly love. At the age of ten, she was placed in a children's home, then a detention center. She was saved by books and poetry. One day a filmmaker came to the center to shoot a documentary about abandoned girls, learned about her poetry, and started to circulate it around Prague. The noted poet František Hrubín labeled her the "Czech Rimbaud" and helped her to get published. Several of her poems show a Beat influence, such as "One-eyed Tomcat," which could easily have been inspired by Ginsberg's "The Lion for Real": "The one-eyed tomcat comes at night" and, as the poet writes, threatens to devour her. But the threat is in vain, as the tomcat licks her off with his eye and jumps away (*Ryba* 46). Another poem, "How's Jazz" (*Ryba* 52), suggests a fondness for Ferlinghetti, equating jazz to three drummers madly drumming their own heads.

Another important poet who, along with Hrabě and Čerepková, formed the "Holy Viola Trinity,"[28] was Inka Machulková (b.1933). She too gravitated to the Beats more as a result of her emotions and lifestyle. She adored Corso, and even wrote him a letter; Corso wrote back, agreeing with her ideas about poetry. However, we find her poems resonating primarily with Ferlinghetti: "Lying silently on the bed you got up from / I commune from you / the creation of our white world" (*Zamkni les* 12). But there are affinities as well with Ginsberg's social empathy ("Tell me why these raggedy grandmas finish up scraps in cafeterias") in the poem "Don't ask me about Marxist philosophy!" (*Zamkni les* 32), and, in the same poem, she speaks harshly against social, political, and racial hypocrisy, noting that the newspapers and the assembly speakers disagree with black race oppression while the chairman of the street committee refuses to live in the same villa with a gypsy family.

Vote for the Beat International

Traces of Ginsberg's and Corso's influences appear in the poems of song-writer Jaroslav Hutka (b. 1947), who said, "We felt ourselves like great Beats"

(Čermák 36). In "To My Generation II," we sense "Howl" especially its messianic attitude:

> I sympathize with people who don't want to work
> and wallow at the museum
> that makes a question of anything it wants
> who wander down the streets and steal rolls at dawn
> are in love with the fantastic party of life
> [. . .] who are afraid to go out
> who bite a passerby in a rush of absentmindedness
> who have themselves locked in asylums
> who commit suicides and love the poetry of independence
> [. . .] I belong to those who bumming around you meet at midnight
> I belong to the generation's holy chosen ones, prepared to die at the
>   martyr's post. (109)

Corso's influence is apparent in Hutka's long poem "Útěk" ("Escape," 1966) in which he writes about marriage in a way that is similar to Corso in his famous poem "Marriage" (published in Czech in 1964), even using the same arguments: "No I wouldn't survive my own marriage / all these uncles and aunts / whom the marriage gives the permission to take part in our hymeneal night / to watch me in the bed" (15). Hutka's poems speak of the same emotions and experiences as did his beloved poets, while retaining originality and freshness.

Another writer influenced in his later writing by Beats is, perhaps surprisingly, Bohumil Hrabal, mentioned above in connection with Midnight Edition. In interviews, Hrabal compared his characters to Ginsberg's Ignu, calling them *pábitelé*, a neologism not easy to translate, resembling "the palaverer": "The palaverers and their life were celebrated by Allen Ginsberg, the ignu poet" (*Pábitelé* dust jacket). Of the Beats' influence on him, he said:

> I'd say I think even more so than anyone could guess. People like Kerouac or Ginsberg definitely fertilized our generation. I'm fascinated by Kerouac and Ginsberg, and Ferlinghetti, by these dharma bums who felt very strongly that the writer should be as far as possible poor, simple, and down to look up. He should be educated and fond of Eastern wisdoms . . . I was with them in their group at a distance. (*Kličky* 69)

There is also a sweet passage, in typical Hrabalian style, of his 1965 meeting with Ginsberg, describing how both of them drank beer and bowed to each other without a word—and of Ginsberg having cut a little of his pubic hair for a guest book (*Kličky* 70).[29]

Hrabal's novels *Taneční hodiny pro starší a pokročilé* (*Dancing Lessons for the Advanced in Age*, 1964) and *Obsluhoval jsem anglického krále* (*I Served the King of England*, 1971) are reminiscent of Kerouac novels: the former is one sentence in an unending stream of consciousness monologue, similar to long passages from the original scroll of *On the Road*, while the latter, like *The Subterraneans*, was written, as he discloses in an afterword (not in the English version), at a single stretch of eighteen days: "The texts are written in fierce summer sun, that heated the typewriter so much it got stuck few times every minute and stuttered. Not being able to look at the white paper I lost control over what I wrote, so I wrote in light's high of automatic method"

(*Obsluhoval* 235). He also expressed his admiration for Kerouac's *The Dharma Bums* (*Kličky* 69). As Tomáš Mazal, Hrabal's biographer, points out, "we may find a certain, both subjective and objective, similarity between Kerouac and Hrabal, not just a kind of programmatic outsidership" (317).

Perhaps the closest to Ginsberg's poetics was that of Milan Koch (1948–1974), a poet whose poems, as Martin Machovec, noted historian of the Czech underground,[30] wrote, could "make an exotic impression. . . . drug inspiration or the theory and praxis of disruption and expansion of the senses, or Buddhism and other Eastern teachings in our country, in the '60s, were acceptable only in deep illegality, anonymity, in the 'underground'" (Koch, *Červená* 7). The poet wrote without any self-censorship, a strategy that proved to be a freeing and positive influence, as it had on Ginsberg when he wrote "Howl." As an underground writer, Koch was not published until after his death.[31] As for his poetics, as Machovec puts it, "the Apollinaire-surrealistic traditions, so popular in Czechoslovakia before the war, mingle with American [Beat] influences" (Koch, *Červená* 7).

We find Ginsberg's influence in many of Koch's poems, above all in "Wheeze for Calliopene,"[32] an openly declared paraphrase of "Howl." The poem (a clear reference to Calliope, Greek muse of heroic poetry, although Koch never mentioned it) remains the only successful effort in Czech poetry to match "Howl," and Koch's work in general ranks as one of, if not the, best variations on Ginsberg in Czechoslovakia. The poem's greatest asset lies in its transfer of "Howl" to Czech reality without the loss of any of its declarative qualities. Like Ginsberg, lamenting his generation's destruction, counting and recounting its physical and emotional wounds, Koch depicts the traumas of his own generation. We see similar surrealistic imagery, including images of torment, but unlike "Howl," we may not perceive the real "models" behind them, which, in Koch's phantasmagorical vision, are all the people of Czechoslovakia. As in Ginsberg's poetry, we sense his strong ethical attitude behind the poem. In addition, the Koch/Bondy connection should be noted. They were friends (Koch even wrote "Quadrofonic Poem for Egon Bondy") and, like Bondy in the 1950s, he was not afraid to point out the hypocrisy and cruelty of the system they lived in.

In "Wheeze for Calliopene," Koch not only used the four-part structure of "Howl" but also successfully employed other design features of the poem. Thus, Part One features the litany-like verses full of horrifying images:

> I saw the hearing scalded in hacking visions of evening bell on worn
> waterfronts of silenced crises [. . .]
> Decrepit faces of political prisoners who chanted, fell and pissed under the regime's
> watchers' truncheons whom the uniform unified their faces –
> The humiliated and insulted who banged with hammers tore with tongs and
> deformed in pneumatic presses their organic hearts
> in praise of falling hell of proletcult's dictatorship – delete (Unpublished ms., n.p.)

When Koch used the "nondimensional ginsbergian verse of litany-like character" (Machovec, "Několik poznámek" 53), it enabled him to multiply his vision of Czechoslovakian reality: one can feel the echo of the horrible 1950s and the Stalinist labor camps and prisons. This reality is intensified through the use of the cumulative effect of adding more and more disturbing images. His control of the form never loses focus or overloads the text. The intensity of these images is almost palpably felt—again, as in the first two parts of "Howl."

The second part of "Wheeze" corresponds similarly to the second part of "Howl," describing the reality from which the threat and darkness arises: "From the bricks and cement, lime and sand, slabs and wires, brass rods / cried through, smashed windows, broken out shitted doors. . . ." Paralleling the third part of "Howl" celebrating Carl Solomon, the fellow patient Ginsberg met in the Columbia Presbyterian Psychological Institute, Koch writes about his friends who frequented Prague's center (in about 250 verses, longer than "Howl")—their activities, travels, and excesses:

> About you who on the National Museum's stairway[33] made dog chases sexual chases psychic chases, smoked grass brought in by guys from Westand East, hustled scrips for fenmetrazin and dexfenmetrazin, reached under girls skirts and lustfully hushed as the journalist discovered you and you posed in front of them in the dreadest tears with naked mouths,with ears buzzing with your own lovely voice in the oldest clothes you could find at home
> You went to visit each other
> and you found the stairways in every city in Czechoslovakia
> You went to visit each other
> and found the stairways in every city in Europe
> You went to visit each other
> and found the stairways in every metropolis of the world [. . .]
> With cuffs threw themselves into the barbwire with torn hands tried
> to abolish the borders and took more electricity into your body
> In attics you dissolved the iron curtain with homemade lysergic acid [. . .] to vote
>   for Beat International" (Červená 11)

In part four, Koch praises hair, understood as a symbol of freedom:

> Hair hair hair hair hair hair hair hair hair
>   hair
>   hair
>   hair
> The manes of infinity – the consonances of infinity
> The madness is hairy homeland
> The hairy-ones for whom the fate with hair is better than with the machine gun
> The hairy community of hairy cross in the middle of hairless world (Červená 27)

Hair became a symbol of freedom for young people, and others, in Czechoslovakia because it was an act of disobedience in a society led by crew-cut politicians and police. As childish as it might seem, hair actually functioned that way, and the hair, the longer the better, was an act of saying, "I'm not yours." It was also not so easy to do (see Note 3). As Jaroslav Hutka put it, "We started to look differently and the battlefield between the young generation and the old world became long hair. It irritated, and that's why hair became so important that it almost equaled the importance of life" (662).

Koch´s poems, such as the long poem "Elections of 1971," contain many references to the burdensome reality of living in Czechoslovakia, and his long prose piece "Be(at)ing" (in Czech *Bytnění*, an untranslatable pun on both "being Beat" and "being") from the late 1960s describes in the style of Kerouac and Snyder a long trip to the Slovak mountains. Koch knew the parts of *The Dharma Bums* and *On the Road* already published in Czech, and there are similarities with Kerouac's writing about "going on the road" in *On the Road* or *Visions of Cody* (although at that time the latter was unpublished):

THERE WAS FEAST IN EVERYTHING AS WE LEFT – in everything was the great excitement opening hearts for the farthest ideals that can't be touched by flesh-and-blood hand even for a second . . . We were so beautifully human . . . We didn't catch the sunrise. There'll be another and realer. It looks [as if] we're about to reach heaven . . . There's a fog wallowing across the Fatra tops and our souls wait until they can return there. (unpublished manuscript, n.p.)

The melded influence of Ginsberg and other Beats can be found often in his lengthy work (almost 700 typewritten pages), no doubt in part because Koch was familiar with them not only as a reader but also as their translator.

The Cage Slams Shut

"The 1960s flowed dramatically into the 1970s, and almost nothing was left of the Prague Beats' individuality. It was getting harder and riskier to hitchhike freely and find communes of kindred souls, the jail cells kept filling with 'parasites' [see Note 9], rolling off the assembly line" (Kozelka 2).

This is an accurate description of the changes after 1968, after the Soviet occupation and the ensuing "normalization"[34]—the repression affected not only the "Beats" but also all of society. As for publishing Beat literature, the complete "Howl" was published in 1969 in the monthly literary review *Sešity pro mladou literaturu* (*Notebooks for Young Literature*), which the regime used as one of the excuses to abolish the journal. After that, Czech aficionados of Beat literature could not find anything in the bookstores. But, yes, there were some "flaws" in the censoring system (see Note 6) and some texts published. The editor and Beats' translator Jan Zábrana still managed to add an excerpt from "Howl" and Ginsberg's notes on writing the poem in the anthology *How a Poem Is Made* (*Jak se dělá báseň*, 1970). The next Beat writer to be published was the not so ideologically undesirable Kerouac. In 1978, a very good translation of the complete *On the Road* was finally published. The 20,000 copies printed sold out in a day, with people signing petitions to print more, which surprisingly happened. An estimated 150,000 copies have been sold to date, and the book remains popular. In 1984, a volume of selected poems by Ferlinghetti was published. Finally, in 1988, it was possible for Ginsberg's poems to be published again, this time in *The Astronomic Clock's Zodiac* (*Horoskop orloje*), an American poetry anthology that also included, among others, Sandburg, Pound, Corso, and di Prima.

One may wonder how these books could get into print in such a culturally restricted state. Is there a contradiction? No, there is not. First, it took a long time for a book to be published, from its conception as an idea to its appearance on the shelves. So books such as *Jak se dělá poesie* or *Jazzová inspirace* were approved in "better" times and then simply flowed through. Second, most of these books were published by Odeon, the best publishing house in Czechoslovakia. Its editors constantly tried to push the limits of what could be printed. Theirs was a steady and exhausting fight with the bureaucrats from the book section at the Ministry of Culture, which was controlled by the Party's Central Committee, and—not only with these titles—required considerable personal bravery. If we say that Odeon was (relatively, of course) a dissident publishing house, it is not far from the truth. Plus, one should not forget that by 1988 the end was near; the Party was losing control and facing problems with dissent. The thaw was proceeding slowly but unstoppably. For example, Odeon had already started to prepare a Czech edition of Burroughs's *Junky* in 1987 and tiptoed around his *Naked Lunch*, eventually published in 1994.

The first of the Beats to visit Czechoslovakia after 1989 was, symbolically, Ginsberg, who came in April 1990 to take part in the King of May 1990 festival. He was accompanied by Anne Waldman, and both of them repeatedly returned. Czechoslovakia (and then the Czech Republic) was visited by Ferlinghetti, Snyder (twice), and Michael McClure. Subsequently, numerous works by Beat writers were published: Ginsberg, Waldman, Ferlinghetti, Snyder, McClure, Burroughs, Kerouac, Corso, and di Prima. There have also been critical studies, television documentaries, and radio programs about the Beats.

The Beats still inspire young poets as they did in the 1960s, although the results are less impressive. One exception is Svatava Antošová (b. 1957), who told me in an interview conducted via written correspondence about Ginsberg's influence on her writing: "Closest to my heart was and still is Allen Ginsberg. We share the same birthday and month. . . . It couldn't leave me unmoved as I began to write." In 1994 she wrote "Please Lady," a lesbian variation on Ginsberg's erotic poem "Please Master." Though openly explicit, hers is more gentle:

> Please lady, touch my forehead with your lips and stay
> Please lady, put your slender arms on my shoulders
> and slowly close to my neck
> smooth it with fingertips till you feel the chill
> running up and down
> Please lady, let me open my eyes and look into yours
> let me push the hair from your face bare the ear and caress its lobe and pinna with
>   my tongue [. . .]" ("Prosím paní" 27)

About the inspiration she told me the following: "Allen's original had a strong impact on me, although I objected to its, let's say, 'undue maleness.' When I later felt the urge to write a poem to my love, I considered approaching it as a kind of female, softer counterpoint to this otherwise fabulous text. The form was given by the opening 'please lady' and I didn't worry after that. It wrote itself." Thus the circle is closed: eroticism served as the excuse for Ginsberg's expulsion, and thirty years later it returns.

To sum up the effect of more than fifty years of Beat texts on the Czech cultural and social environment, we can confidently state that the influence of this relatively small group of writers was and is strong. Most important is the impact of Ginsberg.

In his case, we have to add to his literary influence the trace that his 1965 visit left in the Czech cultural public's consciousness. We cannot but agree with Hrabal who in an interview for a Czech state radio broadcast in May 1989 said, "They [Americans] wondered that in my country anybody taking an interest in literature knows who Ferlinghetti, Ginsberg, and Kerouac are[;] they are here, as I told them, even [as] young people's idols" (*Kličky* 331).

Notes

All translations into English are by Josef Rauvolf.

1. His translator was Jan Zábrana. Since many writers and poets were not allowed to publish their own work, they turned to translating; hence, the high quality of the translations.
2. An important literary review, founded in 1956, publishing prose, poetry, and essays in translation.
3. In August and September 1966, police launched the "Longhairs" campaign. Thousands of young men were affected (often beaten, always cropped), refused service in restaurants, and expelled from public transportation, movie theaters, and schools. The general public supported the suppression.
4. The hazard was made clear in the history of Ginsberg's Prague visit and the aftermath of his expulsion.
5. The translation was completed in the first half of 1959, which makes it one of the first. The Italian translation dates from 1965, as does the French. Only the Danish and German were published in 1959.
6. As Martin Machovec suggests, the name Midnight Edition was Bondy's idea. It should not be seen as referring only to the French wartime underground *Les Editions de Minuit*, but as "surely the symbol of the period's climate, a moment in the middle of a new, another age of darkness" (71).
7. Pilar extends Johanna Posset's short note from her thesis (12) about the Czech literary underground of the 1970s and 1980s and transposes it to the Midnight circle.
8. Bondy's friend, the surrealist and Marxist historian Záviš Kalandra, was sentenced to death and hanged after a 1950 show trial. Bondy himself was a secret police agent from 1953 on, although later expunged for his uselessness.
9. Since they worked only occasionally, they got by on a very low budget. Under the law (abolished in 1989), anyone who did not work, that is, those who did not have the stamp on their ID, could be sentenced as a "parasite" to up to one year in prison
10. Until the early 1990s when Bondy's collected poems and books by other Midnight poets were published (but only a few copies), their work remained relatively unknown, with the exception of Bohumil Hrabal, who was published in the early 1960s. Some of Bondy's poems were set to music by the Czech underground band the Plastic People of the Universe (see note 20) in the late 1970s, released in the West, and circulated in Czechoslovakia on tapes as "musical *samizdat*." Even so, Bondy remained an obscure figure until his death in April 2007. That changed in 2010 with the release of *3 Seasons In The Hell*, a Czech film about Bondy and the Midnight era.
11. Czech writers were aware of the publicity the Beats were receiving in the American mainstream press.
12. Ginsberg's arrival date is unclear. The StB archives say February 18; another source from the same time says February 19; Bill Morgan says February 20 (402).

13. Ginsberg told me in a 1993 interview for a Czech TV documentary that he had had no plans to go to Prague but looked forward to the possibility of seeing the city of Kafka and perhaps visiting relatives in Moscow. But in his letter to his father from Havana on February 5, 1965, he wrote, "I'll stay here another month & go on to Czechoslovakia" (*Family* 227). As far as I know, there is no other proof of his plans to visit Prague, nor did I find any Czech who could confirm or oppose it. Thus, the reasons why he was put on the Czechoslovakian Airlines airplane remain a mystery.

14. Biographies mistakenly state that the fees were for the book. The selected poems were not published until 1990, when Ginsberg came to Prague for the second time.

15. It is strange how deeply the sneakers implanted themselves in people's memories and became a legend. There is an entirely ordinary explanation for them. The poet wore them when he was expelled from subtropical Cuba to snowy wintertime Prague.

16. May Day is an ancient traditional student celebration of the coming of May, often with political undercurrents. Prohibited by the Nazis and the Communists, it was, after clashes with police in the early 1960s, finally permitted in 1965. The next May Day occurred in 1990, again with Ginsberg present.

17. Secret police files provide plenty of information about their surveillance of Ginsberg and their rich web of informers.

18. There are three "Prague" poems in the *Collected Poems*; in addition, Ginsberg wrote the poem "Swan Lake" (published in Czech in *Literární noviny* but not in *Collected Poems*) and at least one poem while sitting on the King of May's throne. Jan Zábrana, who may have known the poems in the stolen diary, writes: "G. kept copying poems from his diary or having somebody else copy them. . . ." (Celý 237). There was a poem Ginsberg wrote in charcoal on the wall for his lover J. S. Unfortunately, there is no copy or photograph of it, and J. S.'s resentful parents immediately whitewashed it.

19. On the same day, at virtually the same hour as Ginsberg was being forced to leave Prague, the evening newspaper *Večerní Praha* published a rave review. Clearly one hand did not know what the other was doing.

20. He is the same author who defended the 1976 arrest of rock musicians connected with the Plastic People of the Universe, whose trial led to the writing of the human rights manifesto Charter 77.

21. The original diary has not been found, although in 1978 it was still in the archives. According to the order, it was there until 1996. A photocopy of the translation was destroyed in 1985. It is hard to believe the police would destroy an item/evidence as important as the diary.

22. In November 1965, President Novotný purged the Czechoslovakian government (approved by the Prague Soviet embassy). Those who were expelled were the ones he considered the most guilty of anti-state actions amongst the students.

23. The censors could be beaten; thus the anthology *Jazz Inspiration* was published in 1966, with the poems of Jack Kerouac, Lawrence Ferlinghetti, and LeRoi Jones. This was possible because production of the book took an unusually long time, and the title was approved prior to spring 1965—and because no one reported it.

24. "Czech Radio broadcast 'Wichita Vortex Sutra' in the 1970s. This poem saved me, I copied its broadcast time and used it in my defense, saying it was against Vietnam, critical of the U.S., etcetera. They could be fooled. Actually I read Ginsberg without any problems then," Miroslav Kovářík says (interview with the author, 2010).

25. Another Beat reference that escaped the censor is Ginsberg's appearance (dubbed simply "the American") in the novel *Age of Lust* by Communist-approved poet Petr Skarlant, published during the toughest times of normalization. The action is set during Ginsberg's visit, and the book is dedicated to Václav Hrabě.

26. Interview with the author, Olomouc 1993, for the Czech TV documentary *Allen Ginsberg*.
27. Quite rightly Ginsberg estimated that his King of May election and subsequent events had great value for Czech people, at first real and later symbolic, as an act of freedom-loving rebellion against totalitarian bureaucratic power (Ginsberg, *Karma* 13).
28. "Neither Václav nor Vladimíra and I could live a double life. The artist's and the everyday one. That's why they called us Beats" (Machulková, *Neúplný čas* 61).
29. There is no evidence of a possible Bondy/Ginsberg meeting in 1965.
30. "Underground" is sparingly used for writers connected with Midnight Edition. It is usually used for the community around the rock group the Plastic People of the Universe, from the early 1970s on, which consisted of musicians, poets, and artists (See Note 20.).
31. He was killed in a streetcar accident on November 18, 1974. His wife, Mirka, vowed to transcribe all he had written and then commit suicide. She followed through on her vows and committed suicide on June 18, 1975.
32. Written in fall 1969, almost five years after the Ginsberg hysteria. No proof of a Koch/Ginsberg meeting can be found.
33. Meeting place of Prague Beats at the city's central Wenceslav Square (Václavské náměstí).
34. Communist ideologists used this term for the years after the "victory over Czechoslovakian counterrevolution" in August 1968.

Chapter 12

Cain's Book and the Mark of Exile: Alexander Trocchi as Transnational Beat

Fiona Paton

Introduction

John Tytell's foundational study *Naked Angels* analyzes the Beats primarily in terms of the American tradition:

> The Beat movement was a crystallization of a sweeping discontent with American 'virtues' of progress and power. What began as an exploration of the bowels and entrails of the city—criminality, drugs, mental hospitals—evolved into an expression of the visionary sensibility. The romantic militancy of the Beats found its root in American transcendentalism. (4)

John Calder, in his introduction to Alexander Trocchi's 1972 poetry collection *Man at Leisure*, asserted that Trocchi "is the British equivalent of the American beats, but the tradition to which he belongs is really more that of the 'damned' French writers, from Baudelaire and Rimbaud to Céline and Genet" ("Preface" v). That the Beat Generation was primarily an American movement is beyond question. However, as the field of Beat studies continues to develop, we are becoming increasingly aware that these two traditions, the European and the American, cannot be separated so decisively. Kerouac may have defined the Beat Generation as "a new group of American men intent on joy" ("Aftermath" 57), but the core of their "New Vision" in the early days drew directly on those "'damned' French writers" as much as the American transcendentalists.[1] Indeed, as this volume demonstrates, a transnational approach to the Beats is highly productive, bringing into focus the heterogeneous mix of cultural traditions that informed their identity and demonstrating the global reach of their influence. A further benefit of this transnational paradigm is the expansion of the Beat line-up to include writers such as Trocchi, whose importance in the postwar literary scene is far greater than the occasional references in Beat biographies would suggest.

Known variously as the "Scottish Beat writer" (Rebel Inc.), "the smack-addled icon of beat literature," (Cumming, "Mean Streets"), and "the most dissolute of the beats" (Home), Trocchi confirms most of the Beat stereotypes with a vengeance. He experimented freely with drugs, embraced poverty in order to pursue his art, affirmed play over work, circulated within the criminal underworld, explored sexual experience freely, and challenged every middle-class value he could identify. Trocchi was also firmly connected to the Beat milieu: he was close friends with Allen Ginsberg and William S. Burroughs; friendly with Herbert Huncke, Gregory Corso, Lawrence Ferlinghetti, and Robert Creeley; and acquainted with Diane di Prima and Michael McClure, among others. When Trocchi left the United States to avoid drug charges in 1961, he became an important disseminator of the Beat ethos in Britain. Jeff Nuttall, a key figure of the 1960s underground, recalls that "Alex rigged up his study like an office. People passing through London dropped in, Jack Michelin, Gregory Corso, Bob Creeley, Ian Summerville" ("Bomb" 186).

But Trocchi was equally involved with the postwar European avant-garde. He founded the influential, albeit short-lived, literary journal *Merlin* in Paris in 1952, and in doing so facilitated the flow from Europe to the United States of writers such as Jean Genet and Samuel Beckett. While there, he honed his radical impulses in the company of Guy Debord in Paris, joining Debord's Lettrist Internationale in 1955 and staying with the group when it evolved into the Situationist International in 1957. His own revolutionary cultural project, sigma, established in London in 1963, would act as a crucial conduit between the Situationists and William Burroughs (T. Murphy, "Exposing" 34). Throughout the 1960s, he remained closely affiliated with Burroughs and Ginsberg, involving them in various counterculture performances and publishing initiatives in Europe, which also included other Beats, such as Corso and Ferlinghetti.

Trocchi resisted the Beat label as he resisted all labels and categories. As he, Richard Seaver, and Christopher Logue wrote in the second edition of *Merlin,*

> Some ways of talking about literature are more useful than other ways of talking about literature. All ways of talking involve the use of distinctions. That is all right so long as those distinctions are not allowed to harden, that is to say, if we abandon them as soon as they cease to be useful. (39)

But even with this caveat, Beat continues to have value as a literary category, for what it primarily denotes is a certain interstitial sensibility that subverts fixed boundaries and borders. Rob Holton has effectively used Frederic Jameson's analysis of postwar standardization to interpret this Beat interstitiality. According to Jameson, "Historically, the adventures of homogeneous and heterogeneous space have most often been told in terms of the quotient of the sacred and of the folds in which it is unevenly invested" (qtd. in Holton, "Sordid" 13). Holton notes that the sacred was one means by which the Beats resisted homogeneity, but that they also "ranged well beyond into a variety of secular cultural spaces that generally remained off-limits to conventional citizens" (13). Holton describes these transgressive social spaces as "the folds of heterogeneity." As even the casual reader of Beat literature knows, such "secular cultural spaces" included voluntary poverty and the rejection of upward mobility, the voluntary crossing of race and class boundaries, experimentation with drugs and sexuality, various criminal behaviors, and uninhibited self-expression that blurred the boundary between literary and vernacular speech. Trocchi powerfully embodies that "state in-between," whether in terms of geographical location, social status, sexual identity, or aesthetics. This interstitial sensibility not only connects Trocchi to the Beat movement, but also helps to deepen our historical understanding of the eclectic forces that brought Beat into being.

Part 1: "Cosmopolitan Scum"

In 1962, the London publisher John Calder invited Trocchi to participate in The International Writer's Conference, which Calder had organized as part of the Edinburgh International Arts Festival. The American contingent included Henry Miller, Burroughs, Norman Mailer, and Mary McCarthy ("1962 International"). Calder recalls that he recruited the unknown Trocchi

> mainly as a Scottish writer to put him into a Scottish day. He was very unlike every other Scottish writer. He'd had years in America and Paris, had been part of the most avant-garde writing scenes everywhere and was in touch with the new Beat writers. . . . He put forward a point of view, on the Scottish Day, of an international culture that was classless, that was bohemian, that was sexually in no way inhibited, that was not prejudiced against things like homosexuality—which was an unmentionable word in Scotland at the time. ("John Calder" 151)

On the first day, Trocchi took part in a forum on "Scottish Writing Today" and created a furor by denouncing the entire proceedings: "The whole atmosphere seems to me turgid, petty, provincial, the stale-porridge, Bible-class nonsense. It makes me ashamed to sit here in front of my collaborators in this Conference, those writers who have come here from other parts of the world, and to consider the level of this debate" ("Scottish Writing"10). Trocchi commenced to go head to head with Hugh MacDiarmid, at that time Scotland's patron saint of literature, calling him "an old fossil" and receiving the epithet "cosmopolitan scum" in return ("John Calder" 151). While Trocchi's fellow panel members were reasonably diverse in their opinions, the seventy-year-old Hugh MacDiarmid, clad in the traditional kilt, aggressively upheld the "Scottish Renaissance"—Scotland's own version of modernism, in which the recovery and preservation of the Scots language were key elements: "So far as I know there is no parallel in literary history to the way in which Scotland has abandoned its own languages, Scots and Gaelic . . .We have tried, for centuries, to build on the things we have in common with the English and now we are seeking to repossess ourselves of our National heritage" ("Scottish Writing" 4).

The next day, Trocchi was in the audience for a session entitled "Is Commitment Necessary?" and was called upon to contribute as he was preparing to leave the hall (probably to give himself a fix in the men's room). Taken by surprise, Trocchi nonetheless immediately defined his own position as "a commitment of the exile. I would claim that for myself as well as for Burroughs, as well as for certain of the beatnik writers in America" ("Is Commitment" 22). Trocchi was not literally an exile. True, he had fled from the United States as a fugitive in 1961, but he was not exiled from his native country, nor were any of the American "beatniks." Rather, Trocchi was identifying a shared condition of alienation from the values of post-industrial Western culture. This disaffection gave Trocchi a feeling of solidarity with the American Beats. Kerouac had described Cold War culture as "a new sinister kind of efficiency" in America, consisting of "supercolossal, bureaucratic, totalitarian, benevolent, Big Brother structures" ("Aftermath" 48–49). Burroughs wrote to Kerouac from Tangiers in 1955 that "[o]ne of my reasons for preferring to live outside of the U.S. is so I won't be wasting time reacting against the cops and the interfering society they represent. Living here, you feel no weight of disapproving 'others,' no 'they,' no Society" (*Letters* 254). Meanwhile, Ginsberg wrote "Howl," he said, to challenge "a sexless and soulless America prepared to battle the world in a defense of a false image of its Authority" ("A Letter to Eberhart" 221). It was this "Authority," that of the nation-state and all of its ideological apparatus, that Trocchi chose to challenge in his own country's capital at the International Writers Conference when he said, "I think the question of human identity is the only central question and it is a question of a man alone and I don't give a damn if he's a Scotsman, or an American, or anything else. It's high time we transcended nationalistic borders" ("Scottish Writing" 12).

Trocchi had done his utmost to transcend his own nationalistic borders both physically and intellectually. Born in Glasgow in 1925 of a Scottish mother and an Italian father, he had been raised in a respectable, middle-class environment that, from an early age, he found stifling. Having enrolled in Glasgow University in 1942, he was called up six months later to serve in the Fleet Air Arm, a branch of the British Royal Navy. He graduated with a degree in English and philosophy in 1949, having made such an impression on his tutors that he was awarded a Kemsley Travelling Scholarship. Foregoing the graduation ceremony, Trocchi, aged twenty-four, immediately left for Europe with his wife and baby girl (A. Scott 24–25). As he stated at the International Writers Conference, "It was Mr. [Henry] Miller's books which helped me get over the Scots Sabbaths, seven days a week normally. And I went to join him in Paris, but unfortunately he had left. But I found other people there" ("Scottish Writing" 10). Some of those other people included Richard Seaver, Jean Cocteau, Guy Debord, Robert Creeley, Maurice Girodias, Christopher Logue, Terry Southern, and George Plimpton. And it was at this point that his real education began.

Trocchi spent several years drifting around Europe with his family before finally settling, alone, in Paris in 1952. His marriage had disintegrated, and Trocchi at this point met Jane Lougee, a young, highly educated, and affluent American with whom

Trocchi subsequently established *Merlin*, now acknowledged as one of the most important literary journals of the post–World War II era (A. Scott 34–35). *Merlin's* other editors were Logue and Seaver. Although the first issue, published on May 15, 1952, was somewhat slight, the magazine would quickly become the main source in English of writers as diverse as Jean Genet, the Marquis de Sade, Eugène Ionesco, Samuel Beckett, and Paul Eluard (J. Campbell, *Paris Interzone* 51–55). The translations of de Sade were authored by the American Austryn Wainhouse, whom Trocchi recruited for *Merlin* as soon as he learned of his solitary, devout labors on behalf of the Marquis. Wainhouse had, that same week, also been approached by Maurice Girodias, who wished to make Wainhouse's translation of de Sade's *La Philosophie dans le Boudoir* one of the first titles of his newly formed Olympia Press (Logue 140). It did not take long for the editors of *Merlin* and Girodias to gather for the first of many business meetings. As Logue recounts in his memoir, Girodias made a simple and irresistible business offer. He would underwrite the publication of the financially strapped *Merlin*, plus the magazine's book imprint, Collection Merlin, and allow Trocchi, Seaver, and Logue to publish whatever they wanted, with the protection from prosecution that Girodias's French citizenship would provide (De St. Jorre 55). In return, they would do a little writing for him:

> Before leaving, Maurice explained that there was a contribution to the future of the Olympia Press he would like us to make. . . . "Let me be candid," he said. "I require simple stories of a wholly pornographic kind. Character drawing, social context are of no importance. Disadvantages even. I want constant, heavy, serious fucking." (Logue 141)

The Merlin cohort was happy to oblige, and Girodias created a special imprint for its endeavors, tastefully named the Traveller's Companion Library.

Girodias is well-known as the man who first published Burroughs's *Naked Lunch* in Paris in 1959. Less well-known is the professional relationship that developed between Girodias and Trocchi in the early 1950s. Trocchi wrote the initial catalogue descriptions (and justifications) for Olympia Press (Cameron, *Paris Interzone* 144) and was one of the most adept pornographers for the Traveller's Companion Library—Girodias referred to him as the first of Olympia's "all out literary stallions" (79). But for Trocchi, these were hack works, churned out for ready cash, all of which went into his magazine. Robert Creeley, who served on the *Merlin* editorial committee, recalls that Trocchi and his fellow editors would diligently search for American women who might be seduced into contributing money to the magazine. But, Creeley adds, "They weren't just going out and lushing; god, it was very severe—I mean these men were *not* self-indulgent. Just witness their activity. They were the first significant publishers of Beckett, for example; they were the first significant publishers of Genet. Collection Merlin, if you look at the titles, shows the whole foundation of Barney Rossett's subsequent activity" (17). Since Barney Rossett was the owner of Grove Press, which, along with its journal *Evergreen Review*, would be one of the most important outlets for Beat literature, we can appreciate, in retrospect, the significance of Trocchi's publishing endeavors.

Creeley's assessment is reinforced by Campbell, who notes that "Although *Notre-Dame-Les-Fleurs* had been translated and published in a limited edition in the

United States in the 1940s, Trocchi himself would be the first to make Genet widely available in English, initially by including extracts of *The Thief's Journal* in *Merlin*, then by issuing the complete novel under the magazine's publishing imprint" (*Paris Interzone* 49). Diane di Prima further substantiates the importance of Olympia Press and *Merlin*. At the time, she was working at the Phoenix Bookstore in New York City: "Both Miller and Genet were being published in France by Olympia Press, and were much sought after in the States. My own first taste of Genet's novels had come while I was carrying Jeanne, when Freddie Herko had stolen *The Thief's Journal* in a limited Olympia edition . . . from his shrink" (*Recollections* 216). She also reveals one of the methods for getting contraband literature into the United States: "The Phoenix had its own underground railroad for books, its own method of importing desired but forbidden literature. Most of it was printed in France by Olympia Press, and book-like packages coming from France to the U.S. would have been suspect"—hence the packages were routed through Turkey and labeled as funeral ashes (217).

Campbell has wittily asserted that "[i]f Miller is the father of the Beat Generation, Genet is its transvestite mother" (*Exiled* 220), and ample evidence exists to support this claim. Carl Solomon had first introduced Ginsberg to Genet in 1948, via a privately printed edition of *Our Lady of the Flowers* bought "in the Gotham Book Mart under the counter" (Solomon qtd. in Burroughs, "The Struggle " 337), but *Merlin* and Olympia Press were the first to make Genet's work widely available in English. Ginsberg included Genet in a list of important influences in a 1966 interview ("The Art of Poetry" 20), as did Kerouac in 1957 (Dolbier 49). Ten years later, Kerouac's opinion had not changed: "Genet is a very tragic and beautiful writer. And I give [him] the crown. And the laurel wreath" ("Interview" 113). Burroughs, in 1974, was equally reverent: "I would think of Beckett in the same way as Genet, as a writer that I admire very much. I've read practically everything Genet has written. He's a very great writer" ("Interrogation" 259).

Trocchi had left Paris by the time Ginsberg, Corso, and Burroughs arrived in 1957, but his reputation remained. In 1969, Burroughs recalled that "Alex's name was a name I had heard quite frequently some years before I'd met him. It was a name I'd heard a great deal in Paris from many people—very contradictory reports. He was described as amoral and unscrupulous" (*Cain's Film*). Such attributes no doubt appealed to Burroughs immensely, and when they first met in 1962, travelling on the same plane to the Edinburgh International Writers Conference, Burroughs found that "we had a lot in common immediately. He was sort of an ally at the conference" ("William Burroughs" 159). At this point, Burroughs already knew *Cain's Book* and thought very highly of it, "one of the best" on the subject of addiction. ("William Burroughs" 161). Ginsberg's first meeting with Trocchi is not reliably documented—Schumacher, for instance, asserts several times that Ginsberg knew Trocchi "from his Paris days" (319, 349), which seems unlikely since Trocchi left Paris in 1956 and Ginsberg's first visit there was in 1957 (Miles, *Ginsberg* 25). There is, however, ample evidence of their long friendship, such as their 1979 tape-recorded conversations, in which they recall events from the late 1950s and 1960s.[2]

Trocchi did live in Venice West, California's version of the Village, for ten months beginning in 1957, and, as in Paris, left a lasting impression.[3] Artist Tony Scibella recalls the challenges of keeping him supplied with drugs: "but it was all kind of gorilla pills like Thorazine, you know. So that's what we kept him on—tongue swollen up—ah, Trocchi. He was a good dude, man. And he worked *all* the time" (Maynard 94). The work Trocchi was doing was writing *Cain's Book*. When he gave the poet Stuart Perkoff a carbon copy of the first one hundred pages, "Perkoff set it up in a spring binder like an icon in his home. Long after Trocchi had gone, Venice poets and artists would continue to talk about his novel as if its existence led validity to what they themselves were doing" (Maynard 97). But Trocchi's mythical stature has led to many factual inaccuracies about his involvement with the Beats. Andrew Murray Scott asserts, "If any one person could be said to have founded the beat community at Venice West, that person would be Trocchi. All the important beats . . . stayed at one time or other in the community" (76). Among many others, Scott names Ginsberg and Kerouac as residing in Venice West, although there is no evidence that either did.

Nonetheless, Trocchi was actively involved in the Beat scene in New York from 1960 to 1961. Herbert Huncke first learned of him after undergoing a drug cure in Jacoby Hospital in the Bronx. The connection came through the artist Bill Heine, whose circle included Elise Cowen and Janine Pommy (later Vega):

> the next person I heard about was the writer Alexander Trocchi, who was supposedly running some kind of college-of-the-streets type of thing on the Lower East Side. Because Trocchi was an experienced and first-rate writer it was natural that he'd come into contact with Ginsberg. Between the two of them they were helping create something of a new scene in the Lower East Side. (Huncke 139)

Huncke actually shared an apartment with Trocchi in 1961, a scene that Huncke describes as "outrageous": "I can remember Trocchi with this knife that must have been a regulation hunter's knife. He had acquired at least two- or three-inch tracks on his arms, as an addict, and he'd allow them to scab over. He had a habit of standing with one of these knives underneath a bright lightbulb picking the scabs off with the point of the knife" (158). Kerouac makes a brief reference in "New York Scenes" to "Bill Heine, he's a really secret subterranean painter who sits with all those weird new cats in the East Tenth street coffee shops" (114). Presumably Trocchi was one of those "weird new cats."[4]

Kerouac's "New York Scenes" describes Times Square as an enormous living room (109), a comparison that evokes a shared camaraderie and a sense of fraternity. In the mind's eye, one can readily see Kerouac, Ginsberg, Burroughs, Joan Vollmer, Huncke, and di Prima drifting through the throng—a community that MacDiarmid would label "cosmopolitan scum." An expanded history of this milieu allows us to spot another figure in the crowd—tall, craggy Trocchi, striding past Bickford's cafeteria, looking to sell his remaining editions of Traveller's Companion erotica to the "little bookshop that specializes in Havelock Ellis and Rabelais" ("New York Scenes" 109). But Trocchi's place in the giant living room of Times Square is not limited to his physical presence there, nor to his pioneering work in Paris bringing writers such as Genet and Beckett there. Trocchi belongs in Times Square because of his own writing, in which we see eloquently magnified Holton's "folds of heterogeneity" ("Sordid" 13) and the interstitiality that is perhaps the most meaningful way of defining Beat.

Part 2: Poet-Adventurer

Trocchi began *Cain's Book* in Paris in 1953 and continued working on it as he moved from France to California to Mexico and then New York City. According to Seaver, Trocchi finally completed it only because Grove Press paid him small amounts for each new batch of pages, which allowed Trocchi to maintain his heroin habit (xvii). The novel appeared in 1960 in the United States, where, surprisingly, it flew under the radar of censorship that would soon catch Miller and Burroughs. Although praised by Mailer—"It is true, it has art, it is brave" (Seaver xiv)—*Cain's Book* received little attention from the mainstream press. It was then published in Britain in 1963, where it generated much more of a stir, one that culminated in an obscenity trial and the incineration of several hundred copies of the book by the City of Sheffield in 1964 (A. Scott 2). Trocchi, called to testify in court, was typically forthright about the book's relation to his own life: "I have taken every drug there is to be taken—but only those from which I know I can safely return. Drugs have an effect and if they did not I do not think I would have written the book" (A. Scott 4). The book was burned.

Cain's Book is usually discussed alongside *Naked Lunch* as an equally powerful and discomfiting record of drug addiction—and some even consider Trocchi's book better.[5] They appeared within a year of each other and were clearly being written simultaneously. Trocchi surely knew something of *Naked Lunch* from the excerpts that appeared in the *Chicago Review* in 1958 and in *Big Table* in 1959, and from Girodias's Olympia Press edition, published in France in 1959. And, for his part, Burroughs likely read the excerpt from *Cain's Book* that appeared in *Evergreen Review* in 1957. The book certainly made an impression on him; in his introduction to Trocchi's *Man at Leisure*, Burroughs talks of its "great vitality": "I remember reading *Cain's Book* for the first time. The barge the dropper the heroin you can feel it or see it. He has been there and brought it back" ("Introduction" viii).

The vitality of *Cain's Book* comes from the sardonic richness and precision of its narrative voice, that of Joe Necchi, an expatriate Scot living in New York who describes with eloquent ennui his life as a heroin addict and scow captain on the Hudson River in the late 1950s. His fragmented descriptions and reflections include the activities of a barge captain, his forays into New York City to score, and memories of his earlier life in Scotland. Much of the narrative takes place in New York, with Necchi wandering the same routes as we find described in many Beat works—and usually with the same purpose: Sheridan Square, Times Square, Harlem, Greenwich Village. As Necchi remarks sardonically, "There was never a wandering Jew who wandered further than a junkie, without hope. Always moving" (73). Trocchi's protagonist traverses "a variety of secular cultural spaces that generally remained off-limits to conventional citizens" (Holton, "Sordid" 13), in the process asserting the value of the perspective offered by such spaces: "To move is not difficult. The problem is, from what posture? This question of posture, of original attitude: to get at its structure one must temporarily get outside of it. Drugs provide an alternative attitude" (236). This deliberate seeking of de-centered positions vis-à-vis the dominant culture connects Trocchi strongly to the Beat sensibility, particularly its shared willingness to enter zones characterized by criminal or "deviant" activities.

Trocchi also demonstrates a similar willingness to cross sexual boundaries and acknowledges borders that are internal or ideological as well as geographical. How apt, for instance, that Necchi, when describing a spontaneous sexual liaison with another man, would state, "I was standing about ten yards from him. Like a man looking on a new continent" (52). For Necchi, the moment of his sexual invitation represents "the ecstatic edge of something to be known" (44). Finding this edge, and crossing it, and continuing onward to test again the boundaries, whether geographical or ideological, is a core element in Beat identity that unites the very different sensibilities of representative figures such as Kerouac, Ginsberg, and Burroughs.

Yet unlike Kerouac or Ginsberg, Trocchi's work does not affirm a transcendent or religious dimension of drug use. Necchi states, "If eternity were available beyond death, if I could be as certain of it as I am sure of the fix I have only to move my hand to obtain, I should in effect have achieved it, for I should be already beyond the pitiless onslaught of time . . ." (239). Compare Trocchi's use of "eternity" with that of Kerouac, who in the second verse of *The Scripture of the Golden Eternity* writes, "One that is what is, the Golden Eternity, or God, or Tathagata-the-name" (23), or with Ginsberg, who brings "Howl" to a close with "Holy time in eternity holy eternity in time" (28). The "heterogeneous fold" of the sacred (Holton, "Sordid" 13) was not a space Trocchi chose to inhabit; in this sense, Trocchi's closest affinity is with Burroughs—both exhibit a much more Sartrean existentialism in which, to quote Burroughs, "[r]eligious truth is always of a categorical and dogmatic nature" ("Sexual Conditioning" 100).

Like Burroughs, Trocchi is unflinchingly direct when describing the ritual of fixing: "Faye's thick, dark, purplish-red blood rose and fell in the eye-dropper like a column of gory mercury in a barometer" (166). Like Burroughs, the text includes didactic addresses to the reader on the subject of drugs, along with various disquisitions on language and ideology. Trocchi's narrative is not so violently disconnected as is *Naked Lunch*, but it is essentially plotless, and consists of a series of reflections, reminiscences, and descriptions that, together, create a work that lies interstitially between fiction and philosophy: "Reading what I have written now, then, I have a familiar feeling that everything I say is somehow beside the point. I am of course incapable of sustaining a simple narrative. . . with no fixed valid categories . . . not so much a line of thought as an area of experience . . . the immediate broth; I am left with a coherence of posture(s)" (231).

But unlike Burroughs, Trocchi allows a degree of rationalization to enter his narrative:

> It isn't simple, any kind of judgment here, and the judgments of the uninitiated tend to be stupid, hysterical. . . . It is not only a question of kicks. The ritual itself, the

powder in the spoon, the little ball of cotton, the matches applied, the bubbling liquid drawn up through the cotton filter into the eye dropper, the tie around the arm to make the vein stand out . . . all this is not for nothing; it is born of a respect for the whole chemistry of alienation. (33)

Sue Wiseman's deconstructive reading of *Cain's Book* emphasizes the contradiction inherent in using heroin, an addictive substance, to disengage from the social addictions of an advanced capitalist culture. As she points out,

Heroin is presented as an acknowledgment, rather than an evasion, of alienation. But—problematically—while heroin is used by the book as a literal addiction to disrupt the addictivity of social organization, and stylistically to disrupt the bankrupt structures of the commodity-novel, heroin in turn attains in the text a ritualized and fetishized treatment. It becomes the ultimate reified commodity. (263)

In some passages, she argues, Trocchi tries to "resolve this contradiction by a retreat into the romantic valorization of the outcast—the insightful heroin addict (unlike the alcoholic) is a significant register and monitor of the society which casts him or her out" (264). But another point needs to be made here: while addiction to heroin may seem just another form of commodity enslavement, it is in fact radically different because the junk subculture is one of those heterogeneous folds that resist the centrifugal spin of mainstream society. Therefore, Trocchi's narrative can be viewed as even more alienated than *Naked Lunch*, in that Necchi remains unrepentant. Trocchi can write about heroin with a sensual introspection that is very different from Burroughs's scabrous indictment, and in doing so he cancels out any moral perspective that might potentially align with the dominant culture. If Wiseman finds this a point of weakness, one might also argue that it is the novel's deepest source of integrity, for it means there is no reintegration possible for the outcast narrator who self-identifies as Cain. The great divide between Trocchi/Necchi and "John Citizen" (77) is as irrevocable as that between Cain and his God. Cain, who was rendered "a fugitive and a vagabond" (Gen. 4:12) by God for killing his brother, Abel, represents for Trocchi not just the exile of the junkie, but existential exile in a much broader sense.

Trocchi not only cites the Biblical story of Cain but also rewrites it. Cain, the first-born son of Adam and Eve and the older brother of Abel, was the tiller of the soil, while Abel was the shepherd. Genesis says that when each offered their first harvests as sacrifices to God, "the Lord had respect unto Abel and to his offering. But unto Cain and to his offering he had not respect. And Cain was very wroth and his countenance fell" (Gen. 4:4–5). The text of Genesis provides no explanation for the rejection of Cain's offering; instead, the Lord reprimands him for his "wroth" (Gen 4:6). And then comes the scene that has achieved such archetypal significance in Western culture: "And Cain talked with Abel his brother; and it came to pass, when they were in the field, that Cain rose up against Abel his brother, and slew him" (Gen. 4:8). Cain's punishment is that he will henceforth till the earth unsuccessfully, and "a fugitive and a vagabond shalt [he] be in the earth" (Gen. 4:12). Cain protests that people will try to kill him wherever he goes, and so the Lord "set a mark upon Cain, lest any finding him should kill him," in which case "vengeance shall be taken on him, sevenfold" (Gen. 4:15). Trocchi's version of this story appears three quarters of the way through the novel.

> I always felt it was strange that the butcher, Abel, should be preferred to the agriculturist, Cain.
>
> Abel waxed fat and rich breeding sheep for the slaughter while Cain tilled. Cain made an offering to the Lord. Abel followed suit with his quaking fat calves. Who'd have gruel rather than a T-bone?
>
> And soon Abel had vast herds and air-conditioned slaughterhouses and meat storehouses and meat package plants, and there was a blight on Cain's crops. And that was called *sin*.
>
> Cain stood and looked at the blight on his crop. And his spade was useless against it in his hand.
>
> And it came to pass that Abel was trespassing there where Cain would carry his spade, which is where land is to be tilled and not where sheep pasture.
>
> And Abel saw his elder brother and he was thin and with a starved look and held the spade to no purpose in his hand. And Abel approached his brother, saying: Why don't you give up and come and work for me? I could use a good man in the slaughterhouse.
>
> And Cain slew him. (180)

Trocchi's retelling is masterful in its rhetorical cadences and trenchant irony. His pronounced sympathy for Cain is apparent in the emphasis on his struggle and starvation, while Abel, far from being the first martyr, is an arrogant trespasser. For Trocchi, Cain is the victim of arbitrary authority and smug complacence. In fact, Trocchi names him "the first poet-adventurer" (231), thus placing himself in the tradition of the French Symbolists and the *poète maudit* or accursed poet, he who lives on the margins of respectable society and whose pursuit of experience and knowledge cause him to cross boundaries and transgress borders. As in Baudelaire's version of the story, "Abel et Cain," in *Les Fleurs du Mal* (which Trocchi knew well), Trocchi sees Cain's plight as one of existential absurdity, whereby the choice is between doomed, isolated struggle or integration into the industrial machine.

Given Trocchi's identification with Cain and the poète maudit, it is entirely fitting that *Cain's Book* should begin with an epigraph from de Sade and a description of the narrator giving himself a fix. The narrator describes this ritual as "Cain at his orisons, Narcissus at his mirror" (10). Cain's offering and prayers are now to himself. For Necchi, "the perceiving turns inward, the eyelids droop, the blood is aware of itself . . . the organism has a sense of being intact and unbrittle, and, above all, inviolable. For the attitude born of this sense of inviolability some Americans have used the word 'cool'" (11). For Necchi, the French poète maudit joins hands with Whitman's loafer as he spends long, solitary days on his scow, writing, getting high, and lounging on the deck waiting for occasional demands of his job. Even in this marginal realm of subsistence labor, cut off from, yet in sight of, the Manhattan skyline, Necchi is an outcast. He compares his own occupation with that of the loader who "originally dislikes the scowman because the scowman doesn't work.

That makes the job unpleasant from time to time, finding oneself having suddenly to deal with the animosity of a man who makes a virtue of his work. It is difficult to explain to the underprivileged that play is more serious than work" (183).

For Trocchi, Cain is emblematic of alienated labor, and his act of murder is a strike not only against his favored brother but also against the entire dehumanizing system represented by the meat-packing factory, the system that Ginsberg decried in "Howl" as "Moloch whose mind is pure machinery!" (*Howl* 17). Hence in passages such as the following, the endorsement of play over alienated labor is associated with the condition of exile represented by Cain: "*I am sitting alone.* It had occurred to me that I was mad. To stare inwards. To be a hermit, even in company. To wish for the thousandth-making time for the strength to be alone and play. Immediately there was a flower on my brow, Cain's flower" (72). But the mark of exile was also a source of strength, for to embrace play, seriously, as the highest expression of human identity, was to embrace a transformative process that would, he insisted, reduce the meat-packing factory to rubble. And, like the Beats, he found places of resistance within the popular culture that America's century of mechanized mass-production had created: "Man is serious at play. Tension, elation, frivolity, ecstasy, confirming the supra-logical nature of the human situation. Apart from jazz—probably the most vigorous and yea-saying protest of *homo ludens* in the modern world—the pin-ball machine seemed to me to be America's greatest contribution to culture; it rang with contemporaneity" (246).

Trocchi's rejection of the work ethic is a key part of his assault on the very foundations of the nation-state. Holton does not explicitly identify voluntary poverty as one of the "heterogeneous folds" occupied by the Beats, but he comes close when discussing Riesman's use of the term "anomic": "that is, the diversity of maladjusted individuals existing beyond—or perhaps beneath—the reach of conformity" ("Sordid" 23). Race and class were often inescapable factors, of course, in determining who occupied the "subcultural folds" of marginal existence ("Sordid" 23), but for the Beats and Trocchi, such border sites were spaces for the poet-adventurer to intentionally occupy and there raise flags of rebellion. For Trocchi, defining one's life in terms of creative play rather than the meat-packing factory became a cornerstone of his utopian vision of an invisible insurrection that would transform the world.

Part 3: Homo Ludens

Trocchi's days of international travel ended with his flight from the United States in 1961, but he remained actively engaged in an international network of experimental aesthetics and social revolution. He was, for instance, the only British member of Situationist International, and one of the most enduring. While others were found guilty of radical insufficiency and asked to leave, Trocchi remained until 1964, when he "resigned" over differences relating to his sigma project (Bowd 9). As Trocchi himself recalled, "Guy [Debord] thought the world was going to collapse on its own, and we were going to take over . . . But you can't take over the world by

excluding people from it!" (qtd. in Marcus 387). Trocchi's crime was his association with "mystical cretins" (Debord's words) such as Timothy Leary and Ginsberg
(Marcus 387).

Nonetheless, Trocchi continued the Situationist agenda through the movement
he called project sigma, and through the printed texts he called the sigma portfolio.
In "Sigma: A Tactical Blueprint," Trocchi described this initiative as "a possible
international association of men" who would work toward a cultural revolution.
(He would later adopt the more progressive noun "wo/man."). The word *sigma*, he
explained, was a mathematical term denoting "the sum, the whole" and hence "it
seemed to fit very well with our notion that all men must eventually be included"
("Sigma" 193). Working from his flat in St. Stephens Street, London, with an electric typewriter and stencils, Trocchi maintained, for several years, a steady flow of
sigma publications. The series included material not only by himself, such as the
influential essay "The Invisible Insurrection of a Million Minds" (published in *City
Lights Journal* and elsewhere), but also by R.D. Laing, McClure, Kenneth White,
Colin Wilson, Creeley, and Burroughs. The individual editions of the portfolio were
circulated by mail to subscribers, for Trocchi was adamant that it be "an entirely new
dimension in publishing . . . outflanking the traditional trap of publishing house
policy" (Subscription Form). That the group was somewhat amorphous, even at the
time, with their documents now obscurely dispersed throughout various archives
around the world, can be attributed largely to Trocchi's insistence that "sigma does
not exist . . . it is merely a word, a tactical symbol, a dialectical instrument. . . .
which we . . . have found useful in the strategic game we have elected to play on an
international scale from now on. . . ." ("Pool Cosmonaut").

The word *international* occurs again and again in the project sigma documents.
Trocchi really did intend a *coup du monde* rather than a *coup d'état*—taking over
the world gradually through a cultural revolution that would, he said, "seize the
grids of expression and the powerhouses of the minds" bringing about an "invisible
insurrection":

> What is to be seized has no physical dimensions nor relevant temporal color. It is
> not an arsenal, nor a capital city, nor an island, nor an isthmus visible from a peak in
> Darien. . . . What is to be seized—and I address that one million (say) here and there
> who are capable of perceiving at once just what I am about, a million potential 'techni-
> cians'. . . is ourselves. ("Invisible Insurrection" 165)

Trocchi's reference to "a peak in Darien" is particularly significant here, bringing
into his discussion in one short phrase the vast enterprise of European colonization
carried out in the name of the nation-state. He is concerned not only with artistic
production within the nation-state but also with all levels of economic and political management, including education and the mass media. He was hopeful, for
instance, that the United Nations represented "the beginning of the end for the
nation state. We should at all times do everything in our power to speed up the
process" (167).

While the idea of homo ludens, or man at play, might seem a feeble platform on
which to build a revolution, as a strategy developed by the Lettrists and Situationists,

it actually played a significant part in the countercultural protests of the 1960s. Gavin Bowd provides an efficient summary of the basic rationale:

> The aim of these rebels against utility was the construction of 'situations': 'A moment of life concretely and deliberately constructed by the collective organization of a unitary ambiance and a game of events.' As incorrigible opponents of the spectacle, the Situationists were for play, involvement, and non-postponement of satisfaction . . . rejecting puritanism and the cult of work, the Situationists also refused 'activism' and the identification with foreign models. (7)

Trocchi utilized his sigma pamphlets to transmit the philosophy of homo ludens, arguing that through developing technology and automation, work time would decrease and leisure time would increase. Adapting Marxist terminology, he coined the phrase "PLAY VALUE" in sigma portfolio # 18:

> What is becoming is *homo ludens* in a life liberally constructed. There is no solution within the contemporary economic framework. . . . If we are not to become so many ants on an ant-heap (or annihilated in a nuclear holocaust) we should do well to explore the creative possibilities of the leisure situation now and adapt our findings to the education of future generations. Such practice in "ludic creativity" is the guarantee of the freedom of each and every one of us. Forced labor, passive leisure: such notions, being in direct conflict with our contemporary revolt, must be consciously transcended. ("Manifesto Situationist")

In Trocchi's advocation of homo ludens, we see again the confluence of the "damned" French poets and the American Beats (Calder, "Preface" v), writers who, although separated by time and space, exhibited the same proclivities for restless wandering and indolent genius. Recall, for instance, Ginsberg's speaker in "America," who admits, "It's true I don't want to join the Army or turn lathes in precision parts factories, I'm nearsighted and psychopathic anyway" (America, *Howl* 34). Kerouac's *The Dharma Bums* is an exemplary model for "ludic creativity." Ray Smith, refusing to submit to either forced labor or passive leisure, realizes, "The only alternative to sleeping out, hopping freights, and doing what I wanted, I saw in a vision, would be to just sit with a hundred other patients in front of a nice television set in a madhouse, where we could be supervised" (121). Nor was voluntary poverty solely the prerogative of the male Beats. Di Prima describes her early days in New York City in terms of artistic freedom bought with "dire poverty" (*Recollections* 127). In *Cain's Book*, Trocchi makes clear his solidarity with those who chose exile rather than a steady job. Through indirect speech, Necchi laconically reports his brother-in-law's view of him: "He would not say he didn't find me difficult to understand sometimes. A man who didn't work, he meant. Oh, he knew I was supposed to be writing or something. But after all I wasn't a child anymore. A man of my age" (56).

Trocchi had several ambitious ideas to make ludic creativity a way of life rather than just a philosophical statement. For instance, Trocchi proposed replacing traditional universities, which "have become factories for the production of degreed technicians" with "spontaneous universities" based loosely on such ventures as the Black Mountain College ("Sigma" 197–199).

More concretely, Trocchi was instrumental in bringing together the participants for the 1965 event known as Wholly Communion, which took place in the Royal Albert Hall. This huge countercultural event was organized in less than a week, but nonetheless managed to effect an impressive program for its capacity audience. Trocchi was the master of ceremonies as well as a featured poet. British poets such as Tom McGrath, Christopher Logue, and Mike Horovitz were joined by the Cuban poet Pablo Fernandez and Simon Vinkenoog from the Netherlands, while Ginsberg, Corso, and Ferlinghetti represented the Beats (Farren 58–59). Since he was unable to be physically present, "a tape recorder played Burroughs's dry ghostly voice reading" (Silesky 140). Horovitz's description of the evening captures its transnational anarchy rather charmingly: "The buds of a spreading poetry international, the esperanto of the subconscious sown by dada & the surrealists & the beats bore fruit—a renewal of light, of 'the Holy Word / That walk'd among the ancient trees'—made flesh" (*Children* 337). Although undoubtedly chaotic at some moments and desultory at others, the event was a remarkable example of ludic creativity within a Situationist performance. The "crazy illuminated hipsters" (Kerouac, "Aftermath" 47) had stormed one of the establishment's most venerable citadels. As Nuttall recalled, "The Underground was suddenly there on the surface, in open ground with a following of thousands" ("Bomb" 179).

Conclusion

With the Wholly Communion event, we see the Beat movement merging with the counterculture, a transition that Kerouac, still its most representative figure, refused to make. As Kerouac told Ted Berrigan in 1967, "I'm bored with the new avant-garde and the sky-rocketing sensationalism" (131). And yet Kerouac's earlier definition of the Beat Generation as "down and out but full of intense conviction . . . subterranean heroes who'd finally turned from the 'freedom machine of the West'" ("Aftermath" 47) resonates strongly with Trocchi's more existentially engaged agenda. Indeed, a few sentences later, Kerouac acknowledges that "the same thing was almost going on in the postwar France of Sartre and Genet and what's more we knew about it" (47). That they knew about it was at least in part due to Trocchi and his indefatigable editorial efforts in Paris in the early 1950s. But the distance between Trocchi and Kerouac is clear, nonetheless. Although Trocchi makes a passing reference to spontaneous prose in *Cain's Book* (60), he omitted Kerouac from the 1963 anthology he co-edited with Terry Southern and Seaver, *Writers in Revolt*, in which Ginsberg, Miller, and Burroughs appeared alongside de Sade, Baudelaire, Dostoevsky, Genet, and Beckett, among others. The original title, *Beyond the Beat*, which the publisher elected to change, is revealing. According to Southern, "This is the period when books by Kerouac and his protégés were very popular and so Alex felt that the literature that he knew of, that is to say of Celine and Malaparte and Jean Genet, and a few others, was much more important, so he wanted to have an anthology that he felt superseded the present vogue" (97). Leaving aside who the trio considered Kerouac's "protégés," he was certainly portrayed as the group's leader by the media. Forced like Sisyphus to shoulder eternally the cursed appellation "King of the Beatniks," Kerouac probably seemed too much associated with the Beat label that Trocchi wanted to move beyond.

Ginsberg and Burroughs, on the other hand, seemed in the 1960s closer to Trocchi's existentialist engagement than to Kerouac's "swinging group of new American men." Both took part in the 1968 protests at the Democratic National Convention in Chicago in the company of Genet and both remained in contact with Trocchi throughout the 1960s and 1970s. Burroughs and Trocchi were particularly close: Trocchi had invited Burroughs to serve as one of sigma's directors in 1963 ("Letter to William S. Burroughs" 207), and Burroughs made several contributions to sigma's broadsheet *The Moving Times*, including the name (*The Moving Times* No. 1). They had planned to write a book on drugs together, which did not materialize, but they did appear together on a Thames TV television documentary in 1964 (A. Scott 127). More significant, however, than collaborations or time spent together was Trocchi's continued role as conduit between the European avant-garde and the Beats. As Murphy has demonstrated, Trocchi was an important point of linkage between Burroughs and the theories of the Situationist Internationale: "The convergence between Burroughs's notion of the reality film and the Situationist theory of the spectacle manifests itself in a number of ways, some of which only become apparent when viewed through the lens of Trocchi's Sigma Project" (34). Murphy identifies Trocchi as the "key to this convergence"—as their "common friend and ally," Trocchi acted as translator between "Debord's primarily political analysis and Burroughs's primarily aesthetic one" (30).

Given the convergences facilitated by Trocchi throughout his life, to describe him as one "who talked a better game than he wrote and who has become a footnote in literary history" (Bair) is not only mean spirited but also woefully inaccurate. Steven Vertovec has defined transnationalism as "a kind of social formation spanning borders" (448), and within the social formation known as the Beat Generation, Trocchi played an important role, far greater than one would suspect from the occasional references to him in biographies of Ginsberg and Burroughs. As John Tytell has noted, "The Beats saw themselves as outcasts, exiles within a hostile culture" (4), and Trocchi's life and work belongs unambiguously within the Beat tradition. Trocchi describes this state of exile in *Cain's Book* with self-deprecating humor, but the pain of exile is also present: "The critics who call upon the lost and the beat generations to come home, who use the dead to club the living, write prettily about anguish because to them it is a historical phenomenon and not a pain in the arse" (224). For the Beats as well as Trocchi, "home" was a perplexed and perplexing concept. The reasons for their collective sense of dislocation are by now well documented, but we are just starting to realize how truly transnational this social formation was, in terms of both geographical wanderlust and cultural influence. As for Alexander Trocchi, he bore the mark of Cain with the pride that comes from refusing to give up and take a job in the meat-packing factory. An incorrigible exile throughout his life, he should not be exiled from literary history.

Notes

1. See Kerouac's *Vanity of Duluoz*: "the soft city evenings, the cries of Rimbaud!, 'New Vision!'" (London: Granada, 1982: 240).
2. These transcripts were published for the first time in Campbell and Niel's *A Life in Pieces: Reflections on Alexander Trocchi* (Edinburgh, Scotland: Rebel, 1997).
3. Laurence Lipton's colorful and creative memoir of Venice West, *The Holy Barbarians*, fictionalizes him as Tom Draegon but provides little insight into his role there.
4. Interested readers are referred to Irving Rosenthal's *Sheeper* for an extended account of the East Tenth Street scene.
5. Ned Polsky says of Trocchi, "Great precision and concision, great insight, I think as much insight certainly into the drug addict's world as Burroughs, and I think a better writer, a better stylist" (Polsky 126). Michael Gardiner discusses Ed Dorn's 1962 *Kulchur* article on *Cain's Book* and *Naked Lunch*, in which Dorn says that Burroughs, for all his genius, "makes less sense about dope than Trocchi does" (qtd. in Gardener 90).

Chapter 13

Greece and the Beat Generation:
The Case of Lefteris Poulios

Christopher Gair and Konstantina Georganta

Underneath, sub roads. On top,
airy tunnels playing jazz.

. . .

We are waiting each at our stop.
We are waiting all in the zinc plated shelter.

— From "Roads," Lefteris Poulios[1]

Lefteris Poulios's twenty-one line poem, "Roads" (1973), is a striking example of the global circulation of ideas in post–World War II poetry. While less overtly indebted to the Beats than his "An American Bar in Athens," which will be the primary focus of this essay, "Roads" draws upon many of the essential Beat tropes—jazz, loneliness, travel, and the road itself—to construct an image that is simultaneously deeply nationalistic and unashamedly transnational in its location of the poetic voice. The opening line's reference to "my land" immediately highlights this doubling ("Roads—lustrous dark octopuses of my land"), coupling a direct avowal of Greek identity with (as becomes increasingly apparent in what follows) a sense of alienation that is expressed through identification with Beat protagonists such as Sal Paradise and the "I" of "Howl." As in *On the Road*, roads connect places and peoples but simultaneously remind them of an existential separation that mere travel is never able to transcend. The poem's closing lines—"We are waiting each at our stop / We are waiting all in the zinc plated shelter"—confirm this isolation and also historicize it. The lines stand apart, separated by the only stanza break in the poem, and, in a formal feature that reinforces the impression of isolation, are written as two separate sentences, each with a full stop. Structure mirrors form, with each individual alone at his or her own "stop," divided, possibly passive or indifferent, but certainly alienated, waiting in the shelter made of zinc. In the Greek original, Poulios uses the word υπόστεγο, a shelter to protect yourself from the elements or in which to stay, crowded or alone, until you are transported somewhere else, which in this context also appears to resonate with images of nuclear annihilation, connoting Bob Dylan's "hard rain" and the inescapable fate that seems to await humanity, whichever road is taken. Given that the poem provides clear information on the actual location of many of the roads it cites—"outside the parliament," "underneath" the main roads, "next to statues"—it is noteworthy that Poulios offers no such direction in the closing couplet. Instead, these lines draw the reader's attention to the verb that, in the Greek original, starts the line: "we are waiting," a present continuous that stresses the twinning of now and forever.

"Roads" is emblematic of the transnational dimensions of Beat that we want to highlight in this essay. While, as suggested above, it resonates with patterns and ideas seen in the work of Jack Kerouac, Allen Ginsberg, Gregory Corso, and many other American writers, it also makes these features specific to national concerns. For example, the poem alludes to "a thousand demonstrations" and the "curse" that has transformed the birthplace of democracy into a murderous dictatorship, alongside the description of "Roads lashed / with pitch and blood. Made from screams / and gravel" in a manner that distinguishes it from the less overtly political (in the specific alignment of poetry and collective street protest) canonical Beat texts of the late 1950s. But—and again we wish to stress this point as fundamental to an understanding of Beat—it does so as part of a global circulation of ideas in which the American Beat Generation serves not simply as the fountainhead for ideas that are adopted by other groups and individuals around the world, but also as a receptor and adaptor of poetic and philosophical traditions from many cultures.

While the Beats can indubitably be seen as a quintessential American movement, looking back to Whitman and Thoreau, celebrating individualism in language generally drawn from the "American Grain" and highlighting aspects of American life threatened by an encroaching and pervasive modernity, this is by no means the whole story. Beat voices are, as with Whitman and Thoreau, also self-consciously pluralistic, drawing upon the aesthetic traditions of (among others) Eastern, European, Greco-Roman, and Native American mythologies to construct their works. Greece, itself, played a role in the development of the Beat consciousness, in a tripartite manner that embraced ancient Greek mythology and literature, British romanticism's engagement with this past and with the revolutionary struggle of the early nineteenth century, and a rather naïve conception of post–World War II Greece as a space in which to escape the crushing pressures of modern America (even though Lawrence Ferlinghetti did organize, in 1972, an evening of poetry in support of the Greek struggle against the Junta, which the poets Nanos Valaoritis and Dinos Siotis also attended).[2] Corso was well versed in the Greek classics from his time in Clinton Prison, and the letters sent during his three-month sojourn in Greece in late 1959 are characterized by allusions to the Acropolis, Homer, and the "Gods of Greece" (210–222).[3] Alan Ansen (On the Road's Rollo Greb) lived in Athens for around forty years, while many of the leading Beats travelled extensively in Greece, celebrating a place of natural beauty and hospitality, where the status of the artist was very different from their experience of mid-century America.

Unsurprisingly, given their affiliations with romanticism and Transcendentalism, many Beat writers were drawn both to the literary and philosophical traditions of ancient Greece and also to the relationship between Byron and the Greek war for independence that led to the birth of the modern Greek nation. When Jack Duluoz meets Sabby Sayakis (Sebastian Sampas) in Kerouac's *Vanity of Duluoz* (1968), he notes how Sabby would "yell Byron at me: 'So we'll go no more-a-roving / So late into the night. . . . .'." Last—but by no means least—the ancient Greeks' concepts of homosexual love between men and of the homosocial relationships that underpin the generation of art serve as direct precursors of the associations that, for Ginsberg, were a necessary precondition for artistic creativity and which, in later life, saw him adopt a role akin to the *erastês* in the *erastês-erômenos* relationship characterizing an ancient Greek education in military and civic—or, in Ginsberg's updated version, artistic—affairs.

The complex circulation of ideas and language within which a Greek Beat aesthetic should be understood is also evident in the role that Greece played in a Beat consciousness whose "Americanness" masks its multifarious global antecedents. When international responses to Beat writing are considered, the paradox continues: a body of writing perceived from within as counter-hegemonic in its critiques of the cultural and political constraints of life at American mid-century is often read by non-Americans as the embodiment of a U.S. freedom unavailable under military dictatorship or where the violent silencing of dissenting voices was the norm. At the same time, the American 1950s was a decade dominated, as Frederick Karl argues, by split personalities and united under "a sense of the counterfeit, the deceptive, the fraudulent, the artificial, and the imitational," forging—in both, contrasting senses of the word—an "American sameness" to counteract "Soviet imperial homogenization" (20–21), while the Cold War and McCarthyism developed a "narrative of authoritarian fear and trembling": the civil rights movement, rock and roll, and the Beats were considered by some as un-American for weakening the population either in the face of an external enemy or debilitating youth, while censorious acts, such as the authorities controlling television images and language, reached deep into the population (59). In Greece, many leftist poets served years of exile in the 1950s, so that their poetry refused to link images to a "a long-lost mythical or historical substratum." Even the sun, Vangelis Calotychos observes, conformed to the daily routine of the concentration camp (206, 208). It was their anti-conformist vision and sarcasm that greatly influenced the 1970s poets (Calotychos 228). For the poets belonging to the Greek generation of the 1970s, as Karen Van Dyck notes, "nationalist chauvinism and foreign dependency went hand in hand: ruled by a dictatorship that called itself a 'Greece for Christian Greeks,' the country continued to integrate itself into the networks of international capitalism with a steady flow of foreign imports and a regime supported by American politicians and the CIA" (*Kassandra* 59).

By the 1970s, Greek poetry—exemplified by the work of Veroniki Dalakoura, Natasa Hatzidaki, Jenny Mastoraki, Pavlina Pampoudi, Poulios, Vasilis Steriadis, and others—drew from both the Greek literary tradition and American dissident and popular cultures to talk about urban alienation, consumerism, and censorship. It exposed the interdependence of a "discourse of deprivation," imposed by censorship, and the "discourse of abundance," induced by consumerism and foreign influence (Van Dyck, *Kassandra* 59).[4] This generation advanced further the desire for resistance against powers of authority and control expressed by the first postwar generation of Greek poets (those born roughly between the years 1919 and 1926, as Alexandros Argyriou groups them, a period that corresponds chronologically to many of the poets of the Beat Generation) and the new rules that they had founded ("νεοτερική ποιητική γραφή," "modernist poetic writing"): a preference for free verse and liberated forms of expression, use of myth to portray grim reality rather than to escape from it, and a focus on the present state of people crowded in cities and drifting misguided (622–623). In the 1960s, the loss of Fotis Kontoglou, Stratis Myrivilis, Constantinos Parthenis, Myrtiotissa, Georgios Papandreou, Manoles Kalomoires, Spyros Melas, and Giorgos Theotokas was registered together with that of Albert Schweitzer, Vivien Leigh, Edith Piaf, Aldous Huxley, Marilyn Monroe, Hermann Hesse, William Faulkner, Winston Churchill, Cole Porter, John F. and Robert Kennedy, Martin Luther King Jr., and Ernest Hemingway in a way that signified the start of a new era headlined with the words "in Paris, students set up barricades," "Elvis Presley, Janis Joplin, Bob Dylan," "the first man is launched in space: Yuri Alekseyevich Gagarin," and "American intervention in North Vietnam" (*60s* 28–34). In the midst of this hullabaloo of images and ideas and sounds and feelings of loss or imminent disaster, what, then, is the role of poetry? "Poetry is dead, long live poetry," Ferlinghetti wrote in his 1976 "Populist Manifesto" (*Rivers* 205), reserving a re-defined role for poets engaged in the political life of a country, and it is this political voice that we hear in the poetry of Poulios, born in 1944, whose poem "An American Bar in Athens" will serve as our case study.

Questions about the power of popular culture, the end of utopianism and its aftermath, and the murder of the poet-artist-visionary mingle in the poetry of Poulios, with deception as part of memory and history and the search for coherence in a mechanistic world, while he himself notes the following about the Beat poets: "This generation of American poetry projects a social dispute with metaphysical content. By registering the malaise of [the] contemporary world, it was an attempt to retrieve the lost human decency" ("Instead of Silence" n.p.). Aligning himself with what Michael Davidson has described as the primitivism of the San Francisco Renaissance vis-à-vis revision of certain forms of romanticism (the ballad, vatic or rhapsodic rhetoric, surrealist juxtapositions, the cult of innocence, primitivism) (31–32), Poulios has described himself as, perhaps, the "primitive of a coming age," citing Nietzsche, Byron, Hölderlin, Rimbaud, Kornaros, Kalvos, and Seferis among the poets he revisits. At the same time, he revealed his affinity with the American Beat Generation: "If the beatniks hadn't existed I might not have managed to write a single worthwhile verse. With their distant influence I managed to set out my own literary demands" ("Instead of Silence" n.p.).

With the Beat attitude a push and an echo, then, his poem "An American Bar in Athens" (1973) becomes emblematic not only for the period that produced it but also for articulation of the fears of the future in postwar Greece. The poem has been compared to Ginsberg's "A Supermarket in California" and to Ezra Pound's "A Pact," both of which depict the poets' relationships with the past that Walt Whitman represents in contrast to that of their own times.[5] Indeed, a first glance at the opening lines of "An American Bar" illustrates the striking similarities between it and "Supermarket," threatening perhaps to undermine the specifics of Poulios's artistic intervention:

> Amongst the wandering, hurried, stupid, faces
> of the street, I saw you tonight Koste Palama,
> Wandering back and forth in my drunken disillusionment;
> Looking for a whore, a friend, resurrection.
> Shop windows and the moon! People of all types
> stroll at night; and iron dogs honk;[6]

Now consider the opening lines from Ginsberg's poem:

> What thoughts I have of you tonight, Walt Whitman, for I walked
> down the sidestreets under the trees with a headache self-conscious looking
> at the full moon.
> In my hungry fatigue, and shopping for images, I went into the neon
> fruit supermarket, dreaming of your enumerations!
> What peaches and what penumbras! Whole families shopping at
> night! . . .
>
> (Howl 29)

The apparent act of homage at work here creates an imitation of an imitation, since Ginsberg, too, is advertising the degree to which the form of his verse replicates that of Whitman's. Likewise, Whitman, Ginsberg, and Poulios all imagine the poet in acts of flânerie, which combine observation, political engagement, and (within their own cultures) dissident or deviant sexual desire. Poulios is also specific in replicating Ginsberg's imagery, noting the moon, the streets and shops, and the presence of the ancestor-poet, in a coupling of anxiety of influence and veneration. Nevertheless, such similarities should not be taken to indicate any lack of engagement with contemporary Greek politics and culture.

The Beat poets placed great emphasis on performance—meaning here, as Davidson uses it, both "'making something happen' (as in Spicer) and in the sociological sense of 'acting out' in a public sphere"—with a focus not only upon the poet's address but upon the reader's active participation with that address (20, 22). Accordingly, the most political Beat poetry was not only polemical in the sense that it criticized American political life or incorporated political convictions into poetry but also inherently political in that by the 1960s the poets themselves became collectively "a kind of oppositional sign" by becoming involved in the civil rights movement, the Vietnam War protest, and the ecology movement, thus synthesizing art, politics, and social theory into a lifestyle promoting personal and societal transformation (Davidson 27).[7] The Beats revived the oral tradition, promoted a utopian dream of a city of art, and celebrated both homo- and heterosexuality. In this way, if not others, the Beats anticipated, as Davidson observes, "the countercultural politics of the New Left [which] saw social responsibility not as a matter of class struggle but as cultural change at all levels of society" (24).

After World War II, in places such as Greece, as well as Poland, Spain, and Russia, where, Seamus Heaney notes, "ideologies warred and solidarities were mercilessly required and equally mercilessly enforced," the question of the role of poetry in saving nations and peoples rose with particular urgency but was to be achieved, paradoxically, "not by ideological counter-punching, not by poems that constituted a counter-revolutionary propaganda, but by poems that were h-e-a-r-d" (37). The cultural function of Greek poetry, in particular, after the 1940s, colluded with what Dimitris Papanikolaou calls "a positive conceptualization of the popular, beyond (or through) its associations with mass production and urban and industrial life" (62). In 1943, for instance, the explosion of national sentiment during the funeral of Greece's national bard, Kostes Palamas (1859–1943), was transformed into an act of resistance against the German Occupation with the poet Angelos Sikelianos's recitation of "Blow, bugles . . . Thundering bells, / shake the whole country, from end to end" (Keeley 41–42). This act later set the stage for the fusion of poetry and politics in the 1960s such that poetry was "h-e-a-r-d" through music. The work of songwriter and composer Mikis Theodorakis became the "prototype for poetically engaged music"—and was consequently banned from public broadcast during the junta—while Dionysis Savvopoulos, the singer-songwriter sometimes called the "Balkan beatnik," fused the personal with the political with albums in which performance showed its own "constructedness": like Bob Dylan's "My Back Pages," Papanikolaou argues, Savvopoulos's songs dealt no longer with clear-cut confrontations but took flight to a "diffuse moment of internalized dichotomies centered on repeating, remembering, playfully relocating and staging the embodied schism as a sign of new times" (93, 113, 127).[8] In September 1971, the funeral of the poet Giorgos Seferis became another such meaningful act against the military junta, with the crowd singing first the Greek National Anthem, then Seferis's poem "Denial" (banned by the junta) as put into music by Theodorakis, and then the Cretan song "Πότε θα κάνει ξαστεριά" ("When will the sky be clear so you can see the stars?" originally sang by Cretan singer Nikos Xylouris).[9]

The political struggles that led to these acts of "h-e-a-r-d" poetry in Greece were tumultuous. The Greek 1950s concluded ten years of foreign military occupation and a civil war that brought terror, famine, and poverty, and in the process introduced, as Thomas Gallant calls it, a period of "reconstruction and retribution" (178). As a result of the civil war that lasted from 1943–1949, a substantial portion of the power of the state was transferred from the government to the armed forces with the army's execution of four Communists in 1952—the so-called Beloyannis Affair, which inspired Pablo Picasso to immortalize leftist leader Nikos Beloyannis in the drawing L'Homme à la fleur—showing, as Mogens Pelt suggests, the army's "room for manoeuvre vis-à-vis the elected government" (42–43).

It was in the late 1950s and 1960s that Greek youth acquired a social consciousness for the first time and came to the forefront of struggles against racism and war (Sakellaropoulos 13). In 1963, the killing of Greek social democrat Gregoris Lambrakis (an event that was fictionalized in Vassilis Vassilikos's 1966 novel Z and revisited by Costas Gavras in his 1969 film of the same name) is considered one of the decade's defining moments: as Pavlos Tsimas wrote,

Days become months, time is condensed, what started as a politicized student movement now influences political developments and, at the same time, a rock scene, concerts, explorations, are gradually created around it – a short-lived rebirth before dictatorship came to stop violently the Greek link between political action and cultural liberation (20).

In 1967, soon after the Rolling Stones performed in Athens, "dictatorship is declared. Junta. And everything changes"; April 21 had become a synonym for the stifling of free political expression (Chronas 58). Like the dichotomies of the U.S. 1950s, which popularized the American Beats, the military junta of 1967 to 1974 provoked the emergence in Greece of a Beat attitude in opposition to an authoritarian regime that considered the use of crude language to be an attack on the colonels' "Greece for Christian Greeks."

The Case of Lefteris Poulios and "An American Bar in Athens"

Three decades after the German Occupation and in the midst of the junta, Poulios used sarcasm and irony to distance himself ideologically from the bleakness he saw around him (Kallerges 96–97). In his poetry, at least until 1978, we find an effect similar to the synthesis of art and politics that the Beats transformed into lifestyle, which involved a rejection of monolithic solutions in favor of personal transformations and an informational role for poetry in moments of crisis, as exemplified in Ginsberg's *Planet News* (1968), "a kind of *bricolage* made out of the swiftly changing cultural values of that period" (Davidson 29).

Davidson also argues that for each of the Beats "place" meant something different but was consistently an allegory for the "myth of an alternative society" and "alternative forms of participation" (Davidson 11). Likewise, Poulios as poet becomes a modern orator talking about cultural change and cultural excess, incorporating in his poetry the sound of the machine that "breaks the stones like bones of a young child" ("Άσμα," "Canto," 1969), of clocks hidden beneath the concrete ("Καβγάς," "Fight," 1973; "Συχνά όταν το Σκοτάδι . . ." "Often when Darkness . . . ," 1977), and images of atomic fog, car exhaust, petrol and tar, addicts, ruined Parthenon, bombs, police cars, tanks, asylums, war, shop windows, television sets, and neon signs. Singing of the loud, void silence of drunken men parading their detachment, Poulios becomes electric in search of a poetry that can shock and shake a decayed society, the Athens that knows you and breaks you with a glance like Circe. Poulios's interest in the ways that roads generate coherence out of disparate elements such as cars, jazz, university campuses, statues, and buildings, as in his short poem "Roads," echoes detail as in *On the Road*, even though for Poulios such unity collapses into demonstrations, murder, and curses.

Poulios transposes American Beat as a means to engage with a tradition of Greek poetry through the figure of Kostes Palamas (1859–1943), a central presence in the Greek literary generation of the 1880s and the author of the words to the "Olympic Hymn," but also a poet who attacked society with his *Satirical Exercises* at the end of the nineteenth and the beginning of the twentieth centuries.[10] As Van Dyck notes, Poulios "politicizes Palamas by dragging him out of the realm of aesthetics into the streets of Athens" (*Kassandra* 58–59). "An American Bar in Athens" converses with Palamas—whose "heavy shadow" molded future generations of poets—and builds on the bonds between grandson and grandfather to create a dam against the nightmarish bleakness imposed by the junta (Πρακτικά Ενάτου Συμποσίου Ποίησης 377). Here, Palamas is significant as the persona chosen to accompany the poet as Polytechneio students protesting against the dictatorship in 1973 in Athens distributed illegal leaflets with his verse. Rather than viewing him here as an object of abuse, the poet is expressing his ideological closeness to the once national bard (Kallerges 89–110). Poulios was, besides, concerned with the degradation of contemporary civilization and the crisis in moral values that failed the aspiration Palamas expressed in his patriotic poems.[11] Like his beloved Pound and Ginsberg, as Haris Vlavianos suggests, Poulios denounces the diminution of poetry's redemptive role in a society that alienates itself from life and from the poet himself (Vlavianos). An "American Bar in Athens" can only then symbolize, according to Kallerges, the most extreme form of alienation and disorientation of traditional values, and nighttime signifies ideological corruption (97–98). As in the bleak 1940s, the stench stretches to the city behind them.[12]

The only icon of the past still admired by both poets, Poulios and Palamas, is Regas Pheraios (1759–1798) whom Palamas considered a person of action who re-established the power of poetry to serve social and national goals (Palamas 17–20). The youth wing of the Communist Party in Greece founded in 1968 was also named after him.[13] Pheraios sought a broader renaissance of the Greek spirit and did not confine himself within the narrow borders of the nation, while he also signified the beginning of a modern transformation of Greek literature, a scheme finally realized, for Palamas, with Dionysios Solomos: "The year Regas died, Solomos was born" (20). Consider the following lines from "An American Bar in Athens":

> I feel your thoughts Koste Palamas; feckless
> old *bon vivant* as you enter the bar
> making eyes at the whores and sipping
> a double whiskey.
> I follow you through clouds of cigarette smoke
> and giggles about my effeminate hair.
> I sit on a boarded stand next to a few
> seated statues and let you buy me a drink.
> We are the liveliest here tonight
> The informers glare with suspicion and
> the lights will go out in an hour.
> Who will carry us home?
> ....
> I feel like a schoolboy whose luck was to have
> a cuss for a teacher. For some time now I wondered
> how we would get along. Hideous aged dog let us go
> and spew up tonight's booze,
> on the doors of closed bookstores.
> Let's go and piss on all the statues
> of Athens; kneeling only in front of
> Regas. And let's part each on his
> way like grandfather and grandson who
> have had a fight. Beware of this madness
> of mine old man; at any moment I could kill you.[14]

Here, reclaiming the distinction between the figural and the literal erased by the regime of 1967 to 1974, "An American Bar in Athens" becomes emblematic of a kind of counterculture Beat ethos applied to Greece. The regime, Van Dyck reminds us,

> sought to eradicate confusion and mixed messages not only through the press law but also through dress codes, curfews, and moral expectations. The corollary of the censor's demand for a perfect fit between what one said and what one meant was the moralist's demand for a perfect fit between what one looked like and who one was. Any kind of undecidability, textual or sexual, was considered subversive. ("Reading" 47–48)

The poet therefore appears with feminine hair, disturbing the passive clientele of the bar, themselves prisoners in a constant state of suspicion and fear; yet it is in that same bar that the poet tries to regain his vague sense of heritage. The end of the poem, with its threat of imminent and sudden death, anticipates a line in one of Poulios's later poems ("Κέντρισμα," "Sting," 1977, from *Selected Poems 1969–1978*, 89)—"A hypothetical death is the shock to rebirth" ("Ένας υποθετικός θάνατος είναι η δόνηση για την αναγέννηση")—and is here appropriately applied to Palamas, who himself wrote about the need to destroy so as to create and be recreated anew.[15] The reader of "An American Bar" is urged to react to the illness at the heart of the community of "informers" and "seated statues" in whose presence the two seemingly unlikely companions perform; the "boarded stand" ("πάνω στο σανιδένιο πάγκο") where they drink together is a bar described in such terms as to resemble another word for stage, namely σανίδι. The line "lights go out in an hour" ("τα φώτα σβήνουνε σε μια ώρα"), apparently a deliberate echo of Ginsberg's "The doors close in an hour" (in "Supermarket"), points therefore both to the control imposed by the regime and to the limited and very specific time slot the two poets inhabit during a performance orchestrated to disturb an involuntary audience populated by the doubly immobile "seated statues." As with Ginsberg's "Supermarket," the poem requires that the reader decipher the literary and the figurative nature of its protagonists' nighttime peregrinations so that we can identify the ailment of the society within the city's inanimate animosity, its bars, closed bookstores, and void statues. The poet depicts trash bins together with storytellers to equate the stench of the city with a society laid to waste, and the poem lays bare the elements that construct it so that it can be itself destroyed and created again.

Reiterating Davidson's remarks on the political engagement of the Beats, to be inherently political means promoting social responsibility in matters of cultural change at all levels of society and offering creation as a means of resistance. It is in this sense that an overview of the main national and international concerns of the 1960s and 1970s and a focus on artistic creativity can help one understand how beliefs are translated into political/poetic discourse and how theory can be produced culturally. Stathis Gourgouris suggests that the twentieth century begins twice—once as a "categorically revolutionary era," then again as an "era of annihilation," bringing together society's radical imagination and the impact of the "atomic age"—and societies control their progress to the extent that they recognize "the effects of their own mytho-poetic production" (250, 254). The period when

Poulios writes his poetry is significant as it bridges the aspirations of the international community in safekeeping "freedom of speech and belief and freedom from fear and want" (proclaimed in the 1948 Universal Declaration of Human Rights) after World War II, and efforts at self-determination and a right to be heard in the 1960s and 1970s.

Translation is a necessary step in the analysis and is in itself a meaningful act. In the twenty-first century, translation scholarship focuses on what can be called post-colonial inequalities—"just as the model for colonialism was based on the notion of a superior culture taking possession of an inferior one, so an original was always seen as superior to its 'copy'"—shifting the focus so that the original and translation are viewed as "equal products of the creativity of writer and translator" (Bassnett 4–6). It is in this way that translation becomes one of the hardest forms of criticism. Our objective here has been the examination of Poulios's poetry as the aesthetic product of a period marked by the Greek Civil War (1943–1949), the exile of many leftist poets within Greece in the 1950s, the social awakening of the young in the 1960s, and the military junta of 1967 to 1974. Poulios tried to make sense of his culture, nationality, and identity by describing a shift in the way we look at these concepts, using as his trope the outlook of a literature not generated solely by a nation and itself representative of split personalities. In his poetry we therefore see railway lines connecting Siberia with Paris and sub-roads linking New York with Beijing ("Χορός πάνω σε σταχτοθήκη" "Dance on an Ashtray"), and, even though the cultural context is important, the texts are significant in their nod to intertextual and transtextual dialogue for "Ugly times / times of automated whips" ("Άσχημοι Καιροί," "Ugly Times") and a price tag on everything ("Το Εμπόρευμα," "The Merchandise").

Notes

1. The translation here is ours, but we consulted the version in *Modern Greek Writing: an Anthology in English Translation*, edited by David Ricks, 441.
2. See Ferlinghetti, *These Are My Rivers*, 13.
3. See, too, Gustave Reininger's 2009 documentary, *Corso: the Last Beat*, in which the sixty-seven-year-old poet returns to Italy and Greece and muses on their significance in the formulation of his Beat persona.
4. This generation came to be collectively known as "the generation of the 1970s" ("η γενιά του '70"), "the generation of protest" ("η γενιά της αμφισβήτησης"), "the pin-ball generation" ("η γενιά των γερανών και των φλίπερς"), or "the third post-war generation" ("η τρίτη μεταπολεμική γενιά"), each term denoting either its chronological placement as regards previous generations of poets or its connection to the cultural and political conditions of the time. The "pinball generation," for example, a phrase referring to the mechanized games that first appeared in Greece in the 1960s, drew attention to the new consumerism and urban alienation of life in Athens during that time. See Van Dyck, *Kassandra* 61–68.
5. Kallerges adds to this the possible influence of Cavafy's poem "Young Men of Sidon (a.d. 400)," where the fifth century c.e. comes in direct contrast to the next century's challenging of tradition. See Kallerges 109.
6. Again, the translation here is ours but we consulted the well-known version by Philip Ramp and Katerina Angelaki-Rooke. See Lefteris Poulios, "An American Bar in Athens,"

in *Modern Greek Writing: an Anthology in English Translation*, edited by David Ricks, 442–443. Ramp and Angelaki-Rooke's translation seems to exaggerate the already strong allusions to "A Supermarket in California": they add the line "While I hold your book in my hand," creating a material presence that serves as a synecdochical reminder of the coupling of anxiety of influence and veneration that we discuss. As is evident in this essay, we believe that translation is one of the hardest forms of criticism and here choose to use the 1973 version but also comment on it and change it.

7. This should not be taken to mean that *all* the major Beat authors became engaged in this way: Kerouac was openly hostile to this representation of Beat, while Burroughs, for example, would hardly match such a description. Nevertheless, even Kerouac was, much against his will and ideological beliefs, repeatedly subsumed within such a vision and made his hostility to it clear in public utterances such as during his 1968 appearance on William F. Buckley's WOR-TV program, *The Firing Line*.

8. Papanikolaou compares Savvopoulos's song "Ωδή στον Γεώργιο Καραϊσκάκη" ("Ode to Karaiskakis," from *A Fool's Garden*, 1969) with Allen Ginsberg's "A Poem on America" (1956) suggesting that what is being proposed in both cases is "iteration and citation, a doubling up of events that already exist as photographs in the mind. Such a simulation of images does not introduce the metaphor one expects to find at the centre of the myth (something representing something else), but a series of signifiers (photographs doubles up) in an endless metonymic chain" (141).

9. See *To Vima*, 23 Sept. 1971. Web.

10. It is interesting to compare Palamas's satirical verses (published in 1908 and 1909) with Poulios's tone in "An American Bar in Athens." Of particular note are the poems that refer to ancestors degraded by the then-contemporary state of politics. See Kokolis 105.

11. For Palamas's use of the image of Greece as a "space-time continuum formed by a synthesis of physical and spiritual elements" (45), see Christopher Robinson's "Greece in the Poetry of Costis Palamas."

12. Compare with Angelos Sikelianos's 1941 poem "Agraphon," which creates a parable for 1940s Athens and its starved inhabitants: as Christ marvels at the white teeth of a dead dog among the stench of the garbage dumb, the poet sees salvation from the Germans, "justice in a time of turmoil and suffering": "If your breath is pure, you'll smell / the same stench inside the town behind us, but / Look how that dog's teeth glitter in the sun: / like hailstones, like a lily, beyond decay." See a discussion of the poem in Keeley, *Modern Greek Poetry*, 3–42.

13. For Regas and the link with the Greek Communist Party, see Van Dyck, *Kassandra* 58. For this and other important dates before and after the civil war, see Neni Panourgia, *Dangerous Citizens: The Greek Left and the Terror of the State*, a chronology which is available at http://dangerouscitizens.columbia.edu/.

14. Again, the translation is ours, but we consulted the version by Ramp and Angelaki-Rooke cited above.

15. Palamas was intrigued by the "never-ceasing periodicity of the seasons and the renewal of life," as presented in the Orphic legends, and in "Ascrean" (1904) he presented the bard Ascraean Hesiod accepting the necessity of death as a prerequisite for renewal after meeting Persephone, "the end of the old and the beginning of the new." Persephone thus accompanies Ascraeus in a "new awakening to a new life like the one he has known of old . . . as a toiler and as a traveller," his longing for her "all-embracing love" reflecting for Palamas, Andreas Karandonis suggests, his own urge "towards youth, towards purification, towards rebirth." See R. J. H. Jenkins, *Palamas: An Inaugural Lecture delivered at King's College, London on 30th January, 1947,* 10; and A. Karandonis, "Introduction to Palamas' *Ascraeus*," in T. G. Stavrou and C. A. Trypanis (eds), *Kostis Palamas: A Portrait and an Appreciation*, 102. Translation of a line from Poulios's poem "Κέντρισμα" is by Konstantina Georganta.

Chapter 14

Japan Beat: Nanao Sakaki

A. Robert Lee

His poems were not written by hand or head, but with the feet. These poems have been sat into existence, walked into existence, to be left here as traces of a life lived for living . . .

Gary Snyder, Foreword, Break the Mirror xi

I

"Anthropological anarchist" (*Nanao or Never*, 134): Nanao Sakaki's self-designation might not exactly win approval for an immigration landing-card. Yet, ironic tease allowed for, it does apt enough justice for the traveler-poet to whom not only nature's expanses of forest, desert, mountain, and river but also metro-lands that include Tokyo's postwar Shinjuku, San Francisco's Mission District, and Amsterdam's Dam Platz became nothing if not his bailiwick. These were worlds for Sakaki, as Gary Snyder rightly emphasizes, to be walked, lived, and felt underfoot. But if that implies drift, mere whatever-comes-along, Sakaki can actually be seen to have lived a life—and with it, the call both to environmental activism and poetry—full of resolution, his own considerable sureness of personal direction. If, too, he continues to attract Western attention as Japan's presiding Beat poet—could there be a more identifying tribute than that of Snyder?—it needs to be said at the outset that Beat and any number of its main players, including Allen Ginsberg, Anne Waldman, and Lawrence Ferlinghetti, as much came to him as he to it.[1]

His interests, not to say creative presence and attractiveness, were considerable. Foremost, always, has to be the poet who launched himself with the slim pamphlet of prose-poetry titled *Bellyfulls* (1961), and whose signature poetry is gathered in *Break the Mirror* (1987), *Let's Eat Stars* (1997), and the translations of *Inch by Inch: 45 Haiku by*

Issa (1985, 1999). His life became famous for its serial movement, the poet as Japanese and Beat counter-cultural foot pilgrim, ever in motion and given to observation of both the local and trans-local perspective. Who more took on the role of itinerant both in his own country and across a sweep of Atlantic and Pacific geographies? These supply the groundswell of his poetry, plays, translations, visual sketches (often of the poet as Orphic-style flautist), and the interviews and reported sayings.

He early took up the mythic Japan called Yaponesia, invented by Toshio Shimao (1917–1986), the novelist of *Shutsokotō-ki* (*A Tale of Leaving a Lonely Island*, 1940) which won the Postwar Literature Prize in 1950, to refract the actual Japan as he saw it from his different wanderings and sojourns at the margin.[2] There was also Sakaki the resolute battler for environmental conservation, antinuclear and antimilitarist campaigner, hater of concrete and dams, green activist against destruction of forests for unnecessary paper or housing or golf courses, founder of a number of ashrams, celebrant of Ainu, Native American, and Aboriginal indigenous cultures, and always the eclectically admired friend and visitor. That does not annul reservations such as those of his daughter, Maggie Tai Sakaki Tucker, who for all her admiration of Sakaki's "patient explanations of how rain works and of where the sun goes at night" also mentions the absenteeism, the odysseys ("I grew up hating the sounds of maps rustling," [*Nanao or Never*, 163]). Nor does it underplay how Sakaki cannily managed his stays, often writing ahead to negotiate readings and performances.

To be sure, and increasingly through to his death in 2008 at age eighty-five, Sakaki also won fame as Japan's best-known Beat, the relished ally besides Snyder, Ginsberg, Peter Orlovsky, and Waldman, of Michael McClure and Joanne Kyger, and the fellow environmentalist and close friend to Beat-affiliated subsequent generation poets such as Gary Lawless of Maine and John Brandi of New Mexico. Even his trademark Whitman-Ginsberg beard, tough wiry frame, sheer unencumbered portability, dropout appearance, and often the vibrant, incantatory voice he gave to readings of his poems suggest Beat style or self-fashioning. The associations with the Beats were many and frequent.

There was the first meeting with Snyder and Ginsberg in Kyoto in 1963 and then Snyder's invitation to him to visit America in 1968 (California and the West Coast of mountain and ocean, Manhattan and Greenwich Village). Subsequent visits include poetry readings with Waldman, Ginsberg, and others, notably at Naropa in 1981. In June 1988 he asked Ginsberg, Snyder, McClure, and Waldman for help in raising money to protect the blue coral reef in Ishigaki-jima against becoming a new airport landing strip. Their poetry reading in San Francisco served as publicity and a fundraiser. Sakaki's message to this Beat consortium was included in his Japanese collection *CHIKYU B* (1989), with a translation into English under the title "Save Shiraho's Coral Reef" in *Nanao or Never* ("this Kamikaze project" he calls the planned landing strip). In April 1990, to select another occasion, he gave a nightclub poetry reading in Prague with Ginsberg and Waldman and with Václav Havel seated in the front row. Overall, Waldman speaks of him as "a major figure in counter-cultural work," "a great presence in our environment," a "pure yet wily presence."[3] Other Beat and associated names to whom he was drawn, and who were drawn to him, include Robert Bly, William Burroughs, Ken Kesey, Georgia O'Keefe, Barry Lopez, and Peter Coyote, the actor-poet and co-founder of the San Francisco Diggers.

In all these respects, the yet more precise biographical contour, from birth in Kagoshima on the south-of-Japan island of Kyushu to demise in old age in Honshu's mountain Nagano, invites careful note.[4] Born of a large family, a school-leaver at age twelve, then an office worker, the outbreak of World War II saw him a navy radar specialist—one who met with departing young kamikaze pilots and at the Izumi Air Base tracked the B-29 on August 9, 1945, as it delivered its bomb on Nagasaki, seeing with his own eyes, albeit at a distance, its toxic mushroom cloud (some of the details appear in his poem "Memorandum").[5] His autodidact's reading of Nietzsche, Schopenhauer, Marx, and Engels, and especially Kropotkin's *Mutual Aid*, along with the memory of friends killed in the war and the immediate unemployment, bombed landscapes, ruined buildings, and food-shortage bleakness of postwar Japan, propelled him ever leftward. As poet-anarchist he tried working in an iron foundry, spent almost two years living in an underpass at Tokyo's Ueno station, took a position for two years as assistant and messenger at the socialist journal *Kaizo*, and from 1955 onward hiked the forests of Japan with the wood sculptor Shin Higuchi in consequence of which the two put on poetry and carving exhibitions in Kagoshima and Ikebukuro (Higuchi gives his name to a Chicago art exhibition center). In the late 1960s Sakaki became one of the founders of The Tribe, sometimes known in the plural as The Tribes (*Buzoku*), the communitarian group that established the Banyan Ashram on the volcanic Ryukyu island of Suwanosejima and where Snyder would spend time.

His Beat-beatnik route famously went beyond Japan to embrace the U.S. southwest of New Mexico (he would live in an old bus in Taos in the 1980s) and Arizona, the Rockies, the Grand Canyon, and the Rio Grande, and especially the Hopi, Navajo, and Pueblo homelands. Further reaches included Alaska, the British Columbia and Washington State Cascades, Maine and Newfoundland, and Mexico. Europe indeed meant Amsterdam and Prague, but also Paris and London. In Australia he traveled the Aboriginal outback, notably Ayers Rock (out of which arose his poem "Chant of a Rock"), and Tasmania's Mount La Perouse, having early become fascinated with bushman arts of survival, hunting, language, and mask and dot-painting.[6] Asia's geographies for him extended to Mongolia's Plains, China's gorges, eastern Siberia, Taiwan's port city of Chi Lung, Korea's Pusan, and Indonesia. It would be hard to doubt transnational Sakaki.

His own appetite for culture rarely diminished, be it for poets of the Tang dynasty (618–907 c.e.), such as Li Bo and Du Fu and the Taoist master Lao Tzu,[7] or Shakespeare, Mozart, and Joyce, or Native American sandpainting and sculpture, or translation (although in a 1988 interview with James M. McCarthy he insists, "I never translate! I just do transformation" [*Nanao or Never* 152]), sometimes even drafting his poems in English. However readily he has been accorded Beat nomenclature, Sakaki always brought both a distinctively Japanese, as well as global, width of appetite to bear. Few figures in his literary-creative formation have played a greater shaping part than Kobayashi Issa (1763–1828), whose haiku he translated with fine care and in reproduced handwritten English in *Inch by Inch: 45 Haiku by Issa*. Inspirational fellow haiku-ists for Sakaki also include the virtuoso Matsuo Bashō (1644–1694), not to mention Bashō the traveler-diarist of *Oku no Hosomichi/The Narrow Road to the Interior* (1694), and the Edo-era poet and painter

Yosa Buson (1716–1783). Sakaki also took full cognizance of a line of antecedent poet-outsiders to include the monk and journeyer Saigyō Hōshi (1118–1190), the vagabond Zen practitioner and eventual abbot Ikkyū (1394–1481), and the humble "great fool" Zen hermit calligrapher and writer Taigu Ryōkan (1758–1831). Each manifested a spare, tensile quality of Japanese idiom at once concentrated yet readily accessible and visual.

He was also always quick to acknowledge heirship to his family's Pure Land Sect Buddhism, hence his commitment to forests and good water, Chinese Taoist philosophy and art, the Indian-Sanskrit mantras and Vedas, and Zen—although he was careful to explain what kind of Zen (Tang dynasty as opposed to Confucian). [8] Sino-Japanese calligraphy and design exercised a lifelong draw. He frequently mentions the impact of the Tibetan yogi-poet Milarepa (1052–1135), whose focus on dharma and tranquility he relished, and a four-page translation of whose work he published in Japanese in 1965. Taken with Sakaki's own interests in artforms to include not only haiku, the seventeen-syllable poetry of concentrated image and perception, but also kabuki, vivid Japanese stage drama, and Edo-era (1603–1867) to Meiji-era (1868–1912) *ukiyo-e*—the so-called "floating world" woodblock painting, and his predilection for continuing Japan's tradition of contemplative-peregrinatory mountain, desert, and island travel and its arising texts, there can be no mistaking his Japanese and other Asian expressive legacy even as it fuses and overlaps with Beat.

II

Working pointers to how Sakaki construes his own identity are to be met with in three first-person poems in *Break the Mirror*, each clearly serious in aim but each possessed of its own seams of playfulness. These all bring to bear his persona as a fusion of Japanese Zen-poet, Beat luminary, and trans-global voice. "Break the Mirror" as the title poem, written in Canberra, Australia, in October 1981 (Sakaki has the helpful habit of dating most of his poems), speaks in a symptomatic voice, his main image quite literally as well as figuratively reflexive:

> In the morning
> After taking cold shower
> ---------What a mistake -------
> I look at the mirror
>
> There, a funny guy,
> Grey hair, white beard, wrinkled skin,
> ---------What a pity--------
> Poor, dirty, old man!
> He is not me, absolutely not. (108)

The speaker's mirror may well report the aging process, and its visible impact on hair, beard, and skin, but his mind's mirror looks for and sees quite a counter-gallery of reflections. These summon the perennial youth inside the veteran, the unaged energy for life taken at the hilt. The listed activity acts to supply both iconography and a working banner:

Land and life
Fishing in the ocean
Sleeping in the desert with stars
Building a shelter in mountains
Farming the ancient way
Singing with coyotes
Singing against nuclear war –
I'll never be tired of life. (108)

The ensuing last lines, those of an inner voice as the poet sits in lotus meditation pose, call for life necessarily freed, fractured if need be, from all fixed consensus as to the world:

"To stay young,
To save the world,
Break the mirror." (108)

This is Sakaki in vintage Buddhist-Beat style, kinetic, appetitive, and given to a matching open poetics.

"Who Am I?," composed in March 1982, and also from *Break the Mirror*, in which the poet looks to his return to Japan "a week ago" from New Mexico-Arizona's Chihuahua desert, does cognate duty:

I'm a poet because they call me so.
Psychiatrist, because
          everybody in the world is insane.
Ecology freak, because I'm Mr. Nature.
Free in love, free in spirit.
Without reason, crazy for music.
Cook dinner for everybody.
Friend of anyone who walks with me.
I'm a Third Stone Age Man. (122)

The effect is to plait into the one creative identity of poet a ply of credentials to include therapist, ecologist, lover, free spirit, music fan, host-cook, rambler companion, and updated primitive. He goes on to connect seeing Native American art and eating venison and black bear meat with being "back home to northern mountain" (122), exhilarated at moonlight, given to song, and moved to be amid the domain of robins. There can be little doubt of the cryptic, which is not to say ungenial, voicing of Sakaki's poem, its frames of reference at once national and transnational, at once here and now and yet beyond. Is not this fashioning also to indicate a Beat-like or at least Snyder-like temperament? More than likely.

"Homo Erectus Ambulant" (undated in *Break the Mirror* 74–75) celebrates human difference even as the Japanese 1980s appeared to be all corporations and strikes, right wing violence, and the 60th-year-warning remembrance of the 1923 Tokyo earthquake. The poem tabulates a better order, be it nature's "clouds and wind," "flowers and seasons," or the writ of the heart over "crazily varicolored . . . human minds" (74–75). For his own part, the poet is to be seen precisely as the title implies, a walker who is at one and the same time Darwinian biped and modern backpack traveler:

> Me, *Homo erectus* ambulant,
> On the way home from a big town,
>   Heavy pack on my back.
> Casually I halt my steps –
> A cloud of horseflies are tempted by my sweaty skin. . .
> In front of me, one meter, a viper wending her way. . .
> In front of me, two meters, two Spanish flies hopping. . .
> In front of me, five meters, a dragonfly and a swallowtail crossing
>   each other. . .
> In front of me, ten meters, three crows flying off. (74–75)

The implication is emphatic, humankind in its better incarnations as one of the planet's many "bouquets" (75), a life-form privileged to be among others, be it horsefly, viper, fly, dragonfly, swallowtail, or crow. "Tomorrow's wind," the poem ends, could be "North, south, east or west" (75), the readiest note of spontaneous possibility.

"Autobiography," written in summer 1993 and included in *Let's Eat Stars*, again faithful to his life's way stations, is also so pitched to be a roll-call of his poet's imaginative beckonings and flights. The poem opens in memory of childhood under wartime conditions:

> Born of a humble & poor family,
> Received minimum education,
> Learnt how to live by himself at fourteen,
> Survived storms, one after another:
> Bullets, starvation & concrete wastelands. (39)

Two succeeding stanzas bespeak an ascetic regimen, brown rice in a cup, fish, and water; pleasure in the work of farmer, fisherman, carpenter, and blacksmith; and an eschewing of the inessentials he enumerates as soap, shampoo, toilet paper, and newspapers. Rather his option, or that of his vatic persona, is one of rhapsody, the "now & again" (39) relish of honeysuckle nectar, coyote song, dragonfly flutter, or the swimming of the humpback whale. The love for earth is located in the wish "to hug rocks in which dinosaurs sleep" (39): nature as time yet always quite undead repository.

In closing, the poem offers a personal map of here and now situatedness and yet transience:

> Feels at home in Alaska glaciers,
> Mexican desert, virgin forest of Tasmania,

Valley of Danube, grasslands of Mongolia,
Volcanoes in Hokkaido & Okinawan coral reefs.
And – one sunny summer morning
He will disappear quietly on foot
Leaving no shadow behind. (39)

The scale of reference is tectonic, inter-hemispheric. It would be hard not to discern a hands-on relish of the world's literal topography of glacier, desert, forest,
valley, grassland, volcano, and reef. Yet all of these coordinates, Alaska to Mexico,
Tasmania to the Danube, Mongolia to Japan's Hokkaido and Okinawa, can also be
thought a species of hieroglyphic, as though the markers of cosmological life geography. If Sakaki as the poet is to be perceived as wholly "at home" (39) in his own
lifetime's time-space, symptomatically, one might say that transcendentally he will
one day "disappear quietly on foot" under sun and without shadow. Sakaki, or his
speaker-persona, so calls upon a deep well of Zen acceptance and tranquility and, as
it were, his own Beat ear and eye roster of the senses.

To these can be added two futurist autobiographical compositions from *Let's
Eat Stars* (1997), the poet projected into a timetable beyond even his own death. In
"Twilight Man" (dated March 1990), wandering along Gifu Prefecture's fog-laden
Nagara River, the speaker discovers among the pebbles "one broken piece of earthenware" (19), Neolithic, perhaps five-thousand-years old. In imagination, river-like,
he conjures up a companion shadow of himself as earthenware maker. That, in turn,
leads into a run of speculation as to both self-legacy and art legacy:

Mingling with pebbles
Mingling with fog
Drifting on river
Drifting into history's debris
I will be a twilight man
Tomorrow

What will be my earthenware? (19)

Each imagistic component delicately inscribes the self in time, pebble, fog, river,
twilight, and earthenware as nature's own clock-hands, a different kind of "history's
debris" (19).

"If I Have Tomorrow" (composed in October 1990 in Santa Fe) creates another
kind of chronological ladder, a series of time-to-come January 1sts, the new year
date of Sakaki's own birthday. Written as though under a full moon from "Nov. 3rd,
1990/Pinacate desert, Mexico" (21), he envisions four January 1sts, each with its fantasy journey. January 1, 1993, three years on from the poem's composition, he imagines himself at seventy, "with donkey, horse and camel" (21), walking across Eurasia
from Korea to England; January 1, 2023, he sees himself climbing Mount Olympus
on Mars; and January 1, 2923, his 1,000th birthday, he imagines himself visiting
"Miranda," one of Uranus's moons, there to encounter the fairy-spirit reincarna-
tion of Prospero's beauteous daughter in Shakespeare's *The Tempest*. For January 1,
11,923, the prospect is even more galactic, an origins-of-the-universe scenario:

Jan. 1st, my, 10,000th birthday.
Work hard for a new solar system
As a grain of stardust in the Milky Way. (*Let's Eat Stars* 21)

Told as though from a geological setting, the Mexican desert, the January 1 time-setting could not evolve into a more symptomatic timetable-to-come.

III

Sakaki as Beat, or at least Beat-allied, yields its own folder of authorship both by and about him. The two poems (both in *Let's Eat Stars*) that explicitly invoke Ginsberg, "Who Needs Allen Ginsberg in Today's Japan?" (written in February 1988 in the East Village when he was reinvited there by Ginsberg and Orlovsky) and "Bye-Bye Allen Ginsberg" (written in the Tokyo region of the Kanto Plain in 1997), underscore a fond mutual intimacy. The former recognizes the author of "Howl" as liberative, Whitman's heir. The latter develops a Buddhist-transcendent requiem to the Ginsberg who had recently died in 1997. Both, in title but also at the same time obliquely in their play of image and allusion, underline Beat as one-to-one friend-ship and yet also literary-creative connection. To these, from *Break the Mirror*, can be added "Gloves / For Allen, sixty-light years old glove" (February 1985), with its reflected sense of himself and Ginsberg as mutually fitting old gloves, and "The Battle of Toads, for Allen Ginsberg" (written in Shinano near the river that con-nects Nagano and Niigata Prefectures, Japan, 1983), in which Sakaki identifies with nature's noble but glandular-ugly amphibian—and with frogs and salamanders—as his figural mode of confronting eco-damage and above all, nuclear contamination ("me, a toad, going to the battlefield," 71).

"Who Needs Allen Ginsberg . . . ?" resembles a Ferlinghetti or Waldman riff, the short phrase or one-word-per-line tabulation of place, animals, politics, and people through which the actually unnamed Ginsberg is to be imagined filter-ing into Japan as though a touchstone spirit. Beginning from "Air / Water / Soil / Coral reefs / Oak virgin forests" (*Let's Eat Stars* 8), the poem invokes grizzlies, otters, and wildcats, and then a concourse of different humanity—specifically the Ainu and Okinawans, gays and lesbians, organic farmers and fishermen, artists and poets. Sakaki is clearly pledged to a realm of creativity over conformism (the ironic dig at "Happy middle class," "Unhappy Millionaires"), a Japan of human variety as against adherence to institutional rules with primacy given to "No Nukes / Free Schools / Children." His ending of "Leaves of Grass – / Roots" (8) points to a Whitman-Ginsberg ethos, the desiderata for a Japan of openness to experience and mindful of its own best nature-centered traditions. It might well pass as a virtual Sakaki manifesto, personal, ecological, imagist, and interactively Beat and Japanese.

"Bye-Bye Allen Ginsberg" (*Let's Eat Stars* 90), far from being a funereal dirge, acts to place the one time of life within cosmological time, again a Zen-Beat schema. The thrust is first to accept the natural order of things ("Don't try what you can't"), to steer beyond mere self ("Sit in the outsider of your meditation! / Take off, leaving your brain behind!"), to understand the world as temporary and an illusion ("The world is just a dream, be crazy"), and to accept that within the universe's chronometer the self endlessly transposes and reincarnates ("It is five minutes to eternity. / Hi, spring wind / When will you return?").[9] The poem's supporting images vividly juxtapose eagle, flower, sprout, sorrel, monkey, deer, wild boar, bear, the body's laughing navel, and even the paradoxical energies of cosmic climate ("The silence thunders in heaven"). All of these elements serve to place the death of Ginsberg inside a universe ever the yin and yang of metamorphosis and sameness, the one temporary human fold inside all time and change. In the poem's lively fashioning, Zen again can be said to meet Beat, East the West, and Sakaki's Japan voice that of his Beat voice.

"Bikki Salmon," written in October 1989 (*Let's Eat* Stars 14–17), although it honors the life and art of the major Hokkaido Ainu wood artist Bikki Sunazawa (1931–1989), whom Sakaki envisages as having becoming one of the salmon imaged in his own woodblocks, carries a further Beat footfall. The poem aligns Bikki, among others, with Black Elk, Issa, Lao Tzu, the Maitreya Buddha, and "Nanao" himself, and as fellow artists-fish "Allen salmon swimming / Gary salmon swimming" (16). Bikki, moreover, wins other plaudits. The cover of *Let's Eat Stars* uses three of Bikki's drawings of salmon, each forward swimming, engraved in traditional indigenous design, and set against a green-and-yellow-rimmed circle. In "Star Bikki" (60–61), written in 1994, a half-dozen years after "Bikki Salmon," Sakaki pays his one creator's salute to the other, seeing Bikki after death metamorphosed into an Ezo spruce as befits a worker in wood (Ezo refers to the Hokkaido region); the tree in its own turn extends upward into the solar system. Bikki so becomes the carver of "the empty sky with his chisel / Something in wood with his soul" to be transposed into "a new star" (60). The closing stanza carries greeting, the good cheer of song and drink, together with Bikki's mythic continuance and powers of communication:

Hi Star Bikki! Nowadays
What are you carving?
What songs are you singing?
What kind of Sake are you drinking?

Hi star Bikki! Sometime
Send me a postcard
Decorated full of stars! (61)

An imagined bridge from Bikki to Ginsberg and Snyder, in both poems and life and art, would be anything but out of keeping.

Sasaki himself as poetic subject has led to little short of a plenty. Snyder deserves first place in the roll-call, comrade of longstanding, fellow environmental poet, Buddhist, another inveterate journeyer. Their meeting, along with Ginsberg (and Kyger), is given confirmatory dating by Sakaki: "In 1963 I met Gary Snyder and Allen Ginsberg in Kyoto" (*Nanao or Never* 174). Rarely, along with his various introductions and interviews, does Snyder better capture Sakaki's ease of passage across country and urban landscapes than in his 1960s poem "Nanao Knows":

> Mountains, cities, all so
> > light, so loose. (98)

Kyger, in a 1998 recollection (she had accompanied, and in February 1960 married, Snyder when they were both at the Zen Institute, Kyoto) says cryptically of Sakaki, "Nanao wasn't one to chat up a storm with me" (*Nanao or Never*, 211). But she goes on to remember his single-minded fascination on one of his visits to California with the authenticity of a Bolinas passion flower, his hospitable cutting-up of a lagoon shark abandoned by local fishermen to make sashimi, his repeated chants of the Vajra Guru mantra in hopes as he said "to get it," the reading of "his famous TOILET PAPER poem" (212)—actually a celebration of natural body functions and an assault on deforestation, and his role in the 1998 campaign to save the Okinawa reef from becoming a plane landing strip.[10] Allen Ginsberg's poem "Nanao," which first appeared on the back cover of *Break the Mirror* and was later published in *Cosmopolitan Greetings*, praises the wanderer poet of "pen & axe sharp a stars," whose brain, legs, eyes, heart, tongue, and hands are connected with earth and sky, whose hands are used for both writing and labor. Sakaki's poetry gives every reason to be thought keyed to the physical world yet also to Buddhist or, again and analogously, Beat spiritual reach.[11] The images do every justice, whether streams-washed brain, four continents cosmopolitan legs, Kagoshima cloudless eyes, heart raw and yet cooked, live Spring salmon tongue, or hands as ready with pen as axe—respectively creative-writing and outdoor-labor implements.

IV

The interplay of directly experienced life encounter (first hand or likelier in his case "first foot") with Zen-Beat expansiveness may well be Sakaki's most recurrent characteristic. Across both *Break the Mirror* and *Let's Eat Stars*, poem after poem gives confirmation within its range of journey and site. Few do so more symptomatically, or winningly, than "Specification for Mr. Nanao Sakaki's House" (composed in Shinano in 1983; *Break the Mirror* 69–70). The opening line, "I want to build my own house on planet earth" (69), immediately involves iconographical as much as verisimilar freight, a double geography of sight and symbol variously glacier, desert, coral, arboreal, polar, islanded, oceanic, peninsular, and volcanic:

> Where would my house stand?
> The high Andes where glacier & desert meet,
> Or Tropic of Cancer where coral reef & rain forest meet,
> Or the taiga where the aurora protects the North Pole,
> Or an island in the East China Sea where great cedars raise
> > young typhoons,

Or northern Yaponesia where beech trees make magnificent shade for
wild beings,
Or a peninsula in the sea of Okhotsk where god blazes in
volcanic crater. (69)

Literal place becomes imaginative place, successively the Andes, the Tropic of
Cancer, the North Pole, the East China Sea, the Sea of Okhotsk, and Japan as the
mythical kingdom Sakaki continues to designate Yaponesia. Each possible architecture, whether native tipi or Mongolian yurt, makes for a home half real, half
emblematic. Construction materials, likewise, bamboo, cedar, clay, coral, limestone
or basalt, are to be "cemented" (a keen irony to the term) of "sweat, wisdom &
friendship" (69). The house so acts as "microcosm" (69), flowered in columbine and
bougainvillea, "statued" by "winter wren" and "golden eagle" (69), and its inhabitants—be they plankton, or sperm whale, or "Myself, the representative of terrestrial
mammals" (70)—collectively all "creatures in unison," "heart rhythm," and "breath
melody" (70). It is a house, in truth, transposed into earth's ark, at once planetar-
ium, reworked Eden, kindergarten ("built for my lovely kids first," 70), and climate
zone. Even so, and allowing for both its mid-winter beauty and its tropical Calypso
call, the poet finds himself beckoned yet further onward—"Leaving snow-covered
new house behind / I start for the unknown land" (70). Sakaki, or his surrogate,
re-assumes the persona of journeyer with pathways yet to be pursued, houses yet to
be built, and futures yet to be met. Once more it is difficult to resist the thought of
journeys inside real time and place, and yet for Sakaki, journeys inside real time and
place co-exist with Zen-Beat journeys into visionary or spiritual further-worlds.

Most of the contributions to *Break the Mirror* work in shared manner. "Urgent
Telegram," an early poem from when he was in Duncun Spring, California, in 1973,
and cast in Sakaki's typical buoyancy of voice, ascends from Japanese breakfast to
Zen and Beat resonance:

> Everything starts with Miso soup, good morning!
> Miso soup is made of shiny spider web
> Life begins with Amazon ocean
> Grand Canyon ends with God-like Odysseus
> His great grandson shall be like Dharma bum
> Your great gran'ma shall be rattlesnake
> Meditation seed of pumpkin pie
> Pumpkin mother of sacred mushroom
> Mushroom father of God
> Good grows with galaxy
> Galaxy is a stolen diamond
> Last night my turkey vulture ate it
> Tomorrow I fly to higher glacier (5)

Miso soup, familiar greeting, ocean, Dharma bum with its Kerouac-title association, meditation, sacred mushroom, galaxy, vulture, ever higher flight: these, Japan
to the Grand Canyon, reflect a poet's self-route from feet-on-the-ground ground
level to the transcendent. The imagery engages both in its juncture and disjuncture,

the everyday of the soup, the metaphysicalism of "Galaxy is a stolen diamond" (5). The mix could not be more vintage Sakaki.

In "Ladies and Gentleman!," a Shinano 1978 poem and one of his longer compositions (*Break the Mirror* 15–18), Sakaki's ludic touch comes notably into play, though as usual at the behest of serious enough purpose. His motif is toilet paper, a modern indulgence he considers tree-destructive, wasteful, and even in its way *contra naturam*. The poem launches with typical brio:

> why too many things in the world?
> most of them, nonsense, ugly, crazy.
> when I go to the supermarket for fish bones
> I'm shaken by so much poor stuff to see,
> most striking
> beyond my imagination,
> TOILET PAPER. (15)

In quick order contrasts are given—the natural droppings of coyote, deer, grizzly, or skunk as against the in-private paper wipe and flush of human evacuation. The question is asked if a Tokyo salamander goes on weekly shopping to Tokyo to buy toilet paper. Why not use "a clean running brook" (15) amid morning glory, camellia, and magnolia? Why not emulate desert processes, trees and their cycle, or use leaves of a root and leaf vegetable popular in Japan such as taro? Rather we have pile-ups of supermarket toilet paper memorably designated by Sakaki as the "gunpowdered ghost skull of trees" (16) and the pulp of an "infernal factory" (16). He looks to broadest land and sea for exemplary processes of ingestion and cleansing, birds such as the winter wren or roadrunner, coral and dry seaweed, limpid streams, and even (another boldly striking trope) Moby Dick's spout—all counters to "lavatory paper," "tissue paper" (17). This, amid "canyon azalea," "a tiny waterfall," "a dipper's song," is the "perfect ceremony of universal circulation" (18), natural waste naturally cycled ("so ancient / so fresh day by day," 18). The poem sidesteps all possible distaste, its images those of healthful, organic process, a personal outdoors, to be set against toilet paper as modernity's true waste, at once the substance and symptom of consumerist eco-damage.

This same refusal to bow to modernity's glut, the loss of organic connection to nature, is again wittily to be heard in "Future Knows" (July 1979, *Break the Mirror* 27). Opening with the line "Thus I heard," the poem's voice gives three instances of the loss of contact with the natural order unwittingly parodied in children's questions and behavior. An Oakland eleven year old asks if the ocean is "a huge swimming pool with cement walls," and a nine year old from Tokyo looking at the night sky from a camping ground complains, "Ugly, too many stars." The third instance calls up Sakaki's own entomological interests, his lifelong fascination with the insect world. He remembers a friend who bought a beetle for his seven year old in a Kyoto store and its upshot:

> A few hours later
> The boy brought his dead bug
> To a hardware store, asking
> "Change battery please." (27)

It might be said that these are easy shots, too ready a set of small exemplary tales. But, if so, do they not also carry well-taken ironic shies—sea, sky, and nature made subject to mechanization, and, in the case of the last example, the well-known Wordsworth dictum as to child being father to the man wryly upended?

War memory almost inevitably weighs in Sakaki's poetry, not least the force of witness born of his own World War II role as radar man. "Blue Open Sky" (undated, *Break the Mirror* 86), the title purposely spaced, looks back with almost documentary exactness to the Japanese aerial suicide missions:

How lovely morning of June!

I send off three Kamikaze pilots
Who head for Okinawa
With a heavy bomb under the wing of
Training fighter, the Shiragiku or White chrysanthemum
At an air base in south Japan, 1945.

The play of a lovely June morning against the pilots' 1945 death flights harbors its own poignancy, not least given the added implication of a plane whose name links to the imperial Chrysanthemum Throne. A "Sgt Goto," his hair long and with a beard and who "looks like me" (86), further personalizes the remembrance, the speaker's haunting double. Immediately the planes are engaged by ten "besieging" (86) American Grumman fighters, a war-in-the-sky scenario that Sakaki leaves little doubt belies all summer mornings. His closing lines possess a haiku-like intensity, and again, carefully spaced verse wonderment at war as burial, fire, derangement:

Three silver winged coffins
Three dazzling fireballs
Three long-tailed question marks
In blue open sky.

Each moving-picture detail, coffins with their silver wings, fireballs with their dazzle, and tail smoke or shimmer as question marks, work in coordinated but discomforting configuration, a death-triad set against the sky's blue canvas. Once again, the local carries the more transcending implication, the kamikaze flights to Okinawa and the counter-action from the Grumman aircraft a pitying human fall. Few U.S. Beat writers address land or air battle in World War II: Sakaki, to an extent, fills a missing perspective, the United States and Japan at war.

Sakaki's Australia poems—to include "Platypus" (Sydney, 1981, *Break the Mirror* 104–105), as an invocation of the original animal-populated continent ("Australia, you platypus! / Don't hesitate / To show your noble spirit" 105), and "Little Captain Cook/Penguin" (started in Tasmania, October 1981, and completed in the southern Rockies, December 1981), in which the penguin embodies "waddling" strength of endurance ("On the southern shore of Tasmania, / Standing motionlessly in dusk / I wait for / The landing of Captain Cook," 109)—have few more impassioned manifestations than "Chant of a Rock" (started in Central, October 1981 and finished at Zuni Village, December 1981, *Break the Mirror* 106–107). Whether this is indeed the Northern Territory's Ayres Rock, Uluru in the local Ananga language, the unnamed rock voices itself as though a dreamtime avatar, seer, archivist.

Opening as though patient Griselda herself, the rock expresses time and welcome:

> So long, so long –
>> Forty thousand years
>>> I wait for you. (107)

This is the rock as body, "tended, caressed, loved," (106) and not by fingers, eye, and heart alone, but "by your songs" (106), the power of aboriginal ceremony and solicitude down "forty thousand years" (107). Thereby, "magical rock" (107), it serves both to emblematize Australia as "a wonderful dreamland forever" (107) and to provide a reflective conduit into the global tragedies of history:

> Remember Wounded Knee in Australia
> Remember Auschwitz in Australia
> Remember Hiroshima in Australia
> Remember a shiny rock in the dreamland!
>
> So long, so long --------
> Forty thousand years
> I wait for you. (107)

Chant indeed it is, Buddhist sutra or Beat ode (with perhaps just a hint of Whitman's "Song of Myself"), or perhaps likelier a hybrid fusion of both. For Sakaki, it makes for a dreamtime-song version of human event set within nature's spectacular patience.

"In and Out," written at El Salto Peak, New Mexico (*Break the Mirror* 123), might well do almost synoptic duty for the whole collection, a menu of interests with the indicative mix of formal and colloquial turns of style that frequently characterize the poetry. The first three lines invoke spiritual touchstones, being as sacred, "your mountain" (123) as truth's dwelling place:

> Your soul is Buddha------
>> Your body, temple,
>> Your mountain, enlightened.

The poem's speaker recalls a previous night's gegenschein (literally counter-shine, the faint sky glow) in which "I sang with coyotes" (123), to be followed by a breakfast of tempeh, cow liver with nettle leaves, and jasmine tea. Noon follows with letter writing and protest as to the world's ills, none more so than the dangers of nuclear arms:

> Stand up to Nuclear War!
> To protect Universal Citizenship of All Living Things,
> To have all out life and death in peace!
> Stand up to Nuclear War!

So much high-mindedness, however, soul or body, diet or nuclear protest, is then brought solidly down to earth immediately and quite literally:

> In the afternoon,
> In the meadow near by,
> A turkey vulture,
> The first one in spring,
> Drops her shit on my hat.

Sakaki once again elides the transcendent, the spirit's mountain, into quotidian life in nature, the vulture's droppings, life as ever a necessary and a playfully chastening balance of contrarieties.

V

Three poems from *Let's Eat Stars* offer an epilogue. "Perennial Treasures" (October 1995 64–66) sets up a working contrast grounded in an about-to-be Nagara River walking trip near Nagoya under "October morning sky" (64) within sight of a new rice crop ("harvesting happiness," 64). He remembers an eighty-nine-year-old woman resolved to exit from the world with her home ("a junkyard— / books, clothes, so many kinds of utensils" 64) and garden (". . . azalea, camphor tree / pampas grass, fern & moss / And nests of snakes, spiders, earthworms & mushrooms" 64) all left in right order. He thinks, too, of Bohemian waxwings who have visited the old lady's home in winter. At an opposite pole lies "21st century Japan," "my mother land" (65). The tabulation is indictment writ large, traduced legacy:

> The number one junkyard on planet Earth
> --Tokyo tower, Nagara River dam,
> Fast breeder reactor Monju
> & Nagano Winter Olympics.
> Leaving such a mess behind
> Who can die in peace? (65)

A letter from Snyder with word of an impending trip to the Himalayas, and Chomolungma (better known as Mount Everest), speaks of the need even for mountains to "stand on tiptoe" (65) above the proliferation of needless buildings, dangerous reactors, and national vanity projects. The poem ends, emblematically, with the poet "straightening my back / Against the northerly wind" as he starts "along the Nagara River" (66). Sakaki could well be a Charles Olson "figure of outward," the pilgrim-poet, ever Zen-inclined, ever in quest of good harmony with the earth.[12]

"How to Live on Planet Earth" (January 1997, *Let's Eat Stars* 84), again environmentalist in subject, colloquial, a verse manual, draws a number of key Sakaki threads into one. Its opening injunction sets the note—"Dwell in the neighborhood / Of stars & rainbows." The consortium of images that follow speak seriously and yet with a typical current of tease, be it listening to the wind "with donkey's ears," hanging about mountains and rivers "with monkey's limbs," or being "rich in wild life" and working with a "hearty sweat." The emphasis then shifts to good hosting, the necessary welcome to friends ("Let's have a daikon dish, home-made Sake & Songs"). The poem finally takes aim at what it calls "shadows," a vista as to the institutions of modern living with a due commentary of his own—"Supermarket, hospital & bank – What a perfect sight" (84). The focus of Sakaki's vision then turns to a more inspirational order of things: "The sun & moon / To look up forever." The Zen-Beat note is hardly to be missed, one of active senses, contemplative wonder.

The title poem "Let's Eat Stars" (written at Mount Taisetsu in central Hokkaido, September 1988) makes a shared plea: "Believe me, children!" it begins (12). His listing of the world's habits bespeak priorities turned upside down, about-face:

> God made
> Sky for airplanes
> Coral reefs for tourists
> Farms for agrichemicals
> Rivers for dams
> Forests for golf courses
> Mountains for ski resorts
> Wild animals for zoos
> Trucks and cars for traffic tragedies
> Nuclear power plants for ghost dance. (12)

These specificities, tellingly paradoxical (especially the turn to nuclear power as potential ghost dance), and on Sakaki's measure as much morally as environmentally antilife, are to be contrasted with a lyric haiku-ist moment, nature as majestic alpha and omega convergence: "Look at the evening glow! / Sunflowers in the garden. / Red dragonflies in the air" (12). Individual vision, best evening perspective, the yellow of the sunflower and the red of the dragonfly as primary colors, growth and flight, all underwrite the twice-spoken ending cry of the child's "Let's Eat Stars" (12). Herein lies Sakaki in characteristic mode, again intimate and vividly imagist, Japan's Beat if we so choose, but always on his own poet-wanderer's imaginative terms of Japan and beyond.

The collection *Nanao or Never* gives a basis for Western reestimation of Sakaki, as do the English-language editions of his poetry. In Japan, he remains both admired and demeaned, either prophetic poet-ecologist or dropout figure from the fringes. The appearance in 2010 of his *Collected Works* in Japanese, under the editorship of Shigeyoshi Hara, should help in redirecting attention to his considerable role in finding his own counter-cultural idiom—at once a celebration of Japanese values and yet a rebuke to their modern yen and consumerist betrayal.[13] Introducing Sakaki at a reading held in The Knitting Factory, New York City, in March 1995, Ginsberg captured the Zen-Beat profile, the foot patroller poet who was able to bridge continents:

> He's an independent desert rat who has spent the last weeks in New Mexico & Arizona – in deserts where he is quite familiar and he'll be headed in a few days up north through Canada and Alaska and then who knows where a wandering classical

Zen-like ah-hm idiot . . . introduced by Gary Snyder, helped me build a house in the Sierras – and been a great adviser in Japanese matters – especially on ecology and the destruction of Japan by the omnivorous capitalist system there – so now I give you Nanao![14]

"Desert rat," Ginsberg's borrowing of one of Sakaki's own phrases, would be unlikely to get the nod of a job offer from some prospective employer.[15] But it speaks aptly, and beckoningly, to Sakaki as the ranking poet of Beat Japan, Japan Beat.

Notes

1. I am conscious that this essay addresses Sakaki's poems as they appear in English. But each translation had Sakaki's approval. I am greatly indebted to Professor Shigeyoshi Hara of Dokkyo University, Tokyo, editor of the recently published Japanese-language *Collected Works*, for great bibliographical and biographical help with the life and translations of Sakaki.

2. See the poem "Memorandum" for an early use of the term Yaponesia (*Break the Mirror* 21). Also the Section II heading of *Break the Mirror*, "Yaponesia Freeway" (55).

3. Personal note from Anne Waldman to author, January 2, 2011.

4. Besides "Who Am I," (*Break the Mirror* 122) and "Autobiography," (*Let's Eat Stars* 39–40), Sakaki's own summaries of his life, in poem and timeline form can be found in "Memorandum," (*Break the Mirror* 20–21), "Specification for Mr. Nanao Sakaki's House" (*Break the Mirror* 69–70), "Break the Mirror" (*Break the Mirror* 108), "If I Have Tomorrow" (*Let's Eat Stars* 21), and the handwritten timeline in *Nanao or Never* (241–243). In "Wowed by Nanao," Steve Brooks provides a helpful transcript of Sakaki's own account of his life (*Nanao or Never* 168–183).

5. "Memorandum," *Break the Mirror* 20–21.

6. "Chant of a Rock," *Break The Mirror* 106–107.

7. See, in this respect, "Cup of Tea, Plate of Fish: An Interview with Nanao Sakaki," *Inch by Inch: 45 Haiku by Issa*, Santa Fe: Tooth of Time Books, 1985. Albuquerque: La Alameda, 1999.

8. In an interview with Trevor Carolan, Sakaki explains very succinctly what kind of Zen he adheres to: "Most Zen is uninteresting to me. . . . It's too linked to the samurai tradition—to militarism. This is where Alan Watts and I disagreed: he didn't fully understand how the samurai class with whom they associated Zen were in fact deeply Confucian: they were concerned with *power*. The Zen I'm interested in is China's Tang dynasty variant with its great teachers like Lin Chi. This was non-intellectual. It came from farmers—so simple. Someone became enlightened, others talked to him, learned and were told. Now you go there and teach; you go here, etc. When Japan tried to study this it was hopeless. The emperor sent scholars, but with their high-flown language and ideas they couldn't understand" (*Nanao or Never* 198).

9. In these respects Sakaki again seems to be invoking the Tang dynasty version of Zen. In his Trevor Carolan interview he explains that his preferred Buddhist Zen "goes beyond human society—to animal life, trees, water, rock. It's easy to relate to the environmental movement." Hence life and death need benign acceptance—"When it's time to sleep, just sleep; when you're sick, just be sick; when you're going to die, just die! Enlightenment!" (*Nanao or Never* 198–199).

10. The poem Kyger refers to is "Ladies and Gentleman!," *Break the Mirror* 15–18. See also "In the Twenty-First Century," *Let's Eat Stars* 76–80.

11. Allen Ginsberg, "Nanao," originally published as a back-cover poem for *Break the Mirror*, 1987, then as the slightly revised version in *Nanao or Never* 144. It is also in Allen Ginsberg, *Cosmopolitan Greetings: Poems 1986–1992* (New York: Harper, 1995).

12. Figure of outward is Olson's term for Robert Creeley in the dedication of his *Maximus* poems.

13. See Note 1 for details of this edition.

14. Allen Ginsberg, "Allen Ginsberg Introduces Nanao Sakaki, The Knitting Factory, New York City, March 11, 1995." *Nanao or Never* 143–144.

15. "Desert rat," another self-description, is also Sakaki's title for Section IV of *Break the Mirror*. In his foreword to *Break the Mirror*, Gary Snyder tells the story of an eminent Buddhist priest boasting of his lineage, to which Sakaki replies, "I need no lineage, I am a desert rat" (xi).

Contributors

R. J. (Dick) Ellis is professor of American studies at the University of Birmingham, head of the department of American and Canadian studies, and fellow of the English Academy. He is the author of over seventy articles and books including *Liar, Liar! Jack Kerouac—Novelist* (Greenwich Exchange 1999) and *Harriet Wilson's Our Nig: A Cultural Biography* (Rodopi 2003), and he is the editor of *Small Beer,* the memoirs of the Communist activist Nan Green. He is working on a new edition of *Our Nig* (with Henry Louis Gates, Jr.) and edited (with others) a collection of essays on post-bellum American women's writing, entitled *Becoming Visible* (Rodopi 2010). He was the founding editor of *Comparative American Studies.* Ellis curated for the Barber Institute in Birmingham in 2008–2009 the only exhibit in the U.K. of the original 1951 manuscript of Kerouac's *On the Road.*

Jane Falk is senior lecturer in English composition at the University of Akron. She has contributed an appreciation of Philip Whalen's *The Diamond Noodle* to *Continuous Flame,* a tribute volume to Whalen (Fish Drum 2005), as well as Whalen biographies to the *Encyclopedia of Beat Literature* (2007) and the *Greenwood Encyclopedia of American Poetry* (2005). An essay on Zen and the poetry of Philip Whalen has recently appeared in *The Emergence of Buddhist American Literature* (SUNY 2009). She is working on an essay about Joanne Kyger's video production *Descartes.*

Jimmy Fazzino is a doctoral candidate in literature and teaches in the literature, writing, and creative writing programs at the University of California, Santa Cruz. He has been a contributor to *The Beat Review* and has several articles on the Beats forthcoming in *The Literary Encyclopedia.* Research interests include twentieth-century American literature and modern poetry and poetics. His dissertation is entitled "Beat Subterranean: Assemblages of Influence and Beat Writing in World Contexts."

Christopher Gair is head of English literature and associate director of the Andrew Hook Centre for American Studies at the University of Glasgow, Scotland. He is the author of *Complicity and Resistance in Jack London's Novels* (Mellen 1997), *The American Counterculture* (Edinburgh UP 2007), and *The Beat Generation* (Oneworld 2008), and is the editor of *Beyond Boundaries: C. L. R. James and Postnational Studies* (Pluto 2006). He edited editions of Stephen Crane's *Maggie: a Girl of the Streets* (Trent 2000) and Jack London's *South Sea Tales* (Random House 2002). He has published essays in *Modern Fiction Studies, Journal of American Studies, Studies in the Novel,* and *Studies in American Literature* and is editor of *Symbiosis: a Journal of Anglo-American Literary Relations.*

Konstantina Georganta is the co-director of the Scottish Universities' International Summer School hosted at the University of Edinburgh. She completed her doctorate in 2009 in the department of English literature at the University of Glasgow. Her thesis, now under contract to the Rodopi Series in Comparative Literature, explores encounters between British and Greek poetry in the period 1922–1952 and considers the work of T. S. Eliot, C. P. Cavafy, W. B. Yeats, Kostes Palamas, Demetrios Capetanakis, John Lehmann, and Louis MacNeice. She has published on T. S. Eliot's "The Waste Land," William Plomer's poetry, and short stories on 1930s Greece.

Nancy M. Grace is the Virginia Myers Professor of English at The College of Wooster, where she is chair of the department of English and the women's, gender, and sexuality studies program. She is the author of *The Feminized Male Character in Twentieth-Century Literature* (Mellen1995), co-editor of *Girls Who Wore Black: Women Writing the Beat Generation* (with Ronna C. Johnson, Rutgers UP 2002), co-author of *Breaking the Rule of Cool: Interviewing and Reading Beat Women Writers* (with Ronna C. Johnson, UP of Mississippi 2004), and author of *Jack Kerouac and the Literary Imagination* (Palgrave 2007). She also published and edited *681 Lexington Avenue: A Beat Education in New York City 1947–1945* (Greater Midwest 2008) by Elizabeth von Vogt, sister of John Clellon Holmes. The Choice Top 100 Title was awarded in 2004 for *Breaking the Rule of Cool* and in 2007 for *Jack Kerouac and the Literary Imagination*. She has published essays on Beat literature, women Beats, Kerouac, and Joyce. Grace is a founding board member of the Beat Studies Association and co-editor of *The Journal of Beat Studies.*

Michele Hardesty is assistant professor of U.S. literatures at Hampshire College. She is the author of "Looking for the Good Fight: William T. Vollmann's *An Afghanistan Picture Show,*" published in the summer 2009 issue of *boundary 2.* Her research and teaching interests concern the intersections of politics and culture in the twentieth- and twenty-first-century United States. She is working on a project concerning U.S. writers who traveled to and wrote about conflicts in the Third World during the Cold War.

Allen Hibbard is professor of English and director of the Middle East Center at Middle Tennessee State University; he has also taught at the American University in Cairo and was a Fulbright lecturer at Damascus University. He is the author of *Paul Bowles: A Study of the Short Fiction* (Twayne 1993) and *Paul Bowles, Magic & Morocco* (Cadmus 2004), the editor of *Conversations with William S Burroughs* (UP of Mississippi 2000), and has published a collection of his own stories in Arabic. Hibbard's research explores the history of interactions, interpenetrations, and cross-pollinations between the United States and the Arab world, from the perspectives of modernism, post-colonialism, globalization, genre, transnational movement, and translation. His current projects include a volume on the modern Arabic poet Adonis, a translation of Syrian writer Haidar Haidar's novel *A Banquet for Seaweed*, and a biography of the gay Jewish American writer Alfred Chester.

Ronna C. Johnson is a lecturer in English, women's studies, and American studies at Tufts University, where she has also been director of women's studies. Her recent publications include *Breaking the Rule of Cool: Interviewing and Reading Women Beat Writers* (with Nancy M. Grace, UP of Mississippi 2004) and *Girls Who Wore Black: Women Writing the Beat Generation* (with Nancy M. Grace, Rutgers UP 2002). She is writing *Inventing Jack Kerouac: Reception and Reputation 1957–2007* (forthcoming 2012, Camden House). She has presented and published on Jack Kerouac, Joyce Johnson, Lenore Kandel, and Brenda Frazer, as well as work on women Beat writers and gender in Beat movement discourses. Johnson is a founding board member of the Beat Studies Association and co-editor of *The Journal of Beat Studies*.

A. Robert Lee is professor of American literature at Nihon University, Tokyo, and formerly taught at the University of Kent, United Kingdom. His recent books include *Designs of Blackness: Mappings in the Literature and Culture of Afro-America* (Pluto 1998), *Multicultural American Literature: Comparative Black, Native, Latino/a and Asian American Fictions* (UP of Mississippi 2003), *United States: Re-Viewing Multicultural American Literature* (U of Valencia 2009), *Gothic to Multicultural: Idioms of Imagining in American Literary Fiction* (Rodopi 2009), and *Modern American Counter Writing: Beats, Outriders, Ethnics* (Routledge 2010). He also edited *The Beat Generation Writers* (Pluto 1996) and has published essays on Beat writers, including William S. Burroughs, Ted Joans, Oscar Zeta Acosta, and international figures including Andrei Voznesenky and Kazuko Shiraishi.

Hassan Melehy is associate professor of French and francophone studies at the University of North Carolina at Chapel Hill. Much of his scholarship has been on early modern philosophy and literature in addition to twentieth-century thinkers. He has published *Writing Cogito* (SUNY 1997) and *The Poetics of Literary Transfer in Early Modern France and England* (Ashgate 2010) and has translated a number of works of philosophy and social science, including Jacques Rancière's *The Names of History* (Minnesota UP1994). He has authored articles on Deleuze, Foucault, Derrida, and Rancière and has also written on the films of Robert Altman, David Cronenberg, Jean-Luc Godard, and Ernst Lubitsch. Melehy's current research focuses on Jack Kerouac's role in Québécois literature of the last forty years.

Fiona Paton is assistant professor of English at the State University of New York at New Paltz, where she teaches American literature and specializes in Beat writers Jack Kerouac and William S. Burroughs. Recent publications include "Monstrous Rhetoric: *Naked Lunch*, National Insecurity, and the Gothic Fifties" (*Texas Studies in Literature and Language* 2010) and "Reconceiving Kerouac: Why We Should Teach *Dr. Sax*" in *The Beat Generation: Critical Essays* (Peter Lang 2002).

Josef Rauvolf is a journalist, writer, and translator who lives in Prague. He studied at the Faculty of Philosophy of Charles University in Prague, and while doing menial jobs worked for *samizdat* editions, and for dissent. After the fall of communism in 1989, he published translations of William S. Burroughs (*Naked Lunch, Nova Express, Junky, Queer, The Yage Letters, The Ticket That Exploded, The Western Lands, The Place of Dead Roads, Wild Boys*), Allen Ginsberg, Jack Kerouac (*Dharma Bums, Visions of Cody*), Charles Bukowski, Hubert Selby Jr., William Blake, William Gibson, and J. G. Ballard. He has published articles about the Beat Generation and made documentaries about the Beats for Czech television and radio broadcasts, and has lectured at universities in Prague and elsewhere.

Jennie Skerl is a founding board member and past president of the Beat Studies Association. She has published *William S. Burroughs* (Twayne 1985), *William S. Burroughs at the Front: Critical Reception, 1959–1989* (co-edited with Robin Lydenberg, Southern Illinois UP 1991), *A Tawdry Place of Salvation: The Art of Jane Bowles* (Southern Illinois UP 1997), and *Reconstructing the Beats* (Palgrave 2004). She edited the Winter 2000 special issue of *College Literature* on the Beats and has published invited introductions to the twenty-fifth anniversary edition of *Naked Lunch* (Grove 1984), *Speed* by William Burroughs, Jr. (Overlook Press 1984), *William S. Burroughs: Time-Place-Word* (ed. Eric Shoaf, Brown U 2000), and the Foreword to *Retaking the Universe: William Burroughs in the Age of Globalization* (ed. Davis Shneiderman and Philip Walsh, Pluto 2004). Skerl retired as associate dean of the College of Arts and Sciences at West Chester University.

Jaap van der Bent is assistant professor at the Radboud University Nijmegen, the Netherlands, where he teaches American literature, with an emphasis on the Beat Generation and African American writing. His dissertation was on the work of John Clellon Holmes, about whom he has also written in a number of British and American publications. He was co-editor of *Beat Culture: the 1950s and Beyond* (VU UP 1999) and contributed to *The Beat Generation: Critical Essays* (Peter Lang 2002) and *Beat Culture: Lifestyles, Icons, and Impact* (ABC-CLIO 2005). He has published many articles on American literature and the Beats in Dutch, British, and American newspapers, periodicals, and magazines. His Dutch publications include introductory essays, accompanied by translations, on the work of Beat-related writers, including David Markson and Douglas Woolf.

Anne Waldman has been an active member of the "Outrider" experimental poetry community for over four decades, as writer, editor, teacher, performer, scholar, infrastructure curator, and cultural/political activist. She is the author of more than forty books, including *Fast Speaking Woman* (City Lights 1975, 1996), a collection of essays entitled *Vow to Poetry* (Coffee House 2001), and several selected poem editions including *Helping the Dreamer* (Coffee House 1989) and *Kill or Cure* (Penguin 1994). She has concentrated on the long poem as a cultural intervention with projects such as the antiwar feminist epic *The Iovis Trilogy: Colors in the Mechanism of Concealment* (Coffee House 2011). She was one of the founders and directors of The Poetry Project at St. Marks's Church In-the-Bowery. She also co-founded with Allen Ginsberg the Jack Kerouac School of Disembodied Poetics at Naropa University, where she is Distinguished Professor of Poetics. She has edited and co-edited many collections based on the holdings of the Kerouac School, including *Beats at Naropa* (Coffee House 2009). Waldman is a recipient of the Poetry Society of America's Shelley Memorial Award and has recently been appointed a chancellor of The Academy of American Poets.

Works Cited

Abbott, Keith. Rev. of *The Blue Hand: The Beats in India* by Deborah Baker. *The Beat Review*. 2:4 (Sept. 2008). Web. 13 June 2011.

Abbeele, Georges van den. *Travel as Metaphor: From Montaigne to Rousseau*. Minneapolis: U of Minnesota P, 1992. Print.

Adams, Rachel. "Hipsters and Jipitecas: Literary Countercultures on Both Sides of the Border." *American Literary History* 16.1 (2004): 58–84. Print.

Alan, Josef, ed. *Alternativní kultura*. Praha: Nakladatelství Lidové noviny, 2001. Print.

Allen, Donald M., ed. *The New American Poetry*. New York: Grove, 1960. Print.

Allen, Donald M., and Warrren Tallman, eds. *The Poetics of the New American Poetry*. New York: Grove, 1973. Print.

"Allen Ginsberg a morálka." *Mladá fronta*, 16 May 1965. Print.

Allnutt, Gillian, Fred D'Aguiar, and Eric Mottram. *The New British Poetry*. London: Paladin, 1988. Print.

Allsop, Kenneth. *The Angry Decade: A Survey of the Cultural Revolt of the Nineteen Fifties*. 1957. London: Peter Owen, 1964. Print.

Anctil, Gabriel. "Les 50 ans d'*On the Road*: Kerouac voulait écrire en français." *Le Devoir* 5.5 (Sept. 2007). Web. 23 Dec. 2009.

———. "'Sur le chemin': Découverte d'un deuxième roman en français de Jack Kerouac." *Le Devoir* 4 (Sept. 2008). Web. 22 Aug. 2010.

Anctil, Pierre. "La Franco-Américanie ou le Québec d'en bas." *Du continent perdu à l'archipel retrouvé. Le Québec et l'Amérique française*. Ed. Dean R. Louder and Eric Waddell. Saint-Nicolas, QC: Presses de l'Université Laval, 2007. 25–39. Print.

———. "Paradise Lost, ou le texte de langue française dans l'oeuvre de Jack Kérouac." P. Anctil et al., 93–103. Print.

———, et al., eds. *Un homme grand: Jack Kerouac at the Crossroads of Many Cultures/Jack Kérouac à la confluence des cultures*. Ottawa: Carleton UP, 1990. Print.

Anderson, M. Christine. "Women's Place in the Beat Movement: Bonnie Bremser Frazer's *Troia: Mexican Memoirs*." *Women's Studies International Forum* 26.3 (May–June 2003): 253–263. Print.

Anderson, Quentin. *The Imperial Self: An Essay in American Literary and Cultural History*. New York: Knopf, 1971. Print.

Antošová, Svatava. Mail interview with Josef Rauvolf. Sept. 2010. TS.

———. "Prosim, paní." *Host*, 5 (2007): 27. Print.

Appadurai, Arjun. *Globalization*. Durham, NC: Duke UP, 2000. Print.

———. *Modernity at Large: Cultural Dimensions of Globalization*. Minneapolis: U of Minnesota P, 1996. Print.

"Aquí los poetas están en el poder." *Barricada* 23 (January 1986): 8–9. Print.

Argyriou, Alexandros, ed. *ΗΕλληνικήΠοίηση: ΗΠρώτηΜεταπολεμικήΓενιά* [*Greek Poetry: First Post War Generation*]. Athens: Sokoles, 1982. Print.

Austin, J. L. *How to Do Things with Words*. Ed. J. O. Urmson and Marina Sbisà. Cambridge, MA: Harvard UP, 1972. Print.

Bacchilega, Cristina. *Postmodern Fairy Tales: Gender and Narrative Strategies*. Philadelphia: U of Pennsylvania P, 1997. Print.

Bair, Deirdre. Review of *Exiled in Paris by James Campbell*. *New York Times* 19 Feb. 1995: BR24. Print.

Baker, Deborah. *A Blue Hand: The Beats in India*. New York: Penguin, 2008. Print.

Baraka, Amiri [LeRoi Jones]. *The Dead Lecturer*. New York: Grove, 1964. Print.

———. *Dutchman and The Slave: Two Plays*. New York: Morrow, 1964. Print.

———. *Home: Social Essays*. New York: Morrow, 1966. Print.

Baro, Gene. *"Beat" Poets*. London: Vista, 1961. Print.

Barthes, Roland. *Empire of Signs*. Trans. Richard Howard. New York: Hill & Wang, 1982. Print.

Basch, Linda, Nina Glick Schiller, and Cristina Szanton Blanc. *Nations Unbound: Transnational Projects, Postcolonial Predicaments, and Deterritorialized Nation-States*. Langhorne, PA: Gordon, 1994. Print.

Bassnett, Susan. *Translation Studies*, 3rd ed. London: Routledge, 2002. Print.

Bayer, Konrad. "hans carl artmann and the viennese poets." Weibel 32–39. Print.

———. *Selected Works*. Ed. and trans. Malcolm Green. London: Atlas, 1986. Print.

———. *The Sixth Sense*. Trans. Malcolm Green. London: Atlas, 2007. Print.

"Bean Train Press Readings." Bean Train Press, n.d. [1963?]. n.p. Print.

Behdad, Ali. *Belated Travelers: Orientalism in the Age of Colonial Dissolution*. Durham: Duke UP, 1994. Print.

Belgrad, Daniel. *The Culture of Spontaneity: Improvisation and the Arts in Postwar America*. Chicago: U of Chicago P, 1998. Print.

———. "The Transnational Counterculture: Beat-Mexican Intersections," Skerl, *Reconstructing* 27–40. Print.

Benjamin, Walter. "On Some Motifs in Baudelaire." *Illuminations*. Trans. Harry Zohn and ed. Hannah Arendt. New York: Schocken, 1968. 155–200. Print.

Berrigan, Ted. Interview with Jack Kerouac. *The Paris Review: Beat Writers at Work*. New York: Modern Library, 1999. Print.

Best, Alan D., and Hans Wolfschutz, eds. *Modern Austrian Writing: Literature and Society after 1945*. London: Oswald Wolff, 1980. Print.

Bettleheim, Bruno. *The Uses of Enchantment: The Meaning and Importance of Fairy Tales*. New York: Vintage, 1977. Print.

Beverley, John, and Marc Zimmerman. *Literature and Politics in Central American Revolutions*. Austin: U of Texas P, 1990. Print.

Bhabha, Homi. *The Location of Culture*. London: Routledge, 1994. Print.

The Bible. Authorized King James Version with Apocrypha. Oxford: Oxford UP, 1998. Print.

Bobo, Jacqueline. "*The Color Purple*: Black Women as Cultural Readers." *The Audience Studies Reader*. Eds. Will Brooker and Deborah Jermyn. London: Routledge, 2003. Print.

Bondy, Egon. *Kádrový dotazník. Básnické dílo Egona Bondyho, svazek V. Básnické sbírky z let 1963–1971*. Praha: Pražská imaginace, 1991. Print.

———. *Prvních deset let*. Praha: Maťa, 2002. Print.

———. *Totální realismus. Básnické dílo Egona Bondyho, svazek II. Básnické sbírky z let 1950–1953*. Praha: Pražská imaginace, 1992. Print.

———. *Ve všední den i v neděli. . .Výbor z básnického díla 1950-1994*. Praha: Dharma Gaia, 2009. Print.

Bowd, Gavin. *The Outsiders: Alexander Trocchi and Kenneth White*. Kirkcaldy, Scotland: Akros, 1998. Print.

Bremser, Bonnie. *Troia: Mexican Memoirs*. 1969. Champaign, IL: Dalkey, 2007. Print.

Bremser, Ray. *Angel*. New York: Tompkins Square Park, 1967. Print.

Breton, André. *Manifestoes of Surrealism*. Trans. Richard Seaver and Helen R. Lane. Ann Arbor: U of Michigan P, 1972. Print.

Briggs, Laura, Gladys McCormick, and J. T. Way. "Transnationalism: A Category of Analysis." *American Quarterly* 60.3 (Sept. 2008): 625–648. Print.

Brown, Pete. "Africa and Small Poem." *Evergreen Review* 3.10 (Nov.–Dec. 1959): 55. Print.

———. "Americans in Albion." *Circuit Magazine* 2 (1966): 16–17. Print.

———. "Few." 1959. *Few*. London: Migrant, 1966. Print.

———. "Riding the River: Jazz and Poetry in the U.K." *Kaleidoscope*. BBC Radio 4.28 (June 1998). Radio.

Buchebner, Walter. *Zeit aus Zellulose*. Graz: Styria, 1994. Print.

Bürger, Peter. *Theory of the Avant-Garde*. Trans. Michael Shaw. Minneapolis: U of Minnesota P, 1984. Print.

Burns, Jim. *Beats, Bohemians and Intellectuals*. Nottingham: Trent, 2000. Print.

Burroughs, William S. *Burroughs Live: The Collected Interviews of William S. Burroughs 1960–1997*. Ed. Sylvere Lotringer. Los Angeles and New York: Semiotext(e), 2001. Print.

———. *Cities of the Red Night*. New York: Holt, 1981. Print.

———. *Everything Lost: The Latin American Notebook of William S. Burroughs*. Ed. and intro. Oliver Harris. Columbus: Ohio State UP, 2008. Print.

———. "Interrogation." *Burroughs Live*. Burroughs 244–260. Print.

———. *Interzone*. Ed. James Grauerholz. New York: Viking, 1989. Print.

———. Introduction. *Man at Leisure*. Alexander Trocchi vii–viii. Print.

———. *The Letters of William S. Burroughs, 1945–1959*. Ed. Oliver Harris. New York: Viking, 1993. Print.

———. *Naked Lunch: The Restored Text*. Ed. James Grauerholz and Barry Miles. New York: Grove, 2001. Print.

———. *Queer*. 25th Anniversary Edition. Ed. and intro. Oliver Harris. New York: Penguin, 2010. Print.

———. "Sexual Conditioning." *The Adding Machine: Selected Essays*. New York: Arcade, 1993: 87–105. Print.

———. "The Struggle Against Censorship." *Burroughs Live*. Burroughs 330–343. Print.

———. "Tangier." *Esquire* Sept. 1964: 114–119. Print.

———. *The Wild Boys: A Book of the Dead*. New York: Grove, 1971. Print.

———. "William Burroughs." Campell and Niel 159–164. Print.

Burroughs, William, and Allen Ginsburg. *The Yage Letters Redux*. Ed. and intro. Oliver Harris. San Francisco: City Lights, 2006. Print.

Butler, Judith. "Imitation and Gender Insubordination." *Deconstruction: Critical Concepts in Literary and Cultural Studies*. Ed. Jonathan Culler. Vol. 2 London: Routledge, 2003. 371–387. Print.

———. *Undoing Gender*. New York: Routledge, 2004. Print.

Butler, Michael. "From the 'Wiener Gruppe' to Ernst Jandl." Best and Wolfschutz. 236–251. Print.

Cain's Film, and Marihuana Marihuana. Dir. Jamie Wadhawan. Chronos Video, 1969–1972. Videocassette.

Calder, John. "John Calder." Campell and Niel 151–154. Print.

———. Preface. *Man at Leisure*. Alexander Trocchi v–vi. Print.

———, ed. *A William Burroughs Reader*. London: Pan, 1982. Print.

Calotychos, Vangelis. *Modern Greece: A Cultural Poetics*. Oxford: Berg, 2003. Print.

Campbell, Allen and Tim Niel, eds. *A Life in Pieces: Reflections on Alexander Trocchi*. Edinburgh, Scotland: Rebel, 1997. Print.

Campbell, Howard. "Beat Mexico: Bohemia, Anthropology and 'the Other.'" *Critique of Anthropology* 23.2 (2003): 209–230. Print.

Campbell, James. *Exiled In Paris*. Berkeley: U of California P, 2003. Print.

———. *Paris Interzone*. London: Minerva, 1994. Print.

Carden, Mary. "'Adventures in Auto-Eroticism': Economies of Travelling Masculinity in Autobiography Texts by Jack Kerouac and Neal Cassady." *Journeys*. 7.1 (June 2006): 1–25. Print.

Cardenal, Ernesto. "Invitación a los poetas norteamericanos." 26 Aug. 1985. Series 8, Box 13, Folder 5. Allen Ginsberg Papers, Department of Special Collections, Stanford University. Print.

———. "Letter to the Editor." *El Corno Emplumado* 5 (1963): 146–147. Print.

Cardenal, Ernesto, Allen Ginsberg, and Yevgeny Yevtushenko. "Declaration of Three Joint Statement on Nicaragua." *Deliberate Prose: Selected Essays 1952–1995*. Allen Ginsberg. New York: HarperCollins, 1982. 52–53. Print.

Carter, Steven, ed. and trans. *Traditional Japanese Poetry*. Stanford: Stanford UP, 1991. Print.

Čerepková, Vladimíra. *Básně*. Praha: Torst, 2001. Print.

———. *Ryba k rybě mluví*. Praha: Československý spisovatel, 1969. Print.

Čermák, Miloš. *Pravděpodobné vzdálenosti: rozhovor Miloše Čermáka s Jaroslavem Hutkou*. Praha: Academia, 1994. Print.

Certeau, Michel de. *The Practice of Everyday Life*. Trans. Steven F. Rendall. Berkeley: U of California P, 1984. Print.

Césaire, Aimé. *The Collected Poetry*. Trans. Clayton Eshleman and Annette Smith. Berkeley: U of California P, 1983. Print.

Charters, Ann. Introduction. *Troia: Mexican Memoirs*. Bonnie Bremser i–vii. Print.

———. *Kerouac: A Biography*. 1973. New York: St. Martin's, 1994. Print.

———. "Variations on a Generation." *The Portable Beat Reader*. Ed. Charters. New York: Penguin, 1992. xv–xxxvi. Print.

Chronas, Giorgos. "Στο περιβόλι των λαμπρών τεχνών: το πάθος της υγείας στην ασθένεια του '60–'70" ["In the Glorious Arts' Garden"]. *60s*. Athens: Sui Generis, 2009. 57–58. Print.

Clifford, James. "Notes on Theory and Travel." *Inscriptions* 5 (1989): 177–188. Print.

———. *Routes*. Cambridge, MA: Harvard UP, 1997. Print.

Connery, Christopher L., and Rob Wilson, eds. *The Worlding Project: Doing Cultural Studies in the Era of Globalization*. Santa Cruz, CA: New Pacific, 2007. Print.

Connolly, Cyril. "Comment." *Horizon* 11 (May 1945): 305–306. Print.

Conran, Terence "Foreword." *From the Bomb to the Beatles*. London: Collins, 1999. 7–8. Print.

Cordova, Cary. "The Mission in Nicaragua: San Francisco Poets Go to War." *Beyond El Barrio: Everyday Life in Latina/o America*. New York: New York UP, 2010. 211–231. Print.

Coronation Street. Granada TV. 9 Dec. 1960 ff. Television.

Coronel Urtecho, José. *Panorama y antología de la poesía norteamericana*. Madrid: Talleres de la Editorial Escelicer, 1949. Print.

Corso, Gregory. *An Accidental Autobiography: The Selected Letters of Gregory Corso*. New York: New Directions, 2003. Print.

———. *Gasoline*. San Francisco: City Lights, 1958. Print.

———. *The Happy Birthday of Death*. New York: New Directions, 1960. Print.

————. *Mindfield*. New York: Thunder's Mouth, 1989. Print.

————. *Mokré moře*. Praha: SNKLU, 1964. Print.

Creeley, Robert. *Tales Out of School: Selected Interviews*. Ann Arbor: U of Michigan P, 1993. Print.

Crown, Joseph H. "Letter to the Editor." *The Nation* 14 July 1979: 40–41. Print.

Cuadra, Pablo Antonio. "Notes on Culture in the New Nicaragua." *The Central American Crisis Reader*. Ed. Robert S. Leiken and Barry Rubin. New York: Summit, 1987. 242–251. Print.

Cumming, Tim. "The Devil? That Was His Own Dark Side," Interview with Marianne Faithfull. *The Guardian* (London) 12 May 2004. Web. 24 June 2011.

————. "Mean Streets." *The Guardian* (London) 7 Aug. 2003. Web. 17 Oct. 2011.

Cunliffe, Dave. "Four Decades of Nomadic U.K.: Jack Kerouac's Enduring Legacy." *Dharma Beat* 7 (Fall 1996): n.p. Print.

————. "Long Forgotten Heroes: British Beat Writers of the Fifties and Sixties." Unpublished essay, n.d., n.p. TS.

————, ed. "The New British Poetry." *Poetmeat* 8 (n.d.; c. 1964): n.p. Mimeographed TS.

————. "Some British Beat History: An Introduction." *The Kerouac Connection* 10 (Apr. 1986): 17–18. Print.

————. "Some British Beat History: Golden Convulsions." *The Kerouac Connection* 19 (Spring 1990): 22–23. Print.

Damon, Maria. *The Dark End of the Street: Margins in American Vanguard Poetry*. Minneapolis: U of Minnesota P, 1993. Print.

Dansby, Andrew. "Another Night at the Opera for Waits." RollingStone.com 3 Nov. 2000. Web. 9 June 2011.

Davidson, Michael. *The San Francisco Renaissance: Poetics and Community at Mid-Century*. Cambridge: Cambridge UP, 1989. Print.

de Lauretis, Teresa. *Technologies of Gender*. Bloomington: Indiana UP, 1987. Print.

De St. Jorre, John. *Venus Bound: The Erotic Voyage of the Olympia Press*. New York: Random House, 1996. Print.

Debord, Guy. *Comments on the Society of the Spectacle*. London: Verso, 1998. Print.

————. "Report on the Construction of Situations." Situationist International Online. n.d. Web. 2 July 2011.

————. *The Society of the Spectacle*. Trans. Black & Red, 1977. *Marxist Internet Archive*. n.d. Web. 10 June 2010.

Deleuze, Gilles, and Felix Guattari. *A Thousand Plateaus: Capitalism and Schizophrenia*. Trans. Brian Massumi. Minneapolis: U of Minnesota P. 1987. Print.

Derrida, Jacques. *Specters of Marx: The State of the Debt, the Work of Mourning, and the New International*. Trans. Peggy Kamuf. New York: Routledge, 1994. Print.

Di Prima, Diane. *Dinners and Nightmares*. San Francisco: Last Gasp, 1998. Print.

————. *Recollections of My Life as a Woman*. New York: Penguin, 2001. Print.

————. *Revolutionary Letters, Etc*. San Francisco: City Lights, 1971. Print.

————. *Various Fables from Various Places*. New York: Putnam, 1960. Print.

Dickens, Charles. "Frauds on the Fairies." *Household Words, A Weekly Journal*. Victorianweb. org. 23 June 2006. Web. 2 July 201.

Dickinson, John, and Brian Young. *A Short History of Quebec*. Montreal: McGill–Queen's UP, 2008. Print.

Dion-Lévesque, Rosaire. "Jack Kérouac, romancier." *Silhouettes Franco-Américaines*. 432–436. Print.

————. *Silhouettes Franco-Américaines*. Manchester, New Hampshire: Association Canado-Américaine, 1957. Print.

————. "Yvonne Le Maître, journaliste de Lowell, Massachusetts." *Silhouettes Franco-Américaines*. 549–553. Print.

Disney Consumer Products. n.d. Web. 26 June 2011.

Dolbier, Maurice. "Beat Generation: Roadster." *Empty Phantoms: Interviews and Encounters with Jack Kerouac*. Ed. Paul Maher. New York: Thunder's Mouth Press, 2005. Print.

"Dva tóny z Violy." *Večerní Praha* 7 May 1965. Print.

Dworkin, Andrea. *Intercourse*. New York: Free, 1987. Print.

Edwards, Brian. *Morocco Bound: Disorienting America's Maghreb, from Casablanca to the Marrakech Express*. Durham, NC: Duke UP, 2005. Print.

Edwards, Brian, and Dilip Parameshwar Gaonkar, eds. *Globalizing American Studies*. Chicago: Chicago UP, 2010. Print.

Egan, Charles. *Clouds Thick, Whereabouts Unknown*. New York: Columbia UP, 2010. Print.

Eleftheriou, Manos, and Niarchos, Thanassis. *ΗΔεκαετίατου '60* [*1960s*]. Athens: Kastaniotis, 2005. Print.

Enevold, Jessica. "The Daughters of Thelma and Louise: New? Aesthetics of the Road." *Gender, Genre, and Identity in Women's Travel Writing*. New York: Lang, 2004. 73–95. Print.

Estridge, Larry. "Poets of the Revolution." *New Haven Advocate* 17 Mar. 1982: 1, 6–8. Print.

Fabre, Michel. *From Harlem to Paris: Black American Writers in France, 1840–1980*. Urbana: U of Illinois P, 1991. Print.

Falk, Jane. "Journal as Genre and Published Text: Beat Avant-Garde Writing Practices." *University of Toronto Quarterly* 73.4 (Fall 2004): 991–1002. Print.

Farren, Mick. *Give the Anarchist a Cigarette*. London: Pimlico/Random, 2002. Print.

Faucher, Albert. "Projet de recherche historique: l'émigration des Canadiens français au XIXe siècle." *Recherches sociographiques* 2.2 (1961): 243–245. Print.

Feinsilber, Pamela. "One Wild Ride." *San Francisco Magazine* Sept. 2004. Web. 24 June 2011.

Feldman, Gene, and Max Gartenberg, eds. *Protest: The Beat Generation and the Angry Young Men*. London: Souvenir, 1959. Print.

Ferguson, Niall. *Colossus: The Rise and Fall of the American Empire*. New York: Penguin, 2005. Print.

Ferlinghetti, Lawrence. *A Coney Island of the Mind*. New York: New Directions. 1958. Print.

————. *Pictures of the Gone World*. San Francisco: City Lights, 1955. Print.

————. *These Are My Rivers: New and Selected Poems 1955–1993*. New York: New Directions, 1993. Print.

————. *Seven Days in Nicaragua Libre*. San Francisco: City Lights, 1984. Print.

————. *Who Are We Now?* New York: New Directions, 1976. Print.

Ferlinghetti, Lawrence, and Alexis Lykiard. *The Cool Eye: Lawrence Ferlinghetti Talks to Alexis Lykiard*. Exeter, Devon: Stride, 1993. Print.

Fisher, Roy. *Poems*. Oxford: Oxford UP, 1988. Print.

Fialik, Maria. *"Strohkoffer"-Gespräche: H.C. Artmann und die Literatur aus dem Keller*. Wien: Paul Zsolnay, 1998. Print.

Fisher, Roy. *Poems*. Oxford: Oxford UP, 1988. Print.

Fountain, Nigel. *Underground: the London Alternative Press, 1966–1974*. London: Commedia/Routledge, 1988. Print.

"The French Canadians." *New York Times* 5 July 1889: 4. Print.

Friedman, Amy. "'I saw my new name': Women Writers of the Beat Generation." Lee, *Beat Generation*. 200–216. Print.

Friedman, Jonathan. "Global Crises, the Struggle for Cultural Identity and Intellectual Porkbarrelling: Cosmopolitans versus Locals, Ethnics and Nationals in an Era of

De-hegemonisation." *Debating Cultural Hybridity.* Ed. Pnina Werbner and Tariq Modood. London: Zed Books, 1997. 70–89. Print.

Friedman, Susan. *Mappings.* Princeton, NJ: Princeton UP, 1988. Print.

Gair, Christopher. *The Beat Generation: A Beginner's Guide.* Oxford: Oneworld, 2008. Print.

Gallant, Thomas W. *Modern Greece.* London: Arnold, 2001. Print.

Galtung, Johan. *The Fall of U.S. Empire—and Then What?* Oslo: Transcend UP, 2009. Print.

Ganser, Alexandra. *Roads of Her Own: Gendered Space and Mobility in American Women's Road Narratives 1970–2000.* Amsterdam and New York: Rodopi. 2009. Print.

Gardiner, Juliet. *From the Bomb to the Beatles.* London: Collins, 1999. Print.

Gardiner, Michael. *From Trocchi to Trainspotting: Scottish Critical Theory since 1960.* Edinburgh, Scotland: Edinburgh UP, 2006. Print.

Gewirtz, Isaac. *Beatific Soul: Jack Kerouac on the Road.* New York: New York Public Library; London: Scala, 2007. Print.

Gilman, Charlotte Perkins. *Women and Economics: A Study of the Economic Relation Between Men and Women as a Factor in Social Evolution.* Boston: Small Maynard, 1898. Print.

Ginsberg, Allen. "The Art of Poetry." Interview by Tom Clark. *Spontaneous Mind.* 17–53. Print.

———. *Collected Poems 1947–1997.* New York: HarperCollins, 2007. Print.

———. *Howl and Other Poems.* San Francisco: City Lights, 1956. Print.

———. Interview by Josef Rauvolf, "Allen Ginsberg." Narr. Josef Rauvolf. Praha: Česká televize, 1993. Television.

———. *Karma červená, bílá a modrá.* Praha: Mladá fronta, 2001. Print.

———. *Kvílení.* Praha: Odeon, 1990. Print.

———. "A Letter to Eberhart." *Beat Down to Your Soul.* Ed. Ann Charters. New York: Penguin, 2001. Print.

———. "Nicaragua Notebook." 22 Jan. 1982. Series 2, Box 37, Folder 2. Allen Ginsberg Papers, Department of Special Collections, Stanford University. TS.

———. *Spontaneous Mind: Selected Interviews 1958–1996.* New York: Harper, 2001. Print.

———. "U.S. Poets to Participate in Nicaragua 'Encounter for Peace.'" 19 Jan. 1986. Box 182, Folder 4. PEN American Center Archives, Princeton University Libraries. Print.

Ginsberg, Allen, and Louis Ginsberg. *Family Business.* New York: Bloomsbury, 2001. Print.

Ginsberg, Allen, and Patrick Warner. "Nicaragua Express: Journal Notes, Photos, Poems and Conversations, January 21–February 5, 1986." 1986. Series 8, Box 13, Folders 7–10. Allen Ginsberg Papers, Department of Special Collections, Stanford University. TS.

Girodias, Maurice. "The Dirty Young Adam: An Afterword." Campbell and Niel 79. Print.

Gourgouris, Stathis. *Does Literature Think? Literature as Theory for an Antimythical Era.* Stanford: Stanford UP, 2003.

Grace, Nancy M. "Artista: Interview with Brenda (Bonnie) Frazer." Grace and Johnson 109–130. Print.

———. *Jack Kerouac and the Literary Imagination.* New York: Palgrave, 2007. Print.

Grace, Nancy M., and Ronna C. Johnson. *Breaking the Rule of Cool: Interviewing and Reading Women Beat Writers.* Jackson: UP of Mississippi, 2004. Print.

Gray, Robert, ed. *Yahahbibi Occasional Word Ensemble.* London: the editor, n.d. Print.

Green, Malcolm. Introduction. Bayer, *Selected Works* 3–13. Print.

———. Introduction. Bayer, *The Sixth Sense* 5–12. Print.

Hájek, Igor. "Americká bohma." *Světová literatura.* Vol. 6. 1959. Print.

———. "Z bradburyovského světa do pražského předjaří." *Literární noviny,* 12 (1965). Print.

Hampson, John. "Movements in the Underground—1." *The Penguin New Writing.* Harmondsworth: Penguin, 1946. 130–135. Print.

Hannerz, Ulf. *Transnational Connections*. London: Routledge, 1996. Print.

Haňťa Press. *Zpravodaj Společnosti Bohumila Hrabala*, č. 8. Praha, 1990. Print.

Hardt, Michael, and Antonio Negri. *Empire*. Cambridge: Harvard UP, 2000. Print.

Harper, Clifford, Dennis Gould, and Jeff Cloves, eds. *Visions of Poesy*. London: Freedom, 1994. Print.

Harris, Oliver. "Introduction." *Queer*. 25th Anniversary Edition. Burroughs. New York: Penguin, 2010. Print.

———. "Introduction." *The Yage Letters Redux*. Burroughs and Ginsberg. San Francisco: City Lights, 2006. Print.

———. *William Burroughs and the Secret of Fascination*. Carbondale: Southern Illinois UP, 2003. Print.

Harris, Oliver, and Ian MacFadyen, eds. *NL @ 50*. Carbondale: Southern Illinois UP, 2009. Print.

Harris, William J. "Introduction." *The LeRoi Jones/Amiri Baraka Reader*. Ed. Harris. New York: Thunder's Mouth, 1991. xvii–xxx. Print.

Hartmans, Pieter. "Press Articles." *The Tom Waits Library*. n.d. Web. 26 June 2011.

Havel, Václav. Preface. *Spontaneous Mind*. Ginsberg ix–x. Print.

Heaney, Seamus. "Homage to Seferis." *Harvard Review* 20 (Spring 2001): 33–38. Print.

Hemmer, Kurt. "Brenda Frazer (Bonnie Bremser)." *Encyclopedia of Beat Literature*. Ed. Kurt Hemmer. New York: Facts on File, 2007. 104–105. Print.

———. "'The natives are getting uppity,' Tangier and *Naked Lunch*." Harris and MacFadyen. 65–72. Print.

———. "The Prostitute Speaks: Brenda Frazer's *Troia: Mexican Memoirs*." *Paradoxa*. 18 (2003): 99–117. Print.

Hendin, Josephine G., ed. *A Concise Companion to Postwar American Literature and Culture*. Oxford: Blackwell, 2004. Print.

Hewison, Robert. *In Anger: Culture in the Cold War, 1945–1961*. Rev. ed. London: Methuen, 1988. Print.

———. *Too Much: Art and Society in the Sixties, 1960–1975*. London: Methuen, 1986. Print.

———. *Under Siege: Literary Life in London, 1939–1945*. London: Weidenfeld, 1977. Print.

Hibbard, Allen, ed. *Conversations with William S. Burroughs*. Jackson: UP of Mississippi, 1999. Print.

———. "Introduction: A Moveable Feast." *Bowles/Beats/Tangier*. Ed. Allen Hibbard and Barry Tharaud. Tangier: International Centre for Performance Studies, 2008. Print.

———. "Shift Coordinate Points: William S. Burroughs and Contemporary Theory." Schneiderman and Walsh 13–28. Print.

———. "Tangier and the Making of *Naked Lunch*." Harris and MacFadyen 56–64. Print.

Hintze, Ide. "Die Schule fur Dichtung/The Vienna Poetry School: Notes for a Lecture, Kerouac School, Boulder, 3 July 1995." n.p., n.d. Web. 17 Oct. 2011.

Hodgins, Paul. "Theatre: Strange 'Magic'." *Orange County Register* 26 Apr. 2006. Web. 4 June 2011.

———. "Theater: 'The Black Rider: The Casting of the Magic Bullets'." *Orange County Register* 27 Apr. 2006. Web. 26 June 2011.

Hoggart, Richard. *The Uses of Literacy: Aspects of Working-class Life with Special Reference to Publications and Entertainments*. Harmondsworth: Penguin, 1957. Print.

Holladay, Hilary. "Parallel Destinies in *The Bell Jar* and *On the Road*." Holladay and Holton 99–117. Print.

Holladay, Hilary, and Robert Holton, eds. *What's Your Road, Man? Critical Essays on Jack Kerouac's On the Road*. Carbondale: Southern Illinois UP, 2009. Print.

Holmes, John Clellon. *Go*. New York: Ace, 1952. Print.

———. "This Is the Beat Generation." *New York Times Magazine* 16 Nov. 1952: 10–22. Print.

Holton, Robert. *On the Road: Kerouac's Ragged American Journey.* New York: Twayne, 1999. Print.

———. "'The Sordid Hipsters of America': Beat Culture and the Folds of Heterogeneity." Skerl, *Reconstructing* 11–26. Print.

———. "The Tenement Castle: Kerouac's Lumpen-Bohemia." Holladay and Holton 60–76. Print.

Home, Stewart. "Young Adam Introduction." n.p. Web. 10 Nov. 2010.

Horoskop orloje. Praha: Odeon, 1987. Print.

Horovitz, Michael, ed. *Children of Albion: Poetry of the Underground.* Harmondsworth: Penguin, 1969. Print.

———. Editorial. *New Departures* 4 (1962): 41. Print.

Houedard, Dom Sylvester. "Beat and Afterbeat: a parallel condition of poetry & theology." *Aylesford Review* 5 (1963): 146–156. Print.

Houston, Libby. *A Stained Glass Raree Show.* London: Allison and Busby, 1967. Print.

Hrabal, Bohumil. *I Served the King of England.* New York: Vintage, 1990. Print.

———. *Kličky na kapesníku. Sebrané spisy Bohumila Hrabala, sv. 17.* Praha: Pražská imaginace, 1996. Print.

———. *Pábitelé.* Praha, Mladá fronta, 1969. Print.

———. *Poupata.* Praha: Mladá fronta, 1992. Print.

Hrabě, Václav. *Stop-Time.* Praha: Mladá frontá, 1969. Print.

Huncke, Herbert. *Guilty of Everything: The Autobiography of Herbert Huncke.* New York: Paragon, 1990. Print.

Hunt, Tim. *Kerouac's Crooked Road.* 1981. 3rd edition. Carbondale: Southern Illinois UP, 2010. Print.

Hussey, Andrew. "'Paris is about the last place. . .': William Burroughs In and Out of Paris and Tangier, 1958–1960." Harris and MacFadyen 73–83. Print.

Hutka, Jaroslav. *Básně.* Praha: Galén, 2008. Print.

International Situationiste #1. Situationist International Online. n.d. Web. 1 July 2011.

Jackson, Alan. "Edinburgh Scene." *Love, Love, Love: the New Love Poetry.* Ed. Pete Roche. London: Corgi, 1967. 55. Print.

Jak se dělá báseň. Praha: Československý spisovatel, 1970. Print.

Jazzová inspirace. Praha: Odeon, 1966. Print.

Jay, Paul. "Beyond Discipline? Globalization and the Future of English." *PMLA.* 116.1 (2001): 32–47. Print.

Jean-Louis [Jack Kerouac]. "Jazz of the Beat Generation." *New World Writing* 7 (Apr. 1955): 7–16. Print.

Jenkins, R. J. H. *Palamas: An Inaugural Lecture delivered at King's College, London on 30th January, 1947.* London: Favil, 1947. Print.

Joans, Ted. *A Black Manifesto in Jazz Poetry and Prose.* London: Calder and Boyles, 1971. Print.

———. "Ted Joans: Tri-Continental Poet." Interview with Henry Louis Gates Jr. *Discourse* 20.1–2 (1998): 72–89. Print.

———. *Teducation: Selected Poems 1949–1999.* Saint Paul, MN: Coffee House, 1999. Print.

Johnson, Chalmers. *Dismantling the Empire: America's Last Best Hope.* New York: Henry Holt, 2010. Print.

Johnson, Kent. "Interview with Ernesto Cardenal." *A Nation of Poets: Writings from the Poetry Workshops of Nicaragua.* Los Angeles: West End, 1985. 7–24. Print.

Johnson, Rob. *The Lost Years of Williams S. Burroughs: Beats in South Texas.* College Station: Texas A&M P, 2006. Print.

Johnson, Ronna C. "Mapping Women Writers of the Beat Generation."Grace and Johnson 3–41. Print.

Johnson, Ronna C., and Nancy M. Grace, eds. *Girls Who Wore Black: Women Writing the Beat Generation*. New Brunswick, NJ: Rutgers UP, 2002. Print.

———. "Visions and Revisions of the Beat Generation." Johnson and Grace 1–24. Print.

Kallerges, Herakles. *Διαδρομέςστη Νεοελληνική Ποίηση* [*Peregrinations in Modern Greek Poetry*]. Athens: Kastaniotis, 2001. Print.

Kaplan, Amy. *The Anarchy of Empire in the Making of U.S. Culture*. Cambridge: Harvard UP, 2002. Print.

———. "Manifest Domesticity." *American Literature* 70:3 (Sept. 1998): 581–606. Print.

Kaplan, Amy, and Donald E. Pease, eds. *Cultures of United States Imperialism*. Durham: Duke UP, 1993. Print.

Kaplan, Caren. "Deterritorializations: The Rewriting of Home and Exile in Western Feminist Discourse." *Cultural Critique* 6 (1978): 187–198. Print.

Karl, Frederick R. "The Fifties and After: An Ambiguous Culture." Hendin 20–71. Print.

Kastrinaki, Aggela. *Η Λογοτεχνίαστην Ταραγμένη Δεκαετία 1940–1950* [*Literature in the Troubled Decade 1940–1950*]. Athens: Polis, 2005. Print.

Kaufman, Bob. *The Ancient Rain: Poems 1956–1978*. New York: New Directions, 1981. Print.

———. *Solitudes Crowded with Loneliness*. New York: New Directions, 1965. Print.

Keeley, Edmund. *Modern Greek Poetry: Voice and Myth*. Princeton: Princeton UP, 1983. Print.

Kenner, Hugh. *The Sinking Island*. London: Bearnes, 1987. Print.

Kern, Robert. "Mountains and Rivers are Us: Gary Snyder and the Nature of Nature." Skerl, *College Literature* 119–138. Print.

Kerouac, Jack. "Aftermath: The Philosophy of the Beat Generation." *Good Blonde & Others*. Kerouac. 47–50. Print.

———. *Desolation Angels*. 1965. New York: Riverhead, 1995. Print.

———. *Dharma Bums*. New York: Viking, 1958. Print.

———. *Doctor Sax: Faust Part Three*. 1959. New York: Evergreen, 1987. Print.

———. *Empty Phantoms: Interviews and Encounters with Jack Kerouac*. Ed. Paul Maher Jr. New York: Thunder's Mouth, 2005. Print.

———. *Good Blonde & Others*. Ed. Donald Allen. San Francisco: Grey Fox, 1993. Print.

———. Interview by Ted Berrigan. *The Paris Review: Beat Writers at Work*. New York: Modern Library, 1999. 98–133. Print.

———. Jack Kerouac Papers, 1920–1977. Henry W. and Albert A. Berg Collection of English and American Literature, New York Public Library.

———. Letter to Neal Cassady. 22 May 1951. *Selected Letters* 315–317. Print.

———. Letter to Neal Cassady. 10 January 1953. *Selected Letters* 395–96. Print.

———. Letter to Yvonne Le Maître. 8 September 1950. *Selected Letters* 227–229. Print.

———. *Maggie Cassidy*. London: Granada, 1982. Print.

———. "New York Scenes." *Lonesome Traveller*. London: Granada, 1982. Print.

———. *La Nuit est ma femme*. Jack Kerouac Papers 15.20. TS.

———. *On the Road*. 1957. New York and London: Penguin, 1991, 2005. Print.

———. "On The Road, écrit en Francais." 1951 or 1952. Jack Kerouac Papers 2.41. TS.

———. *On the Road: The Original Scroll*. New York: Viking, 2007. Print.

———. "The Origins of the Beat Generation." *Good Blonde & Others*. Kerouac. 55–65. Print.

———. *Říjen v železniční zemi*. Praha: Mladá fronta, 1963. Print.

———. *Satori in Paris*. 1966. *Satori in Paris and Pic*. New York: Grove, 1985. 5–118. Print.

————. *The Scripture of the Golden Eternity*. San Francisco: City Lights, 1994. Print.

————. *Selected Letters, 1940–1956*. Ed. Ann Charters. New York: Viking, 1995. Print.

————. *Sur le chemin*. 1951. Jack Kerouac Papers 39.10. TS.

————. *The Town and the City*. 1950. New York: Harcourt, 1978. Print.

———— *Vanity of Duluoz: an Adventurous Education, 1935–46*. St. Albans: Granada, 1982. Print.

————. *Visions of Cody*. 1960. New York and London: Penguin, 1993. Print.

Khan, Nyla Ali. *The Fiction of Nationality in an Era of Transnationalism*. New York: Routledge, 2005. Print.

Knight, Brenda. *Women of the Beat Generation: The Writers, Artists, and Muses at the Heart of a Revolution*. Berkeley: Conari Press, 1996. Print.

Koch, Milan. Unpublished manuscript. Libri prohibiti Archive. Praha. n.d. TS.

————. *Červená karKULKA a jiné básně*. Praha: Vokno, 1992. Print.

"Kocovina s ginsbergem." *Rudé právo* 17 May 1965. Print.

Kokolis, K.A. *Κωστής Παλαμάς, Σατιρικά Γυμνάσματα* (Kostes Palamas: Satirical Exercises). Athens: Metaixmio, 2005. 105. Print.

Kozelka, Milan. "Když byla poezie divokým životním stylem." *Host* 5 (2007): 2. Print.

Kyger, Joanne. "Congratulatory Poetics, Joanne Kyger Interview." *Convivio*. Ed. John Thorpe. Bolinas: New College of California, 1983. 109–120. Print.

————. Interview by David Chadwick. "Crooked Cucumber Interviews, Joanne Kyger." *Cuke.com*. 29 September 1995. Web. 14 Nov. 2005.

————. Interview by David Meltzer. "Joanne Kyger." *San Francisco Beat*. San Francisco: City Lights, 2001. 122–132. Print.

————. Interview by Linda Russo. "Particularizing People's Lives." *Jacket Magazine* 11 (Apr. 2000). Web. 14 Nov. 2005.

————. Interview by Nancy M. Grace. "Places to Go." Grace and Johnson 133–153. Print.

————. Letter to the Jane Falk. 10 Aug. 2010. TS.

————. *Strange Big Moon*. Berkeley: North Atlantic, 2000. Print. Rpt. of *The Japan and India Journals 1960–1964*. Bolinas: Tombouctou, 1981.

————. *The Tapestry and the Web*. San Francisco: Four Seasons Foundation, 1965. Print.

LaFeber, Walter. *Inevitable Revolutions: The United States in Central America*. New York: W.W. Norton, 1983.

Lawless, Gary, ed. *Nanao or Never: Nanao Sakaki Walks Earth A*. Nobleboro, Maine: Blackberry, 2000. Print.

Le Guin, Ursula K. *The Lathe of Heaven*. 1971. New York: Scribner, 2008. Print.

Le Maître, Yvonne. "The Town and the City." *Le Travailleur* 20.12 (23 Mar. 1950): 1–2. Print.

Lee, A. Robert, ed. *The Beat Generation Writers*. London: Pluto, 1996. Print.

————. "Beat International: Michael Horovitz, Andrei Voznesensky, Kazuko Shiraishi." *Modern American*. Lee. 70–83. Print.

————. "Black Beat: Performing Ted Joans." Skerl, *Reconstructing* 117–134. Print.

————. "Black Beats: The Signifying Poetry of LeRoi Jones/Amiri Baraka, Ted Joans, and Bob Kaufman." *Beat Generation*. Lee. 158–177. Print.

————. "Chicanismo's Beat Outrider." Skerl, *College Literature* 158–176. Print.

————. *Modern American Counter Writing: Beats, Outriders, Ethnics*. New York: Routledge, 2010. Print.

Lennon, John. "John Lennon, Man of the Decade Interview." 2 Dec. 1969. Web. 25 Aug. 2010.

Leonard, Tom. "The Locust Tree in Flower, and Why It Had Difficulty Flowering in Britain." *Invisible Shivers: Selected Works, 1965-1983*. Newcastle-upon-Tyne: Galloping Dog, 1984. 100–103. Print.

Levitt, Peggy, and Sanjeev Khagram. *The Transnational Studies Reader: Interdisciplinary Intersections and Innovations*. 1994. New York: Routledge, 2007. Print.

Ligairi, Rachel. "When Mexico Looks Like Mexico: The Hyperrealization of Race and the Pursuit of the Authentic." Holladay and Holton 139–154. Print.

Lindberg, Kathryne V. "Mister Joans To You: Readerly Surreality and Writerly Affiliation in Ted Joans, Tri-Continental 'Ex-Beatnik.'" *Discourse* 20.1–2 (1998): 198–222. Print.

Linders, Jan. Interview, August 1992, Convidados de Piedra, Madrid 1992. *Tom Waits Library*. n.p. Web. 10 June 2011.

Lipton, Lawrence. *The Holy Barbarians*. New York: Messner, 1959. Print.

Literární archiv XXV. Praha: Památník národního písemnictví, 1991. Print.

Logue, Christopher. *Prince Charming*. London: Faber and Faber, 1999. Print.

Lott, Deshai E. "'All things are different appearances of the same emptiness': Buddhism and Jack Kerouac's Nature Writings." Skerl, *Reconstructing* 169–186. Print.

Lovelock, Yann. "Bluejeans and Gowns: The Beat Scene in Oxford, 1959–62." Unpublished essay, n. d. [1995]. Print.

Lydenberg, Robin. *Word Cultures: Radical Theory and Practice in William S. Burroughs' Fiction*. Urbana: U of Illinois P, 1987. Print.

Lyon, Janet. *Manifestoes: Provocations of the Modern*. Ithaca, New York: Cornell UP, 1999. Print.

MacDiarmid, Hugh. "Scottish Writing Today." International Writers Conference. Edinburgh. 20 Aug. 1962. Print. Transcript. WP5. 205. 586. National Library of Scotland.

Machovec, Martin. "Několik poznámek k podzemní ediční řadě Půlnoc." *Kritický sborník*. Číslo 3. Praha: Vesmír, 1993. Print.

Machulková, Inka. "Já, beatnička, jsem číslo jedna v Obci spisovatelů!." *Host* 5 (2007): 7. Print.

———. *Neúplný čas mokré trávy*. Brno: Host, 2006. Print.

———. *Zamkni les a pojď*. Brno: Host, 2009. Print.

Mainx, Oskar. *Poezie jako mýtus, svědectví a hra: kapitoly z básnické poetiky Egona Bondyho*. Ostrava: Protimluv, 2007. Print.

Malmgren, Carl D. *Fictional Space in the Modernist and Postmodernist American Novel*. Lewisburg, PA: Bucknell UP, 1985. Print.

———. "*On the Road* Reconsidered: Kerouac and the Modernist Tradition." *Ball State University Forum* 30.1 (Winter 1989): 59–76. Print.

Mao, Douglas and Rebecca L. Walkowitz. "The New Modernist Studies." *PMLA* 123.3 (2008): 737–748. Print.

Marcus, Greil. *Lipstick Traces: A Secret History of the Twentieth Century*. Cambridge: Harvard UP, 1990. Print.

Marinetti, F. T. *Let's Murder the Moonshine: Selected Writings*. Ed. R. W. Flint and trans. Flint and Arthur A. Coppotelli. Los Angeles: Sun & Moon, 1991. Print.

Martinez, Manuel Luis. *Countering the Counterculture: Rereading Postwar American Dissent from Jack Kerouac to Tomas Rivera*. Madison: U of Wisconsin P, 2003. Print.

———. "With Imperious Eye: Kerouac, Burroughs, and Ginsberg on the Road in South America." *Aztlán* 23.1 (1998): 33–53. Print.

Maynard, John Arthur. *Venice West: The Beat Generation in Southern California*. New Brunswick, NJ: Rutgers U P, 1991. Print.

Mazal, Tomáš. *Spisovatel Bohumil Hrabal*. Praha: Torst, 2004. Print.

McDowell, Linda. "Off the Road: Alternative Views of Rebellion, Resistance, and 'The Beats'." *Transactions of the Institute of British Geographers* 21.2 (1996): 412–419. Print.

McGlathery, James J. *Grimms' Fairy Tales: A History of Criticism on a Popular Classic*. Columbia, SC: Camden, 1993. Print.

McHale, Brian. *Postmodernist Fiction*. London: Routledge, 1987. Print.

McMillan, Ian. "Performance Poetry." *Oxford Companion to Twentieth Century Poetry*. Oxford: Oxford UP, 1995. 415–416. Print.

McNeil, Helen. "The Archaeology of Gender in the Beat Movement." Lee, *Beat Generation* 178–199. Print.

Mead, Philip. "The American Model II." *Assembling Alternatives: Reading Postmodern Poetries Transnationally*. Ed. Romana Huk. Middletown, CT: Wesleyan UP, 2003. 169–191. Print.

Miles, Barry. *The Beat Hotel: Ginsberg, Burroughs, and Corso in Paris, 1958–1963*. New York: Grove, 2000. Print.

———. *Ginsberg: A Biography*. New York: Simon, 1989. Print.

———. *Jack Kerouac: King of the Beats*. New York: Henry Holt, 1998. Print.

———. *William Burroughs: El Hombre Invisible, A Portrait*. New York: Hyperion, 1993. Print.

Millett, Kate. *Sexual Politics*. New York: Ballantine, 1969. Print.

Mills, Katie. *The Road Story and the Rebel: Moving Through Film, Fiction, and Television*. Carbondale: Southern Illinois UP, 2006. Print.

Miner, Earl, ed. and trans. *Japanese Poetic Diaries*. Berkeley: U of California P, 1969. Print.

Mitchell, Adrian. "Moon Over Minnesota." *Circuit A* spring/summer 1967: 24–27. Print.

Mlakar, Heike. "Jack Kerouac's and Brenda Frazer's Shared 'Romantic Primitivism': A Comparative Study of *On the Road* and *For Love of Ray*." *Neo-Americanist* 3.1 (2007) 1-11. n.p. Web. 24 June 2011.

———. *Merely Being There is Not Enough: Women's Roles in Autobiographical Texts by Female Beat Authors*. Boca Raton, FL: Universal, 2008. Print.

Mondragón, Sergio, Margaret Randall, and Harvey Wolin. "Editors' Note." *El Corno Emplumado* 1 (1962): 5. Print.

Morgan, Bill. *I Celebrate Myself*. New York: Viking, 2006. Print.

Morgan, Peter, ed. *C'mon Everybody: Poetry of the Dance*. London: Corgi, 1971. Print.

Morgan, Ted. *Literary Outlaw: The Life and Times of William S. Burroughs*. New York: Holt, 1988. Print.

Mottram, Eric. *Allen Ginsberg in the Sixties*. Brighton: Unicorn Bookshop, 1972. Print.

———. (Featured on) "The British Beats." Narr. Ian McMillan. *Kaleidoscope*. BBC Radio 4, 26 Oct. 1991. Radio.

———. "The British Poetry Revival 1960–1974." *Modern British Poetry Conference*. Ed. Eric Mottram. London: Polytechnic of Central London, 1974. 66117. Mimeographed TS.

———. "A Pig-headed Father and the New Wood." Rev. of *An Introduction to the New American Poetry*. Ed. Donald M. Allen. *The London Magazine* 2.9 (1962): 63–73. Print.

———. *William Burroughs: the Algebra of Need*. Buffalo: Intrepid, 1971. Print.

Moyse, Arthur, ed. *The Golden Convolvulus*. London: Screeches, 1965. Print.

Müllerová, Veronika. "Ostermannova Viola." Thesis. Praha: Literární akademie, 2008. Print.

Mullins, Greg. *Colonial Affairs: Bowles, Burroughs, and Chester Write Tangier*. Madison: U of Wisconsin P, 2002. Print.

Mulvey, Laura. "Visual Pleasure and Narrative Cinema." *Screen* 16.3 (1975): 6–18. Print.

Murphy, Cullen. *Are We Rome: The Fall of an Empire and the Fate of America*. New York: Houghton Mifflin, 2007. Print.

Murphy, Timothy S. "Exposing the Reality Film: William S. Burroughs among the Situationists." Schneiderman and Walsh 29–57. Print.

———. *Wising Up the Marks: The Amodern William Burroughs*. Berkeley: U of California P, 1997. Print.

"Na besedě s Allenem Ginsbergem." *Rudé právo* 3 March 1965. Print.

Nadel, Alan. *Containment Culture: American Narratives, Postmodernism, and the Atomic Age*. Durham: Duke UP, 1995. Print.

Nattier, Jan. "Who is a Buddhist?" *The Faces of Buddhism in America.* Ed. Charles Prebish and Kenneth Tanaka. Berkeley: U of California P, 1998. 183–195. Print.

Nicosia, Gerald. "A Lifelong Commitment to Change: The Literary Non-Career of Ted Joans." *Teducation.* Ted Joans i–vii. Print.

———. *Memory Babe: A Critical Biography of Jack Kerouac.* 1983. Berkeley: U of California P, 1994. Print.

Nielsen, Aldon. *Black Chant: Languages of African-American Postmodernism.* Cambridge: Cambridge UP, 1997. Print.

"1962 International Writers Conference Program." *Reality Studio: A William S. Burroughs Community.* n.d. Web. 8 Feb. 2011.

Notley, Alice. "Joanne Kyger's Poetry." *Coming After.* Ann Arbor: U of Michigan P, 2005. 15–26. Print.

Nuttall, Jeff. *Bomb Culture.* London: MacGibbon, 1968. Print.

———. "Bomb Culture." Campbell and Niel 176–189. Print.

———. (Featured on) "The British Beats." Narr. Ian McMillan. *Kaleidoscope.* BBC Radio 4, 26 Oct. 1991. Radio.

Okano, Haruko. "Women's Image and Place in Japanese Buddhism." *Japanese Women.* Ed. Kumiko Fujimura-Fanselow and Atsuko Kameda. NY: Feminist Press, 1995. 15–28. Print.

Ortner, Sherry B. "Is Female to Male as Nature is to Culture?" *Woman, Culture and Society.* Ed. M. Z. Rosaldo and L. Lamphere. Stanford, CA: Stanford UP, 1974. 68–87. Print.

Palamas, Kostes. *Complete Works.* Athens: Govostes, 1969. Print.

Panourgia, Neni. *Dangerous Citizens: The Greek Left and the Terror of the State.* New York: Fordham UP, 2009. Print.

Papanikolaou, Dimitris. *Singing Poets: Literature and Popular Music in France and Greece.* London: Legenda, 2007. Print.

Parkinson, Thomas, ed. *A Casebook On the Beat.* New York: Thomas Y. Crowell, 1961. Print.

Patchen, Kenneth. *Poems of Humor and Protest.* San Francisco: City Lights, 1955. Print.

Peabody, Richard, ed. *A Different Beat: Writings by Women of the Beat Generation.* London: High Risk. 1997. Print.

Pease, Donald E. "American Studies after American Exceptionalism? Toward a Comparative Analysis of Imperial State Exceptionalisms." Edwards and Gaonkar 47–83. Print.

Pelt, Mogens. *Tying Greece to the West: US-West German-Greek Relations 1949–1974.* Denmark: Museum Tusculanum, 2006. Print.

"PEN Charter." *PEN International.* n. p. Web. 2 July 2011.

Pennell, C.R. *Morocco: From Empire to Independence.* Oxford: Oneworld, 2003. Print.

Perkins, Michael. "Bonnie Bremser." *The Beats: Literary Bohemians in Postwar America. Dictionary of Literary Biography.* Vol. 16. Ed. Ann Charters. Detroit: Gale, 1983. 33–35. Print.

Perloff, Marjorie. *The Futurist Moment: Avant-Garde, Avant Guerre, and the Language of Rupture.* Chicago: U of Chicago P, 1986. Print.

Petříček, Miroslav. "Padesátá." *Roky ve dnech.* Praha: Arbor Vitae, 2010. Print.

Pickard, Tom. "Serving My Time for a Trade." *Paideuma* 9 (Spring 1980): 156. Print.

Pilař, Martin. *Underground.* Brno: Host, 1999. Print.

———. *Vrabec v hrsti.* Praha: Dokořán, 2005. Print.

"Poetry in Motion" prospectus. London: Poetry in Motion poets' collective, n.d. [1967]. Mimeographed TS.

Poláčková, K. A. "Ginsberg objevuje Československo." *Svobodné slovo* 21 March 1965. Print.

Polsky, Ned. "Ned Polsky." Campell and Niel 100–102. Print.

Poore, Charles. "Books of the Times." *New York Times* 2 Mar. 1950: 25. Print.

Posekaná, Dana, and Zdenka Šťastná. "Gaudeamus igitur." *Mladá fronta* 2 May 1965. Print.

Posset, Johanna. *Česká samizdatová periodika 1968–1989.* Brno: Reprografia, 1991. Print.

Poteet, Maurice, et al., eds. *Textes de l'Exode: Recueil de textes sur l'émigration des Québécois aux Etats-Unis (XIXe et XXe siècles).* Montreal: Guérin Littérature, 1987. Print.

Poulios, Lefteris. *Ποιήματα: Επιλογή 1969–1978* [*Selected Poems 1969–1978*]. Athens: Kedros, 1982. Print.

———. *Αντίτηςσιωπής* [*Instead of Silence*]. Athens: Kastaniotis, 1993. Print.

Pound, Ezra. "Date Line." *Literary Essays of Ezra Pound.* New York: New Directions, 1968. 74–87. Print.

———. *Patria Mia.* Chicago: Seymour, 1950. Print.

Powell, Neil. *Oxford Companion to Twentieth Century Poetry.* Ed. Ian Hamilton. Oxford: Oxford UP, 1995. Print.

Pratt, Mary Louise. "Arts of the Contact Zone." *Profession* 91 (1991): 33–40. Print.

———. *Imperial Eyes.* London: Routledge, 1992. Print.

Proceedings from the Ninth Poetry Symposium at the University of Patras, 7–9 July, 1989 [*Πρακτικά Ενάτου Συμποσίου Ποίησης. Κωστής Παλαμάς: Η Εποχή του και η Εποχή μας. Πανεπιστήμιο Πατρών,* 7–9 Ιουλίου, 1989] [Kostes Palamas. His Time and Ours]. Patra: Achaikes Endoseis, 1992. Print.

Prothero, Stephen. Introduction. *Big Sky Mind: Buddhism and the Beat Generation.* Ed. Carole Tonkinson. NY: Riverhead, 1995. 1–20. Print.

———. "On the Holy Road; The Beat Movement as Spiritual Protest." *Harvard Theological Review* 84.2 (Apr. 1991): 205–222. Print.

Puchner, Martin. *Poetry of the Revolution: Marx, Manifestos, and the Avant-Gardes.* Princeton, NJ: Princeton UP, 2006. Print.

Purdy, Anthony. "Shattered Voices: The Poetics of Exile in Quebec Literature." *Literature and Exile.* Ed. David Bevan. Amsterdam and Atlanta: Rodopi, 1990. 23–36. Print.

Ramazani, Jahan. *A Transnational Poetics.* Chicago: U of Chicago P, 2009. Print.

Randall, Margaret. *Coming Home: Peace Without Complacency.* Albuquerque, NM: West End, 1990. Print.

———. *Risking a Somersault in the Air: Conversations with Nicaraguan Writers.* San Francisco: Solidarity, 1984. Print.

Rebel, Inc. *Young Adam* Advertisment. End matter. Campbell and Niel n.p. Print.

Rebhandl, Bert. "Clean Up Your Act." Web. 6 April 2011.

Rexroth, Kenneth. *Thirty Spanish Poems of Love and Exile.* San Francisco: City Lights, 1955. Print.

Rich, Adrienne. "Notes Toward a Politics of Location (1984)." *Blood, Bread and Poetry, Selected Prose 1979–1985.* NY: Norton, 1986. 210–231. Print.

Richardson, Mark. "Peasant Dreams: Reading *On the Road.*" *Jack Kerouac's* On the Road. Ed. Harold Bloom. Philadelphia: Chelsea House, 2004. 207–231. Print.

Ricks, David, ed. *Modern Greek Writing: an Anthology in English Translation.* London: Peter Owen, 2003. Print.

Riedlbauchová, Tereza. "Básnické podvědomí může předpovědět události, které teprve nastanou..." *Host* 11 (2009). Print.

Robinson, Christopher. "Greece in the Poetry of Costis Palamas." *Review of National Literatures* (Fall 1974): 41–65. Print.

Roby, Yves. *The Franco-Americans of New England: Dreams and Realities.* Trans. Mary Ricard. Sillery, QC: Septentrion, 2004. Print.

———. *Histoire d'un rêve brisé? Les Canadiens français aux Etats-Unis.* Sillery, QC: Septentrion, 2007. Print.

Roche, Pete, ed. *Love, Love, Love: the New Love Poetry*. London: Corgi, 1967. Print.

Rosaldo, Renato. *Culture and Truth: The Remaking of Social Analysis*. Boston: Beacon 1989. Print.

Rose, Gillian. *Feminism & Geography: The Limits of Geographical Knowledge*. Minneapolis: U of Minnesota P, 1993. Print.

Rosenthal, Irving. *Sheepers*. New York: Grove, 1967. Print.

Routhier, Adolphe-Basile. "Le rôle de la race française en Amérique." *Fête nationale des Canadiens-Français célébrée en Québec en 1880*. Ed. H.-J.-J.-B. Chouinard. Quebec City: A. Côté, 1881. 282–295. Print.

Rühm, Gerhard. "the phenomenon of the 'wiener gruppe' in the vienna of the fifties and sixties." Weibel 16–29. Print.

Rushdie, Salman. *The Jaguar Smile: A Nicaraguan Journey*. London: Picador, 1987. Print.

Said, Edward. *Culture and Imperialism*. New York: Vintage, 1994. Print.

———. *Humanism and Democratic Criticism*. New York: Columbia UP, 2004. Print.

Sakellaropoulos, Tasos. "*ΗΕλληνικήΔεκαετίατου* '60" ["The Greek 1960s"]. *60s*. 13–14. Print.

Sakaki, Nanao. *Break the Mirror: The Poems of Nanao Sakaki*. 1987. Nobleboro, ME: Blackberry, 1996. Print.

———. *Inch by Inch: 45 Haiku by Issa*. Albuquerque: La Alameda, 1999. Print.

———. *Let's Eat Stars*. Nobleboro, ME: Blackberry, 1997. Print.

Saldana-Portillo, Maria Josefina. "'On the Road' With Che and Jack: Melancholia and the Legacy of Colonial Racial Geographies in the Americas." *New Formations* 47 (2002): 87–108. Print.

Sasaki, Ruth Fuller. "Letter from Kyoto: Dear Everyone." *Zen Notes* 7: 4 (April 1960): n.p. Print.

———. "Rinzai Zen Study for Foreigners in Japan." *Zen Pioneer*. Isabel Stirling. Emeryville, CA: Shoemaker and Hoard, 2006. 180–246. Print.

Sauvy, Alfred. "Trois mondes, une planète." *L'Observateur* 118 (4 Aug. 1952): 4. Print.

Sawyer-Lauçanno, Christopher. *Continental Pilgrimage: American Writers in Paris, 1944–1960*. San Francisco: City Lights, 1992. Print.

Schireson, Grace. *Zen Women: Beyond Tea Ladies, Iron Maidens, and Macho Masters*. Boston: Wisdom, 2009. Print.

Schneiderman, Davis, and Philip Walsh, eds. *Retaking the Universe: William S. Burroughs in the Age of Globalization*. London: Pluto, 2004. Print.

Schulman, Grace. "Introduction: Poetry of a New Heaven and Earth." *Poets of Nicaragua: A Bilingual Anthology, 1918–1979*. Ed. Steven F. White. Greensboro: Unicorn, 1982. i–v. Print.

Schumacher, Michael. *Dharma Lion of Allen Ginsberg*. New York: St. Martin's, 1994. Print.

Scott, Andrew Murray. *Alexander Trocchi: The Making of a Monster*. Edinburgh, Scotland: Polygon. 1991. Print.

———, ed. *Invisible Insurrection of a Million Minds: A Trocchi Reader*. Edinburgh, Scotland: Polygon, 1991. Print.

Scott, J. D. "In the Movement." *Spectator* 1 Oct. 1954: 400. Print.

Seaver, Richard. Introduction. *Cain's Book*. Trocchi xi–xx. Print.

Seyhan, Azade. *Writing Outside the Nation*. Princeton, New Jersey: Princeton UP, 2000. Print.

Shepard, Odell. *The Lore of the Unicorn*. New York: Harper, 1979. Print.

Silesky, Barry. *Ferlinghetti, the artist in his time*. New York: Warner, 1990. Print.

60s, τοροκτουμέλλοντόςμας [*60s, rock of our future*]. Athens: Sui Generis, 2009. Print.

Skarlant, Petr. *Věk slasti*. Praha: Melantrich, 1977. Print.

Skerl, Jennie, ed. *Reconstructing the Beats*. New York: Palgrave, 2004. Print.

———, ed. Spec. issue of *College Literature* 27.1 (2000): 1–274. Print.

———, and Robin Lydenberg, eds. *William S. Burroughs at the Front: Critical Reception 1959–1989*. Carbondale: Southern Illinois UP, 1991. Print.

Skinner, Jonathan. "Generosity and Discipline: The Travel Poems." *Jacket Magazine* April 2000. Web. 15 Nov. 2005.

Šlajchrt, Viktor. "Ginsberg v Praze." *Literární noviny* 20 April 1990. Print.

Smethurst, James. "Remembering When Indians Were Red: Bob Kaufman, the Popular Front, and the Black Arts Movement." *Callaloo* 25.1 (2002): 146–164. Print.

Smith, Keven Paul. *The Postmodern Fairytale: Folkloric Intertexts in Contemporary Fiction*. New York: Palgrave, 2007. Print.

Snyder, Gary. *The Back Country*. New York: New Directions, 1968. Print.

Sollors, Werner. *Amiri Baraka/LeRoi Jones: The Quest for a "Populist Modernism."* New York: Columbia UP, 1978. Print.

———. *Multilingual America: Transnationalism, Ethnicity, and the Languages of American Literature*. New York: New York UP, 1998. Print.

Southern, Terry. "Terry Southern." Campbell and Niel 76–79. Print.

Spengler, Oswald. *The Decline of the West*. Vol 2. Trans. Charles Francis Atkinson. New York: Knopf, 1937. Print.

"Statement on Nicaragua." 12 Jan. 1986. Box 177, Folder 6. PEN American Center Archives, Princeton University Libraries. Print.

Stavrou, T. G., and Trypanis, C. A., eds. *Kostis Palamas: A Portrait and an Appreciation*. Minneapolis: Nostos, 1985. Print.

Stirling, Isabel. Message to the Jane Falk. 27 July 2010. E-mail.

Strasser, Kurt. *Experimentelle Literaturansätze im Nachkriegs-Wien: Konrad Bayer als Beispiel*. Stuttgart: Heinz, 1986. Print.

Suzuki, D. T. *Zen and Japanese Culture*. New York: MJF, 1959. Print.

Takemura, Ken-Ichi. "Foreigners in Kyoto." *The Mainichi* 9 April 1960: 7. Print.

Tambimuttu, Thurairajah. "Fourth Letter—The New Moderns." *Poetry London NY* 1.4 (1960): 1–12, 52–62. Print.

Tatar, Maria M. *The Annotated Classic Fairy Tales*. New York: Norton, 2002. Print.

Tietchen, Todd F. *The Cubalogues: Beat Writers in Revolutionary Havana*. Gainesville: UP of Florida, 2010. Print.

Tolkien, J.R.R. *Tolkein On Fairy-stories: Expanded edition with Commentary and Notes*. Ed. Verlyn Flieger and Douglas A. Anderson. London: HarperCollins, 2008. Print.

Trigilio, Tony. "'Will you please stop playing with the mantra?': The Embodied Poetics of Ginsberg's Later Career." Skerl, *Reconstructing* 187–202. Print.

Trocchi, Alexander. *Cain's Book*. New York: Grove, 1992. Print.

———. "The Invisible Insurrection of a Million Minds." Campbell and Niel 164–176. Print.

———. "Is Commitment Necessary?" International Writers Conference. McKewan Hall, Edinburgh, Scotland. 20 Aug. 1962. Print. Transcript. WP5. 205. 586. National Library of Scotland.

———. "Letter to William Burroughs." A. Scott, *Invisible* 207–209. Print.

———. *Man at Leisure*. 1972. London: Oneworld Classics, 2009. Print.

———. "Manifesto Situationiste." Sigma Portfolio # 18. 6.1825. 1964. TS. National Library of Scotland.

———. "Merlin." Campbell and Niel 39–42. Print.

———. *The Moving Times*. 7.87. National Library of Scotland. Print.

———. "Pool Cosmonaut." Sigma Portfolio # 37. n.d. TS. 6.2030(27[2]). National Library of Scotland.

——. "Scottish Writing Today." International Writers Conference. McKewan Hall, Edinburgh. 20 Aug. 1962. Print. Transcript. WP5. 205. 586. National Library of Scotland.

——. "Sigma: A Tactical Blueprint." A. Scott, *Invisible* 192–203. Print.

——. "Subscription Form." Sigma Portfolio # 12. n.d. TS. 6.1825. National Library of Scotland.

——, Terry Southern, Richard Seaver, eds. *Writers in Revolt*. New York, Frederick Fell, 1963. Print.

Tsimas, Pavlos. "Τα φοιτητικά κινήματα στα "σίξτις", οι μέρες που λαχτάρησα θα'ρθουν;" ["The Student Movements of the 1960s"]. *60s* 19–23. Print.

Tully, David. *Terry Southern and the American Grotesque*. Jefferson, NC: McFarland, 2010. Print.

Tuma, Keith. *Fishing by Obstinate Isles: Modern and Postmodern British Poetry and American Readers*. Evanston: Northwestern UP, 1998. Print.

Turner, Steve. *A Hard Day's Write*. New York: Harper, 1994. Print.

——. *Jack Kerouac: Angel-Headed Hipster*. London: Bloomsbury, 1996. Print.

Turner, Victor. *The Ritual Process*. Ithaca, NY: Cornell UP, 1977. Print.

Tye, Larry. *The Father of Spin: Edward L. Bernays and the Birth of Public Relations*. New York: Holt, 1998. Print.

Tytell, John. *Naked Angels: the Lives and the Literature of the Beat Generation*. New York: McGraw-Hill, 1977. Print.

Tzara, Tristan. *Approximate Man and Other Writings*. Ed. and trans. Mary Ann Caws. Detroit: Wayne State UP, 1973. Print.

van der Bent, Jaap. "Holy Amsterdam Holy Paris: The Beat Generation in Europe." *Beat Culture: The 1950s and Beyond*. Ed. Cornelis A. van Minnen, et al. Amsterdam: VU UP, 1999. 49–60. Print.

——. "'O fellow travelers I write you a poem in Amsterdam': Allen Ginsberg, Simon Vinkenoog, and the Dutch Beat Connection." Skerl, *College Literature* 199–212. Print.

Van Dyck, Karen. "Reading Between Worlds: Contemporary Greek Women's Writing and Censorship." *PMLA* 109.1: 45–60. Print.

—— *Kassandra and the Censors: Greek Poetry Since 1967*. Ithaca, NY: Cornell UP, 1998. Print.

Varley, H. Paul. *Japanese Culture: A Short History*. NY: Praeger, 1973. Print.

Vega, Janine Pommy, *Tracking the Serpent: Journeys to Four Continents*. San Francisco: City Lights, 1997. Print.

Vertovec, Steven. "Conceiving and Researching Transnationalism." *Ethnic and Racial Studies* 22.2 (1999): 447–462. Print.

Vine, Ian. "Beatnik as Anarchist." *Anarchy* 31 (1963): 283–287. Print.

——. *Cascades, etc*. Bristol: the author, 1965. Mimeographed TS.

Vlavianos, Haris. "ΛευτέρηςΠούλιος: Είναιθαυμάσιοναγτραγουδάς'" ["Lefteris Poulios: 'It is wonderful to sing'"]. *ΤαΝέα* 9 Feb. 2008. Web. Sept. 2010.

von Franz, Marie Louise. *The Interpretation of Fairy Tales*. Dallas: Spring Publications, 1970. Print.

Von Hallberg, Robert. *American Poetry and Culture 1945–1980*. Cambridge: Harvard UP, 1985. Print.

Waddell, Eric. "Kérouac, le Québec, l'Amérique. . .et moi." Anctil et al. 1–17. Print.

Wagnleitner, Reinhold. *Coca-Colonization and the Cold War: The Cultural Mission of the United States in Austria after the Second World War*. Chapel Hill: U of North Carolina P, 1994. Print.

Waits, Tom. "Lucky Day Overture." *The Black Rider*. Island Records, 1993. CD.

Waine, Anthony and Jonathan Wooley. "'Blissful, Torn, Intoxicated': Brinkmann, Fauser, Wondratschek." Skerl, *College Literature* 177–198. Print.

Waldman, Anne. Message to A. Robert Lee. 2 Jan. 2011. Email.

———. *Outrider: Essays, Poems, Interviews*. Albuquerque: La Alameda, 2006. Print.

———. *The Romance Thing: Travel Sketches*. Flint: Bamberger,1987. Print.

Waley, Arthur, trans. *The Pillow Book of Sei Shonagon*. London: Allen, 1957. Print.

Watson, Steven. *The Birth of the Beat Generation*. New York: Pantheon, 1995. Print.

Weibel, Peter. *Die Wiener Gruppe/The Vienna Group: A Moment of Modernity 1954–1960*. Vienna: Springer, 1997. Print.

Wiener, Oswald. "the bio-adapter." Weibel 690–699. Print.

Weinreich, Regina. "The Beat Generation is Now About Everything." Hendin 72–94. Print.

Weston, J. L. *From Ritual to Romance*. 1920. Bath: Chivers, 1980. Print.

Whalen, Philip. *Highgrade: Doodles, Poems*. San Francisco: Coyote's Journal, 1966. Print.

———. *Scenes of Life at the Capital*. San Francisco: Maya Quarto Ten, 1970. Print.

———. *Scenes of Life at the Capital*. Bolinas: Grey Fox, 1971. Print.

———. "Tiger Whiskers: Interview with Anne Waldman (1971)." *Off the Wall*. Ed. Donald Allen. Bolinas: Four Seasons Foundation, 1978. 5–27. Print.

———. "Zen Poet: Interview with Yves Le Pellec (1972)." *Off the Wall*. Ed. Donald Allen. Bolinas: Four Seasons Foundation, 1978. 50–67. Print.

Whisnant, David E. *Rascally Signs in Sacred Places: The Politics of Culture in Nicaragua*. Chapel Hill: U of North Carolina P, 1995. Print.

White, Steven F. *Culture and Politics in Nicaragua*. New York: Lumen, 1986. Print.

Wilentz, Elias. *The Beat Scene*. New York: Corinth, 1960. Print.

Williams, William Carlos. *Kora in Hell: Improvisations*. San Francisco: City Lights, 1957. Print.

Wilson, Colin. *The Outsider*. London: Victor Gollancz, 1956. Print.

Wilson, Robert, Tom Waits, and William S. Burroughs. *The Black Rider: The Casting of the Magic Bullets*. Thalia Theatre Program. Hamburg, Germany, 1990. Print.

Windling, Terry. *Married to Magic: Animal Brides and Bridegrooms in Folklore and Fantasy*. n.d. Web. 26 June 2011.

Wiseman, Sue. "Addiction and the Avante-Garde: Heroin Addiction and Narrative in Alexander Trocchi's *Cain's Book*." *Beyond the Pleasure Dome: Writings and Addiction from the Romantics (Writing on Writing)*. Ed. Sue Vice, Matthew Campbell, and Tim Armstrong. Sheffield, England: Sheffield Academic, 1994: 256–266. Print.

Wolff, Janet. "The Invisible *Flaneuse*: Women and the Literature of Modernity." *Theory Culture & Society* 2.3 (1985): 37–46. Print.

———. "On the Road Again: Metaphors of Travel in Cultural Criticism." *Cultural Studies* 7 (May 1999): 224–239. Print.

Woodson, Yoko. "Hokusai and Hiroshige: Landscape Prints of the Ukiyo-e School." *Hokusai and Hiroshige*. San Francisco: Asian Art Museum of San Francisco, 1998. 31–43. Print.

Wullschlager, Jackie. *Hans Christian Andersen: The Life of a Storyteller*. Chicago: U of Chicago P, 2000. Print.

Wyatt, William. "monk theme." Horovitz, *Children* 314. Print.

Yahahbibi Occasional Word Ensemble. Ed. Robert Gray. London: the editor, n.d. Print.

Yampolsky, Philip. ed. and trans. *The Platform Sutra of the Sixth Patriarch*. New York: Columbia UP, 1967. Print.

Young, Cynthia A. *Soul Power: Culture, Radicalism, and the Making of a U.S. Third World Left*. Durham, NC: Duke U P, 2006. Print.

Zábrana, Jan. *Básně*. Praha: Torst, 1993. Print.

———. *Celý život*. Praha: Torst, 2001. Print.

"Zen." *Shambhala Dictionary of Buddhism and Zen*. 1st ed. 1991. Print.

Zipes, Jack David. *Why Fairy Tales Stick: The Evolution and Relevance of a Genre*. New York and London: Routledge, 2006. Print.

Index